The Greens and Cornbread of Wakulla County: Historical Stories Told by the People

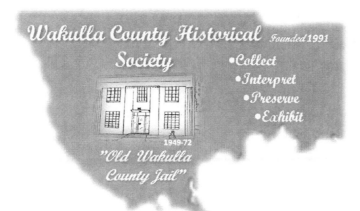

Wakulla County Historical Society Founded 1991

•Collect •Interpret •Preserve •Exhibit

1949-72 "Old Wakulla County Jail"

Compiled by:

The Wakulla County Historical Society

Southern Yellow Pine Publishing

Published by
Southern Yellow Pine (SYP) Publishing
4351 Natural Bridge Rd.
Tallahassee, FL 32305

www.syppublishing.com

ISBN-10: 0985706228

ISBN-13: 978-0-9857062-2-7

Photographs in this book owned by the original submitter unless otherwise noted.

Cover art Credit ©2011 Jo Ann Palmer, Cathy Frank, Allison Frank-Green. Permission to reprint this portion given.

Cover graphic design: Taylor Nelson

Back cover photo: The Osprey Excursion boat in St Marks, FL, owned by E.W. Roberts, photo courtesy of John Roberts.

Printed in the United States of America
First Edition
September 2012

Dedication

This book is dedicated to the pioneer spirit of so many courageous men and women who risked all to seek a new life in what would become Wakulla County. The migration began primarily when Florida became a U.S. territory in 1821. These intrepid folks cleared the land to establish small farms and engaged in commercial fishing. Life was not easy. Frequent destructive hurricanes, the second Seminole War from 1835 to 1842, Malaria, and the dreaded yellow fever took many lives. But our strong willed, God fearing forebears never gave up and many, as well as their descendants have become prominent citizens of our community and state. Today, many of our people, black and white, can connect directly to those early settlers.

Lastly, we honor those who support the Wakulla County Historical Society as they constantly strive to insure that our colorful history lives on and is not forgotten. John Roberts

Table of Contents

Acknowledgements

This book was compiled by the Wakulla County Historical Society. That being said, this is the type of book that it takes a team of people with a purpose to complete. The following list includes many, but surely not all of those who helped and played a part in the production.

The Wakulla County Historical Society Book Committee; Betty Green, Tanya Lynn, Terri Gerrell, Carolyn Harvey,

All the contributing authors. Many individuals around the county took time to write their stories or histories and get them to us.

Cover work artists; Jo Ann Palmer, Cathy Frank, and Allison Frank-Green. Credit also goes to Taylor Nelson who took that artwork and turned it into a marvelous graphic cover.

The WCHS Board for supporting this project.

Editing staff which included many WCHS members; Betty Green, Tanya Lynn, Terri Gerrell, Linda Thompson, Cathy Frank and then our final SYP Publishing editor Lindsay Marder.

Southern Yellow Pine Publishing LLC who facilitated the project and helped with book formatting.

HERITAGE VILLAGE PROJECT

The Heritage Village Project is a dream for Wakulla County. The Wakulla County Historical Society has worked for many years towards finding a place to build a historic park. The goal was to save some of the older historical structures and our history and culture related to them. The first step towards that goal was finding and obtaining some land. Over the years many options were explored. Recently we were able to solve that part of the problem. The following is a Press Release that was written by Murray McLaughlin.

The Heritage Village is a plan of the Wakulla County Historical Society that calls for relocation of some 12 historic homes that have been donated to the Society. The homes would become the focus for a park featuring not only the historic homes, but a representation of the life and times of early Wakulla families. An educational center, signage and kiosk, interpretive exhibits, amphitheater, hiking trails and other amenities would make the Park a tourism destination.

The largest barrier to establishment of the Park was the lack of land suitable for the Village. There is an old adage, "timing is everything". Mr. Ben Boynton, a local developer was sitting in the audience when Murray McLaughlin of the Wakulla County Historical Society made a presentation to the Wakulla County Board of County Commissioners in early 2011 regarding the WCHS vision for a Heritage Village. As a result, Mr. Boynton communicated to Mr. McLaughlin that he would be interested in talking to the Society about a donation of up to 40 acres for location of the Village. Soon, members of the Heritage Village were out walking on a beautiful piece of property ideally located and well suited for the Village vision.

Mr. Boynton advised the Society that he would file a revised land use plan for Bloxham Plantation to include approximately 40 acres for the Society. The gift to the Society would help him meet requirements for conservation easements and green space and simultaneously help the Society with location of the Heritage Village. It would then be up to the County to look favorably upon the change. On March 11, 2011, the first formal action by the Commission began a journey of many staff meetings, Planning Commission meetings and three meetings of the Board of County Commission. This culminated in a final Board meeting on July 16th which approved Mr. Boynton's project and cleared the way for transfer of the land to the WCHS.

The transfer will take place on Aug. 17, 2012 at the Zion Hill United Methodist Church adjacent to the property. To locate the site, drive one mile south of SR 267 on US 319 and turn right on Zion Hill Road. This road ends at the church.

The Boynton Family, County Officials, members of the Historical Society and the general public are invited to celebrate this historic event. An official of the Historical Society will be available to lead interested parties on a short tour of the property.

Mr. McLaughlin stated, "This is a tremendous opportunity for the WCHS and will go a long way toward making our dream a reality. We are very grateful to Mr. Boynton for his generosity and for considering our vision worthy of this gift. We can now begin the planning and fund raising needed, knowing we have a home."

On Aug. 17, 2012

Wakulla County Historical Society Accepted a Gift Conveyance of Land for Heritage Village from the Ben Boynton family

The Wakulla County Historical Society would like to say Thank-you to the BOYTON FAMILY

Mr. Ben Boynton

We now have the land! Ben Boyton and the Wakulla County commission have made this dream for Wakulla County a possibility. Our next step is to raise the money. All the homes will need to be transported to their new home. Once there, they will need to be repaired and restored. It will take time and money but, we believe it can be done.

The following pages show some examples of the homes & buildings and the history we are trying to save. A few photos and some floor plans are included. Precious history will be lost if the homes are not saved.

Cathy Frank, President WCHS with Ann Boyton at the Conveyance

The Carter House aka The Langston/Gamble/Carter House

The Elie and Beatrice Carter Home was built by Irvin Langston about 1905 and served as the home to Irvin and his wife, Ida Strickland and their six children. Mr. Langston managed the Panacea Mineral Springs Hotel but following the death of his wife he remarried and moved to Spring Creek where he built the large building over the water known today as the Willie Spears house. The Langston house became known as the Gamble Place as the Gamble of Proctor and Gamble, Inc. of Atlanta bought the house and land, creating a hunting lodge. In 1943, Elie Carter and his wife, Beatrice Revell, bought the house and 100+ acres to farm and raise their eight children. During WWII, German prisoners of war were interred at Camp Gordon Johnston and were allowed to work on surrounding farms. The prisoners agreed readily to come to the Carter farm because there was good food and fresh air. Elie died in 1978 while preaching a sermon at the Congregational Holiness Campground in Panacea. His widow remains near the house and several children live nearby. The Langston/Gamble/Carter house is very unique with unusual and unexplained etchings and paintings on the walls.

This house remains in the ownership of the Carter family and the Historical Society can only hope the family will save this very special building.

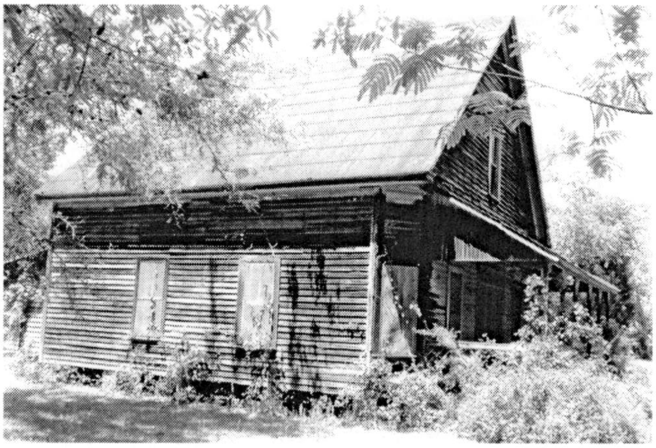

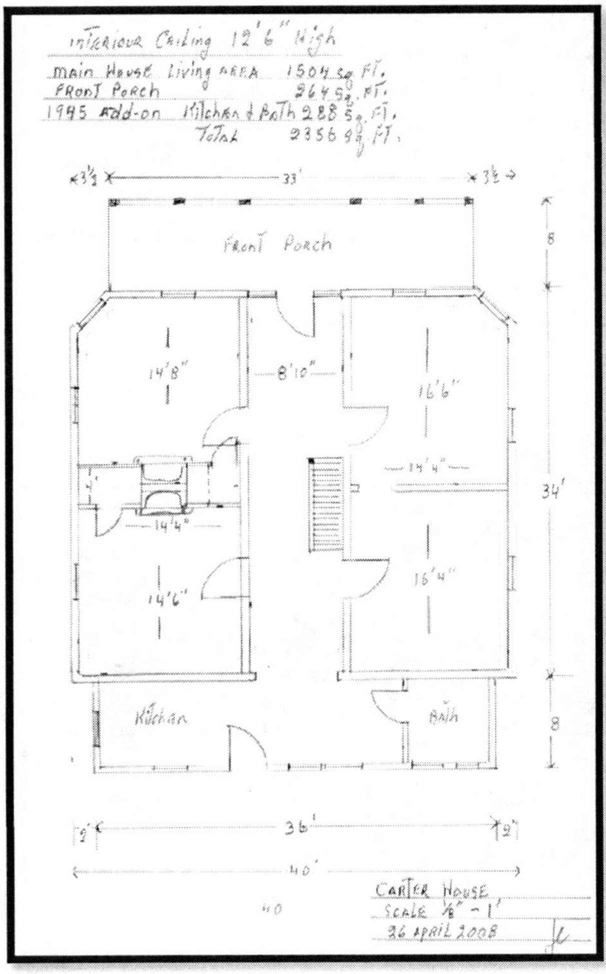
Interiour Ceiling 12'6" High
Main House Living Area 1504 sq. ft.
Front Porch 264 sq. ft.
1945 Add-on Kitchen & Bath 288 sq. ft.
Total 2356 sq. ft.
3½
33'
3½
Front Porch
8
14'8"
8'10"
16'6"
14'4"
14'4"
34'
14'6"
16'4"
Kitchen
Bath
8
2'
36'
2'
40'
Carter House
Scale ⅛" - 1'
26 April 2008

McLaughlin House

First known as the Tully place, as George W. Tully who lived in Crawfordville on a large farm but who preferred building, including the construction of the Old Wakulla County Courthouse, built the original building as a "bunkhouse" for his sawmill that he operated in Medart. George Tully and his family resided in the historic home just behind Crawfordville's former Wakulla Bank. The Tully men would travel to Medart on Mondays to work at their sawmill and return to Crawfordville for the weekend…or at least for Sunday. The Medart building was later sold to John Archie McLaughlin and his wife, Annie Carraway, parents of nine children. They added rooms to the building and established a store nearby. One of the sons, Alton James "Buddy" and his wife Sedav Raker, lived and operated a store near the old home for more than half a century. In recent years the house was vacated and the land sold to a developer. It is now parked "temporarily" on a site nearby owned and kindly shared by a friend and neighbor, Marshall Spears.

The Wakulla County Historical Society and several family members have already invested money in moving the building to its present location and are looking forward to its journey to the Heritage Village site.

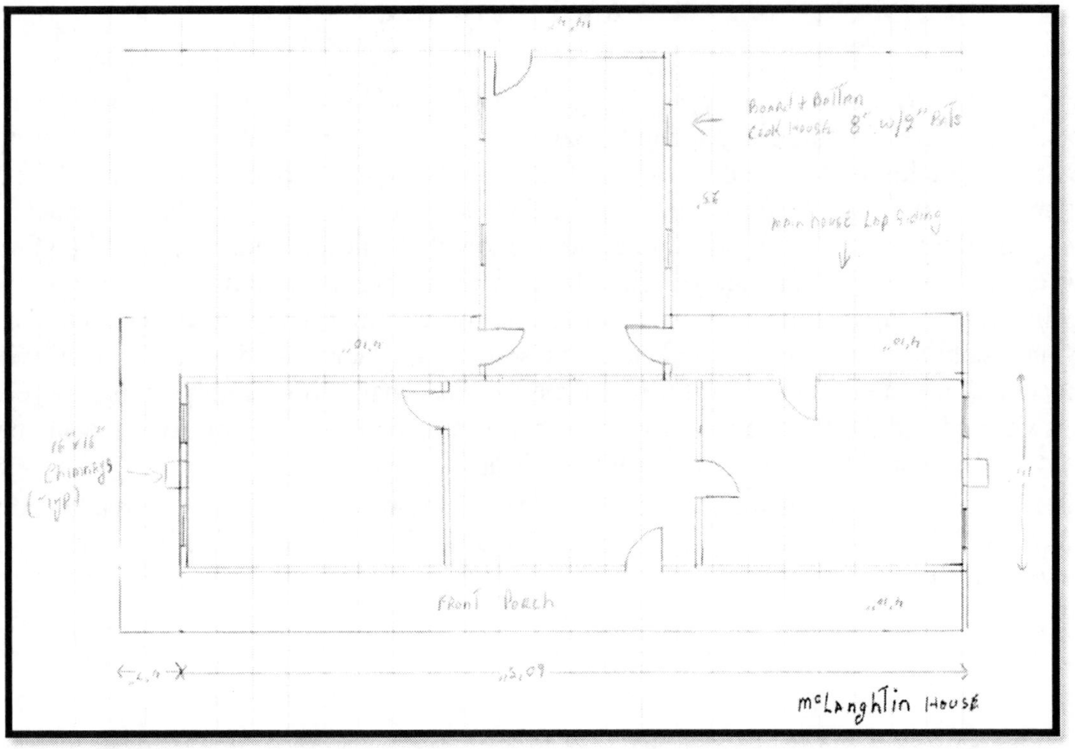
Board + Batten
16"x16" Chimneys (Typ)
Front Porch
McLanghlin House

Family of
John and Annie Carraway McLaughlin
Back row, left to right: Buddy McLaughlin, Willie V. McLaughlin Harvey,
Rosebud McLaughlin White, Lena McLaughlin Harvey
Front row: Selma McLaughlin McKenzie. John McLaughlin.
Quintus McLaughlin, Annie Carraway McLaughlin,
Yvonne McLaughlin Harvey (Baby), Johnnie McLaughlin Smith

We are hopeful that the Wakulla County Historical Society can save this home. There is more than a morsel of history here.

Epsie Strickland House

The house was built and completed in November of 1889 by Moses Strickland. He and his wife, Fannie Hester Strickland moved into the house on November 27, 1889, the day before their son, Hubby, was born. All the material used in the building was cut on the property. The cypress siding was grown in the ponds near the house. Mr. Jeff Gowdy hand planed the boards inside and probably helped Moses and others to build the house. Moses and Fannie had six children and often had their Lynn nieces stay with them. When Moses died, their son, Isaiah and his wife, Epsie Rayburn, moved in the home to take care of Fannie until her death. Isaiah met an untimely death in the Merchant Marines in November of 1941 and Epsie remained with her children in the house. Therefore, it's known today as the Epsie Strickland house. It is another sturdy farmhouse that housed a family for a century.

Front row: L-R; Isaiah Strickland, Herbert "Hubby" Strickland, Virgil Lynn (Watkins), Moses Strickland, Thelma Strickland (Forbes), Fannie Hester Strickland, Dorcus "Dossie" Strickland (Raker)
Back row: L-R; Ethel Lynn (Spears), Freida Strickland (McCallister)
Note: The names in parentheses are the girls married names when they grew up.
Photo taken in front of Moses Strickland house. Original photo shared by Marjorie Raker Lovell

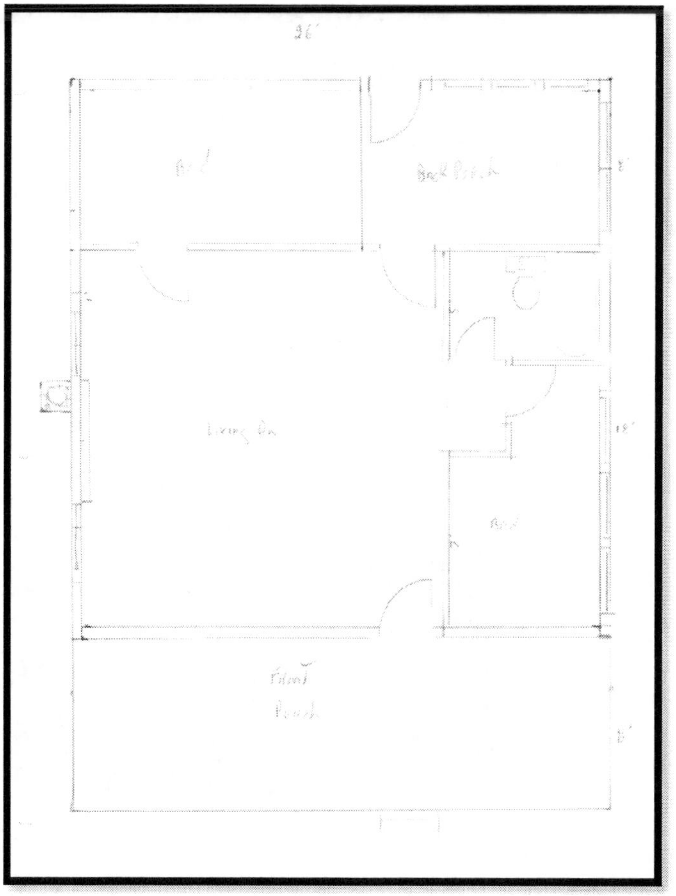
26'
Back Porch
8'
Living Rm
18'
Front
Porch
8'

Alligood-Council House

This house was built by Jasper Alligood in 1908. His daughter, Grace Alligood, was listed as ten years of age in 1910. She grew up to marry Dillon "Dill" Council in 1920 and they remained here with Dill being listed as a farmer in a community of many farms in 1930. This was a small farm house typical of homes built in Wakulla County in the early 1900s. The current owners of the house, Mike and Carolyn Harvey, would like to see it saved as part of our Heritage Village.

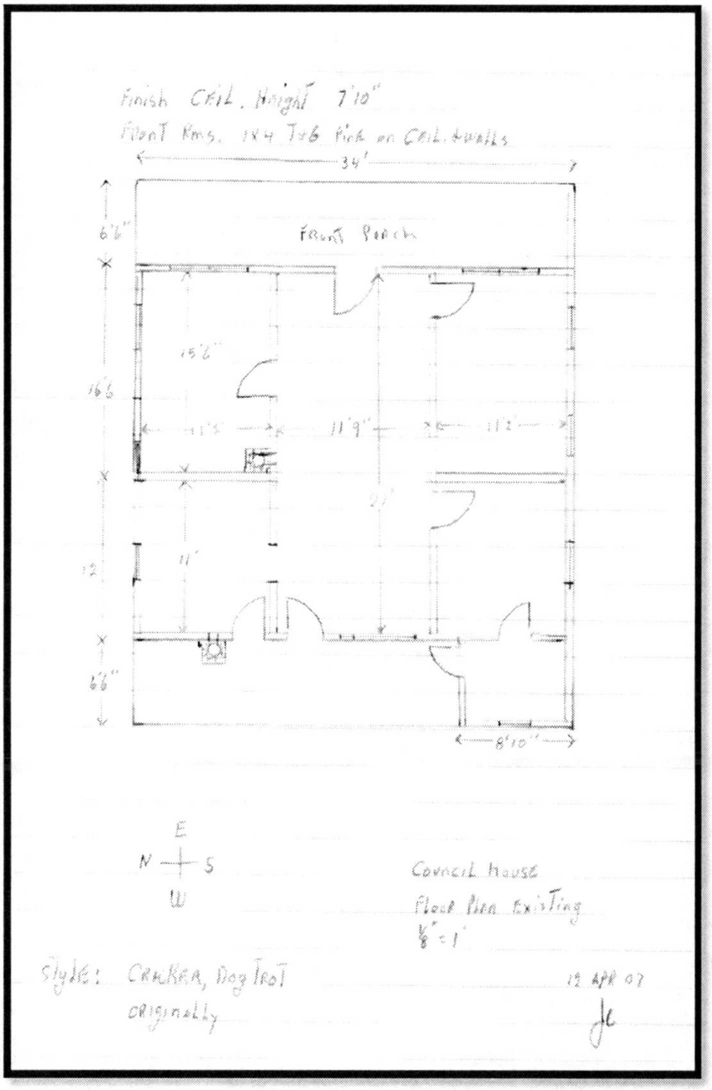

The original construction style is cracker, Dog Trot.

Coggins House

The Coggins House, known in more recent years as the Miley Place, has an extensive, though sparsely written history. Jesse Coggins and his wife, Mary Ann, were listed in the Wakulla Census in the years 1850, '60, '70. The Coggins family acquired extended land-holdings in the Medart area and their youngest son, William Nicholas (1865—1933) and his wife, Alberta Allen (1876-1956) lived in the large home set in a garden-like surrounding with the beautiful old live oaks, flowers and ponds surrounding it. In the early 1900s Alberta operated the "Pineview Boarding House" here where boarders stayed as they worked on the Panacea bridge and at least one man came from St. Marks to board there and attend the Medart School under the widely respected teacher, C. K. Allen, who became School Superintendent in 1912.

The home has been allowed to languish for many years but still exhibits a quiet elegance representing the hardworking and thrifty pioneers of the late 1880s and early 1900s.

Smith Creek School

Mr. Freeman Ashmore, 1908-2003, attended this school as a youngster and described it in detail in his book, *Looking Back*, published the year before his death. The building was erected on an acre of land donated to the county by Lorenzo Cox for that purpose. It was 16 feet wide and 27 feet long with three six foot high windows on each side, two doors in the front, one in the back and a seven foot porch stretched across the front with a water shelf on the end. The roof had a steep pitch being six feet from the crown to the center of the building and was originally cypress shingles. There were no restrooms or running water. Water was brought by buckets from a nearby spring and placed on the water shelf near a gourd dipper. Restroom breaks had girls dismissed to the woods on one side of the building and later, boys would go to the other side.

Following consolidation in the 1930s, the building served the Smith Creek community as its voting precinct and community building. Today, the Volunteer Fire Department has its building next door. The building belongs to the county and may well remain in the community but we trust it will be preserved as the little school house residing in the stories of pioneer Wakulla County.

This school building from Smith Creek was built by 1920 and possibly earlier. School records have not indicated the date it came into service. We do know however, that it was in use in the 1920s. Mr. Freeman Ashmore attended that school when he was a boy. He died in 2003 at the age of 94. He had previously written stories of his school days in this little one room school house.

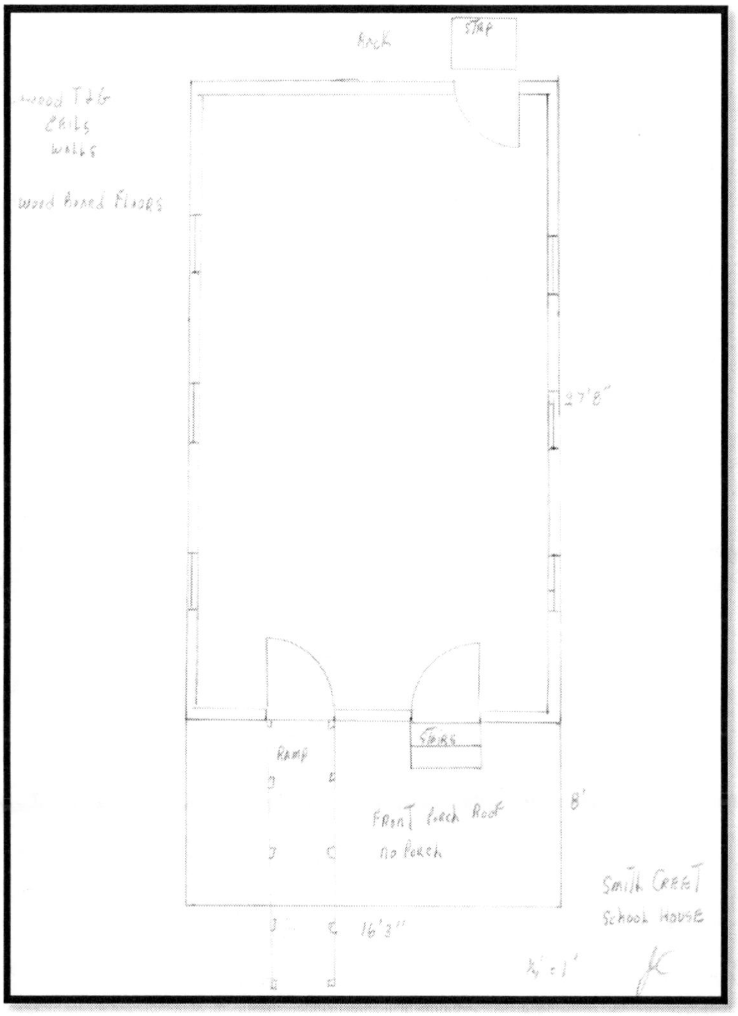
BACK
STEP
Wood T&G
Ceilings
Walls
Wood Board Floors
27'8"
STAIRS
RAMP
8'
FRONT Porch Roof
no Porch
SMITH CREEK
School HOUSE
16'3"

Ross Linzy House

Ross Linzy House: Not as old as it looks! Built by Ross and Amy Linzy as their first home after their marriage in 1928, it was a 2 bedroom house with a front porch and one fireplace. A kitchen, dining room, pantry and pot-belly stove were added in 1938. This house is special because it was built by a couple who didn't really know anything about building but dreamed of being self-supporting for themselves and their family. They built, by hand, including making the blocks that were laid, a country store that was quite successful for many years on the land that now harbors Walmart. They raised their four children, supported themselves and contributed to the welfare of the Ivan Community for well over a half century.

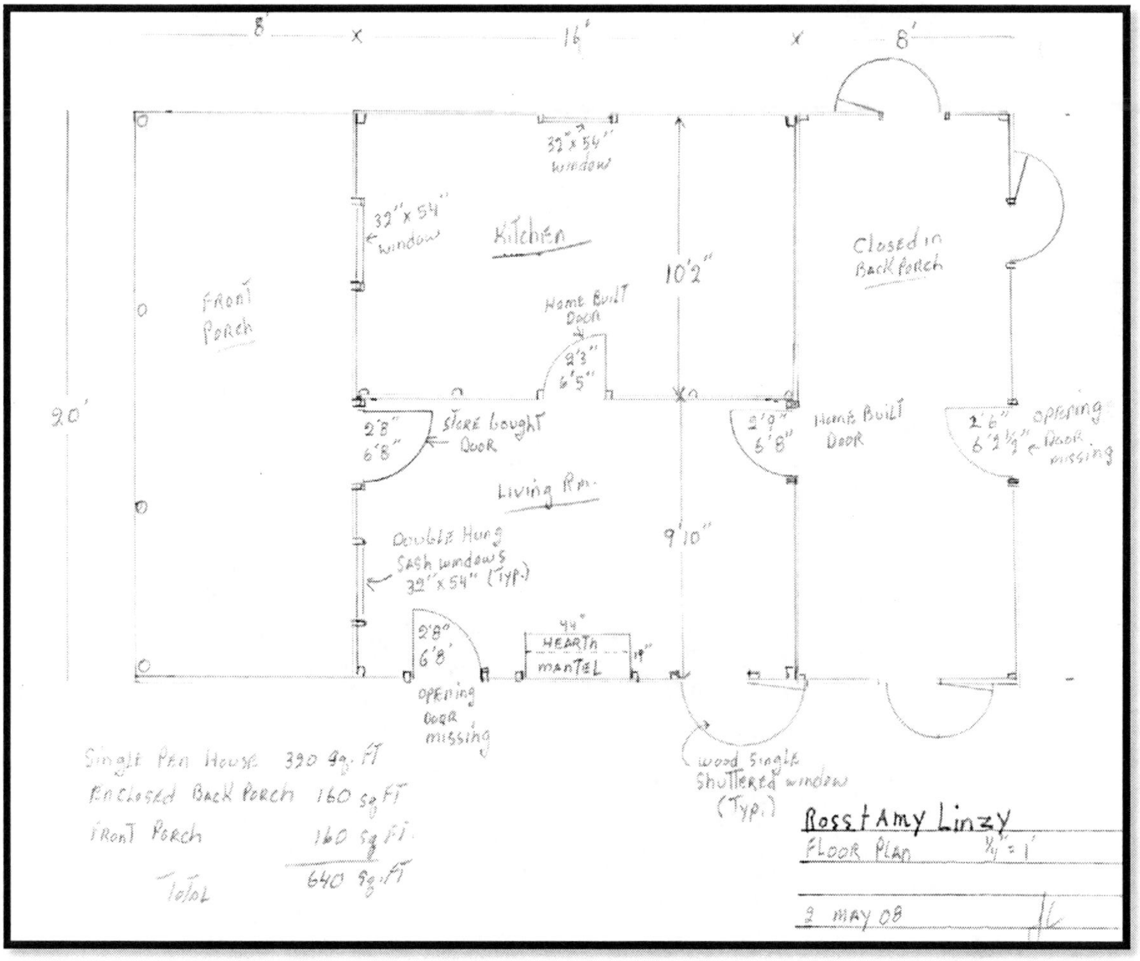

8'
16'
8'
20'
32" x 54" window
Kitchen
10'2"
Closed in Back Porch
Front Porch
Home Built Door
2'3" 6'5"
2'8" 6'8"
Store bought Door
2'9" 6'8"
Home Built Door
2'6" 6'2 1/2"
opening Door missing
Living Rm.
Double Hung Sash windows 32" x 54" (Typ.)
9'10"
44"
HEARTH
MANTEL
19"
2'8" 6'8"
opening door missing
wood single shuttered window (Typ.)
Single Pen House 320 sq. FT
Enclosed Back Porch 160 sq FT
Front Porch 160 sq FT
Total 640 sq. FT
Ross + Amy Linzy
FLOOR PLAN 1/4" = 1'
3 MAY 08

Heyward R. and Maude Strickland Linzy House

Married in 1904, Heyward and Maude Linzy built their home north of Crawfordville near Jump Creek and Leland Gowdy's place. When their first son died in 1909, they thought they lived too near the creek and it was a "sickly area" so they dismantled the house and transported it to the present site where it was rebuilt. In 1959, the house was covered with asbestos shingles and, at the same time, the separate kitchen was joined to the house by an enclosed passage.

The couple remained in the house until their deaths and their granddaughter, Kelly Harvey, who lived there shortly after her marriage and decorated it with red ribbons for Christmas, 1984, would like very much to see this very special home saved.

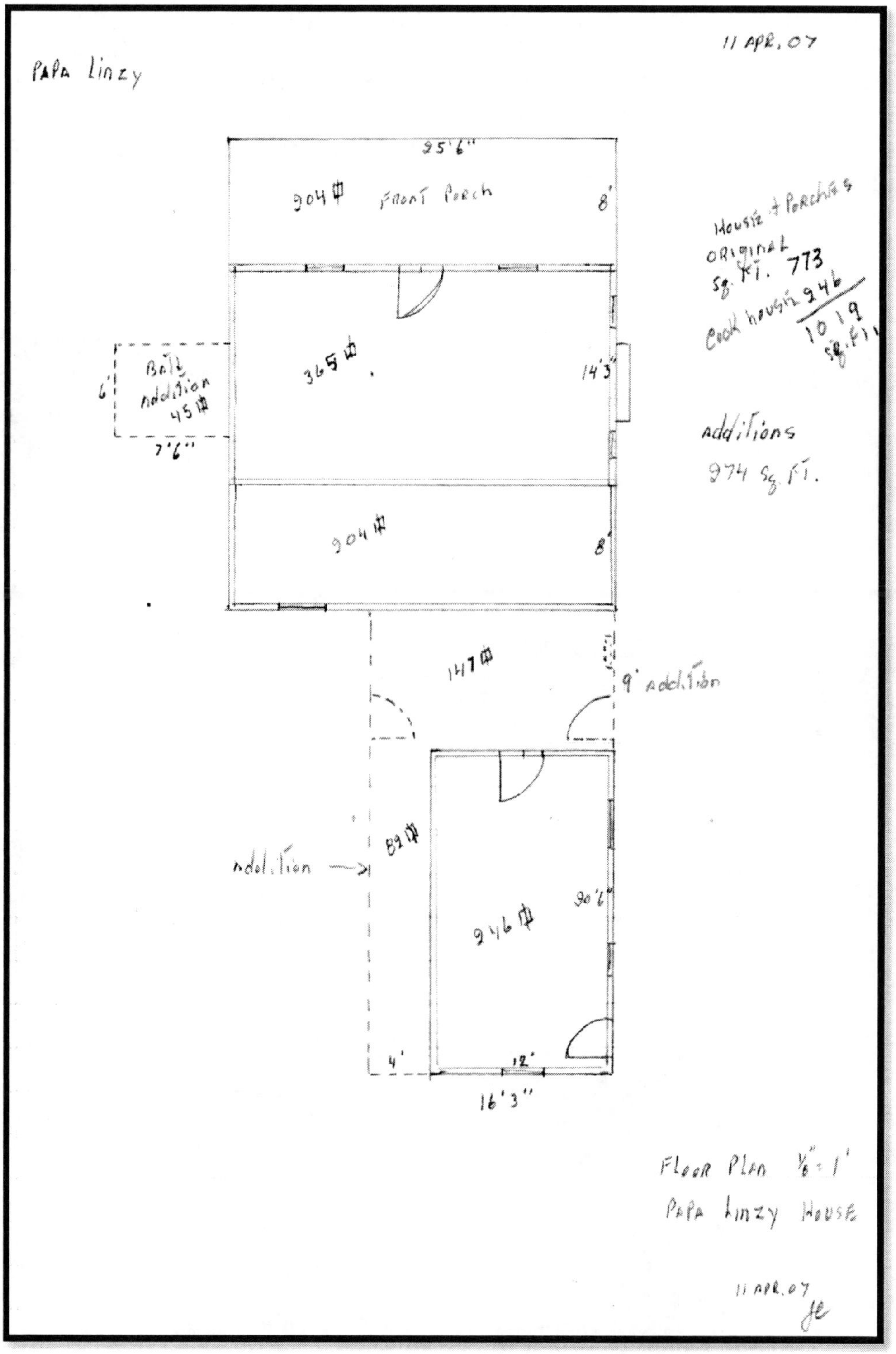
Papa Linzy
11 APR. 07
25'6"
904 ⌀ Front Porch
8'
House + Porches
original
sq. ft. 773
Cook house 246
1019
sq. ft.
Bath addition
45 ⌀
6'
7'6"
365 ⌀
14'3"
additions
974 sq. ft.
904 ⌀
8'
147 ⌀
9' addition
addition
82 ⌀
246 ⌀
20'6"
4'
12"
16'3"
Floor Plan 1/8" = 1'
Papa Linzy House
11 APR. 07

Bill and Clora Mae Gray Laird Home

James Laird and Nellie Pearl Eubanks were married February 11, 1900. We do not know when this little house was built in the Hilliardville Community, but we do know that Jim and Nellie lived there until their deaths. After his death in 1947, his youngest son, Bill, and his wife, Clora Mae Gray moved into the house and there they raised their family of nine children. One of those children, Kathy Roberts, owns the building now and would like to see the structure moved and returned to its state of a small farm home in the early 1900s. The main part, before additions, is quite old and sturdy and worthy of restoration.

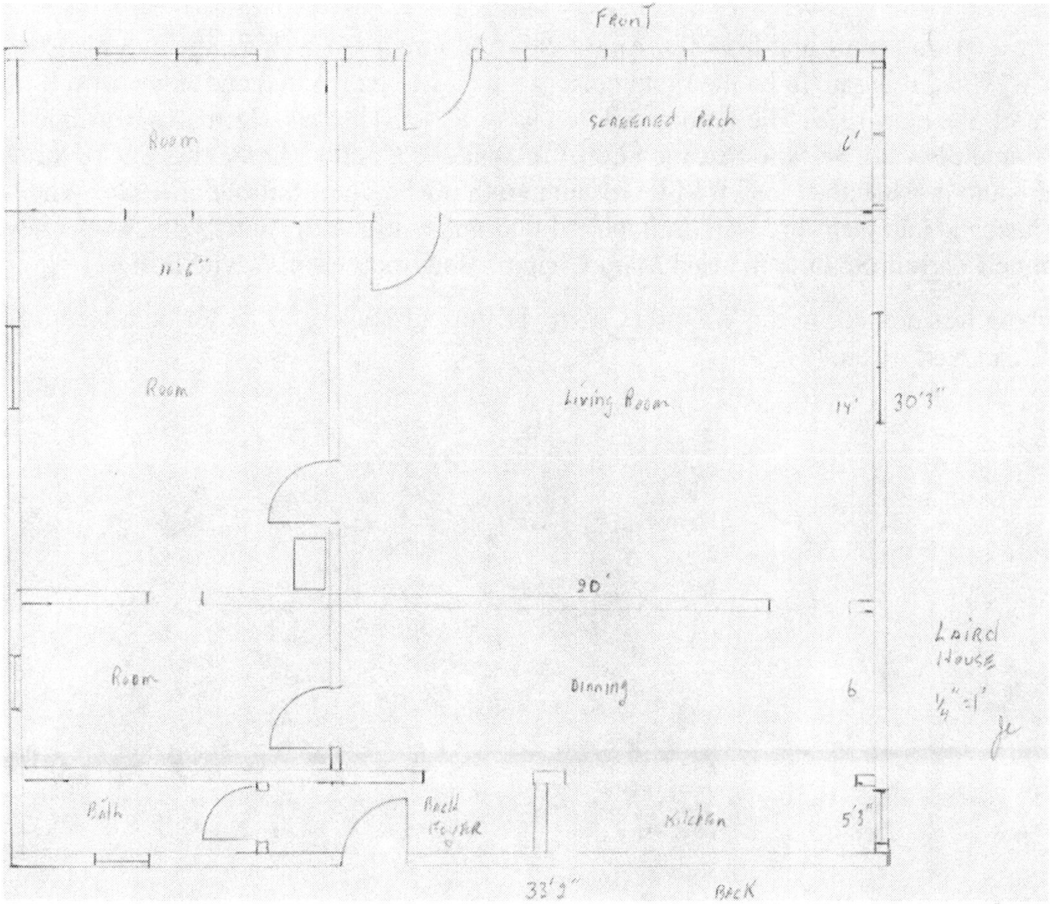
FRONT
SCREENED Porch
6'
Room
11'6"
Room
Living Room
14'
30'3"
90'
LAIRD HOUSE
1/4"=1'
Room
Dinning
6
Bath
Back Foyer
Kitchen
5'3"
33'2"
BACK

"June" Moore House

Junior Leaston Moore and his wife, Annie Pigott Moore lived in this large and well built house in the early 1900s. It is said to be the first house in the area to be painted and it was a well kept home and yard until the heirs died. The Moore children were Steve, Thomas, Herman and Annie. Annie married Emmett Ferrell, Sr. who became Sheriff of Wakulla County. Annie was one of three victims of the train/auto crash at the Gossett Mill crossing on the G.F. & A. Railroad in 1926. When Annie died, her husband and their three children moved into this house with Annie's parents for several years. Emmett Ferrell, Sr. later married Mary Coggins Bell, mother of Wayne Bell.

The home was donated to the Wakulla County Historical Society by its former owners Mr. and Mrs. S. A. Coxwell in 2007.

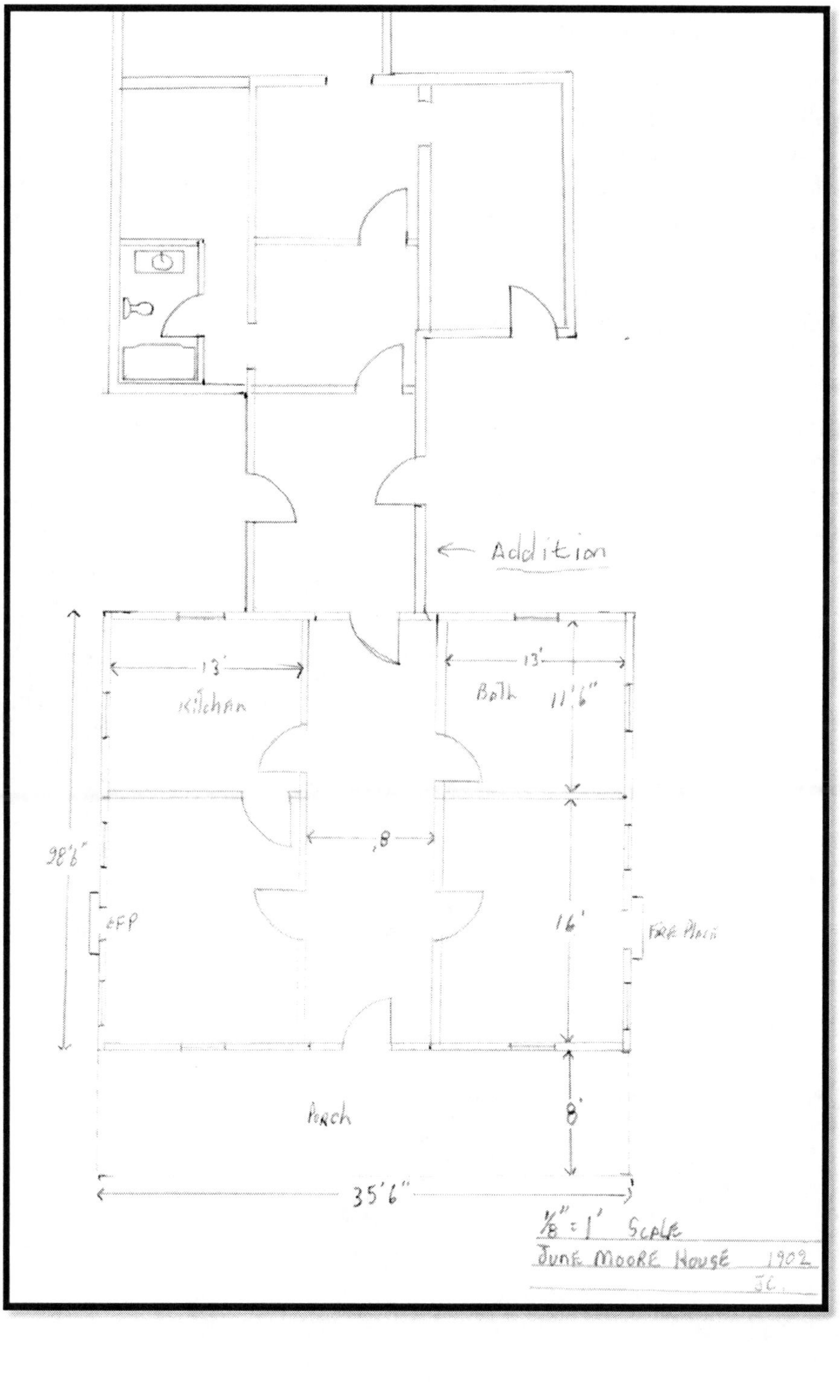
Addition
13'
Kitchen
13'
Bath
11'6"
8'
98'6"
FP
16'
Fire Place
Porch
8'
35'6"
1/8" = 1' Scale
June Moore House 1902
J.C.

Crawfordville School Lunch Room

In July of 1939, Arran citizens chose to join other schools in the county in a consolidation movement. Their vote led to the closing of the Arran School and the beginning of busing their children to Crawfordville High School, for grades 1-12. In September of that year the School Board decided against advertising the Arran school building for sale. We find in the School Board minutes in August of 1941, the motion to purchase the Sopchoppy lunchroom ceiling as "they had furnished all materials for the Crawfordville Lunchroom." Lonnie Dispennette in his article here says the materials came from the old Arran School. In September of '41, Ernest Roddenberry of Sopchoppy had the low bid of $184.30 for painting the Crawfordville Lunchroom as well as the lunchrooms for Sopchoppy, Buckhorn, and Shadeville Schools!

The Crawfordville Lunchroom served not only in that capacity but it was also the home for community square dances and in later years for the special reading program for Crawfordville Elementary School. It housed the Wakulla News when that building burned several years ago.

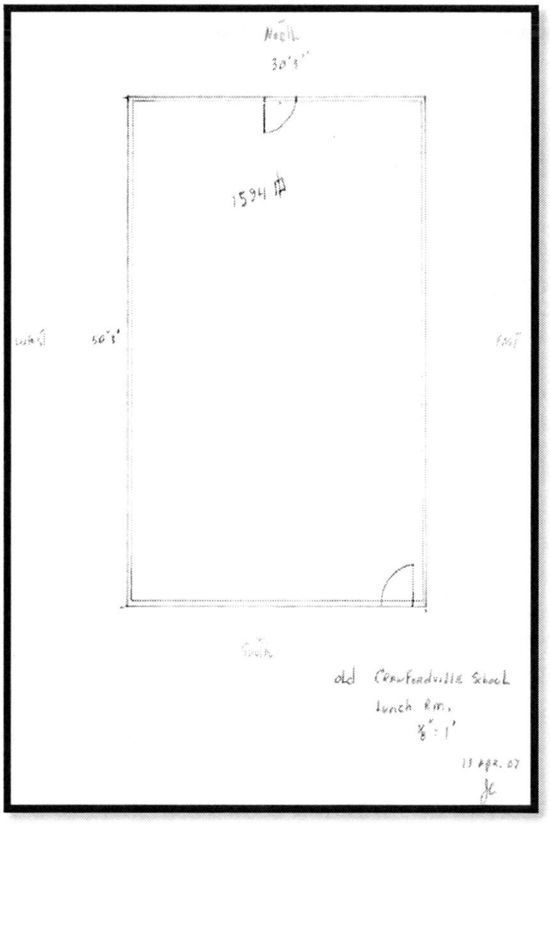
North
1594 ft
West
East
South
old Crawfordville School
Lunch Rm.
13 Apr. 07

EARLY TIMES

Drew Crawford Adams & Adams Plantation

John Wesley Adams and his wife Caroline Powell Adams first settled in Wakulla County during the early 1840s on property located on the west side of the Sopchoppy River, where they built a home, church and post office. They had four children: Sara Iona, Caroline, Drucilla and John Wesley Adams II (11/24/1848 - 5/20/1913). He married Julia E. Crawford, daughter of Dr. John Lovic Crawford.

The Adams family remained in Sopchoppy until 1876, when John Wesley acquired the Gavin Plantation. It later became known as the Adams' Plantation with the home located two miles east of Crawfordville on the Lower Bridge Road.

John Wesley and his wife prospered here farming and timbering and gaining vast acreage. They had five children: Drew Crawford (12/14/1876 - 01/04/1952), Joseph, Henry Clay, Charles Yancey, and John Lovic (12/12/1879 - 11/21/1935). At the death of Joseph Adams, Drew Crawford Adams became the sole heir to the Adams Plantation and the last of the Adams family to live there.

Drew married Maggie McMillen (09/04/1874 - 03/10/1974). They had two sons, McMillen Crawford, who died at the age of eleven, and Samuel Pitt.

Drew and Maggie were professional photographers with their studio over the old Bennett Drug Store at the corner of College and Monroe Streets. Their son Sam joined them in the business. Sam (1905 - 1985) married Alice Beaty (1908-1985). They had five children: Mary Elizabeth, John Wesley, James Drew, Alicia and Richard.

The Adams Studio remained in Tallahassee, adding a smaller campus studio on West Pensacola Street. They received a commendation from Eastman Kodak and have pictures archived in the Florida State Museum.

Sam and his family moved to Anna Maria Island in 1946. His mother and father retired a few years later and moved to Anna Maria Island to a lovely home on the beach.

Adams Plantation House

Sam worked at the Post Office, was a City Commissioner for two terms, was the first Fire Chief of Anna Maria and was appointed by Governor Leroy Collins to the Erosion Control Board. He also served in the US Navy from 1943-1945 and 1951-1953. He and wife Alice both died in 1985. Their children, grand-children and great-grandchildren still live in the Anna Maria area.

Drew Adams sold the Adams Plantation to Earl J. Stephens, who sold it to St. Joe Paper Company in 1960. The original house (which I think was built in the early 1880s) is still standing but has been but has been remodeled, such as closing in the big breezeway and adding a kitchen. Several families have owned the house after it was sold to St. Joe Paper Company.

Submitted by: Carmen D. Corley, 940 Shadeville Road, Crawfordville, FL

Richard Alexander Shine; Builder of Tallahassee

Richard Shine was one of Tallahassee's leading pioneers. He came to Tallahassee when Leon County included what is now Wakulla and Jefferson Counties. He is listed as voter number 58 for Tallahassee in 1829. He built Tallahassee literally, politically, militarily and religiously. He was Tallahassee's leading builder of homes and civic buildings in the 1830s to 1860s. He served 8 terms on the city council, from 1830 to 1850. He also served in the Territorial Legislature as well as the State House after statehood as a member of the Wig party. Richard served as captain in the Leon Riflemen and was an elder in the First Presbyterian Church in the 1840s.

Richard had a large brickyard in Tallahassee. Best that I can determine, using vague descriptions, the brickyard was located between Leon High School and Goodwood Plantation. This area also has the clay needed for making bricks. He supplied the bricks for building the First Presbyterian Church and the Capitol building built in 1845. He was contractor on several of the downtown historic homes extant as well as for Goodwood Plantation. The historic marker in front of the Bloxham House at 410 N. Calhoun St. list him as the builder. The Chittenden House on Park Avenue, then 200 Foot Road, is said that he built that home from materials from the Capitol building that was torn down for the one he built. One of his most notable engineering feats is the "deep cut" or "long cut" for the railroad where it runs under Magnolia Dr. by the Tallahassee Democrat. This was done in the late 1850s and early 1860s just before the War Between the States. He also engineered and rebuilt the railroad to St. Marks. In 1843 most of downtown Tallahassee burned. It was determined that to rebuild, it should be done using bricks. Richard Shine supplied most of the bricks in this rebuilding effort. Richard, also had losses during this fire, more than any other downtown property owner. He was part owner in buildings that housed businesses on the west side of Monroe Street. They were A.M. Hobby, M.L. Baker, Sentinel Office, Ward and Whites law office, Ward and May's Saddlery. He was also part owner in buildings that housed businesses on Clinton Street (Now College Ave.); Thompson and Hagner's Law Offices, F. Flagg's Watch Shop and Life and Trust Bank.

Richard Shine also helped build the population of Tallahassee. He and his wife, Mary Ann had 10 children. His son R.A. Shine, Jr. was a local business man and a county collector. His son William Francis Shine was a prominent surgeon for the Confederate Army during the War Between the States. His son, Francis Eppes Shine was also a doctor. Three of Richard Senior's sons married 3 of Francis Eppes daughters. Francis Eppes was the grandson of Thomas Jefferson and the founder of what was to become Florida State University and was a six times mayor of Tallahassee both before and after statehood. Richard Shine Senior's direct descendants are full of medical doctors, with some buried at Monticello, the Jefferson home in Virginia.

Richard Shine Senior is buried in the Old City Cemetery. His tomb along with his wife and other family members is on the "Walking Tour" and is featured on the front of the Walking Tour brochure. These tombs are very distinctive in that they are double arched and have carved tablets for the enclosures. These tombs are just inside the gate as you enter the cemetery off of Martin Luther King Blvd.

My lineage with Richard Shine is through my 6th great-granddad, Maj. Daniel Shine born 1690. He was Richard Shine's great-granddad. Richard's granddad was John Shine born 1725. His dad was Frances Stringer Shine born 1760. My line of course is more lengthy. My mother is Mary Frances Andrews Pearson. She came to Tallahassee with her mother and father back in the 1930s. Her mother was Mary Rebecca Wilkinson Andrews. Mary Rebecca was the daughter of John Lawrence Wilkinson, CSA. He moved to Wakulla County in 1903 from Sumter County, Georgia. His children attended the school in Woodville. His line follows the Shine line through his mother Elizabeth Jane Miller Wilkinson. Her mother was Sarah Williams Shine Miller. Sarah's father was John Shine born 1759 who served in the Revolutionary army. His dad was Daniel Shine born 1729. His mother was Barbara Franck who was friends with George Washington and had him in her home when he toured the States. Daniel Shine born 1729, his dad was Maj. Daniel Shine born 1690.

My own personal history in Tallahassee starts when I was born at Tallahassee Memorial Hospital in 1956 to Lawrence Murray Pearson and Mary Frances Andrews Pearson. I attended Leonard Wesson School and Tallahassee Christian Schools. I lived at 112 Polk Drive until I went off to school in Lynchburg, Virginia in 1973. There I met my wife the former Sallie (Penny) Pendleton Eubank. When Penny and I first met, my sister Lauren asked her, when was her birthday, she said Feb. 22, 1956. This being my birthday as well my sister thought she was fooling around. When we compared our birth certificates we found out she was born an hour and 33 minutes before me. We moved back to Tallahassee after being married June 12, 1976 the U.S.A. bicentennial year. After about four months we moved to Wakulla Station in Wakulla County. My history with Tallahassee does not stop there. I have continued to work in Tallahassee ever since. My Son Kent and daughter Carrie were both born at Tallahassee Memorial Hospital. My daughter is now attending TCC and working in Tallahassee as well. My mother still owns the house I grew up in on Polk Drive and still lives in Leon County. My youngest brother Dana also still lives in Leon County.

I am proud to know that my family has not only been a builder of Tallahassee but of our nation as well. I have at least 2 ancestors that fought in the Revolutionary Army. My 6th great-grandparents were the first settlers of New Bern, South Carolina from Germany and my Andrews ancestors were pioneers to Holmes County, Florida.

Shawn Pearson, 4521 Bloxham Cut Off Road
Crawfordville, Florida 32327, *sspearson@comcast.net*

Excerpts From In Search of The Diamond Brooch; Hall Family

There are many Gerrells in Wakulla and Leon Counties now, in modern days. The earliest branches of the family were all in the area by 1850. The following are excerpts from *In Search of The Diamond Brooch*. This book will be published by SYP Publishing, LLC later this summer. The book relates and chronicles periods of the family history as well as that of Leon & Wakulla County's.

Elizabeth Hall-North Florida.

Elizabeth Byrd Hall came to Wakulla County from North Carolina after the death of her husband, Enoch Hall. Family lore states she wanted to be closer to her younger brother Benjamin Byrd. They were direct descendants of William Byrd, founder of Richmond, VA. Her husband died in 1825. We believe she arrived in Wakulla County in 1827.

Mary Jane Moore Hall
As a Child she buried her doll with a real diamond brooch on it.

She arrived; *imagine this*, with her children and six Negro slaves along with her wagons of household goods. That would have taken guts, strength and stamina to move away from a civilized area to go to the wilderness as a widow. She established a home here in the woods east of the St. Marks River. Her brother Benjamin Byrd was a merchant in the town of Magnolia on the St. Marks River. He was also postmaster and a councilman for the city. Elizabeth and her family settled on land about a mile from Magnolia on the east side of the St. Marks River. She had an 80 acre land grant on the east side of the River, a bit north of Magnolia. Elizabeth raised her family in the area and added to her land holdings in the Newport census district. In 1860, the Newport census district was the fifth largest in Florida. The people were located along the river between St. Marks and the county line just south of Natural Bridge. Carving a home out of unsettled North Florida wilderness would have been difficult to say the least.

Her children were Hiram, Lewis, Ahijah, Enoch, Elijah, Mahala, & Mary. Hiram moved back to Georgia. The others stayed in the area. Ahijah was one of the first sheriffs in the county from 1845-1853. Family stories claim him as the first sheriff. I am not sure of that; he may have been the second. Ahijah was very active in county politics and activities. He owned land in the area now known as Wakulla Station. It was known as Oil Still Station at the time. He built and ran a turpentine fire still there close to the St. Marks Railroad. His holdings in the turpentine business were sold to Newton Culbreath who formed the Wakulla Turpentine Company that operated until the end of the industry. In 1866, Ahijah was one of six people named by the Florida Legislature to act as a Commissioner to permanently choose a location for the county site of Wakulla.

Various members of the family were active in Magnolia and Wakulla County. Elizabeth's son Lewis married Sarah Faircloth. They had seven children. One of their children was Lewis Franklin, our direct ancestor. Lewis and his son Lewis Franklin were blacksmiths, farmers, gunsmiths and coopers. They were resourceful doing everything they needed to do to provide for their families. Mary married John Coleman who I will mention later. Elijah is listed as a farmer in the 1860's census.

Elizabeth later remarried a man by the name of Aaron Johnson in 1835. It is believed he was a farmer as a younger man. In the 1850's he was working for the Georgia-Florida Plank Road Company. He built a home at the intersections of the Tallahassee and Chaires branch of the road at Johnson Springs, later known as Rhodes Spring. He was the keeper of the Plank Road toll station until it closed in the late 1850's. The Plank Road's demise was caused by the reconstruction and conversion of the Tallahassee - St. Marks Railroad to steel rails and steam locomotive power.

Lewis Franklin was also a gunsmith during the time guns were being changed from flintlocks to cap and ball. We know where the home site was. A photo follows. and the memories of Jessie French Gerrell and Frankie French Blackburn have allowed us to identify outbuildings such as the barn and the buildings used for blacksmithing and gun repair. We have found many artifacts at this site including farm tools and 100s of antique gun parts.

Lewis Franklin married Mary Jane Moore on August 27, 1867 shortly after the Civil War. They had known each other all their lives. At the time Mary Jane was a widow. She had previously been married to Matthew Burns, a Civil War veteran, who died just after the war. He was 23 at the time. She already had two children from her first marriage. All the families had been neighbors and friends.

When Mary Jane was a little girl she was responsible for the title of this book.

In Search of The Diamond Brooch

Pete Gerrell was fond of saying, "I've spent my life in search of the diamond brooch." When he said that, he was referring to the favorite family story about little Mary Jane Moore. Our home is full of artifacts excavated from various pioneer home sites. People would frequently ask Pete what in the world inspired him to go around digging up all this stuff. This story was told to Pete when he was just a young child. The story inflamed a young boy's imagination and fanned a love of history and family.

Pete's great-grandmother, Mary Jane Moore, was a young child of perhaps 4 or 5. When she grew up she married Lewis Franklin Hall who was Elizabeth Hall's grandson. For this story, she was young enough that she played with dolls frequently and had limited communication skills, perhaps 3-5 years of age.

The Moores were neighbors living just down the Pinhook Road. There was a death and thus a funeral where the families were together. Mary Jane Moore went to the funeral with her family. At the funeral, which was open casket, she observed the deceased woman dressed in all her finery with a brooch pinned to her dress. The funeral proceeded and the woman was buried. The mourners went home and returned to their daily lives.

A few days later, Great Great, Grandma Sarah Faircloth Hall, noticed a piece of jewelry, *her diamond brooch*, was missing. A search began. With questioning, Mary Jane admitted she borrowed the brooch to play with. She dressed her favorite doll and pinned the brooch to her and had a funeral. She told the family she buried the doll. The problem was she was not sure where she buried it. It might have been around the yard or, it might have been out there in the corn field. The family searched high and low. It is said they even dug up part of the nearby corn field. In the days of plowing with a mule, this was not done lightly. As the story goes neither the brooch nor the doll were ever seen again. Little Mary Jane was just not sure where she buried that doll baby.

Pete Gerrell, c 1995. Excavating Hall Family Artifacts In those days there was no trash pick-up. They buried it.

And thus, Pete Gerrell spent his life "in search of a diamond brooch" digging for family history and family artifacts.

Dr. William Saffold Kendall

William Saffold Kendall was born in Roan's Prairie, Texas in 1862. As a young man he was living with an uncle on his deceased father's property before he decided to leave Texas. He traveled for two weeks by coach to Washington, Georgia where another uncle resided. This uncle persuaded William to attend the Medical College of Georgia in nearby Augusta. William received his degree in 1888.

Dr. Kendall began his medical career in the small town of Washington but soon returned to Texas where he set up practice in Anderson, a town near Roan's Prairie. He traveled to Galveston, Texas in 1900 to assist in the care of victims of the hurricane and great flood. His next move was back to Washington, Georgia where he re-opened his practice. After a short period, he moved to Atlanta and began practicing there.

In Atlanta, a condition in his legs worsened until he was unable to walk. He knew of the potential healing effects of the mineral springs in Florida and elected to move his family there and avail himself of the springs' qualities. He relocated to Newport in Wakulla County, was brought there on a stretcher and began drinking water from the springs as well as using them to soak his legs. He was soon able to walk and began practicing his skills in the town of Newport. He later practiced in Crawfordville and eventually moved to Sopchoppy where he continued to administer to the ill until he died in 1928. Lacking driving ability, he was driven to homes of the ill by his sons until they began their own careers and then he was driven by his step-son. He performed all necessary procedures required by ailing individuals - dental as well as medical.

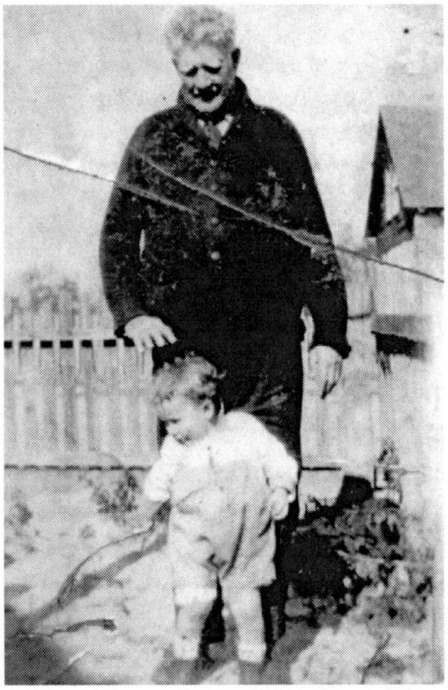

Dr. W.S. Kendall with Harry Kendall, 1927

Dr. Kendall brought with him from Atlanta his wife Emma Ware, daughter Ruby, and sons Saffold and Carl. He had been friends with Dr. Harper in Atlanta and was influential in Dr. Harper's decision to relocate to Crawfordville. After the passing of his wife, Dr. Kendall married Jessie White Carraway and together they produced a son, Harry White Kendall. Ruby married and lived in Tallahassee, Florida. Carl, with wife Gertrude, moved to New Jersey where he worked as a machinist and developed an automatic bottling machine which he built and sold until his health failed. Saffold, with wife Hortense, moved to Los Angeles, California where he practiced law. Harry studied and obtained a PhD in Physics after which he was a professor and department chairman at the University of South Florida. He and his wife Lauranne presently reside in Marianna.

Submitted by: Harry W. Kendall, PO Box 313, Greenwood, FL 32443

The Journey Story from England, A King, To Wakulla County

Back row: Maxie, Gerald Allen, Dorothy Nell, Timothy Floyd, Walter Glen Middle row: Rodney, Frances Carole, Cathy Marlene, Latrelle, Ronnie Center: Marjorie Clarice Sanders Gray Bottom row: Patricia Lynette, David Ray, Suzanne Circa 2001

Trice Ancestry and Links to Kings of England

Our Trice ancestors are descended from a King of England - No Kidding. Ludusky Trice's mother, our 3rd great-grandmother was a Wilcox descended from several Wilcox families who are direct descendants of the Plantagenet Kings. We are going to share with you the time when they left the Carolinas, and Georgia. The ancestry of so many Wakulla County and the surrounding area folks are tied together by these great adventurers looking for the promise of a better way of life, religious freedoms, and wealth. This is the ancestry of our mother, Marjorie Clarice Sanders Gray, a fine lady indeed! Beginning with the House of Plantagenet, a branch of the Angevins, a royal house founded by Geoffrey V of Anjou, father of Henry II of England.

The Plantagenet Kings Ruled England more than 300 years. Plantagenet Kings first ruled the Kingdom of England in the 12th century. Their paternal ancestors originated in the French province of Gatinais and gained the County of Anjou through marriage during the 11th century. The dynasty accumulated several other holdings, building the Angevin Empire that at its peak stretched from the Pyrenees to Ireland and the border with Scotland; in total fifteen Plantagenet monarchs ruled England from 1154 until 1485 before losing power in the Wars of the Roses.

Edward I	King of England
Reign	16 Nov 1272 -7 Jul 1307
Spouses	Eleanor of Castile m. 1254
	Margaret of France m. 1299
Father	Henry III of England
Mother	Eleanor of Provence
Birth	17 June 1239 Palace of Westminster, London, England
Death	7 July 1307 Burgh by Sands, Cumberland, England buried at West Minster Abbey, London, England

Edward I went to war to suppress rebellions in Wales and Scotland. He imposed English rule in Wales, but the Scots won their war with England. When he died he left to his son, Edward II, an ongoing war with Scotland and many financial and political problems. *Source: Wikipedia, the free encyclopedia on the World Wide Web.*

Edward II	King of England
Reign	7 July 1307 – 25 January 1327
Spouse	Isabella of France
Father	Edward I of England
Mother	Eleanor of Castile
Birth	25 April 1284, Caemarfon Castle Gwynedd
Death	21 Sept. 1327 Berkeley Castle, Gloucestershire buried at Gloucester Cathedral, Gloucestershire

Edward II's reign was disastrous for England, and was marked by incompetence, political squabbling and military defeats. Edward was deposed by his wife Isabella in January 1327. *Source: Wikipedia, the free encyclopedia on the World Wide Web.*

Edward III	King of England
Reign	1 February 1327 - 21 June 1377
Spouse	Philippa of Hainault
House	House of Plant age net
Father	Edward II of England
Mother	Isabella of France
Birth	13 November 1312, Windsor Castle
Death	1377 Buried in Westminster Abbey, London

Edward III is noted for his military success transforming the Kingdom of England into a military power in Europe. Source: Wikipedia, the free encyclopedia on the World Wide Web.

In the 1800s the Trice family was moving south from North Carolina to Georgia and on to Florida. In 1820 the Ezekiel Trice family (not Ezekiel the preacher) was in Orange County, North Carolina.

Ezekiel had three sons: Abner, Mann, and Henry. Trice families born Orange County, North Carolina, are found in Jones County, Georgia including an Ezekiel. In 1840 in Decatur County, Georgia, there was an Ezekiel Trice, who was born in 1760 and died in 1770, and a Henry Trice born 1800 and died 1810. In Gadsden County, Florida, a Mann Trice is born in 1810. A second Trice family was in Gadsden County in 1840 and had four children. *Source: Florida Roberts Trice March 2010.*

Ancestry Links to Plantagenet Kings	
Name (Date of Birth -Date of Death)	**Ancestry Link***
Edward III King of England (1312 -1377)	17th great-grandfather
John Gaunt Lancaster Plantagenet (1340 -1399)	Son of Edward III
John (Marquis Somerset) Beaufort (1373-1410)	Son of John gaunt Lancaster
Joan Beaufort (1406 -1465)	Daughter of John
Thomas Wilcox (1450 -1500)	Son of Joan
Robert (1470 -1530)	Son of Thomas
Thomas Wilcox (1515-1560)	Son of Robert
Christopher Wilcox (1565 -1595)	Son of Thomas
John Wilcox (1596 -1651)	Son of Christopher
John Wilcox (1620 -1676)	Wilcox Son of John
Israel Wilcox (1656 -1689)	Son of John
Thomas Wilcox (1689 -1779)	Son of Israel
John Wilcox (1728 -1793)	Son of Thomas
John Wilcox (1777 -1852)	Son of John
Elizabeth L Wilcox (1826 -1893)	Daughter of John
Ludusky Elena Trice (1857 -1924)	Daughter of Elizabeth L
William Thomas Roberts (1875 -1949)	Son of Ludusky Elena
Gladys Thelma Roberts (1899 -1997)	Daughter of William Thomas
Marjorie Clarice Sanders (1923 -2008)	Daughter of Gladys Thelma
Patricia, Rodney, Ronnie, David, Dorothy, Latrelle, Timothy, Carole, Cathy, Gerald, Glen, Maxie and Suzanne Gray	Daughters and sons of Marjorie Clarice

Figure 1 Armorial of Plantagenet

John Wilcox and his daughter, Elizabeth, are in Laurens, Georgia in 1830. In 1850, Mann Trice and John Wilcox are in Leon County, Florida. (Source: Florida Roberts Trice March 2010).

We also know that our ancestors, the Abner Trice family were living in Wakulla County as early as 1941. We do not know if this Abner is the son of Ezekiel in Orange County, North Carolina. It is entirely possible that he is, but we cannot confirm it without additional information.

* Additional information in the (Gray-Sanders-Pigott-Roberts Family Tree)

Trices and Roberts in Wakulla County

The Trice's were in Wakulla County in the 1850, 1860, and 1870 census data. Ludusky's parents, Abner from North Carolina and Elizabeth from Georgia, lived in Shell Point in 1850. Abner is buried in the Sanders Cemetery in Curtis Mills. The gravestone shows he was a soldier in the Civil War and was a Private in Company P (Eland's Company) in the 7th Florida Mounted Infantry. His family is buried with him in the Sanders Cemetery as follows: Wife Elizabeth (Wilcox) Trice, born 1824 and died 1893, Grandson, George Dewey Trice, child of 1. S. and Nancy Trice, born May 9, 1899, died January 11, 1904, Granddaughter, Elizabeth Roberts, child of 1. S., and Nancy Trice, cannot read birth and death dates on the gravestone

Military records for Abner are on file through the Family History Centers of the Latter Day Saints. Record 1303475 is the film number for his service in the Florida War, 6th Regiment, Florida Militia. Record 1835-1836 J-Y A-I FHL US/CAN Film is for service in the Florida War, 7th Florida Militia. Record 1303476 FHL US/CAN Film is for services in three Seminole Wars.

• Florida War, 9th Regiment, Florida (Drafted) Militia, 4 months, 1836

• Florida War, 7th Regiment Florida Militia, 1836

• Florida War, 7th Regiment (Mounted) Florida Militia, 4 months, 1837

Source: Florida Roberts Trice March 2010

Ludusky Elena Trice came from a family that was in Florida as early as 1841 before Florida became a state. The 1850 U.S. Census for Shell Point shows all the Trice children were born in Florida. Joseph was the oldest child at nine years old in 1850. Abner was born in North Carolina, and Elizabeth was born in Georgia.

We have a record of William Theodore Roberts' parents in the 1870 U.S. Census for Apalachicola, Florida. The census shows James Roberts, age 45, born in North Carolina, living in Franklin, County. James was a farmer with land valued at $100 and a personal estate valued at $175. The household included his wife Elizabeth who was 43 years and born in South Carolina. They had four children living with them in 1870. All of the children were born in Florida indicating the family had been in Florida since at least 1850 and maybe even earlier. William Roberts is nineteen and working on the farm. His siblings living with James and Elizabeth in 1870 were (1) Sarah age 14. (2) Louisa age 12 and (3) George age 10.

The U.S. Census data shows the Roberts in Carrabelle in 1880, 1900, 1910, and 1920. William Theodore married Ludusky Elena Trice and the family actually lived in McIntyre across the Ochlockonee River from Curtis Mills. McIntyre is about ten miles from Carrabelle. The family started out in Apalachicola then moved to McIntyre to work for the sawmill. Later, many of them left the McIntyre-Curtis Mills area; I think the likely reason for leaving the area was the lack of jobs once the sawmill and the railroad line to Tallahassee closed.

William and Ludusky made a wise decision to leave Apalachicola and move to McIntyre to provide a better life for their family. Curtis Mills was a booming community with a thriving lumber industry. Lumber was shipped on the Ochlockonee River and the railroad that ran between Tallahassee and Curtis Mills. The lumber industry played out when all the large cypress trees were cut. With the lumberyard work experience and/or working for the railroad, many in the Roberts family continued in careers similar to the work they had in Curtis Mills.

William Theodore Roberts' son, William Thomas Roberts (B: 16 Nov 1875 in Florida, D: 08 APR 1949 in Wakulla County, Florida) is our 2nd great-granddaddy. He married Martha Louise "Lou" Sunday (B: 20 AUG 1880 in Florida, D: 08 May 1948 in Wakulla County, Florida). I heard a lot about him when we were growing up. He was a kind, gentle man to all of his grandchildren. He was known for being one of the best log walkers in the area. He would roll the logs to control the flow of the logs. After he retired, he would spend hours working on his wood lathe. It was told that he would sit on the porch for a while visiting, then would slip away and you would find him out working on his lathe. Mama said Grandpa Tom was a hard worker and happy as long as he was doing something like gardening or chopping wood. He was a tall quiet even tempered man. She said that he was estimated to weigh 16 pounds at birth. You see, there were no scales to weigh babies with at that time.

The adage that opposites attract holds true to Grandpa Tom and Grandma Lou. She loved to socialize and Tom was quiet, making it easy for him to slip away so he could do the things he loved. Mama said that Grandma Lou liked to talk and visit with family. She was also remembered as a kind grandmother.

William Thomas and Martha Louise Sunday Roberts Circa 1935

Family folklore tells that Grandma Lou was a Midwife and used either moonshine or whiskey to help with her practice. She would take a sip for herself, one for the mother, and a drop for the baby.

Our Grandmother, Gladys Thelma Roberts (B: 26 Dec. 1899 in McIntyre, Franklin County, Florida, D: 10 Dec. 1997, Tallahassee, Leon County, Florida) married Nathaniel Walker Sanders III, (B: 05 May 1891, in Curtis Mills, Wakulla, Florida, D: 13 March 1977, Medart, Wakulla, Florida) was the oldest daughter of Tom and Lou Roberts.

Grandma Sanders' was the mother to 11 children: Mildred (Willis), Marjorie (Gray), Madelyn (Crowson), Nathaniel, Marcia (Raker, Vause), Dorothy Mae (died young), Mahalia Ruth Hurly, Smith) Norris (died young), Robert "Bobby", Janelle (Gray then Crawford), and Donna Gail (Deese).

Gladys Thelma Roberts Circa 1919

Gladys Sanders 1927 with Mildred, Nathaniel, Marjorie, and Madelyn – So Cute!

Our mother spoke of the fun, happy childhood she enjoyed; parents, brothers, sisters, aunts, uncles and all the community that loved and supported each other. When the grandchildren came along, they also have many happy memories of that loving environment. One of the favorite activities was jumping on Grandma's feather bed. We would take turns falling back onto the bed and lifting each other in the air. Latrelle's favorite thing to do was to stay with Grandma, not only Latrelle, but every Grandchild either lived with Grandma or visited often.

Grandma's food was always awesome! We had to work for our dinner; we would kill our chicken for good ole' Chicken and Rice, along with vegetables from the garden, and of course, some type of bread. The funny thing was that Grandma didn't have enough pots, so she would cook her Chicken and Rice and then rinse out the pot to make a chocolate cake. How we miss those wonderful days.

After all of Grandma's children and grand-children were grown and spending less time with her, Mom brought her to all our family gatherings. Grandma was always quiet in a crowd and spent a lot of time whistling songs like 'Amazing Grace'. She told Mom that we (her children) loved her very much and that is so true! Another bit of wisdom from Grandma.

We all loved Grandma too. We all loved Granddaddy Sanders too. He made all of us feel very special.

One-on-one Grandma talked a lot. She kept up with each one of her grandchildren with help from Mom and her sisters who needed someone to talk to when her children shared their joys and difficulties in raising their own children. We spent a lot of time with our cousins, because Mom and her siblings frequently brought their kids to visit Grandma.

Grandma and Granddaddy

Gladys Thelma Roberts and Nathaniel Walker Sanders circa 1980

Our cousin, Brenda Crowson, told a story at Grandma's funeral; she said a snake was after Grandma's chickens, and Grandma killed the snake with her walker. Now that is a woman with spirit! At the funeral we had a huge photo of her and she was quite the matriarch looking out at her family. Her family filled up the little Pentecostal Church in Sopchoppy. We were proud to be a part of that family. Grandma died at the age of 99 and was a gentle sweet spirit until the end of her days.

Our Mother, Marjorie Clarice Sanders Gray (B: August 26, 1923 Curtis Mills, Wakulla, Florida, D: October 23, 2008, Tallahassee, Leon County, Florida), was their second daughter. She married Rev. Walter Floyd Gray (B: 26 Sep 1916, Medart, Wakulla County, Florida, D: 21 April 1998 Leon County, Florida). She was a kind gentle soul like her predecessors. It is true that "the apple does not fall far from the tree". Never an unkind word was heard from her. She could always be found working with her hands, gardening, sewing, and always in the kitchen cooking to feed such a large family. She had many challenges as she was the mother of 13 children and the wife of a minister for 50 years. She always greeted us each morning with a smile and a sweet angelic voice telling us to "rise and shine"!

We were only allowed to do a few things which included going to school and school activities, church, working hard, playing hard, and when it was time to eat, we enjoyed that because we were starving from working and playing all day. We learned to enjoy life's simple pleasures. What a blessing!

Several of the children wrote about Mama in our last WCHS book, "The Heritage of Wakulla County". Several of the children spoke on our fond memories of special things that she would do for us. She had a knack of making each one of us feel special. Our brother Timothy mentioned how she would get up early in the morning to prepare a big pot of crabs and flounder after Daddy went fishing the night before. Dorothy shared how Mom was our rock. We could count on her to be

Marjorie 3rd from left with friends and relatives circa 1938

there for us. We never had to stay with a sitter. Every morning, we got fresh biscuits, grits, bacon or fat back, and eggs made to order.

Sitting around table all 15 plus visitors circa 1967

When we got home from school, Mom had something cooked for us. She was also famous for her chocolate cakes with chocolate icing. We had that frequently. That is still a favorite recipe. Mom's breakfast and after school treats were truly a gift of love. Another gift was her ability to let us be ourselves; not trying to change us. We could play for hours uninterrupted. We had to get into a big fight to get her attention. She ignored the little squabbles.

Our Daddy always loved "his Margie". In an interview with a Wakulla County News Reporter, our Daddy, Rev. Walter Floyd Gray, said about Mom, "Marjorie was an ideal preacher's wife, very gracious and loving; a quiet, gentle woman who bore my 13 children." He went on to say, "She supported me without complaint and worked just as hard as I did, even when we pastored churches many miles from home." He also said, "All the

Marjorie Clarice Sanders and Rev. Walter Floyd Gray Circa 1980

Marjorie Sanders Gray's Hershey's "Perfectly Chocolate" Chocolate Cake

2 cups sugar
1-3/4 cups all purpose flour
3/4 cup Hershey's cocoa
1-1/2 teaspoon baking powder
1-1/2 teaspoon baking soda
1 teaspoon salt
2 eggs
1 cup milk
1/2 cup vegetable oil
2 teaspoons vanilla extract
1 cup boiling water"

Heat to 350°. Grease and flour 2- 9 inch round baking pans. Combine dry ingredients in a large bowl. Add eggs, milk, oil and vanilla extract, beat on medium speed 2 minutes. Stir in boiling water (batter will be thin) pour into pans.

Bake 30-35 minutes (or until a wooden toothpick inserted into the center comes out clean)
Cool ten minutes. Remove from pans to wire racks. Cool completely.

Frost with "Perfectly Chocolate Frosting

The Perfectly Chocolate Frosting can be found on the next page if desired.

Marjorie Sanders Gray's "Perfectly Chocolate" Chocolate Frosting

1 stick (or 1/2 cup) butter or margarine
3 cups powdered sugar
1 tsp vanilla extract
2/3 cup Hershey's Cocoa
1/3 cup milk

Melt butter, stir in cocoa. Alternately add powdered sugar and milk, beating on medium speed to spreading consistency. Add more milk , if needed. Stir in vanilla.

We put our cake in a 9" x 13" pan, topped with frosting, and served it from the cake pan since we always served around 15 people. On special occasions, we would double the cake and frosting recipes and make a four layer cake.

churches always thought that she was wonderful. They used to call her "Sister Preacher".

Mom and Dad, and Latrelle are gone on to be with the Lord now and the large Gray home is filled with another happy family that loves our place as much as we did.

All of the Gray Children are proud of the heritage that has been passed on to us from the King of England, through our ancestors, to Wakulla County.

I want to say a special thank you to our sister Dorothy Nell Gray for the many years of tireless research to document our family history.

**The full source is housed at the Wakulla County Museum and Archives "The Gray-Pigott-Sanders-Roberts Family Tree" January 2012, Created by Dorothy N. Gray; Submitted By Dorothy N. Gray and Cathy Gray Frank. Recipes submitted by; Cathy Frank*

William Chitwood

William Chitwood's family has been traced all the way back to John De Chetwode in, 1082, from Buckinghamshire, England. The surname was Chetwode for twenty generations until Thomas Chetwode, born in 1630, moved his family from London, England to Lancaster, Virginia, where he died in 1684, at the age of 54 years old. Thomas and Elizabeth Chetwode's son, Thomas changed the spelling of his last name from Chetwode to Chitwood. The family migrated from Virginia to North Carolina, from North Carolina, to Williamsburg County, South Carolina and then on to Georgia.

William Chitwood was born in 1835 in Williamsburg County, South Carolina. His father was Charles Chitwood. William married Louisa Weeks on July 18, 1851, in Troup, County, Georgia. Louisa's parents were Toliver Weeks and Matilda Cotney Weeks. William and Louisa were listed on the, 1860 census records of Coffee, County, Alabama. Their children were Martin Alexander, Thomas Toliver, Mary Jane, and James W. Chitwood.

William Chitwood fought in the Civil War with the Gulf Rangers. The "Gulf Rangers" were formed of friends, neighbors and kin, on September 14, 1861, in Geneva, Coffee County, Alabama. After mustering in Montgomery, Alabama, they became part of Company D, 4th Confederate Infantry, 1st Regiment, made up of men from Alabama, Tennessee and Mississippi. (Became Co. E. 54th Ala. Inf. Regt.) They served at the battle

of "Island Ten," in Tennessee. This battle was fought as a holding action; 7,000 Confederate troops were to hold General Pope and 40,000 Union soldiers in check long enough for General Albert Sydney Johnson to attack Grant at Shiloh. After about a month, on April 8, 1862 the outnumbered Confederates formally surrendered. William C. Chitwood died in prison on May 29, 1862, Camp Randall, Madison, Wisconsin at the age of 28 years old. He was buried at Forest Hill Cemetery in Madison, Wisconsin. There is a headstone marking his grave.

After William's death, Louisa Weeks Chitwood married Jack Hughes. They had one son William Henry Hughes. She later married a man named Crosby.

After his death, she moved to Curtis Mills, Wakulla County, Florida to live with her daughter Mary Jane. She is buried in the Sanders Cemetery in Curtis Mills, Florida.

William and Louisa Chitwood's daughter, Mary Jane Chatwood (*note name change again*) married John Henry Sanders.

William and Louisa were my 2nd great-grandparents. William Chitwood died at the young age of 28 years old but he left a very large legacy. Every Sanders from Wakulla County, Florida and every Chatwood from Jackson County, Florida are part of that great legacy.

Submitted and written by, Louise Thomas, 419 Buckhorn Creek Rd. Sopchoppy, FL 32358

The following is a poem written about William Chitwood & Mary Jane of the previous article.

Poppa

Mama received a letter today From The War Department CSA. Poppa was captured at Island Ten. Will he ever come back home again?

I remember the day Poppa left home, Sitting up high on his chestnut roan, So handsome in his uniform of gray, I cried, "Poppa, please don't go away."

Poppa said, "Mary, you're my brave little girl, Mind your Mama, She'll need help with the farm Watch out for your brothers, try to keep them from harm."

Poppa, where were you, the day the Yankee's came to our house? We were so scared. Mama said, "Ya'll be quiet as a mouse." We climbed on the roof and jumped to the ground. We hid in the woods, so we couldn't be found.

The Yankee's rode off at the break of dawn, It was such a relief to finally see them gone. They took all our chickens, our two pigs and the goat, got our potatoes, and everything else they could tote.

We still have the silo filled with black eyed peas, and our milk cow Bessie, we hid in the trees. Poppa, we love you, miss you and wish you were here. Tomorrow you will have been gone for one year.

Mama received another letter today, From The War Department CSA. She said you went to Heaven, to be a soldier for our Lord, And in the sheath upon your side, You carry a golden sword.

Submitted and written by, Louise Thomas, 419 Buckhorn Creek Rd. Sopchoppy, Fl 32358

History of the Pelt Family Homestead

Durant John Pelt was born to Jonathan Van Pelt and Susannah Gwaltney Van Pelt on January 6, 1818 in Craven County, North Carolina. Jonathan and Susannah Van Pelt's children, Durant, Caroline, and Henry, used the surname Pelt instead of "Van Pelt." Caroline married a Gwaltney and remained in North Carolina until her death in 1900. Henry is listed in the 1860 Putnam County, Florida census. Confederate service records indicate that Henry was born in North Carolina, enlisted in 1861 and died of disease in Richmond on July 29, 1864.

Durant Pelt moved to Wakulla County circa 1848. He told his son G.W. Bostic Pelt that he came from North Carolina to Florida with a wagon, a mule and a feather bed. More than likely he traveled with some of his Gwaltney relatives. The Gwaltney name appears in several historical accounts of the time. A store in Arran, Florida was run by a family of Gwaltneys.

After arriving in Wakulla County, Durant married Melvina Posey, daughter of Noah and Feribay Shepherd Posey, on March 16, 1855. The 1860 Wakulla County census lists Durant, age 43, and Melvina, age 23, living with their three children, ages five, three, and seven months. It appears that they were living on the Posey property at the time of the census. The baby did not reach one year of age and is buried in the Pelt family cemetery. Durant enlisted in the Confederate Army in 1864 in the Captain John Tupperville Company, First Regiment of Florida Reserves. The regiment was detailed to retrieve lumber from the swamp to build barrels. In 1863, Noah Posey transferred to his daughter Melvina 190 plus or minus acres of land. On January 1, 1867, Noah conveyed to Melvina and her heirs another 190 plus or minus acres "in consideration of love and affection, as well as $5," witnessed by J. L. Crawford. Later in 1867, Melvina bought 160 acres from John Beard. Durant and Melvina's descendants are still living on this property, which is west of Crawfordville.

Durant and Melvina had nine children: Henry Ellis, who married Sallie Giles; Columbus Crawford, who married Mary Elizabeth Lawhon; Shoalt, who died before one year of age; Andrew Jackson, who married Mary Frances Stevens; Virginia, who married James Coleman; Noah Jackson, who married Theodocia Lawhon; Peter, who married Emma Eubanks; Melvina Adelia, who married William Everett Whaley; and George Washington Bostic, who married Emma Ruth Pigott.

The original house was built up the road from the present site where Janice Pelt Brown now lives. The house was given to the youngest male child (George Washington Bostic) as was the custom in the family. Bostic married Emma Ruth Pigott in 1898, and they had ten children who were raised in this house. Their children were Senia, who married Calhoun Taff; John Durant, who married Ethel Vause; Noah Bostic, who married Mary Morris; Emma Lee, who married Henry Green; Andrew Jackson, who married Elva Tucker; George Cajer, who married Debra Council; Oma Lee, who married Halley Lawhon; Carmel, who married Etta Mae Council; Harry, who married Carolyn Knight; and Mary Ruth, who married Elmo White.

The house was taken apart and moved to the present location sometime around 1920 or 1921. When my father, Carmel, was a very young child, he recalled riding on the wagon with his baby brother, Harry, and his sister, Oma Lee, who was holding her doll. It is the belief that the home site was relocated for better farm land. After the death of his mother, Emma Ruth Pigott Pelt, Carmel and his wife Etta Mae lived in the family home and raised six children: Berlin, who married Ellen Bruce; Etta Jo, who married Ralph Oliver; Willie, who married Janis Wester; Vera; Brenda who married Gene McCarthy; and Carmen, who married Broward Sapp.

The house was built out of heart pine, and it has gone through numerous renovations over its 140 plus years of life. Three generations of Pelts have lived in this house. Our mother, Etta Mae, who is now 88, still lives in the Pelt House. It is not a grand old house, just a typical Florida Cracker house that has sheltered many babies, children, young and old people of the Pelt family. Many of life's lessons have been taught in this old house. Honesty, being kind to your neighbor, and having a good name are but a few. Perhaps the most important lesson the people of this house were taught was to be proud of our Southern heritage and to love and honor God. The house has been a home to the Pelt family and their heirs who are now living all over the world.

Pelt, Michael and Pelt, Malcolm. (2004). Van Pelt Genealogy, North Carolina Origins, Volumes 1 and 2. Salem, Massachusetts: Higginson Book Company. Pelt, Chester H., Sr. (1992). A Genealogy History of the Pelt Family Branch of the Van Pelt Family Tree. Salem, Massachusetts: Higginson Book Company; Florida State Archives ; Brenda Pelt McCarthy, Crawfordville, Florida

The Pigott's Branches and Tributaries

Great-grandfather John Ervin Pigott Jr. & Great-grandmother Mary Ann Ellen Durrance

The Rev. Walter Floyd Gray and Marjorie Clarice Sanders Gray children are often asked, "Are you related to everyone in Wakulla County"? We usually laugh and reply that, "Well, maybe half of the county". As I tell our story, you will see that many of the citizens of Wakulla County are related to us.

Our Grandmother Iseybel Pigott was a good story teller and could keep the grandchildren's interest for hours with her tales. Rev. Walter Floyd Gray, our father was good at telling stories too. They could keep your interest for hours with tall tales mixed in with some truth. I was amazed at his ability to keep up with the ancestry of our family members; you could ask our father about anyone in the county and he would tell you their ancestry line for three generations.

This knack for storytelling and research has been passed down to many of our relatives and many of the Gray children.

I am going to share with you our Journey Story of amazing facts about the Pigott family and our relatives.

The early history of the Pigott family can be traced back to the 1600s. Quaker meeting records show John Pigott married Margery Brown whose family was involved in establishing the first Quaker settlement in America. Our 6th great-grandfather, James Brown left England as a young man along with his brother William. They worked with William Penn to establish the first Quaker settlement in what is now Salem County, New Jersey. It is believed that Penn set aside 40 acres in 1701 for "public worship, the right of burial, and the privilege of education". Among the original owners, certainly the Brown brothers (James and William) represented the strong religious values of the community. They are believed to have held the first Quaker meetings in their homes about 1704 prior to the building of the Meetinghouse. By 1751, six members of the Brown family, four men and two women, were ministers in Nottingham. William Penn founded Pennsylvania in 1682 with Chester County, PA representing the most western frontier at that time, and the lands were mostly tribal and unsettled by Europeans.

John Pigott was in Chester County as evidenced by the genealogy and biographical sketches of the family of Samuel Painter, who came from England and settled in Chester County. William Penn wrote as follows, "In 1707, I bought off John Piggott 100 acres of land in Birmingham, Chester Co., PA.". Additional evidence of John Piggott's Quaker activities recorded in notes from a Nottingham

Monthly Meeting held 08 August, 1730, states "collections to purchase books resulted in the shillings placed in the hands of John Piggott and another member". It further reports, "Said books were purchased as requested".

The earliest Pigott relative of record was born in 1634 in West Sussex, England showing ancestry links to present day Pigott's.

Name	Birth-Death	Ancestry	Birthplace
Thomas Pigott	1634-1693	7th great-grandfather	West, Sussex, England
John Pigott	1654-Unknown	6th great-grandfather	Nottingham, Cecil, Maryland
John Pigott	1689-1743	5th great-grandfather	Nottingham, Cecil, Maryland
John Pigott	1717-1743	4th great-grandfather	Susquehanna Hundred, Cecil Maryland
Charles Pigott	1776-1816	3rd great-grandfather	Darlington, SC
John Ervin Pigott Sr.	1810-1885	2nd great-grandfather	Darlington, SC
John Ervin Pigott Jr.	1848-1914	great-grandfather	Darlington, SC
Iseybel Pigott	1872-1961	grandmother	Medart, Wakulla, FL
Walter Floyd Gray	1916-1998	father	Medart, Wakulla FL
Patricia Lynette 1941, Ronnie 1943, Rodney 1943, David Ray 1944, Dorothy Nell 1946, Latrelle 1947-2011, Timothy Floyd 1949, Frances Carole 1950, Cathy Marlene 1952, Gerald Allen 1953, Walter Glen 1955, Maxie 1958,		children of Walter Floyd	Medart, Wakulla, FL
Suzanne Gray 1960			

Many of the folks in Wakulla County are related through the marriage of Rev. John Ervin Pigott Sr. and Mary Elizabeth Revell, married on March 4, 1838**.** According to family Bible records, the Pigott and Revell families came from Darlington, South Carolina together around 1854.

According to family Bible records, the Pigott and Revell families came from Darlington, South Carolina together around 1854.This information in the family Bible was written with blackberry juice. The Bible has been passed down through the Rev. Stephen Thomas Pigott line.

The first census of record showing John E. Sr., and Mary Elizabeth in Wakulla County was in 1860. It shows him with his wife Mary Elizabeth, and children and others in the household. It listed the following: William N., Mary J., Robert R., Stephen T., John E. Jr., Eliza A., James C., Sarah P. The census spelled Pigott Pigat.

The earliest Revell relative of record was born in 1630 in Northern England, Scotland and died in Virginia showing ancestry links to present day Pigott's.

Name	Birth-Death	Ancestry	Birthplace
John Revell	1630-1693	8th great-grandfather	Northern England (Scotland), D: Virginia
John Joseph Revell	1655-1720	7th great-grandfather	Virginia, Surry County D: 1720 Isle of Wright Co. VA
Randall Revell	1683-1739	6th great-grandfather	Isle of Wright Co. VA
Joseph	1704-	5th great-	Isle of

John	1784	grandfather	Wright Co. VA D:Wayne Co. NC
John Revell	1754-1830	4th great-grandfather	Darlington Co. SC D: Unknown
Stephen Revell	1790-1857	3rd great-grandfather	Darlington Co. SC D: Interstate
Mary Elizabeth Revell	1816-1894	2nd great-grandmother	Darlington Co. SC D: Wakulla Co. FL
John Ervin Pigott, Jr.	1848 - 1914	great-grandfather	Darlington Co. SC D: Wakulla Co. FL
Iseybel Pigott	1872-1961	grandmother	Medart, Wakulla Co. FL D: Same
Walter Floyd Gray	1916-1998	Father	Medart, Wakulla Co, FL D: Same
Patricia Lynette 1941, Ronnie 1943, Rodney 1943, David Ray 1944, Dorothy Nell 1946, Latrelle 1947-2011, Timothy Floyd 1949, Frances Carole 1950, Cathy Marlene 1952, Gerald Allen 1953, Walter Glen 1955, Maxie 1958, Suzanne Gray 1960		children of Walter Floyd	Medart, Wakulla Co. FL

Mary Elizabeth's father *Stephen Revell*, son of John and Mary Revell, married our 3rd great-grandmother, *Quinta Jerusha Kirby* on March 5, 1812. Jerusha was the daughter of *James Kirby* and *Margaret Brown.*

A proof of the birth and death of Stephen, and Jerusha and their children is recorded in the old family Bible that belonged to their son, Stephen Calvin Revell.

Stephen's occupation was a planter. He died intestate. His estate contained one thousand two hundred eighty (1,280) acres located on the northeast side of Lynch's Creek in the Darlington District. The Revells' were members of Bethel Baptist Church in Olanta, SC and then Sardis Baptist Church in Sardis, SC.

Jerusha sold all of her real estate in South Carolina and joined her children in Wakulla County in 1859. Evidence of Jerusha in Wakulla County, Florida is in the February 21, 1859 minutes of Mt. Elon Baptist Church in Smith Creek, Wakulla County, FL. Jerusha lived with her daughter Mary Elizabeth and John E. Pigott, Jr. until her death in 1884.

Children of Stephen and Jerusha Kirby Revell:

1. William Wesley Revell (1814-1874) M 1-Margaret McClary M 2- Mary B. McClary M 3-Eliza Butler
2. Mary Elizabeth Revell (1816-1894) M-John Ervin Pigott Sr.
3. Margaret Maria Revell (1818-1892) M-Ephraim Vause
4. John Nelson Revell (1820-1885) M-1 Permelia Ann M-2 Arcadia Chandler (Roberts)
5. Matthew James Revell (1823-1880) M-1 Charity Anderson M-2 Margaret Lawhon M-3 Nancy Miller
6. Sarah Ann Revell (1825-1891) M-Lazarus Hudson Mims
7. Stephen Calvin Revell (1828-1912) M-Mary Adeline Anderson
8. Harriet Jane Revell (1830-1916) M-James P. Langston
9. Sidney Eli Revell (1832-1864) M-Mary Elizabeth Bradham
10. Samuel Kervin Revell (1835-1902) M-1 Melvinia Bradham M-2 Rosanna Jennie Bradham
11. George Washington Revell (1837-1880) M-Harriett E. Keels
12. Susannah Angeline Revell (1839-1859) M-John D. Askins
13. Elijah Alexander Revell (1841-1864)

Our 3rd great-grandmother Quinta Jerusha Kirby Revell parents were James Kirby and Margaret Brown; James was born November 23, 1751, married Margaret Brown September 6, 1771 in SC; he died around the end of 1820 in Darlington County, SC.. Margaret was born about 1756 in SC. The last record of Margaret is a deed gift to her children on February 8, 1840. She most likely died in Sumter County, SC where she had been living with her son Nelson.

The 1880 census shows James Kirby's two living children (Jerusha Revell and Nelson Kirby) say their father was born in SC. But on the 1880 Mortality Schedule for his son Benjamin Kirby, it says his father was born in VA.

James fought in the Revolutionary War and was granted 100 acres of land by the United States Government for his service. He was listed on a muster roll of the St. David's Parish SC Militia formed as a unit in 1776. He served under Captain Elias Dubose. Captain Dubose's company served with General Francis Marion in 1781 and 1782.

Children of James and Margeret Brown Kirby:

1. Nancy Ann Kirby (1755-1852) M-Alamon White, 2-Thomas C. Nesom
2. Molly Kirby (1778-1825) M-John Chandler
3. William Kirby (1780-1835) M-Melicia Bryan
4. George Kirby (1782-1843) M-1-unknown 2-Mahala Fountain
5. Abraham Kirby (1785-1850)
6. Louanza Kirby (1788-1853) M-Abraham Nesom
7. Benjamin Kirby (1791-1880) M-Deborah McCree Pilkington
8. Margaret Kirby (1793) M-Mr. Philips
9. *Quinta Jerusha Kirby* (1796-1884) M-Stephen Revell
10. Elizabeth Kirby (1797-1840) M-Mr. Hickson
11. James Kirby, Jr. (1799-1870) M-Elizabeth Courtney M 2-Laura Eliza Belew
12. John Kirby (1800-1854) M-Nancy Moore
13. Samuel Kirby (1802-1879) M-Frances Harriet Cook
14. Nelson Kirby (1803-1881) M-Hester Richardson M 2-Nancy

Our 3rd great-grandparents John Ervin Pigott Sr. and Mary Elizabeth Revell came from North Carolina to Florida with a group of people who had seven horses and two-wheeled carts. They slept in carts and tents which consisted simply of a piece of canvas thrown over a ridgepole. It took three weeks to make the trip.

After arriving in Wakulla County, they purchased land from Henry Nash, a large plantation owner, for whom John Ervin, Sr. served as foreman. According to a story by our Aunt Emma Pelt, they lived in a four-room log house which was locked with a chain.

John Ervin, Sr. was a farmer (including raising sheep), fisherman, carpenter, and brick mason. Bricks in those days were made of oyster shells from Old Skipper Bay. They were burned then water thrown over them to slick them into lime. The lime was mixed with sand, put into molds, and turned out, four bricks at a time. The bricks were used for chimneys and house pillars.

It was very common for the children to work in the fields picking cotton and corn. Children would quilt, spin wool and cotton, and work hard along with the adults.

They made their beds with Spanish moss that was gathered from the trees. The trash picked out, then boiled and dried on the fence.

She said the bustles worn by girls were made of sacks of cotton tied around the waist with a belt. The hoops women wore resembled barrel hoops and were fastened by elastic, holding the skirts out like tents. One time a girl fainted in church and the ladies present formed a screen around her. It was considered disgraceful to wear less than 3 or 4 petticoats.

The Pigott Family has always been a family with Christian values with many pastors and servants of the Lord as indicated by their early Quaker start. John Ervin, Sr. started Friendship Primitive Baptist around 1856. He donated the land, built the church, and served as the pastor. John Ervin Pigott, Jr. and Mary Ann Ellen donated the land to start Lake Ellen Baptist Church in Medart in 1869. They are Charter members and are buried at Lake Ellen Baptist Church. Lake Ellen in Medart, and

Lake Ellen Baptist Church were named after Mary Ann Ellen Durrance.

Rev. Robert (Bob) Pigott and our Uncle William Elijah Gray also pastored at Lake Ellen. Rev. Steven Thomas Pigott pastored at Beulah Primitive Baptist Church in Lost Creek.

Churches used to meet every other Sunday. The folks in Medart were all family and would meet one Sunday at Friendship and the other Sunday at Lake Ellen.

When John Ervin Sr. died, he passed the land to his sons. According to our father, Rev. Walter Floyd Gray, the land was divided accordingly: Steve owned all the land around Lake Ellen Church and the Recreation Park over to Hwy. 98. John Ervin Pigott, Jr. owned land from the site of the old pastorium across from Lake Ellen Baptist Church, back to Little Lake. Jim Pigott joined him on the South and owned all the land from Friendship Church, Pigott's Pond, over one-half the way to Lake Ellen and reaching to the Molly Branch on the west side; it went due North to the Sassar Landing (now Vause's Landing). Another cousin Bernard Pigott joined the Pigott property on the South side of Pigott's Pond.

Ancestry line for Rev. John Ervin Pigott, Sr., March 4, 1810 in Darlington Dist., SC, Died Nov. 22, 1885, Medart, Florida, buried in Pigott Cemetery, Medart.

Mary Elizabeth Revell, March 4, 1838 in Darlington Dist., SC, Died Jan 2, 1895, Medart, Florida, Pigott's Cemetery, daughter of Stephen and Mary Revell.

Children of John Ervin Pigott Sr. and Mary Elizabeth Revell Pigott

1. William Pigott (1837-1862) Killed in Civil War service at Murfeesboro, TN
2. Mary Jane E. "Molly" Pigott (1840-1926 M-James William Wood
3. S. Charles McCall Pigott (1842-1852)
4. Robert Reid Pigott (1844-1926) M-Mary Elizabeth "Puss" Reynolds
5. Stephen Thomas Pigott 1846 – 1921M-Nancy Elizabeth Whaley
6. *John Ervin Pigott, Jr.* (1848-1914) M-Mary Ann Ellen Durrance 1870
7. Warren C Pigott (1851-1853)
8. Eliza Ann Pigott (1854-1926) M-Newt Wood
9. James Calvin Pigott (1857-1943) M-Nancy Fairby Raker
10. Sarah Cornelia Pigott (1860-1936) M-John Knox Whaley
11. Winnie Jerushia Pigott (1862-1935) M-Enoch David Thomas
12. Minty Jane Pigott (1862-)

Our great-granddaddy John Ervin Pigott, Jr. married Mary Ann Ellen Durrance in Medart, FL in 1870; Mary Ann Ellen's parents were Jesse W. (Washington?) Durrance and Catherine Stephens. The first Durrance in Wakulla County, Jesse (1814-1858) was our 2nd great-granddaddy. He was born in Georgia and moved to Wakulla County between 1840 and 1844 prior to the first state election in 1845. He married Catherine in 1833. They lived in what is now Purify Bay in Medart. Together they had eight children: James Stephens (1830), William Henry (1834), Thomas Jefferson (1836), William Augustus (1838), John Alexander (1840-1891), Martha Jane (1843), Mary Ann Ellen (1848-1922) M-John Ervin Pigott, Jr., Sarah Eliza (1852).

Jesse and family members are believed to be buried in a cemetery somewhere in Purify Bay. We don't know where the cemetery is, but it was recorded in a WPA work project Register of Deceased Veterans Florida No. 65 Wakulla County. Washington Durrance, veteran of Indian Wars, is listed as buried in this cemetery. Records of Jesse and Catherine and children come from the Pigott family Bible which was in the possession of Mary Ann Ellen Durrance Pigott.

<u>Ancestry line for John Ervin Pigott, Jr. and Mary Ann Ellen Durrance</u>

John was born 20 September, 1848 in Darlington, South Carolina and died 15 June, 1914 in Medart, Wakulla, Florida. Mary Ann Ellen Durrance was born on 24 November, 1846 in Medart; Wakulla, Florida died 26 October, 1922 in Wakulla County, Florida

Children:

1. Lanie Catherine Pigott (1868-1942)Solomon Haddock
2. Iseybel "Isey" Pigott (22 September, 1872-28 June 1961) M-Walter Fleming Gray
3. Charlie N. Pigott (1874-1919) M-Sally Hartsfield
4. Jan Oaks Pigott (1876-no information)
5. Mary Cornelia Pigott (1876-1907) M-Thomas Jefferson Williams
6. Emma Ruth Pigott (1878-1956) M-George Washington Pelt
7. James Ervin Pigott (1879-1968) M-Latisha Clemmons
8. Warren C Pigott (1882-1884)
9. Pearl Pigott (1884-1972) M-Franklin Frederick Green

Our sister Dorothy Nell Gray said that her first memory of Grandma Gray is when she stayed with our family.

We lived in the old house. It had three bed-rooms, with one for the girls and one for the boys and wall-to-wall beds (2 doubles in each room). At that time she was bedridden and got a double bed for a month in the boy's bedroom. Latrelle and I got to sleep in the other double bed.

Grandma entertained us with stories and always had some grandkids around listening to her. I wish I could remember the stories.

She talked a lot about how wonderful Daddy (Floyd Gray) was and how she wished she could live with us, but "Poor ole Margie" had too much on her already. She always said "Poor ole Margie" when she talked about Mama.

You may wonder how our Grandma Gray met Granddaddy Gray living in such a rural area as Medart, Florida. Daddy said that his Uncle Joel Hartsfield and Aunt Lizzie (Pigott) Hartsfield, from Leon County, visited Lake Ellen Baptist Church for a Fifth Sunday Meeting. Aunt Lizzie talked our great-grandpa John Ervin Pigott, Jr. into letting our Grandma Iseybel go spend the week with her Hartsfield relatives. Our Grandfather Walter Fleming Gray was visiting his Uncle Joel Hartsfield. When grandma got to Uncle Joel's house, the first thing she saw was Walter in the woodpile cutting wood. She decided right then and there that she was going to have this good looking man for her husband. They married and had nine children with our daddy being the baby.

Children:

1. John Elisha Gray (1901-1958) M-Mary Hamilton
2. Mary Pricilla Gray (1904-1973) M-Nathaniel Porter
3. William Robert Gray, Sr. (1905-1960) M-1 Hannah Stephens M-2 Annie Harris
4. Vera Lucille Gray (1907-1924) M- Council Gray
5. William Melton Gray (1908-1977) M-1 Myrtle Lindsey M-2 Louise Smith
6. Verdie Bell Gray (1910-1991) M-1 James Ross Eubanks M-2 Ellis Theodore Oaks
7. Annie Christine Gray (1912-1995) M-Rufus Crum
8. Rev. Truman Lee Gray (1914-1992) M-Susie Willis
9. Rev. Walter Floyd Gray (1916-1998) M-Marjorie Clarice Sanders March 30, 1940 see England, a King, to Wakulla County in this publication.

Daddy was the baby of a big family. His nickname was "Beauty By" and "Steel Wool" because of his curly, wiry hair.

His daddy, Walter Fleming Gray, died young and left Grandma Gray with a large family to raise by herself. He tells of the mischief that all those kids got into while "running the roads" of Wakulla County. Grandma Gray worked day in and out to keep them with life's necessities. But he also loved to tell of the slower, gentler times when they had so much love and support of a large family.

They attended school at the two room schoolhouse in Medart that was later the White home place. Grades one through four were in one room, and five through eight in the other room; he only finished the 7th grade. He would go in late and then get out early so he could help Grandma Iseybel do the jobs she took in which included washing clothes, chopping wood, and working on farms. He shared with me that she had to work the farms at night with a lantern. It is hard to believe that a small woman could accomplish such hard task. She was only 4'10" and weighed around 100 pounds.

Rev. Walter Floyd Gray Pastor at Aenon Baptist Church 1954

Daddy said that his favorite things to do were playing ball, fishing, and swimming in Lake Ellen and Pigott's Pond.

In later years Daddy moved to Tallahassee with his Gray relatives. He became a dance instructor in Tallahassee and loved to attend all the area dances. That is where he met our mother Marjorie Clarice Sanders. After a short courtship, they married and had 13 children (see chart above).He always said that he married the prettiest woman in Wakulla County and I agree.

Later he became a pastor and served as a Southern Baptist Minister for some 50 years.

Daddy's words of advice he left to his grandchildren were, "Always be kind, honest, and love the Lord with all your heart. The most important thing you can do is put God first in your life and always serve Him". Daddy lived those words out by example.

We miss those days of hard work, playing hard, good food, and fellowship. The swim in Pigott's Pond and Lake Ellen, playing ball and the camaraderie of a big family.

Mom, Dad and our sister Latrelle have gone on to be with the Lord. It is a reminder to be thankful for our loved ones and for the heritage that has been passed down to us through the generations. We should strive to make our children proud of the heritage that we leave behind for them.

Sources: Gray-Pigott, Sanders-Roberts Family Tree; THE REVELL FAMILY by Devota Durrance Hodge and Etta Maude Rouse Kirkland; THE VAUSES by Tanya Watts Lynn and JoAnn Roberts Hadland; U.S. Census Records; Stephen Calvin Revell Bible Records; Stephen Revell Plat Partition, Darlington County, SC; Bethel Baptist Church Records, Olanta, SC; Mt. Elon Baptist Church Records, Smith Creek; Wakulla County, FL; U.S. Civil War Records and Pension applications; Rene Rylanders Roots Web World Connect; Surry County, VA Land Records; Surry County, VA Tithables and Poll Taxes; Isle of Wright County, VA Land Records; Will of Randall Revell dated 1733, Isle of Wright County, VA; Will of Joseph John Revell, Wayne County, NC; Wayne County, NC Land Records; Wayne County Poll Tax and Voter Lists; Research Information provided by Russell Johnson; Surry County Court Records; John Revell Equity Records, Darlington County, SC; Revolutionary War Records; James Kirby Probate and Estate Records, Darlington County, SC; Margaret Brown Kirby, Deed Gift, Sumter County, SC; James Kirby Descendant DAR Application; Information from Claudia Brumbalow; Ancestry.com ; texasrhino added 14 February 2010; Pigott Family Bible; Sylvia Durrance Excerpts taken from "The Heritage of Wakulla County" pg. 119; Robert Warwick Day, Ph.D. The Nottingham Lots and Early Quaker Families

Special thanks to our sister Dorothy Nell Gray for the many years she dedicated to tracing our ancestry and researching the family history. To learn more about the Gray-Pigott, Sanders-Roberts Family Tree and many other families, visit The Wakulla County Historical Society Museum and Archives.

Submitted By: Cathy Gray Frank, 15 Stanley Dr., Crawfordville, FL

John Manning and Arcadia Roberts

John Manning Roberts was born about 1817 in South Carolina. Arcadia "Cadey" Chandler was born January 22, 1820 in Darlington District, South Carolina. Cadey was the youngest of six daughters born to John and Molly Kirby Chandler. Cadey's mother, Molly was the daughter of James and Margaret Brown Kirby.

Cadey's mother died when she was a young child and several years later, in 1830, her father died. Her four oldest sisters were married by that time and so Cadey and her sister Millie went to live with their oldest sister Margaret and her husband, Wright Langston in Williamsburg County, SC. John Chandler's estate paid for Cadey and Millie to board with Margaret and Wright until each of them married. The Langstons were members of Bethel Baptist Church in Olanta, SC. Arcadia joined the church and was baptized on September 14, 1837. John Manning Roberts joined the church and was baptized on September 9, 1839.

John Manning Roberts and Arcadia Chandler married about 1838. They were listed on the 1840 census in Williamsburg County and on the 1850 census in Darlington County. John and Cadey had eight children. They were: (1) Benjamin Marion "Med" born about 1839; (2) Margaret Elizabeth born about 1841, married Edward Miles Houston; (3) John Pinkney born April 14, 1843, married Ella J. Bostick; (4) Andrew Sylvester born April 4, 1845, married Letitia Holland; (5) Almira Jane born 1847, married James Franklin Duggar; (6) Lewis Abraham born April 3, 1849, married 1st Harriet Caladonia "Donie" Revell and 2nd Catherine Elizabeth "Cat" Barineau; (7) Eli M. born about 1851, married Angeline "Ann" Syfrett; (8) Joseph Emory born June 10, 1859, married 1st Lilla E. Gregory and 2nd Mary Affleck.

Andrew Sylvester Roberts born 4 April 1845 in Darlington County, South Carolina, died 9 June 1925 in Sopchoppy, Wakulla County, Florida. He served in the 11th FL Infantry Regiment, Co. I, C.S.A. Andrew was a farmer and also had a store in Sopchoppy at one time. He was Sopchoppy postmaster from 1895 to 1900. Andrew served as a deacon at the Sopchoppy Baptist Church for many years.

Letitia Holland born 22 March 1841 in Leon County, Florida, died 11 Sept. 1927 in Sopchoppy, Florida. She was a schoolteacher in Leon County before marrying Andre.

In December 1854, the John Manning Roberts family came to Florida with many other families from Darlington County. The Roberts family settled in Sopchoppy. John was a carpenter and a farmer. One day in 1859, John and some other men headed to Tallahassee to purchase some supplies. Back then, this was a three day trip. The first day they would go part of the way and camp for the night. On the second day they would go on into Tallahassee, conduct their business and then head back and camp again. They would make it home on the third day. John and the others were in Tallahassee when John suddenly fell down dead in one of the stores. The men were bringing him back to Sopchoppy for burial, but the weather was warm and he began to decompose, so they had to stop and bury him along the way. This story was told to me by the sons of John Manning Roberts, II (Uncle Johnny). Uncle Johnny was the grandson of John and Cadey.

Arcadia Roberts was listed on the 1860 Florida Agricultural Census. She had 25 acres of improved land and 20 unimproved. The cash value of her farm was $200. She had a horse and 20 swine, with the livestock valued at $80. She had 150 bushels of Indian corn, 100 pounds of rice, 2 bales of ginned cotton of 400 pounds each and 30 pounds of honey.

When the War Between the States broke out, most of the eligible young men in Wakulla County enlisted in the Confederate Army to fight for southern independence. Among these men were Benjamin Marion, John Pinkney and Andrew Sylvester Roberts, Edward Miles Houston and James Franklin Duggar. Andrew Sylvester Roberts was my great-great-grandfather. I am very proud of all of the brave soldiers who fought so valiantly for the South.

In the 1870s, Arcadia married her first cousin, John Nelson Revell, and moved to Liberty County with him. His wife, Permelia Ann, had died sometime after 1870. John Nelson was the son of Stephen and Jerusha Kirby Revell. He was born September 13, 1820 in Darlington District, SC. John and Permelia had one son named Stephen Jacob Revell born December 6, 1843. Stephen married Mary Savannah Strickland of Wakulla County. John Nelson Revell was a farmer and a Baptist preacher. Stephen Jacob was also a preacher and was the founder of Lake Mystic Baptist Church in Bristol. Cadey was a midwife and delivered many babies in Liberty County. The Revell home place was on the site of what is now Liberty County High School.

John Nelson Revell died November 9, 1885 in Bristol. Arcadia Chandler Roberts Revell died July 30, 1900 in Bristol. Arcadia and John Nelson Revell are buried in Bristol Cemetery, Liberty County, Florida.

A couple of well-known descendants of John Manning and Arcadia Chandler Roberts are a great-grandson, B.K. Roberts who was a Florida Supreme Court justice from 1949 to 1976; and a great-great-grandson, Glenn "Fireball" Roberts, the legendary racecar driver.

John Manning Roberts and Arcadia Chandler were my great-great-great-grandparents.Their son Andrew married Letitia Holland. Andrew and Letitia's daughter, Almyra Letitia Roberts married John Pleasant Grant. Myra and Pleas had a daughter named Marcia Grant who married Claxton Vause, Sr. My parents are Claxton Jr. and Vonita Haskett Vause.

Sources: U.S. Census Records; John Chandler Will and Estate Papers; James Kirby Estate Papers; Margaret Brown Kirby Deed Gift; Bethel Baptist Church Records, Olanta, SC; FL Marriage Records; FL Death Records; Cemetery Records; U.S. Civil War Records and Pension Applications; Information from Roberts and Revell descendants. Submitted by Arlene Vause, 89 Rose Street, Sopchoppy, FL 32358; phone (850) 962-2210.

Mary Jane Chatwood Sanders: (Mammy)

Mary Jane Chatwood was born in Geneva, Coffee County, Alabama on June 10, 1853. Her parents were William C. Chitwood and Louisa Weeks Chitwood.

Mary Jane was eight years old at the onset of the Civil War. One of her earliest memories was when the Yankees came to their house. She jumped out an upstairs window and caught her hair in the window, when running to hide from the Yankees.

Her father William Chitwood was killed in the civil war in 1863, leaving her mother with four children. Her mother married again, had one more son, and her second husband was killed in the civil war. They lived near her parents. Her mother married the third time to a man named Crosby and left with him, leaving her children behind.

Her brothers Martin Alexander and Thomas Toliver were old enough to do public work splitting rails, making 25 cents per day. Mary Jane was about 12 years old and small for her age. She worked all day in the fields, taking her little brother with her. She dug up roots for them to eat. She took care of the house. They made just enough to buy meal to make corn bread. A lot of people were starving to death.

One day while they were working in the field splitting rails John Henry Sanders walked up. He went to work with them. They invited him to stay with them as he had no place to stay.

Mary Jane married John Sanders in 1871, when she was 18 years old. They had five children while they lived in Geneva, Alabama. One child, a boy, died and is buried in Geneva, Alabama. Their other children were Emma, John, Jim, and Bill.

In April 1880, John got into some trouble and almost got killed. Mary Jane loaded John and the children in the wagon with everything she could load up and went to her brother Tom's house in Marianna, Florida. Her brother Bill and his wife went with them. They later moved to Syfrett Creek, Florida along with Bill and his wife. Bill and his wife got Pneumonia and died leaving a small daughter, Lelia, who was raised by their neighbor Sampson Roddenberry and two of his spinster daughters.

Mary Jane and John later moved to Curtis Mills, Florida; where John traded his team of oxen for 200 acres of land, a house and a barn, owned by John Trice. John and Mary Jane had seven more children. Richard (Dick), Andrew, Nathaniel, Mahaley, Viola, Pink and Rosena. Mary Rosena died at the age of 7 months and "Pink" died at the age of 7 years.

In their later years they moved in with their daughter Mahaley Sanders Brown. They were living there when John Henry died in 1930. My mother Mildred Sanders Willis spent a lot of time at Aunt Mahaley's house. That was like her second home. She always slept in the room with her Grandmothe r, Mary Jane, more lovingly referred to as Mammy.

Mary Jane Chatwood Sanders

Mammy always slept on a big soft feather bed with lots of quilts. She dipped "3 Thisles Snuff." She would cure the kids from smoking cigarettes by giving them snuff. The snuff would make them sick. She was always tight with her money. She didn't believe in wasting anything. She did not think anyone should pay a nickle for a Coca-Cola, but it was alright to spend money on snuff. She always carried two pocketbooks, one for medicine and one for money.

In 1944, Aunt Mahaley died and a few months later her husband Carl Brown died. Mammy moved to Crawfordville to live with another daughter, Viola Sanders Revells. I remember Mammy sitting in a rocking chair, with her snuff can beside her on the floor. She was only about 5 foot tall and her white hair was pulled back into a ball on the back of her head. She died on September 17, 1950 at the age of 97 years old.

Submitted and written by, Louise Thomas, 419 Buckhorn Creek Rd. Sopchoppy, Fl 32358

Joshua Franklin Spears

I was recently asked to write about my paternal grandfather and his career of making chairs. Joshua Franklin Spears was born March 25, 1866, the son of Daniel L. Spears and Rebecca. "Josh" was a farmer, a Primitive Baptist preacher, a blacksmith, and a maker of chairs. He lived a short distance southwest of Whiddon Lake in Ivan, Wakulla County,

Rocking chair without arms.

Florida. Slightly north of his wood framed home was a large work-shop where he built hundreds of chairs of various sorts and sizes. There was a large rocking chair with arms, a smaller rocking chair without arms, a child's rocking chair with arms, and a high chair for children to sit at a table. There were also straight chairs without arms for use at the dining table. He made a few straight chairs with arms for use at each end of the dining table.

Large Rocking chair with arms

The chair frames were of white bay and swamp hickory. Granddad would go into the surrounding woods to pick out the tree he wished to use for making a chair. If he wanted the tree, he would either mark it with a cut and get it later, or would cut the tree and take it with him at that time. He would have the tree cut into lumber and would begin work on making the frame.

Granddaddy made his own tools. He used a lathe that he pumped with his foot, and a chisel to shape the chair frame

The seat of the chair was made of cowhide. The cowhides were soaked in Whiddon Lake until they were soft enough to work with. Then they were hung on the side of the workshop until ready for use. When placing the hide on the chair seat platform, the edges of the hide were folded to fit underneath the seat and were intricately threaded together with cowhide strips in such a manner that the seat was secure and sturdy. The chairs were very durable and comfortable to sit in. Many are still in use today. I have a small rocker that Granddad made for me when I was about two years old. I am eighty-five so the chair was built more than eighty years ago.

Childs Rocking chair with arms made by; Joshua Franklin Spears

My parents always kept four large rockers on the front porch, which reached across the front of the house. There were two chairs on each side of the porch and we enjoyed sitting and relaxing in them.

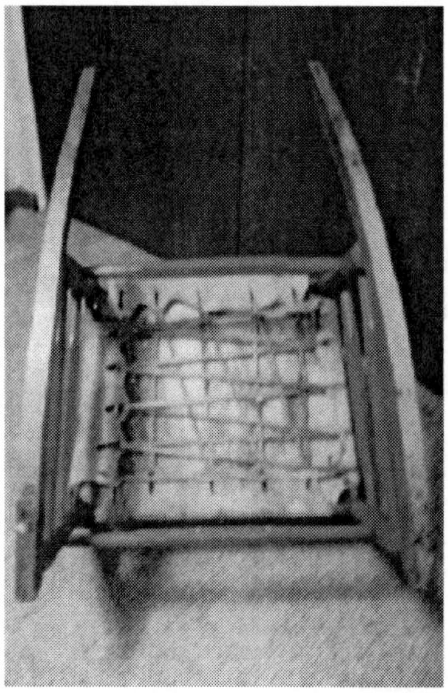

Underside of Large Rocking Chair with arms

We grandchildren loved to visit the workshop. Granddad was always busy but he did not mind us being there as long as we did not bother anything. There were wood shavings all over the floor and we enjoyed playing with them and putting them in our hair. I have many fond memories of those days.

Submitted by Jewell Griner 3001 S. Meridian St. Tallahassee, FL 32301

Ephraim and Margaret Vause

Ephraim and Margaret Revell Vause and their children moved from Darlington County, South Carolina to Wakulla County, Florida in 1854. They were my great-great-great-grandparents. They traveled in wagons along with many other families from Darlington County. Ephraim and Margaret's daughter Jerusha said that they camped at Wakulla Springs on their way down to the property that they had purchased from the Apalachicola Land Company. Representatives from the Apalachicola Land Company had gone to Georgia and the Carolinas selling Wakulla County land to many families. The Vause family's property was located about halfway between the towns of Sopchoppy and Smith Creek on the Ochlockonee River.

Ephraim was born in Sumter County, SC on October 12, 1818. He was the son of James and Charlotte Engram Vause who were both born in North Carolina. James and Charlotte had four sons and two daughters. Margaret Maria Revell was born in Darlington County, SC on April 27, 1818. She was the daughter of Stephen and Jerusha Kirby Revell who were both born in SC. Stephen and Jerusha had eight sons and five daughters. Ephraim and Margaret were married on January 10, 1840.

Margaret and Ephraim were members of Bethel Baptist Church in Olanta, SC. Ephraim was mentioned several times in the Bethel church minutes, but there were a couple of humorous excerpts. March 6, 1841: Charge against Ephraim Vause for trading horses on the Sabbath. April 3, 1841: Ephraim Vause confessed to selling horses on Sabbath and he was restored to full fellowship. February 28, 1857: Charge against Bro. Ephraim Vause for allowing fiddling and dancing in his house, also a charge against John D. Sessions for dancing. May 2, 1857: Ephraim Vause excluded from church for allowing fiddling and dancing in his house. Records indicate that he was later restored to the fellowship, but he returned to Florida shortly after this.

After moving to Wakulla County, the Vause family settled on a place which came to be known as Vause Branch. Ephraim and Margaret joined Mt. Elon Baptist Church in Smith Creek in April 1855. However, they apparently returned to SC for a short time as indicated by Bethel Church minutes in 1857. Seven of Margaret's brothers and one sister and their families also settled in the Wakulla County area. Margaret's mother, Jerusha

Revell, moved to Wakulla County and joined Mt. Elon Baptist Church in February 1859 by letter from Sardis Baptist Church in South Carolina. Margaret's father died in April 1857 in Darlington, SC.

Ephraim was listed on the 1860 and 1870 Wakulla Agricultural Census. In 1860 he had 45 acres improved and 600 unimproved. The cash value of his farm was $1,200, value of farm implements and machinery was $15 and value of livestock was $500. He had 2 horses, 11 milk cows, 2 working oxen, 30 other cattle and 35 swine. He had 300 bushels of Indian corn and 3 ginned cotton bales of 400 pounds each. In 1870 Ephraim had 1000 acres: 60 improved, 900 woodland and 40 unimproved. The cash value of his farm was $500, value of farm implements and machinery was $15 and value of livestock was $394. He had 3 horses, 5 milk cows, 18 other cattle and 30 swine. He had 160 bushels of Indian corn, 25 bushels of oats, 50 bushels of sweet potatoes, 1400 pounds of sugarcane and 120 gallons of molasses.

Ephraim and Margaret had ten children: (1) William James Washington born October 1840; (2) John Engram born August 1842, married Penelope Jane Baker; (3) Francis Marion "Med" born July 1844, married 1st Antoinette "Ann" Marie Kersey and 2nd Martha "Mattie" Powell; (4) Thomas Evander born March 1846, married Frances Elizabeth "Fannie" Langston; (5) Harriet Jerusia born January 1848, married Luther Tucker; (6) Stephen Calvin born February 1850; (7) Ephraim Wesley born May 1852, married Harriet "Hattie" Tucker; (8) Margaret Ann Elizabeth "Lizzie" born June 1854, married S. Hiram Cox; (9) Mary Jane born July 1857, married Joseph Clinton Harvey; and (10) Elijah Bostick born December 1860, married Isabelle Amanda "Belle" Spears. The two youngest children were born in Wakulla County. Stephen Calvin died when he was five years old.

The four oldest Vause sons enlisted in the Confederate Army and fought for southern independence. William James Washington Vause was killed in the war. He was wounded in the battle of Murfreesboro, TN and was captured at Stones River and died nine days later while being held prisoner by the Union. John, Med and Tom returned home after the war.

Margaret died on June 1, 1892 and is buried at

Vause Family tree was Created by: JoAnn Roberts Hadland

Vause Branch Cemetery, Wakulla County. After the death of his wife, Ephraim went to live with one of his children in Arran. Ephraim died in 1898 and is buried in Arran Cemetery, Wakulla County.

By Arlene Vause Great-great-great-granddaughter Sources: Ephraim Vause Bible Records; U.S. Census Records; FL Agricultural Censuses; U.S. Civil War Records; Bethel Baptist Church Records; Mt. Elon Baptist Church Records; THE VAUSES compiled by Tanya Watts Lynn and JoAnn Roberts Hadland.

Jincy Ethel Griffin Willis

She was born on a farm in Calhoun County, Florida in 1888. Her parents were John Mitchell Griffin and Jincy Stone Griffin. She was one of ten children. Her father raised corn, yams, cane and nearly everything but cotton. He served on the school board in Calhoun County for twelve years. Her father died when she was 15 years old.

After her father's death her mother and four of her brothers took over the farming. The farm land was a good distance from their house and they would camp out for several days at the time while working the farm. Ethel had to drop out of school to stay home and take care of the younger children. She did all the cooking, cleaning and sewing. She made all their clothes, even the underwear. She wanted to be a teacher as long as she could remember. At the age of twenty she went to Blountstown and took the teachers exam, even though she had not been in school for four years. To brush up for the test she borrowed books from the principal. She did well enough to get a third grade certificate which entitled her to teach for two years before she would have to take another exam.

She could not get a job in Calhoun County. Her sister lived near Crawfordville, so she moved to Wakulla County. She taught her first year at the Rehwinkel School, on the Spring Creek Road. The next year she taught at Honeyville, near Wewahitchka. Then she came back to Wakulla County and taught at the Curtis Mills School and The Oak Park School. When she taught at the Curtis Mills school she lived in the home of John Henry and Mary Jane Sanders. He was on the school board. *(My grandmother Ethel lived in the home of my great-grandparents John Henry and Mary Jane Sanders and taught my grandparents Nathaniel Sanders and Gladys Roberts.)*

Jincy Ethel Griffin Willis

When she was teaching in Oak Park she met James Walter Willis. He was a woods rider. They got married in 1914 at her family home in Wewahitchka, Florida. They spent their honeymoon at the Gibson Inn in Apalachicola, Florida and then took the GF&A train back to Oak Park where they made their home. They later moved to Ashmore.

They had two children. Griffin O'Neil Willis who married Mildred Sanders and Ethel Hazel Willis who married Norwood Willis.

Griffin did not go to school until he was in the fourth grade. She home schooled him. She said he was too little to walk all the way to the Sopchoppy School from Ashmore. When Ethel Hazel started to school, her daddy drove the bus. Her first year of school, she would cry every day if he left her in the class, so he sat in the class with her.

Teacher Jincy Ethel Griffin Willis & Her Students at Oak Park School

She loved her family and was always very proud of them. She always said she was of Dutch Irish descent. The following people are part of her linage.

Thomas Stone was born in 1735 in Charles Town, South Carolina. Thomas Stone and family resettled in 1768 in St. Phillip's Parish, Georgia. In March 1774, he took the oath as Justice of the Peace of St. Phillip's Parish and served to 1778. In March 1778, upon creation of the Commission for Confiscated Estates, he was appointed a commissioner from Chatham County. He appeared as # 34 on Governor Wright's black list, excepting leaders from the general order of amnesty. In 1782 he was elected as a Representative from Chatham County to the Commons House of Assembly. He gave material aid and support to the cause of the colonies in the Revolutionary War. (Charles Town had fallen to the British in May 1780.) In 1783 the name of the city was officially changed from Charles Town to Charleston.

During the war, Thomas had his land and all his assets valued at $7,000. Taken by the British and a price put on his head because he was the "Rebel Counsillor" to the Sons of Liberty and fled to Savannah, Georgia. There he owned plantations and ran a coffee house on Factors Walk, next door to the cotton exchange. In this coffee house, he and others formed the charter for the first public college, called the University of Georgia. After the war, Thomas was on the "Georgia Roll of Honor," formerly called by the King "The 153 most abhorred" (with death by hanging if caught.)

Henry Dessex Stone, son of Thomas Stone was born in 1767 in Charles Town, South Carolina. Henry was a member from McIntosh County of the Georgia Constitutional Convention of 1795. He served as Sheriff, Glynn County, Georgia from 1799 to 1801. He later moved to the Mississippi territory, and became a resident of Alabama in 1817 with the division of the territory. He was appointed as Chief Justice of Orphans Court, and served for several years.

Henry was commissioned Colonel on March 28, 1820. He had been elected Colonel of Alabama Militia, 24th Regiment of Infantry, Montgomery County. He was mentioned in July 1821 as Colonel commanding the Regt. of Augusta Militia.

Colonel Stone and family moved to Florida about 1824 and settled in the town of Iola. He was listed as one of the county's first settlers. He was a Veteran of the Revolutionary War and the War of 1812. He served with Andrew Jackson and was later President of the Territorial Council of Florida. He served for a number of years as clerk of the Superior Court at Marianna.

Lewis Maxwell Stone, grandson of Colonel H. D. Stone was born in 1819. He graduated from Harvard University with a Law degree in 1841. He represented his country in the Alabama House from 1849-50 and 1851-52 and the Alabama Senate from 1859-63. He was a member of the Constitutional Convention of 1861 and again represented his country in the House from 1868-69 in which he was Speaker of the House. In 1875 he was a member of the Constitutional Convention. He represented his country also in 1888-89.

Lewis's brother, Thomas Oswald Stone was

born in 1834. He graduated from Medical College in Philadelphia. In the spring of 1862, during the War Between the States, he enlisted as a lieutenant of Co. G. 40th Alabama Infantry Regiment, and was elected Major of the regiment. Later he was promoted to Lieutenant

Revell Family of Sopchoppy with Jincy Willis standing in the back on the far right

Colonel, which rank he held at his death.

James Bennett Stone, grandson of Colonel H. D. Stone, and also my great- great-grandfather was born in, 1823. He was Sheriff of Calhoun County from 1855-59. He served as Clerk of Circuit Court from 1860-62. He served in the House of Representatives from Calhoun County in the sessions of 1868, 1869, 1870 and 1877 and in the Constitutional Convention in 1885. He also served as County Commissioner for three terms. He lost a leg in a sawmill accident and could not enlist in the Confederate Army.

Terrell Higdon Stone, son of James Bennett Stone, also my great-great uncle moved to Port St. Joe, Florida in 1904. His family was the first to move back to St. Joe after the Yellow Fever epidemic. He was listed as the founding father of Port St. Joe. He served in a number of public offices. Postmaster, Justice of the Peace, County Commissioners, Mayor of Port St. Joe and represented Gulf County in the Florida House from 1933-35. He owned a large tract of land on St Joseph Bay. He donated this large tract of land to the state. He was honored by having the state park on the peninsula he once owned named for him. The T.H. Stone Memorial State Park and the highway leading to it as the T.H. Stone Memorial Highway.

Joseph Seaborn Stone, grandson of Colonel H. D. Stone was twice elected sheriff of Calhoun County and represented Calhoun County in the Florida House of Representatives in the session of 1895.

Lachland McIntosh Stone, son of Colonel H. D. Stone was an attorney and often associated politically with Richard Keith Call and the "Nucleous," the political ring of Andrew Jackson's old army cronies. He was elected to the Legislative Council of Florida in 1828. Representative Stone secured passage of a bill to establish Marianna as the county seat. In 1830, he was commissioned by President Andrew Jackson for a four year term as Marshal of the Southern District of Florida.

Lewis Maxwell Stone, born in 1844 and grandson of Colonel H. D. Stone became an ordained Baptist minister. In 1873 he took charge of the Meridian Baptist Female College. In 1877 he became president of the Gainesville, Alabama Female College. In 1879 he moved to Shuqualak, Mississippi where Professor Stone with the aid of citizens founded the Shuqualak Female College, with him as proprietor and president.

This is just a part of the people who make up my heritage. I also am very proud to come from such a long line of patriots.

Submitted and written by, Louise Thomas, 419 Buckhorn Creek Rd. Sopchoppy, Fl 32358

Visiting Wakulla Springs in the Early 20th Century

The above photo is Winifred Weeks Apthorp. She was the ancestral grandmother of Wakulla County resident George Apthorp. The following letter was written by her in the early 20th century.

- A Trip to Wakala Springs -

Among the many places of beauty and interest which Nature has given us, Wakala Springs is well worthy of mention.

These remarkable springs are located out in the country at a distance of perhaps eighteen or twenty miles from Florida's capital city, and so a strong pair of horses and a reliable driver offer the best means of paying them a visit. For years Wakala Springs have afforded one of the best picnic grounds that can well be imagined, surrounded as they are by a fine old forest, notwithstanding the long, tiresome carriage drive of nearly twenty miles. Evidently Southern picnicers knew how to make the most of that long ride, however, for a certain Tallahassee lady, well known as the original "Tallahassee Girl" in the book of that name, once said that it was an understood fact that two or more young people never went to Wakala Springs without coming back engaged.

After leaving Tallahassee, the road for the most part lies through the turpentine regions — a dreary, desolate, level stretch of country, whose only growth consists of tall limbless pines and scrub oaks. There are a few small settlements and occasionally a negro shack to break the monotony and to keep one from feeling that he is completely isolated from all human life. At last the road enters a fine hard wood growth where the great old oak trees bend over, forming arches with waving garlands of gray Spanish moss. Soon the tired horses are resting in the shade, while the party eagerly make their way through the undergrowth down toward the place where they had caught the gleam of water.

And when the visitor has finally reached the spot, and looks out upon what seems like a small lake surrounded by a low, swampy shore, with a fringe of ghostly looking cypress trees rising out of the mud or shallow water, and numerous inlets where partly submerged logs afford an excellent place for snakes and alligators, he begins to wonder if this is all that he has come so far to see. But no, the next thing is to await the arrival of the negro boatman,

2

who is to take the party out to the middle of the water. The boat soon appears, and as soon as the party have embarked, makes its way slowly out through the tangle of water-grass and lily pads until at last it reaches clear water. And there the boat stops in the midst of the tiny lake, or spring as it really is, surrounded on every side, except where the outlet starts, by dense forest trees. The bluest of blue Southern skies are above, — for it is useless to go if there is the least little cloud in the sky, or ripple upon the surface of the water, — and below — what the party have come to see — the wonderful, changing colors of Wakala Springs.

The party kneel in the bottom of the boat and with eyes as near as possible to the surface of the water, look down into the depth below. Down, down, for hundreds of feet, through an almost measureless expanse of water clear as crystal, the gaze penetrates until at last it rests on a glistening shelf of white limestone, which partly reveals the secret of the clearness of the water and the reflected light with its wonderful, changing colors.

In some places shelf after shelf can be seen, one jutting out beneath another, or visible through a hole in the one above, and the gazer begins to wonder whether there really is any bottom to this strange lake, or whether he is not looking into some enchanted region. Let some one drop a coin or a round piece of tin into the water, and then watch as it goes down, radiating through the water above all the colors of the rainbow, until at last it rests on some ledge. The waters close to the shore, too, in many places are of the richest and most glorious shades of blue and green ever seen.

These wonderful changing colors are what have made Wakala Springs noted among lovers of Nature, and of her many marvelous exhibitions often hidden, like these same Springs, in the midst of some great forest.

FAMILY MILITARY MEMORIES

Charles Boykin, USN

When I was a boy in the early 1950s, although we lived in Tallahassee, I spent all my summers down in St. Marks. For a young fellow like me, how happy I was when summertime rolled around. I could escape the "city" and take my shoes off. I had many good friends in St. Marks too. One of my best friends was Charles Boykin. He was my age, and he had two older brothers, good friends of mine too, Tommy and Allen.

Charles and I used to work together getting the small boats ready for their early morning runs out to the flats for a day of trout fishing. When they would return late in the afternoons, Charles and I would help the people unload their boats. We'd then use a large wench to hoist the boats up out of the water, turn them over on their sides, and hose them down good so they'd be sparkling clean when we put them back in the water, ready for the next trip. Charles and I also worked as helpers on deep sea fishing boats, me on the Jenny Lee, and Charles on the Ramona. So like most of the young boys in St. Marks, our work was in and around the fishing business, which dominated.

After graduating from high school, Charles and I, having been around boats and the water most of our lives, and looking to serve our country by military service, naturally gravitated to the Navy. I had always admired Charles's brother, Tommy, who joined the Navy sometime around 1955 or '56, and I was mighty impressed when he'd come home on leave in his Navy uniform.]Tommy served aboard destroyers and to do the same was my goal. Never will I forget the tailor made dress blues Tommy gave me when I enlisted.

After we enlisted, I learned Charles had become an "airdale", which meant he worked with aircraft, and my dream came true as I asked for service aboard a destroyer, and I went to the USS Eugene A. Greene (DDR-711). Since Charles was working with aircraft, I didn't think too much more about seeing him since I didn't think we'd be anywhere near each other. Charles, on the other hand, found out I was aboard the "711". Charles, which I may have known, but had forgotten, had taken orders to the Naval Air Facility, Naples, Italy.

As luck would have it, in 1961, my first port of call was Naples. Excited about being overseas for the first time in my life, I went ashore on liberty as soon as I could. Boy, was I in for a surprise, being a naive young boy from Leon/Wakulla County, Florida. Things I saw as I stepped ashore and spent that first full day and half the night cannot be repeated here! Sure wasn't anything like St. Marks and Tallahassee, I can tell you that.

Naples was a port city and I immediately learned the lower elements follow the fleet and wait eagerly for young fellows such as me to step ashore. The goal was to separate that young man from his entire wallet, or at the very least, the contents of that wallet.

Mothers and Daddys, you may rest easy. The Navy took mighty good care of your sons. Prior to making that first port of call, we were required to watch "training films". One film impressed me to the point that as I write this 50 years later, I still vividly remember it. I think the title was "The Horrors of Venereal Disease". It was so bad I could hardly sleep for several nights in a row. I don't know where they found those poor wretches who starred in the film, ravaged with all manner of pocks and sores all over their bodies. They could barely be distinguished as human. Then to top that off, my Chief Petty Officer, D. R. Bronson, RMC, USN, a tough old veteran of World War II, told me it was his policy that any of his men who contracted a social disease would be forced to write a letter to their mother advising her of that fact. So between that film and my good Chief Bronson, no way was this boy going astray.

After my first liberty ashore, I wasn't all that impressed with Naples, and had pretty much settled on remaining aboard, with the knowledge that other ports would be more attractive. And that brings me to the point of this story, and it has to do with Charles Boykin.

One day some shipmates returned from shore liberty and told me a fellow was on the Fleet Landing and had asked them if I was on the ship. They told me he told them his name was Boykin, and he would wait there for an hour or so in case they were able to locate me. Fortunately I was in the liberty section, so quickly changed into my dress whites and took the motor whale boat to the Fleet Landing. Luckily, Charles had seen my ship, with the large "711" on the hull, anchored out in the bay.

What fun Charles and I had in Naples. He had been stationed there for about a year and knew of the more attractive parts of the city, away from the port area. So many sailors never made it more than a block or two away from the Fleet Landing, and Charles taught me right away that the "real" culture of the city was to be found far from the areas populated by sailors and other mariners down in the port district. How fortunate that two good friends from Wakulla County would meet up and enjoy the sights together in Naples, Italy. Never will I forget.

Eleanor's Story

My name is Eleanor Elizabeth Nelson Beal. I was born on October 11, 1920, at home, in Rochester, New York. My mother was Elizabeth Boch Nelson and my father was Henry Nelson. My parents told me that I inherited my beautiful, brilliant red hair from my grandfather Boch.

During the Depression, my dad had a regular job with the New York Central Railroad for which we were very lucky. That was rare in those days. But the Depression was very difficult for us, I can remember that. Our food and what we ate was so different from what people eat now. We ate potatoes, potatoes, potatoes. We had oatmeal for breakfast, soup for dinner and potatoes for supper. We made the soup out of anything we could get our hands on, so needless to say, we ate lots of potato soup. There were two boys and me. Of course you know, we were just kids, we didn't care. We were playing outside most of the time, jumping rope and playing jacks, things they don't do anymore. I used to love to do those things. But my favorite thing to do was to climb trees.

When I was nine years old, everything changed. My mother and baby brother died during childbirth. I could hear her upstairs, screaming in so much pain. It was awful. My dad never thought this would happen; it hit him so hard. I can remember him sitting in the corner all by himself, crying. Because of his job, he traveled, so he didn't think he could take care of my brothers and me and the house. So I remember him packing us all up, putting us in the car and driving us to an orphanage. It was an awful place, just like you see in the movies. We were all crying. He couldn't bear to leave us there, so my Aunt Millie, an adopted sister of my mother, came and took care of us. My dad did the best he could.

It was very difficult. My aunt was jealous of me and my father because I was very close to him. She was so hard on us. My dad had one of those old fashioned straps that you sharpened razors on and she used to beat us with that strap. My dad was away on business trips a lot so he didn't know. She told us if we said anything, we'd suffer for it. She was a very messy person, but we kids continued to try to keep things clean like our mom did. I scrubbed the steps every Saturday morning.

The holidays were very difficult for my dad and for us children. We never really got over the death of our mom. Many of my dad's family and some of my mom's family would come together on the holidays to make sure we kids enjoyed whatever holiday it was. On Easter, we kids made our own egg coloring stuff because when our mother was alive she loved all that and we remembered. We had the same Easter baskets, year after year, from before my mom died. We carried it forth. My brothers and I stuck together.

I never had time for anything but schoolwork as far as my dad was concerned. He had promised my mom that I would go to a Catholic School. In the city of Rochester we only had two schools. My brothers went to the public school. He explained to them about my mom, and that she wanted me to go to a Catholic school and get a good education. I appreciated that, even until this day. It was a good education. The nuns were very strict and they were very knowing. They were great people, I thought. They taught me how to write. We had a regular class in writing where they drilled us. I used to have beautiful penmanship, right up until the last few years.

Anyway, I wanted to get away from home, so right after high school I joined the nursing group at St. Mary's Hospital in Rochester. They did all the training and we lived there at the hospital. I don't think they do that anymore, but we lived at the nursing facility there and had our training from the nuns, the Sisters of Charity. The nuns trained us, they babied us, and they watched us just like we were their own children. We couldn't have radios or a lot of things. We were there to train, and that was it, that's the way it was. I didn't go into the training because I loved it, I just wanted to get away from home so that's the way I did it. But as it turned out, I just loved it! I graduated from there in October of 1941. In December, World War II broke out and I immediately signed up for the Army, the 19th General Hospital there in Rochester. From there we went anywhere and everywhere, but mostly on the European front. I had all kinds of experiences. But before leaving the states to go overseas, they kept us, everyone who was a part of the 19th General Hospital, in a section of a mental hospital in New Jersey. We only stayed there a couple of days. We were not allowed to leave. The middle floor was empty, so that's where we stayed. We were there until we left for overseas. We listened to the patients yelling and screaming at night. It was terrible. We slept in our clothes with our possessions in our bed rolls so we'd be ready to go at a moment's notice. We stayed there about three or four days until one morning, at about three or four o'clock, they got us all up and put us into trucks. It was so cold. We wanted to go but we didn't want to go, we didn't know what to expect. They didn't tell us what we were headed for, they didn't tell us anything. We didn't know just how big it all was. We were so frightened. They boarded us onto our ship and we set out across the Atlantic Ocean. As we approached international waters, suddenly the ship turned around, and took us back to shore. Why? We didn't know. We were taken right back to where we were previously quartered, the hospital, and that's where we stayed. We were just following orders. Later we found out that there had been a German U-boat trailing us, with torpedoes. We stayed for days until we could go safely. Those boys were so nice about it all. We'd sing, play cards, and do anything we could do to pass the time. Then all of a sudden, we just went. They didn't tell us because we would have been scared to death if we knew what was going on.

We landed in Scotland, then traveled to Wales where they put us through physical fitness training. They made us march through the mountains to make us physically fit. Some of the nurses were older so they would stop and sit off the trail, then on our way back down the mountain, we picked them up.

We left there for parts unknown and ended up in the hills of Malvern, England. We lived there in Nissen huts, which are very similar to a Quonset hut. There were six of us in each hut. We lived in these for awhile. The thing I remember the most from there is a very sad memory. My Nissen hut was very close to the mess hall where we ate and in the morning I would hear this noise. I couldn't imagine what it was, I thought at first it was animals. So one morning I came out and I saw these little children scrambling through our mess hall to get food. What they had for shoes was a block of wood tied on with rags. That has stuck with me through all these years, I felt so bad. There was nothing I could do. I used to bring them things I could get from the mess hall. I was friendly with the guys at the mess hall and they used to do a lot of favors for me.

We moved on to St. Lo, France. Oh, god, what those people went through! Everything was demolished, everything! We went up into the pill boxes where the Germans would get under the ground with their guns and do their shooting. The Germans were gone by then but the pill boxes were still there. I went inside one and looked around. It was gruesome. They left things that they would use for survival, food – anything. I smelled death everywhere I went, especially Rommel's headquarters in Nancy, France, that we took over for our hospital. They left Germans behind, injured Germans. It didn't matter if they were Germans, English, whatever they were, when we saw somebody suffering like that you can't just ignore them, we helped them all we could. That's what we did. We stayed there and took care of them. I don't know what happened to them when we were done.

We nurses stayed in tents and had to march through the snow. We had a pot belly stove in the middle of each tent and put our cots as close to it as we could get them. The cots were a nice size, so my friend and I slept together. Can you see the two of us in a cot? We were both tall and well built women. We'd put enough wood in the stove to last until morning, or so we thought. But the fire would go out and we would have to take turns getting up and restarting the fire. We had to do this to keep warm because the weather just kept getting colder and colder. We would get our wood from the local community by trading American goods for wood and coal. That's how we kept warm. The morale was not good at times, but then we would see who we were helping and that would cheer us up. The patients would come and talk to me, they had to talk to somebody. My door was always open, I never shut it.

Our uniforms were just a wraparound dress with brown and white stripes and a matching cap. It was easier than trying to keep a uniform clean. We went through a lot of them.

Time didn't mean anything. We would just take care of those guys. I came in one Sunday morning and the hallways were lined with soldiers on litters. We didn't know where they were coming from. Of course they would not give any information at all, in war they never talked about details. But I did find out that my brother had been killed and I took it very hard. I'd been so close to him. I later found out that he had been killed at the Battle of the Bulge. I kept working, you had to. How do you take care of that many people? We had to keep taking care of our wounded soldiers, no matter what. I went to different outfits to find where my brother was buried but I couldn't get any information from anybody, nothing, not a dog tag, not anything. Everything was closed tight. You didn't know who you were talking to, you might give something away.

After I found out about my brother, I was very ornery. I looked down at every German and wondered if he was the guy that killed him. I wasn't thinking straight, but that's the way I felt. Wouldn't you have felt the same? I guess it was immaturity. I spent many a tearful night. My brother and I were so close. I wasn't allowed to date or anything at home, so I used to go to dances with him. His name was Joseph. I called him Joey, but he didn't like it. He wanted to be called plain old Joe. He was a good boy. He always had a job, from the time he was thirteen or fourteen. In those days, groceries were delivered and that's what he did.

The German patients had to go to church before we went on Sundays because we couldn't meet them, they were afraid there would be a fight or something. So we'd be getting ready to go to church and we'd listen to those German soldiers marching to church. They'd march with their goose step and they'd sing hymns to it. It was interesting to listen to. Actually, prayer was what saved the day. We had a chaplain who traveled with us. I am Catholic and so was the chaplain. He was so good to me. I wanted a missal so he brought me one. It had all the words just like he was saying. One side was Latin and the other was English.

That's where I started giving anesthesia. They were short handed and somebody asked me if I would do it and I said "sure". I was glad to learn something else, you know. The doctor taught me and stood right behind me the whole time, I will never forget him. So many of the people we took care of were so young, talking to us about their high schools. We did Emergency Room work and there wasn't always a doctor there. But when you work with a doctor long enough you know what they are going to order, so that's what we did. Then the doctor would come in and sign off on it. You had to do that, it was emergency work. That part of it interested me, I liked it. We used to have to take care of two or three litters of patients at a time, giving anesthesia. It was very exciting, but in some cases, very tearful as well. Before that, I was a charge nurse in the orthopedic section. There were forty beds, twenty on each side. And those soldiers would get ornery! This one GI was making passes at me, you know, and he did it once too often so I went to the doctor who was in charge and told him. He said, "Okay, I'll take care of it". Well, he laid him low! He never said anything to me after that. I don't know how he did it, but many years later, I was living in Orlando and he was in the hospital there. He remembered me and the next thing I know, he was knocking at my door. I was married by then and had children, so he was a little late!

My first anesthesia case was an officer who'd taken shrapnel in his eye. They wanted to remove it, but no one could get in his eye socket to do it. The instruments could not get in that eye. I was giving the anesthesia and the patient went into convulsions. Oh my Lord!! But the surgeon saved me. He came up behind me and gave him some kind of drug that calmed him down. They were digging in his eye with their little fingers trying to get that shrapnel out with no success. There was a little nurse there, she hardly stood five feet tall; she was so small. "Let's see your fingers", the doctor said. They took her little finger and dug out that shrapnel. We just didn't have the things we have today. The doctors worked very hard on him and as far as I know he was alright, despite losing his eye. That was my first case. The Chief Anesthetist came and gave him something. I was so upset at the time that nothing registered. I was a young gal and all this happening. And the officer was so young, the whole crew was young, it didn't seem the fair thing to do to anyone.

I remember this one young man. He had just gotten into the Army, and had just arrived over there to fight in the battles. I was about to give him anesthesia and he wanted to talk to me a minute, so I did. He had already lost a leg, and he did not want to lose anything more. He begged me not to let that happen. I told him I didn't have any say about it. You know, I was young, and to have something like this put on me! Well, the surgeon that was going to operate was known as The Butcher. When I saw him come in I knew what was going to happen. He removed an arm. It impressed me so, I will never forget that young face looking up at me from the table talking to me. I told him I didn't have the last word, I wasn't responsible for whatever happened. My attitude seemed so cruel to him, I guess. But what could I do? I was thinking of how I could get through it myself. But that will always remain in my mind.

The Germans left behind the patients they couldn't carry. We went in this one room and there was this soldier that was hurt so badly. It was his leg. We gave him the primary medicine. He was crying. We unwrapped his dressings and the leg and all came off in our hands. The stench was awful, gangrene. They must have let him lay there, I don't know how long. He was in his thirties, I think. He was afraid of what they were going to do, afraid he was going to die. We had a lot to deal with, and we did not have the proper training for this. But neither did they know what they were going to face. So we did what we could. We were such young nurses trying to face things like that.

I had a lot of experiences during the war. I made a lot of friends among the French and the Germans, whom I couldn't understand half of the time! But they were good to me. The French invited us into their homes. In one of them, I gave anesthesia. They related to me the experiences they'd had during the war with the Germans, you know, and how difficult they'd made it for them. They had to hide things. This one family had beautiful paintings and pictures and they hid them under rugs, under anything when the Germans were coming. It was pathetic. I saw some of it. A French nurse anesthetist had invited me to her home so I went over there and I saw some of these paintings, they were beautiful. They were Jewish, and of course "Jews" was a bad word over there then. They were trained to hate them, and some of them to hate the Americans. It was a royal battle to acquire some good memories there, because a lot of them were not very nice to us. We were interfering with them as far as winning the war.

Playing tennis in England? I did! And I liked to play ball a lot, softball, so I belonged to the team there. I played shortstop. We had a lot of fun with that. I am very sports minded and I loved my sports! Oh, here's a naughty story—The Chief Nurse got a call from the fly boys over in England where they were training. They wanted a few young nurses to go over, they were having a dance. "And make them young," they said, "and desirable!" Ha Ha! Anyway, she called me and asked, "Would you go?" I said, "Sure." She picked some others, there were five of us altogether, and we went over there. They flew us from France to England. Well, time to come home and the boys didn't want to let us go. The Chief Nurse called and wanted to know when the girls were getting in. They begged her to let us stay. They had to have a good excuse, so they said, "The weather over here is really bad, it's not very good flying weather. We'd just as soon keep them here for safety's sake if you don't mind." She knew better but she had to give in to them. And we did, we stayed overnight! When we got back, we found that the whole hospital was grounded, no passes until we showed our faces. And boy, did we get the works from the other nurses! They had passes cancelled and all. But we'd had a good time and it was worth it!

My husband, James Stanley Beal, was a bombardier in the Air Force. All those missions, it's a wonder he got out of all that alive. But he loved it. He was a patient of mine in England, that's how I met him. We were signing in people from the front, calling out their names. When I got to his name I said, "Bell", and he said, BEAL!" He was staring me down with those dark brown eyes, you know. I thought, boy, he was good lookin'! Whenever I did roll call I'd say "Bell", and he'd get so mad! He knew I was just doing it, you know. He was very friendly and gregarious and I got to know him pretty well. One time I went to the clothing room where they had to check their clothes in, and I turned around and there he stood. He grabbed me and gave me a big kiss! I mean, this was a very shocking thing to happen to me! I told him, "Don't you ever do anything like that to me again, you know I can be court-martialed!" He was an enlisted man and we were not even allowed to say "Hi" to them, but we had places and areas where we talked. He wanted to go on a bicycle ride in the countryside. I had a bike, and I asked a good friend if I could borrow her bike, so that's where we got the second bike. We got to be the talk of the town, shall we say, they were all knowing what was going on. And the doctor knew too. He came up to me on the last roll call and said, "Spike", (that was my nickname) "I'm awful sorry but I gotta take your boyfriend away." They had to follow the rules too. He'd been keeping him there as long as he could.

He stayed in England after that, because he'd been wounded and wasn't able to continue. But we kept in touch. He would get a phone call to me. I don't know how he did it and he never told me. He was a very aggressive man. He was determined and knew how to get what he wanted. He got his family in on this, and his mom sent me care packages and everything you could think of. Because "He was still gonna marry me, no matter what," he said.

I had been going to school to learn about the diseases that we nurses would encounter in Japan, that's where we were going. It was an entirely different area. But the day we graduated was the day the war ended, so I didn't have to go. Jim and I got home around the same time, finally.

Once we got home from the war, Jim went back to Ohio and I went back to Rochester. We were both unsettled and were unsure about our future. I still got letters from him and his family and in one letter he invited me to come to Ohio to visit. Well, that's all I needed to hear. I packed up a few things and headed to central Ohio. It was there I met most of Jim's family and spent time getting to know them. The next thing I knew, we are engaged and I had to plan our wedding in just a few months, so back to Rochester I went.

The thing that I remembered most about my wedding, and really, it bothers me to no end, is the fact that my Aunt Millie had cats and dogs and what have you. I had a beautiful dress. The day of the wedding came, I went into the room where my gown was spread out on the bed and I saw this great big blue mark on my gown. It was big! The cat had done a number on it. Oh, I was just sick! So my dad grabbed the gown and went down to the dry cleaners with it. You could only do a certain amount, so it still showed a touch. I think only I knew. Oh boy, talk about red-headed temper, I was MAD! I not only disliked my aunt, now I had reason to. Ha! Ha!

My wedding was beautiful, in my Catholic church. I asked for the organist who played there since I was a little girl and went to school there. He taught me what I knew about the Mass. He was very good and very nice. He was part of my childhood right on up. He played "Ava Maria" as I walked down the aisle. A lot of my friends from the Army came. They didn't know how I put together a big wedding in such a short time. This was January 26, 1946. I had only been home 2 months. That's where I pulled my friendships in order, I got it done. But if that cat had been around there, he'd have been a dead duck! In those days, a hundred dollars was a lot of money and that's what I spent on my dress.

But that's not what bothered me; it was just that I had to look at that spot. My dad's sister was there, and she cried and cried. I carried a combination of white lilies and red roses. My Maid of Honor and bridesmaids wore a beautiful deeper than pink color. Their dresses had velvet on top and silk on the bottom. And my dress was satin with openings for flowers. My aunt was crying because she thought I'd torn it.

After the ceremony we went across the street to get our picture taken. It was cold and windy and I was trying to hold onto my big dress and veil! I'd rented a bunny fur coat, it was so cold.

We stayed in town at a hotel. I put my flowers on the windowsill to keep them fresh. But sometime during the night they blew off, and someone found them in the street and brought them in. The fellow at the desk downstairs gave them to me in the morning.

Jim and I had six children, three boys and three girls. I just went into nursing in different areas, different hospitals, trying to stay married and raise my family. My husband became ill. He was sick with heart disease and had shrapnel in his right knee from the war. He finally lost his leg and had to be in a wheelchair most of the time. I was taking care of him. He died not long after losing his leg, in 1976. I don't feel sad about any of it, because I had a good marriage. We had a lot of happy years, he made them happy. He was a fun man.

My oldest son Jim was in the military when my husband died. He was stationed in Rome with the military police. He invited me over there to stay, but I came back after about seven months. While I was there, one of my favorite memories is the day I met Pope Paul. I happened to pick a seat right where he was coming down the aisle. He looked just like his pictures. The tears were coming down my face; it was such a thrill to see him. I had just bought a pair of rosaries. He stood up on the podium and asked if anyone wanted theirs blessed. I held mine up and he blessed my rosaries.

I had come back from spending months with Jim and spent the next couple of years with the rest of my children and grandchildren. In 1978, I went back overseas to see Jim, in Germany this time. We spent six wonderful weeks together, traveling around the countryside. He took me back to several places I was at during the war. It was precious time I was able to spend with him and his family. At the end of my visit, he had taken me to the airport, for me to head back to the states. It was then, on his way home from the airport, that he was killed in an automobile accident. I was told he hit the back of German truck going up a hill. They had a hard time locating me to tell this news. He was my oldest and my closest child, at that time. My heart was broken. That is a pain no mother should ever have to feel. I still haven't gotten over it, I think of him so often. I had more time with him on that visit than I did during most of his teenage years. He was a busy teenager, doing his thing, playing sports, building his cars. I am sure God let us have that precious time together. It was almost impossible to my mind at the time, but I prayed my way through.

A lot of happy memories, a lot of sad memories, but they are all my memories.

Submitted by: Eleanor Elizabeth Nelson Beal

The Pigotts

In 1922 the old Pigott's cash and carry was a Gen'l Merchandise store with clothing on one side of the store and groceries on the other side with hardware in the back. John was born there in August of that year. His mother died in 1930 during childbirth after creating a family which gave John five brothers and one sister.

These kids went to school at the old schoolhouse in Medart until 1930. They moved to Cedar Springs, GA up on the Chattahoochee River near Dothan. They lived there until 1936 when they moved back to Wakulla County. (across from Wakulla Manor). John graduated from Sopchoppy High School in 1941. Notice the rural southern upbringing being shown here.

But, then war looms in the minds of many as news of a war-torn Europe and Japanese atrocities in China makes the daily news. In September of 1941 John, along with Walter Tulley, joins the U.S. Navy in Macon, Georgia. Many young Americans were joining up to "serve their Country" during this period of time. After that it was off to boot camp at Norfolk, Virginia. Later he would go to Aviation Mechanic School in Pensacola.

All this time another background history was developing. It was an opposite from the rural setting described above in that it was the life of a city girl.

Margie Earlene Ives was born in 1926 in Council Bluff, Iowa (across the Missouri River from Omaha). Living in a family which included three brothers and a younger sister, she graduated from Thomas Jefferson High School in Council Bluff. Her father worked as an electrician for the Kimball Elevator Company. Perhaps that is why after graduation Earlene worked as an elevator operator at J.C. Penney.

As was the custom in this time our military men were treated well as they were the defenders of both ourselves and our way of life. Military men were always looked on as underpaid volunteers who were trained to protect our country. Therefore soldiers on stopover in train stations, etc. were frequently treated to cakes, cookies and punch or coffee. Earlene was part of a group who would volunteer in tending to the usual cake and cookies for such occasions.

On Christmas Eve, 1943, she was on such duty handing small gifts, in keeping with the season, to the weary traveling soldiers and sailors. On that day, on his way to San Diego, John was handed a small gift containing stationery by a winsome young lady. He got her name and soon sent her a thank you for the gift. The two corresponded for some two years. Rural Wakulla County John had met city girl Earlene.

During that time John was being shipped around the Pacific. He had been at Pearl Harbor on December 7th 1941! He was on the U.S.S. Saratoga just prior to the battle of Midway. He was back aboard the Saratoga later and found his old comrade, Walter Tully, was also there. They spent time together on Espiritu Santos, New Caledonia.

By the end of the war in 1945, John was a Chief Petty Officer on his way to see the girl he had corresponded with for some two years. He got back to Council Bluff about 9pm one evening. Earlene met him at the door but, as he reached to kiss her, her mother introduced herself. They later went out to help him find lodging. Five days later they were engaged. After he returned to the West Coast a letter came from Earlene's mother asking if he intended to return!

And return he did, for John and Earlene were married February 10, 1946. He took her to the West Coast, but got orders to report to Hawaii for "sea pay" (shipboard duty) again. The first of their children, Stephen Earl, named for both his grandfathers, was born in 1947 in the Naval Hospital at Foley, Alabama. Linda Ruth was born in 1950 at the Mare Island California Naval Hospital. Johnny was born in 1951 in Redding, California.

In the late forties, he served in Okinawa and again in Hawaii, he also spent some time in Council Bluff. One realizes that perhaps those among us who are veterans of wartime military service can truly comprehend the meaning of being "shipped around" away from your family not knowing if you will ever return to them.

At one time he was stationed in the Mediterranean but had return to try to sell his house in Sanford which had been up for sale. It had not sold and they were worried that school would start before they could get the kids settled into a new house, as he had to go back in a few days. Seated at supper that evening, they were surprised by a man who wanted to buy the house right then. He put half the purchase price down and paid the other half the next day.

Chief Petty Officer Pigott retired from the Navy in April 1961 to Crestview, Florida. He found out the old Pigott's store was for sale by his Aunt and Uncle. He made a deal right away to purchase it. He put $2000 dollars down and a note for the rest of the $12,000. Pigott's Store would continue in the family.

Later they had a store over by the high school but had problems with anything left outside. The store was then moved back into the old store building site. The added wing was built over concrete slabs poured in stages as surplus concrete became available. Pigott's store has a long history, and so does its owners. In 1995, they celebrated 49 years of marriage and more than a few years of hard work in Wakulla County. The ole rural boy from Wakulla County had brought the big city girl, the love of his life, to the small town rural life in a big way. The store closed in 2002.

Written by: Franklin D. Howard © 1994. Permission to print by: Susan Sapronetti, Tallahassee, FL

Willie Carmel Pelt

Willie Carmel Pelt, third youngest child and second youngest son of ten children born to George Washington Bostic Pelt and Emma Ruth Pigott Pelt was born and reared in the old Pelt house that was home to at least three generations of the Pelt family. Carmel Pelt was born July 24, 1916, went to school in Arran in his early years and then rode the school bus which his brother, John, drove to Crawfordville. He stopped school after the eighth grade to help his father with farming and to work at a number of jobs to earn money to help the family. One of those jobs was to cut railroad cross-ties, without the benefit of modern saws and technology.

Carmel met Etta Mae Council at school when she was fourteen and he was sixteen. They courted off and on until she was nineteen and he was twenty-one when they were married by Judge A.L. Porter at the Judge's home on May 13, 1938. Virgie and T.E. White served as witnesses to their marriage. The newly-weds returned to the Pelt family's home to live until they could build their own house. That house is located on the Harvey Mill Road facing the Bostic Pelt Road. Moving into the house before it was completed inside, Etta Mae recalled placing a wire across the partition beams and draping sheets for their walls.

C.1941-45 Carmel W. Pelt

In December of 1940, Carmel received his draft notice from the local draft board. He was inducted into the Army at Camp Blanding and sent to Spartanburg, SC for training. He was drafted for a period of one year but three days before that time lapsed, Pearl Harbor was bombed, the US went to war and Carmel remained in the Army. He was stationed at several bases around the nation before shipping overseas including Camp Gordon Johnston at Carrabelle, a base in Texas, and Fort Lewis in Tacoma, WA. Somehow he managed to come for one day in December of 1943, from Tocama, to see his second child, Etta Jo, who was born on his birthday in 1943! She was five months old before her father saw her. After this quick visit with his family, he went back to Fort Lewis and from there to New York City where he shipped out to England. There he joined the vast numbers of Americans, Canadians, and British, being trained for the massive assault on the European continent which had to take place to defeat the enemy.

Carmel went in on the D-Day assault, June 6, 1944. He served under General Patton and Carmel's wife and daughters recall stories and bits of information he told them about this tremendous undertaking. Many men drowned when they came off the landing craft in rough seas and water over their heads because they were so heavily weighted with their packs and weapons that they could not swim.

Carmel and the men he served with admired and respected Gen. Patton. He was known for defying and daring the enemy. One episode Carmel told was about the General relieving himself from a bridge in full view of the enemy, daring them to try to shoot him! Carmel's assignment in the Army was the Military Police and he had achieved a sharpshooter's medal. He told of guarding German prisoners as they were forced to dig up victims of the concentration camps with their bare hands. The soldiers went for long periods of time without warm food but even then they would give part of their rations to the children, especially candy. Carmel had a special place in his heart for the children.

May 8, 1945, saw the end of hostilities in Europe and Carmel was soon on his way home. He thought, though, that he wasn't going to make it. Two bombers were being used to bring his unit of soldiers back and Carmel told his family about the plane having sandbags loaded in bomb bays with the men seated in such a way as to have them balanced from side to side and front and back. Before landing in Miami, the sandbags had slipped to the back and the plane could not get the nose down to land. They circled for two hours while the officers in charge tried to correct the problem. Finally the men were told to all move forward as close to the cockpit as they could, which enabled the plane to land.

Carmel's buddy was not as lucky. When they were loading the two planes in Europe, the men were divided into two equal groups. Carmel went on one plane, his buddy on the other. The other plane crashed and the men were lost. After going through the war and all its hardships, they still did not make it home!

Carmel did make it back without a scratch. His family gives credit to his mother's prayers for her boys (Carmel in Europe and Harry in the Pacific) to return home safely. Records report that Carmel's rating was Tec. Sgt. and he participated in five major battle campaigns: Normandy Campaign, Northern France, Ardennes Campaign, Rhineland Campaign and Central Europe. He came back to his wife and two children and joined his father in farming. Carmel's parents became ill and he decided he should move back in their house to help care for them, so in 1949, he and his family moved back in the old home place. They sold the house he had built to H. D. Lawhon and his wife, Martha Posey, who later moved to Tallahassee, selling the place to Guy Lawhon and his wife, Lucille Causseaux Lawhon.

Carmel went to work with Wakulla County Road Department as the Superintendent of Roads. When there was talk of layoffs, he left to work with Rhett Taff in his surveying business and later returned to the Road Department where he worked until his illness and death from cancer at age 58.

Carmel and Etta Mae had six children. Berlin married Ellen Bruce of Tallahassee and their sons are Travis and Chad. Berlin died at 32 due to injuries received in an explosion at Olin Corporation; Etta Jo married Ralph Oliver and their children are James, Wendy and Wesley; Willie Bostic married Janis Wester of

Tallahassee; Vera married Eric Mathis and their children are Chris and Becky; Brenda married George Carraway and their children are Brook and Diana; Brenda is now married to Gene McCarthy; Carmen married Broward Sapp of Tallahassee and they have two children, Amy and Cody.

Etta Mae lived in the old Pelt homestead until her death at age 90 in 2008. She deeded the old farm to her 6 children and all of them live around the homestead. She participated in the war effort while Carmel was gone. She was trained to cut metal in sheets and to rivet those sheets of metal in building airplanes. She left her only child at the time, Berlin, with Carmel's parents while she worked in Orlando, Wakulla's own Rosie the Riveter!!

An interesting note about Etta Mae added by her daughter, Etta Jo telling of her mother making her two dresses out of a German flag that Carmel had wrapped around a gun he had brought home. Etta Mae said the cloth of the flag was extremely strong and she thought it would make a fine dress. The swastika emblem had been removed. The remnants from the flag were used to make patchwork quilts.

A note from daughter Etta Jo: When our daughter, Wendy was stationed with her Army pilot husband, Tim, in Germany, we visited them and in our travels, staying in a hotel that had been one of General Patton's headquarters, appropriately named The General Patton Hotel. Our next visit coincided with the celebration of D-Day. We actually crossed the English Channel while the D-Day Observances were made and saw Air Force One at one of our bases in Europe.

Submitted by: Etta Jo Oliver, Brenda McCarthy and Betty Green PO Box 969, Crawfordville, FL 32326

Jerry Reeves, Hero of Forgotten War

In April of 1991, Mays Leroy Gray wrote the combat experience of a Wakulla County native who served in the so-called "Forgotten War" forty years earlier. This article was clipped to be stored in a history folder and is now a reminder of the thousands of Americans who served, and for the families of those who died or were crippled in that war, it was not, and never will be forgotten.

This is an abbreviated account of the original article but we are grateful for Mr. Gray's account, which reminds us not only of this hero but of the many who have served and continue to answer the call to preserve freedom throughout the world.

June 25, 1950. The Communist North Korean Army invaded the Republic of South Korea. Armed with Russian tanks, heavy artillery, Russian YAK fighter planes, attack bombers, and tanks, the well-trained and equipped 135,000 strong Army poured into South Korea whose 95,000 men were inexperienced, poorly trained and with poor equipment.

June 30, 1950. President Harry S. Truman ordered American Ground Forces into action.

July 1, 1950. Part of U. S Army 24th Infantry Division flew from Japan to Pusan, Korea as a U. S. stopgap measure to slow the North Korean offensive movement.

July 2, 1950. The U. S. 24th Infantry Division began to move into battle positions near Taejon, about 75 miles south of Seoul. Jerry Reeves was in I-Company, 21st regiment, 24th Division, Eighth Army. From Wakulla County, Jerry had enlisted in the Regular Army (RA) on Jan. 10, 1949. Soon, Jerry was promoted to Platoon Sergeant.

Jerry is quoted as telling to the best of his memory:

"At Pusan, we were completely surrounded by the North Korean Army and were fighting for our lives. Later, our regiment of about 3,000 men advanced to Taegu and we engaged the North Korean forces and fought a holding pattern."

"During the fierce Naktong River Battle, I was wounded by shrapnel from enemy mortar fire. For three days and three nights we were under very heavy enemy fire; fire from artillery, tanks, mortars, and machine gun fire. At the Naktong River Battle, our entire regiment was overrun. As an infantry machine gunner, I was firing a .30 cal. Machine gun, and at times a Browning automatic."

"The North Koreans kept coming every place I looked; our fire was stacking up enemy soldiers, but they kept coming. I, as well as all my buddies, ran out of ammunition. Then we fought them in hand-to-hand combat. Knives, bayonets, bun butts, anything we could get our hands on. Again, I was wounded in the leg from an enemy bayonet. Finally, our entire regiment was overrun."

"As we were being overrun by the North Korean forces, we began to fall back to regroup. While carrying my weapons in my arms, I turned and saw something I will never forget. Without notice, I had stepped across the body of an American soldier that had been cut in half from enemy machine gunfire. For a moment, I stopped and stood there in shock. After a pause, I regained my sense of danger, training and reality of the situation; then I moved out with what was left of my outfit."

" Out of our Company (I-Company) of about 200 men, only 26 survived; and those of us who survived were taken prisoner by the North Korean forces. I saw General Bill Dean in the area, leading the fight. He was also taken prisoner."

"As prisoners of war under heavy guard, we were started on a long, forced march into North Korea and marched straggling into a barbed wire holding pen. During the forced march, we were treated very brutally by the North Korean soldiers. If an American soldier fell sick or fell down, you were bayoneted or shot."

Jerry Reeves at Ft. Benning, GA in 1952

"As prisoners of war, we were beaten, hit with rifle butts, and some men were bayoneted. We were tortured by the North Koreans in their efforts to get information. After three weeks of prison brutality and starvation (we were given one handful of trashy rice per day,) we planned an escape. We killed the North Korean guards, broke out and scattered. Of the 200 American POWs in our group, only eight of us made it out. Many were killed and some recaptured."

"Upon our escape, the eight of us walked and crawled through very rough terrain. Finally we found a stream. Knowing that all rivers and streams flow south in Korea, we followed the direction of the water flow, and finally made our way back south to U. N. forces. Then we almost got shot by them as we were trying to identify ourselves as American soldiers."

"Finally we were rescued and flown to a hospital in Japan for treatment of our wounds and to recuperate from our combat and POW ordeal. After a short stay at the hospital, we were sent back to combat duty in Korea with our old outfit, the 24th U. S. Army Infantry Division."

For his combat services during the Korean War, Jerry Reeves was awarded the following military decorations:

The Silver Star: For gallantry in action.

The Bronze Star: For heroic and meritorious achievement during military operations.

Three Purple Heart Medals: For wounds in combat, three times, three separate wounds.

The Korean Meritorious Unit Citation: awarded by the Republic of South Korea.

Jerry was in combat from June, 1950, to the last part of 1951, about 16 months. He was quoted as follows: "I have always looked upon my combat sacrifices and military experience with pride. I am very proud of my military experience, proud to be an American, and proud to have served my country in its hour of need. I look upon the American flag as the most beautiful thing in the world, and will defend it to my death".

Mr. Mays Gray also served us, and our nation, by his research and writing of this conflict. His article concludes with the following:

"American casualties as a result of the Korean War are as follows: total casualties, 162,708; dead, 54,246; wounded, 103,284; prisoners or missing, 5,178.

As freedom-loving Americans, we should never view these casualties as mere statistics. We should view each one of them as part of America's existence, a part of our heart and soul, a part of our national conscience, and defenders of a free America; a freedom we would not enjoy today except for their sacrifices.

A free nation does not maintain freedom through osmosis, freedom requires defending and continuous vigilance, and freedom doesn't come free!"

Note: Jerry Reeves still lives in Crawfordville and still loves his family and country.

Submitted by Betty Green, PO Box 969, Crawfordville, FL 32326

MODERN TIMES

Adron Anderson

April 6, 1959

Adron Anderson was killed in a tractor accident. Mr. Bonner called Hardy, Adronna and Dottie to his office to let them know what had happened. He had Hardy sit on his knee and Dottie and Adronna stood by his desk as he slowly looked at his wrist watch and said in such a caring voice, "Kids I need to tell you something. Today around 11:30 am, your Daddy went to be with Jesus."

I'll never forget growing up in a school where the principal was a Christian and certainly how he told a group of kids about their Daddy's passing!

By Adronna Anderson Kenbrinck 18541 NE Live Oak Lane,Blountstown, FL 3232, 850-674-8478

Our "Garden Of Eden"

H. Palmer Carr and Madeleine H. Carr

We found our way to Wakulla County through an English contact who had bought a very small A-frame structure in a subdivision called Wakulla Gardens. Those were the waning "hippie" days of the late 1970s when FSU students and faculty "hung out" in the woods smoking dope and growing their own organic gardens. It was happening all over Wakulla County and one assumes this couldn't be avoided with the close proximity to two universities in Tallahassee.

That small A-frame in the "gardens" was where we had our wedding reception on New Year's Eve 1979. Palmer is from Macon, GA, Madeleine a British native who grew up in Switzerland. Nothing had ever been further from our minds than "homesteading" on what was a jungle to us.

We bought 20 acres behind Wakulla Gardens (this was subdivided in the 1960s to fleece the Yankees). After a year of roaming among the hardwoods, we decided on a location to put an octagonal house for which no bank in its right mind provided a loan. As Madeleine continued promoting Florida with the Dept. of Commerce, Palmer began contracting laborers to help build the house.

Whenever there was enough money we'd buy supplies and Palmer consulted more books about plumbing, electrical wiring, and how to fell a large tree. It took seven years to complete and we grew to hate the mildew, the chiggers, and the ticks. But we loved the feathery and mammalian wildlife more. We loved the solitude and the ability to be free to decide how we wanted to structure our own environment.

Living in the Wakulla woods provided once-in-a-lifetime experiences. Such as when hundreds of Wood ducks decided to forage for acorns during one entire December month; or the time an otter crossed the land, and an alligator, or when a deer was born in our driveway, and a bear stood there wondering what all this was about, with a grey and red fox, and a bobcat walking past the house. By

2012, after 30 years, this octagonal tree house has become part of the environment, a curiosity no more to the wildlife.

We've grown to love our "yard deer" and the large variety of Woodpeckers, the loud Blue Jays, and hoot, screech and Barn owls. Even the Katydids' cacophony that keeps us awake during hot summer nights is a sign that our environment is hanging on even as the thousands of Canada geese, the mullet, the Fox squirrels and frogs and toads are either already gone from here or simply cannot stand the increasing population.

There has been tragedy as well. Roaming dogs caught a deer and ripped off its leg as we heard the awful bleaching. An owl ensnared itself in a tree crevice trying to capture a lizard only to die trapped by nature. A human family came out of nowhere one day looking for a lost little boy, who was found, thankfully.

Linking us to the antebellum days back here on the western edge of Tiger Hammock are the meager remains of a slave cabin, judging by the few metal artifacts and the hearth-like configuration of limestone. We wonder if the adjoining Tiger Hammock was named for the panthers we have seen only a few miles south?

In retirement, we notice the trees are aging also. Weakened Oaks simply fall over; dogwoods do likewise apparently having rotted in the ground. Life in these humid jungles has provided plenty of wood to heat, plenty of shade, and the insects are still a bother. We've also enjoyed meeting others who can tell us what a true bug is, how to grow blueberries, but alas, not how to deal with a voracious grasshopper population.

And we learned that mildew inside the house is a result of modern kitchens and plumbing. Apparently those early pioneers who had a kitchen set away from the main house and walked to an outhouse did not have that moldy problem. We still appreciate the solitude, and above all air conditioning.

Submitted by: Palmer and Madeleine Carr, 223 Iroquois Road, Crawfordville

Wakulla County Salt Works

A friend & I fly our tiny ultra light aircraft out of the Panacea airport in Wakulla County. These aircraft fly at such low speed that they are almost helicopter-like in their short & rough field performance but extremely economical to operate. Mine in particular has a set of huge tires that allows it to land in just about anything but high marsh grass. Deep sand, mud & rough fields are no problems. One bright sunny morning in the Spring of 2005, my friend & I were flying low & slow over the marsh & near the tree line just west of Spring Creek. Looking carefully, I spotted what looked to be big stacks of karst & brick formations all along that area of the coast in extreme southern Wakulla County. These strange stacks of rock debris had something in common. They were mostly all overgrown with Spanish bayonets, Palm, old Cypress & Pine trees but the bricks & karst underneath were clearly visible from the air. Interesting enough for me to land & take a look!

Since there was plenty of places to land in the sand near the big piles of bricks & karst, I carefully lined up an approach that would land me right near the stacks. My friend with smaller tires also landed when I signaled to him that the ground was firm enough for his smaller tires.

When he unbuckled from his ultra light, we then walked over to the now huge piles of bricks & karst. It always amazes me how things look so small from the air yet when you get on the ground you fully realize the true size of objects.

Slowly wading through the marsh grass surrounding the stone mounds, we noticed a lot of old rusted metal. We said to each other, what can this be? This big heavy metal out here in the middle of nowhere surrounded & mostly covered by large chunks of karst & old red bricks! How & why could it have been hauled out here? Upon looking further we found that there were as many as 20 to 30 other stacks of this same material scattered in various places!

This called for some expert help from Google research! Thanks to the internet, we were able to quickly discover that these sites were from the Civil War era! They were actually Salt Boiler sites built by locals from the surrounding area! These Salt Boiler sites were very important to the Confederate war effort! They supplied salt used in the Civil War for meat preservation, gunpowder & other uses. The going rate for a bushel of salt was $12.50 in Confederate dollars! A large amount of money at that time & a great incentive for many people to risk their lives in support of their beloved South!

We also discovered through our research that one of our local citizens had a Confederate forces relative who was captured in this area by Union forces raiding the Salt Boiler sites. A young CSA Private named Noah Posey who was later sent to Ship Island off Alabama as a POW. Unfortunately, young Noah later died at Ship Island possibly of malnutrition or disease.

This information now whetted my appetite to see if more Boiler Sites were located further east to St. Marks. To my great delight, I flew to the marsh between the St. Marks River & East River & discovered a motherload of Boiler Sites located in this very isolated area. To me it looked like nobody had been in there in ages except wild pigs, which were plentiful & deer which were few in number.

I flew over this area at first & took plenty of photos & video of more boiler sites than I'd ever seen! There were also old roads & trails visible only from the air! I spotted small, shallow, square & round shaped ponds that later I could only figure were collection ponds where the ground was dug to collect salt water from the very low water table. I can only assume that they did this to prevent them from having to lug the water from the far away East River & St. Marks Rivers. There was also a very old trail visible from the sites to Port Leon where again I can only assume that the salt was loaded onto barges & blockade runners for shipment north to the war effort.

After a very extensive inspection of possible landing sites, I landed safely in several areas here. You have to be extremely careful doing this, as any mishap can cause a very long walk to civilization & possibly many days of recovering the aircraft.

The wild pigs here love to dig deep ruts in the ground to feed on roots & whatever else they can find. They can make landings hazardous. Take it from me, the wild pigs eat well as many looked to be 300 pounds or more with many piglets learning the trade. I kept a watchful eye on my fellow explorers!

Eventually I flew as far as the Aucilla River in search of more boiler sites but was unable to find any further sites. Viewing this particular terrain from the air, it seems this area from the St. Marks Lighthouse eastward was not accessible for salt boiler site construction due to the lack of immediate river transportation for the salt & needed supplies.

What dawned on me as we ended our exploration was the fact that all the salt boiler sites were completely destroyed! All of them! A lot of these sites were difficult to find even from the air. We found it almost incomprehensible how Union forces could have found & destroyed all of them! They must have had help! Thank you!

Submitted by: William L. Catalina P.O. Box 422 Crawfordville, FL 32327 Email: blumax008@aol.com

Homer Harvey And His Vehicles

Homer Harvey with 1954 Ford Station Wagon used for family vacations

In March of 1991, a magazine article entitled "Homer R. Harvey, Jack of All Trades" was circulated in Wakulla County. The subject of the article lived his entire life in Wakulla only traveling for business or vacation. Yet, evidence of his life is witnessed every day by all who travel Highway 319 south of Crawfordville.

Perhaps you have noticed a clearing on the west side of 319 about ½ mile north of the Wakulla County Public Library with a semicircle of more than a dozen old cars and trucks facing the highway. You may have seen a wedding party with the photographer in charge; perhaps an advertising photographer arranging a scene for display or any of many individuals with cameras taking pictures to be arranged, painted or even sold! These old cars have given St. Marks Lighthouse competition in the photographic subject category.

These old vehicles represent the travels of Homer as he farmed, raised cattle and hogs, collected pine sap to be taken to turpentine stills and made a living for his family. This is not a field of dreams but a field of memories. There is the Dodge cattle truck used to take cattle to market in Monticello and occasionally Marianna. There's the '39 Ford truck used to haul turpentine gum from the woods to Homer's place where he had an office and a ramp built for loading and unloading barrels of gum. The gum was collected by workers who poured it into barrels that were then sold to Homer who loaded a 40 foot trailer which he used to haul the drums to Valdosta to a dealer. His trip was made once a month during the dipping season.

A talented man, Homer Harvey, known to be rancher, farmer, electrician, plumber, truck driver and carpenter, truly lived through more than one era of history. As a young man on horseback, he herded cattle throughout most of Wakulla County on the open range from the Ochlockonee Bay to Jackson Bluff in Leon County. In those days most of what was done on the farm was labor intensive with little aid of machinery. Homer's mechanical talents allowed him to make early use of the farming and building improvements throughout his life. He died in 2011 at the age of 95 leaving a legacy of accomplishments. The cars and tractors, as well as buildings he built, remain as monuments to that life.

Homer is buried in Lake Ellen Cemetery just south of where he lived and the cars are parked. His son said he never sold or traded a

Homer Harvey's Gift to Wakulla

vehicle but when he bought the new car or truck, he parked the old…and there they are today, offering a glimpse into several journeys of life!

Submitted by; Betty Green, PO Box 969, Crawfordville, FL 32326 original magazine article printed in Wakulla Times

Betty Ann Korzenny,

Betty Ann Korzenny, Resident of Wakulla County currently living in Hunters Glen, a gated community located between Shadeville Road and Highway 98, East of the Wakulla River.

My husband, Felipe Korzenny, and I moved to Wakulla County in November 2005 after living for the two prior years in Tallahassee. While we enjoyed living in Tallahassee, we were attracted to the acreage available and the beauty of the property we saw in Hunters Glen. Since my husband is a professor at Florida State University, and I teach as an adjunct faculty there, we needed a location accessible to the University. On the other hand, we had at that time four miniature donkeys that drove our considerations for the type of property that could provide adequate pasture land for them, and a beautiful natural environment for our home. We looked in several locations around Tallahassee, but fell in love with the woods in Wakulla County. We hired a local contractor, Ted Beam, and worked with him on the design and building of our home. While we had owned many homes in our lives, this was the first time that we ever built one to fit us and the wild beauty of this land.

Compared to many of our friends and neighbors here in the County we are newcomers. Many in this area have extended families of numerous brothers, sisters, aunts, uncles, and cousins who even share their last names. People know each other and share life histories. Little by little we have built our friendship networks, but our families are far-flung and visit only occasionally when they can during the year. We treasure our neighbors who share our interests in nature and the lifestyle which can be built when you can enjoy these surroundings. We now also have two Paso Fino horses, one bought from a neighbor in Hunters Glen. Another neighbor has her horse living with ours on the property bringing our equine number to six. Our animals are our daily family, including the

Betty Ann Korzenny

horses and donkeys already mentioned, our two cats, and our fish.

I am deeply appreciative of the beauty of where we live and the lifestyle in this beautiful county. We ride our horses on our own and nearby paths, we bike on the old railroad trail between Tallahassee and St. Marks as well as in the St. Marks Wildlife Refuge, we treasure Wakulla Springs and go there often for a boat ride on the Wakulla River, and I am frequently shopping and exercising at my gym in Crawfordville. St. Marks is important to us. We belong to the Yacht Club, eat at the restaurant on the River, and start and end our bike rides at the trail's head there.

I am originally from Troy, New York and have lived in many places in the United States; New York, Virginia, North Carolina, Colorado, Michigan and California, as well as internationally in Mexico, Italy, Nigeria, and Germany. When people ask, *What is the favorite place where you have lived?* My answer is; *I have enjoyed them all, some of them I have indeed loved very much.* Each location has had its valuable qualities and influenced the person I am. So, my home in Wakulla County is indeed special for me and I'm very thankful to be a part of all of this natural beauty and for the friends I have made.

Submitted by: Betty Ann Korzenny, 424 Hunters Trace, Crawfordville, 32327; 925-7977

Memories of Ora Harper & Annie Haddock Posey

This article appeared in the Wakulla Area Digest January 1995

Wakulla County lost two very special ladies in early November 1994. To attend their funerals within two days was to be doubly blessed because those services honored such remarkable women and reflected in their extraordinary strengths and characters.

Mrs. Ora Harper died Friday, November 7, 1994 at the age of 96. The mother of five sons and one step-son, she is survived by only one, Clifton Harper of Crawfordville. Her other children were Johnny, who died as a boy; Newman, never married, was Voter Registration Officer and died in 1971. Clifton, retired from Florida Power Corporation, still lives in Crawfordville with his wife, Ruth Poli. George married Naomi Enfinger, became a lawyer and Wakulla County Judge before his death in 1990. Ray, who died in 1973, was a refrigeration engineer with the State of Florida and was married to Ann Kepler. Miss Ora's step-son, Joseph E. Harper married Sally Eubanks whose family moved from Wakulla County to Bradenton. He was buried there following his death in 1982.

Dr. Joseph Harper, twice widowed and with one son, Joseph, came to Wakulla County in 1907. He was from Atlanta where he boarded the train and disembarked at Arran. He first rented a house from Wright Walker, Jr. that was located where the county health clinic now stands in Crawfordville. He later bought it but the house burned and years later he gave that land to the county for the Health Department. Many local people still feel that building should be named in honor of Dr. Harper and his 35 years of service to the county. After building another house which also burned, Dr. Harper moved across the street into the home just south of the Crawfordville Baptist Church known then as the Wright Walker House. Presently the Harvey-Young Funeral Home, this building is referred to as the Harper House because of Dr. Harper's practice and residency for so many years.

Miss Ora Allen from Tallahassee married Dr. Harper on September 17, 1916 when she was 19 and he was 51. She was wife, mother, doctor's assistant and sometimes substitute doctor or nurse. Although her life's story remains in the shadow of the good doctor's contributions to the county, yet she was a strong supporter and co-worker with him in his practice. She not only kept the house, raised the children and tended the garden but often she would accompany him as he went to deliver babies or minister to the sick and if he was needed in more than one place at a particular time she would fill in for him in one of those places. She delivered many babies on her own, among them the Fulford twins in St. Marks. Her house served as a clinic when necessary where broken bones were set, wounds cleaned and bandaged and advice was given.

In conducting memorial services for Miss Ora, Brother Emmett Whaley recalled many of her talents. He told how the Doctor and his wife would minister to people regardless of their ability to pay. They would accept pay in almost any form it was offered. It might be chickens, a ham, eggs or perhaps fish or vegetables. When doctor Harper died, he and his wife had delivered 7,000 babies in Wakulla County – more than Wakulla's population at that time. They had many thousands of dollars owed to them throughout their lifetime although a few people kept paying on their debt for years after his death in 1942.

Following her husband's death, Miss Ora went to work at Camp Gordon Johnston where she worked until the base closed following the war. She would leave before day to walk from her house to the post office to catch the bus picking up people from Tallahassee to Sopchoppy to take to the base as civilian workers. After the war, she went to work in Tallahassee with the state's Motor Vehicle Department where she remained until her retirement. Her favorite pastimes were fishing and gardening. Her son, Cliff, says she always kept a garden and seemed she planted enough to feed Crawfordville, if necessary. She also loved to fish and went often in those earlier retirement years with her grandsons. She was ill for many years before her death but she will always be remembered as a strong, capable and generous person.

Mrs. Annie Haddock Posey died November 6, 1994 at the age of 93 years, 10 months. Her life had been blessed with such good health that she had never been hospitalized and her final days were blessed by being able to live at home, get around and go out to eat with her children. On the morning of her death, she had unlocked the door, laid out her clothes and was waiting for her son, Nolan, to bring her breakfast and her paper. She leaned her head back and went to sleep just before her son arrived. There was no evidence of trauma. What a blessing!

Her funeral was held at Lake Ellen Baptist Church with Rev. H. D. Lawhon and Elder Emmett Whaley conducting the services. H. D., who was married to Martha Posey until her death in an automobile accident, spoke of his mother-in-law as a very special and dear friend. He related that she had left instructions for her services to be held at this church where she and her husband, Arthur Posey, had made their commitment to Christ and where her husband and first son had been buried more than fifty years ago. In his remarks, H. D. told briefly of the challenges she had faced and overcome in her lifetime and of her faithfulness to her children, to her jobs and to her Christian duties.

We look back now at the life of "Miss Annie." She was born in Jesup, Ga., January 6, 1901, to Solomon Monroe Haddock and Lannie Kathleen Pigott from Medart. Solomon had met his future wife when he came to work with his uncle in a turpentine still at Medart. After being married by Judge R. Don McLeod in Crawfordville, they went to Georgia to live but returned to Wakulla County when Annie was five months old. She and her sisters, Ollie, who married T. S. Barrow, and Omalee who married Bob Spears, and her brother George who never married, lived and went to school in Medart.

Miss Annie and Noah Arthur Posey were married by Judge R. Don McLeod, April 11, 1923, in Crawfordville. They moved to Fort Myers where their first child Noah Monroe was born. When they returned to Wakulla county, they lived in Shadeville just past and to the left of where Michelle's Grocery is now. This house remained Miss Annie's home for her lifetime although she changed its location in 1949 when she had it moved to Crawfordville between where Wakulla State Bank and the Junior Food Store are located today. Their house was moved the same year the "new courthouse" was dedicated.

While living in Shadeville, Arthur had supported his growing family by fishing- he was a gill-net fisherman and a farmer. It was while living there that their first son, Noah Monroe, was killed by being hit by a truck as he left the school bus. This tragedy happened December 14, 1932.

Arthur had served in the US Army in France in the latter part of World War I and because of being gassed, suffering double Pneumonia and frostbite, his health grew worse and he was admitted to the Veteran's Hospital in Lake City, FL a few times before his death there in 1941.

Following her husband's sickness and death, Miss Annie was left with a young family of eight children to feed, clothe and educate. Without welfare, food stamps or Medicaid she shouldered the tremendous responsibility. She was blessed with an inner strength, good health, a willingness to work, her love for God and her family and her talents as a seamstress. While still a child, she had taught herself how to sew and make clothes for herself, her mother and her sisters and later for her own family.

Submitted by; Betty Green, PO Box 969, Crawfordville, FL 32326

OUR PEOPLE AND LIFESTYLE

Treasured Memories of Bea Andrew; Some of my treasured memories of childhood and growing up.

You see, I was born between two brothers, so I grew up with them as my playmates. Dan was two years older than I but I thought there was nothing he didn't know about. We grew up on a farm and never had much wealth but there was one thing that we did have and that was LOVE.

I remember once when our grandmother came to stay with us, and she dipped snuff.

One day Dan and I thought that was so cool the way she put that snuff in her bottom lip, so we stole her snuff and hid it in the chicken nest. After we got through with supper, we went out to dip us some snuff. Well, you can imagine what happened. We got so sick when we swallowed that juice and started vomiting.

Sister Brother; Beulah /Bea Green & Daniel Green

Grandmother knew we got her snuff. She said, "You little rascals, you deserve what you get for stealing my snuff!"

Our dad was a great one for buying old cars; the only problem was that none of them ever would run. Well, one time he brought home an Austin car. It was so little that we used it for a toy and would push it around the house and pretend we were going to town.

I remember once Daddy had this old mule and his name was "Old Bob". Well, we would take turns riding him. When it came my turn to ride, Dan played a joke and lifted Old Bob's tail and tickled him with a cattail weed and Old Bob threw me off into a bed of sandspurs that had my legs glued together. Well, you know what happened to Dan. Yep, he got a whipping!!

Buddies 1950; Dan Green & Bo Andrew

One time our dad had a Model-T car and the gas tank was up beneath the windshield. Dan opened the gas tank cap and inhaled the gas. Of course, you know who had to follow, yep, me, and I got so drunk I rolled off to the ground and hit the dirt! I don't know how we ever got grown, but by God's grace we did!

That thought brings me to another escapade in our older years. I was going with Bo Andrew at this time and Dan and he built a car from scratch. I mean from nothing. They found an engine and an old chassis with wheels. They also found an old car body in the woods and put it on the frame. The gas tank was a 5 gallon can, wired to the frame and it didn't have a hood. It was such a pretty car that we named it *Pretty Boy.*

Dan Green & Betty Jo Oaks
1950

We were so proud of that car that we drove it to the Governor's Mansion for the inauguration of the Governor. (Don't remember which one.) Anyway, when we were going home the car was about to stop running so Dan told Bo to get out on the fender and choke the carburetor to keep it running and, oh, my goodness, was it cold that night!

There are so many memories that I don't have time to write them all down at this time but we did grow up and of course, you know I married Bo and Dan married Betty Jo Oaks and even after we married and went different ways, we continued to be the best of friends. The four of us, at least now, Betty and I, have fond memories of our times together as our loved ones are waiting for us on the other side. Some day we will all be together again!!

Written and submitted by Beulah "Bea" Green Andrew, P. O. Box 1015, Crawfordville, FL 32326

Childhood Memories Annie Maude Harris Browning

I was born Annie Maude Harris, October 9, 1920, in Wakulla County.

My Mother was Annie Lee Lewis. She was born August 30, 1887 and died September 15, 1960. Annie was the daughter of Howell (H.G.) Lewis and Victoria Dikes Lewis. Howell Lewis was born in 1858 and died in 1928. Victoria Dikes Lewis was born in 1858 and died in 1908. Mother had one sister, Nancy, and four brothers, Bloxham, Charlie, Pickens, and Johnny.

Howell Lewis was the first Postmaster in Woodville. Mother used to help him in the post office.

Granddaddy Lewis was a farmer in addition to being Postmaster. He owned a lot of property in Woodville. I was told he gave the land for the Woodville School, White Church, and White Church Cemetery. My Mother's youngest brother Johnny L. Lewis was born on October 10, 1896, and died on January 3,1897. He was the first person to be buried in the White Church Cemetery in Woodville.

After Grandmother Victoria died, Granddaddy Lewis remarried Joanna Alligood. There were five children born of this marriage, three sons, Felkel, Wilson, and Bobby, and two daughters, Inez and Mary. Wilson was born in 1907 and is the only living child of this marriage.

My mother married my father, William Harris. William was one of four sons of Rebecca Winburn Harris and James D. Harris. He was born October 4,1878 and died June 15,1957. His Mother, Rebecca, was born July 21, 1858 and died October 19, 1933. His father, James, was born May 24, 1840 and died August 21, 1924.

William's father, James D. Harris, fought as a Confederate soldier in the Civil War and returned from the war to continue farming in Woodville. His tombstone in the White Church Cemetery in Woodville, reads "He Was True To His Loved Ones, His Friends and His Country".

James and Rebecca Harris lived in the Arran area. Rebecca moved from Arran to Woodville some time after his death. In Arran they lived close to the Council family. Nora and I always played with the Council's two girls Debra and Etta Mae when we visited our grandmother.

My parents, Annie Lewis Harris and William Harris, had five boys and four daughters, Billy, Manard, Nora, Estelle, Annie Maude, Norman, Oliver, Horace and Theo. I am the only living daughter of Annie Lewis Harris and William

Harris. My brother Theo, born in 1927, is their only living son.

Wakulla County has always been special to me.

My sister, Estelle, married Troy Eubanks's from Wakulla County. They lived in Medart where they raised two girls, Eula and Annabel. We visited them often.

My parents moved our family to Arran when I was 6 years old. My brother Billy, sister Nora, and I attended the one room school out in the country. All grades were taught in the single room of the school house.

We lived next door to the Vause family. Their son, Deawood and I played together all the time. We used to hunt bottles which we took to the general store where we traded them for candy. I still have a picture taken in the hall of our home there.

Before I finished first grade we moved from Arran to Crawfordville. We lived on Trice Rd. across from the Trice family. Mrs. Trice gave me a big, beautiful doll. I remember two girls from first grade, twins, Eloise and Louise. My teacher, Etta Maude Rouse, lived in a rooming house in Crawfordville. It is now the funeral home on Hwy 319. Miss Rouse invited me to spend a weekend in Sopchoppy where she lived with her parents. This was the highlight of my first grade year, we had a wonderful time.

My Granddaddy Lewis owned property on Natural Bridge Road. My mother inherited property from him that was about a mile and a half from the Woodville School. After I finished first grade in Crawfordville we moved back to Woodville and lived on the property on Natural Bridge Road.

I attended Woodville School from then through the 10th grade. My second grade teacher was Mrs. Nomie Howard. Before classes started each morning we had Bible reading and prayer. One day Sara Harris and Doris Lawhon came to school wearing pants. Principal Arlie Rhodes sent the girls home to put on dresses. How things have changed. I was on the basketball team, a sport I really loved.

Annie Harris Browning

My father grew vegetables. We all had to get up early on Saturday to shell peas and beans. Our parents took the produce by wagon to the Tallahassee curb market to sell.

At age 19, I married George Browning. We had four boys, James, Glen, Wayne, and Michael, and no girls, although I nearly had my girl. My first baby, James, was born in the little Johnson's Hospital in Tallahassee. When I was discharged from the hospital, the orderly carried me out and put me in the back seat of the car. A basket with the baby was placed on the front seat. As we drove up to our house, another car pulled up behind us. They had given me the wrong baby. They took my baby girl. This was as close as I ever came to having my little girl. And that is when they started putting name tags on the babies.

Submitted by; Annie Maude Browning P.O. Box 268 Woodville, FL 32362

The Council Family As I Remember It

I am Beverly Council, the second daughter born on September 16, 1946, to Owen R. and Eleanor Jones Council. But my story begins years before then.

My great-grandfather was John C. Council, a pioneer of Wakulla County. He had two wives and two families. His first wife, Frances DeLaura Posey, died, and he remarried Missouri Redd, my great-grandmother. Their first child, Lawrence E. Council, born July 23,1892, was my grandfather. They lived in Crawfordville. When granddaddy was a young man, he and his brother, Whit, decided to go down south and get rich. They ended up in Manatee County, just south of the Tampa Bay area, and that is where they found their fortune. They met two pretty sisters, Margaret and Josephine Dole. Whit married Margaret and my granddaddy married Josephine, my grand-mama. Granddaddy and Grandmama had seven children. My father, Owen, was their second son and fourth child.

I want to tell you a little about my grandmama's history. In 1883 Eben Dole, a native of Massachusetts, brought his young Kansas bride, Margaret (Maggie) Niles Dole, to Terra Ceia Island, Florida, a lush, subtropical area. Terra Ceia is Spanish for "Heavenly Land". They built a two-story house on the island not far from the bay. They had eight children, four boys and four girls, all born in the old house. The house and its furnishings spoke eloquently of a gracious way of life that is vanishing from the southern scene.

Lawrence E Council & Josephine Chalmers Dole on their wedding day. April 14, 1916

Grandmama was the third child born on May 29, 1897. They lived well by growing citrus trees. One day my great-grand-mother, Maggie, brought home a small sapling which one of her sons planted in the front yard, not too far from the front porch of the house. At that time the sapling was about as big around as a pencil. Quite a few years ago, at least 30 or more, it was measured and had reached the height of a five story building, 30 feet around the trunk, and its limbs spread 345.7 feet. Of course it has continued to grow since then. It is a rubber tree, aka as a banyan tree. They drop vines, and if allowed to take root, the vines quickly become like another tree. It is a sight to see. At any rate, back when it was measured, it was considered the largest tree in Manatee County and probably in Florida. It took possession of the yard years

Banyan Tree approx 30-40 years ago

Council Banyan Tree

ago. The front porch had to be torn down. The roots of the tree extended underneath the house and pushed up the hearth stones in the fireplace. At one time it was necessary to cover the roof of the house with tin to prevent the roots taking hold in the roof. Years ago a tree expert was consulted about removing the tree. He said it would be cheaper and easier to move the house away from the tree. The Dole homestead was eventually sold to a very good friend of the family, Willis Underwood, who died March 2012 at the age of 99! I called him Uncle Willis, even though he wasn't my uncle. He was a very special person to the Dole and Council families. He let us visit him and the old Dole home place any time we wanted which we did as often as we could. The place just seemed to draw you to it with its history and memories. He got a lot of visitors who liked to sit in the rocking chairs on the screened front porch. A lot of articles have been written over the years in several newspapers and magazines about the island, the Dole homestead and the tree.

Gary and the mule Jack

Granddaddy and his family moved to Crawfordville on Daddy's 7th birthday, August 5, 1929. This was during the great depression and they moved back to Crawfordville hoping life would be better. Unfortunately, it didn't get a whole lot better. Granddaddy farmed on a small scale and anybody who knows anything about farming knows it's a tough job and you are at the mercy of the weather. He also took any other jobs that were available in the area. If they had stayed in Manatee County, life would have eventually been good for them financially, but Granddaddy couldn't get that Wakulla County sand out from between his toes and had to "go back home". Grandmama was really homesick for a few years, but Wakulla County eventually became her home and she stayed here the rest of her life. She and Granddaddy were tough, honest, hardworking, Christian pioneers and I loved them with all my heart.

I remember Granddaddy as an easy going, sentimental, friendly, jovial man, always finding something to laugh about. I remember him most sitting in his favorite rocking chair in the living room, smoking his pipe and reading the newspaper. I spent a lot of time in his lap in that rocking chair, which I still rock in myself today. He had a nickname for everyone. Unfortunately, he died when I was 15 years old so my memories of him are few, but precious.

Grandmama was a little more serious than Granddaddy but still a "sport" as daddy would say, and just as loving as Granddaddy. She was the rock of the family.

I spent a lot of time at their house, where I live today. I have fond memories of waking up to them stirring around in the early mornings. I would lie in bed, content and happy listening to the sounds they made, and recognizing from those sounds what they were doing, like Granddaddy building a fire in the fireplace, or Grandmama cooking breakfast in the kitchen. She always cooked a good breakfast and I would he there waiting with anticipation, my mouth watering from the wonderful smells that wafted throughout the house. Then we would all sit at the old wood table passed down from past generations, eating grits, fresh fried eggs, fried salt bacon, homemade biscuits, homemade syrup, jellies and jams, and drinking hot, sweet tea. Sometimes she would make homemade candy for us, sassafras tea and swamp cabbage.

Their door was always open to anyone, and everyone was treated with the same respect. And if you did go for a visit, you always left with something. The old dirt road from Crawfordville used to run right in front of their house, before it was moved to where it is now.

They made a living by hard labor, Granddaddy farming and taking any other job that came along. Grandmama sold eggs, vegetables, pears, relishes, etc., whatever she could grow and whatever she could can. She continued to do this after Granddaddy passed away. She made hickory nut cakes that were delicious. I remember seeing her sitting in front of the fireplace picking the meat out of hickory nuts. That's a long, hard job. I've done it. We usually got something handmade or home cooked as presents on special days, and we appreciated whatever it was just as much, or more, than any store bought item. She put a lot of love in everything she did.

Owen cleaning and packing eggs.

When she was 80 years old, I saw her plow a little garden with a push plow. She always wore a straw hat and long sleeved shirts when she worked outside. I saw her several times during the day and night outside with her gun looking for whatever was after her chickens. I've seen her crawl under her house during the day and night, with a gun, after snakes, or whatever was after the chickens. She did what she had to do to protect her chickens, because they provided her eggs and on special occasions, good fried chicken and chicken & dumplings. Back then, chicken was usually reserved for company and Sundays. Also, back

Grandma picking hickory nuts for Christmas cakes.

then, we called our meal times breakfast, dinner and supper.

One day she and I went down to Skipper Bay to cook and eat fish. She took some rocks and an old grill out of an old stove. She built a fire pit with the rocks, then built a fire in the pit After the fire burnt down to hot coals, she put the grill on the rocks and cooked mullet on the grill. We had a fine picnic. She was a survivor and never failed to impress me over and over. Whenever I would visit her, I would always leave feeling better and blessed to have her as my grandmama. She taught me a lot about life in the way she lived.

My father's nickname was Cotton because when he was a small child his hair was almost white. He told me a lot of stories about growing up in Wakulla County. Back then their transportation was a mule named Jack and a wagon. They mostly walked, especially the kids, whenever they went somewhere. He said he and his older brother, Lawrence E. Council, Jr., nicknamed Major, walked all over the county. Sometimes they would get lucky and catch a ride with someone. He talked a lot about walking to the seine yard at Fiddler's Point to help catch mullet. They had to hunt and fish for their meat then. They grew what fruits and vegetables they could in the summer and canned them for winter.

Daddy had five other siblings besides Major: Dorothy, Josephine, Joyce, Ernest and Gary. I don't know the particulars but I remember hearing Aunt Dorothy talk about meeting Clark Gable in person. She was the eldest of the seven children. She married Wade Loftin and they had four children.

Aunt Josephine became a nurse and worked at the Florida State Hospital in Chattahoochee while going to FSU to become a teacher. While working at the hospital, she met and married George Smith, a carpenter from that area. Aunt Josephine was born on July 9, 1918. She and Uncle George were married on Sept. 28, 1939. They lived just north of the Georgia state line on Smithtown Road between Chattahoochee and Faceville. The road was called Smithtown because most of Uncle George's family lived on that road. He had eight brothers and one sister. They weren't far from Wingate's Lunker Lodge on Lake Seminole. They never had any children of their own, but they treated every child they came in contact with as their own, especially their nieces and nephews, and we all loved them. They were special people, well respected in their community. Aunt Josephine was always sweet and soft spoken. She was another pioneer like Grandmama. She was a lady and a firm Christian. She loved to hunt and fish. I have a letter postmarked July 2, 1941 from her to Grandmama telling her "I traded three setting hens for two years of the ladies Home Journal, one year of the Saturday Evening Post, and five years of the Country Gentlemen." I spent a lot of time with her and Uncle George when I was around 2 and 3 because I was a breech birth and my younger sister was a breech birth and Mama was not in good health. They wanted to adopt me but Mama and Daddy wouldn't agree to it. Aunt Josephine would keep any child that needed a temporary home, and a lot of tender loving care. My sisters and I spent some summers with them. They were very memorable times because we were always treated very special. They would sit us on their front porch and tell us stories about Brer Rabbit and his family that lived just down in the hollow. They described everything in detail and as I sat there on the porch, looking down is the hollow, I believed every word. I could imagine every detail they described. Aunt Josephine was very artistic and did some painting. Whenever we would visit and start to leave, she and Uncle George would stand out in their yard and wave bye to us until they couldn't see us anymore. We always hated to leave them. In their later years they decided to sell out and move into a nursing home. Unfortunately, before they could do that, Aunt Josephine got very sick and ended up in the hospital in Bainbridge and died there on Feb. 11, 1993. Uncle George died a few years later. They are buried in Sylvania Cemetery not far from where they

Joyce(Joy) in front of the USO Building

Ernest Council and Frank Andrews in the stern of the Georgia Queen are now operating the facilities at Shell Point Beach and invite all of their friends to come and see them. Photo by Keightley.

lived.

Uncle Ernest married Lois Forbes and they had three children. He and Frank (Bo) Andrew leased the skiff boats, deep sea boat, the Georgia Queen, cottages and cafe from A. B. Taff years ago before that area was developed. Daddy worked there with them too. Daddy said one day a group of people came to the marina that had never seen the gulf before and one of the women in the group put her hand up over her eyes while looking out at the gulf and exclaimed "wow, what a lake!"

Ernest & his dog while working at Shell Point

Joyce, who we called Aunt Joy, after graduation, worked at Wakulla Springs and lived on the property while she worked there. After several years, she moved to Ft. Walton Beach where she was administrator of the USO for many years. Then she became a realtor. She eventually bought a bungalow across from the gulf in Destin where she could always hear the waves and go for long walks on the beach. She never married but loved all her nieces and nephews as if they were her own.

Gary was the baby of the family. My older sister Judy says she remembers when she and Uncle Gary got home from school; they would each get a biscuit from Grandmama's old wood stove (there was always biscuits left over from breakfast), stick a hole in the biscuits with their finger and put syrup in the hole. That was always the after school snack. Then they would get on Uncle Gary's bicycle, with Judy on the handlebars, and off they would go with their snack visiting neighbors. He married Joyce Hall and they had five children.

I can remember the ice truck delivering ice blocks to my grandparents' house, they would put big chunks of ice in the bottom of their "ice box" to keep the box cool. This was before refrigeration was invented. I also remember a man coming by in a vehicle occasionally selling coffee, tea, candy and some other items.

Daddy joined the Army when he was 18. He started out as a radio operator but eventually became a paratrooper. While stationed at Fort Benning in Augusta, Georgia, he met my mother, Eleanor Alice Jones. She and her family lived on Railroad Street. She had three sisters. Their house faced a cotton factory where they all worked. The factory was a big, red brick building for about as far as you could see. Just behind the factory was a railroad track, then alongside it was a dirt road that went down to the end of the row of houses, and then a sidewalk going down the row of houses, with a walkway to each house. All the houses were built alike, all painted white. Each one had a little front porch. A levy that held water was behind the houses. All the children were warned not to ever go up to the top of the levy because we might drown. They scared me enough that I never attempted to see for myself, but I knew it was there because we had to cross a small bridge to get on Railroad St., and under that bridge was always rushing water flowing into the levy. That was enough to convince me. There was probably, 50 ft. between the factory and the front of the houses and maybe 30 feet from the back of the houses to the top of the levy. Mama was making thread for soldier's uniforms at the factory when she met Daddy. They met in September and married in November 1942. I have the letter from Daddy to Grandmama telling her about them getting married. In the letter he says: "We went to town to get us supper and go to the show. Well, we went in a cafe to eat but didn't eat much and then we left and were just walking the streets. It started raining and we were standing in it. Within a half minute's time we decide we would get married. Well that's the story and I am really proud of my wife." Daddy had just found out that he was going to be transferred to Columbus, GA, and they also knew by then that he would eventually have to go overseas. I guess they decided the only way they could be together was to get married.

While Daddy was on a ship on his way overseas to train for the highly secret D-Day invasion, their first child, my older sister, Judith Patrell Council, was born on October 21, 1943. Daddy didn't get to see Judy until he returned home from WWII, sometime in May of 1945.

One story Daddy liked to tell that I thought was unique was while they were overseas training for the D-Day invasion, during one of their furloughs he and another soldier went to see a movie. Back then when you went to a theater to see a movie, you watched the world news, a cartoon and then the movie. Daddy said during the news they were showing a lot of young, beautiful women in bathing suits standing on top of a big sign that said Wakulla Springs. Of course that was the last thing he expected to see. He recognized a lot of the "girls back home". He said he couldn't help himself and had to shout with glee in the theater. And of course all of us older, local folks remember the big sign advertising Wakulla Springs and the row of bathing beauties that stood on top of it. What's the chance of being on the other side of the world, homesick, knowing you are not far from plunging into war, and seeing a news story about the very county you are from and seeing people you know on a big screen in a theater. I'm so glad Daddy was fortunate to be in the right place at the right time.

Last photo of family before Major & Owen went overseas. Back: L-R: Major & Owen, 2nd Row: Dorothy, Lawrence, Jo, Eleanor, Joy, Josephine, George. Front Row- Gary and Ernest.

A lot has been written about Daddy's involvement in WWII. Most of you have already read that story. But I have to repeat some of it because it was such a big part of our lives. I grew up hearing a lot about the war and his involvement in the D-Day invasion and being a POW. I saw firsthand the injuries he incurred fighting in this war. I can only imagine what it must have been like for him to finally come back home, a free man, but forever changed mentally and physically. It must have been a tremendous challenge for everyone.

I have numerous letters from family members to Daddy and from Daddy to family members, while he was in service. One is a letter from Daddy to his Mama asking her "to send him a peck of penders if it's not too much trouble" - which she did a couple of times. For those that don't know, penders was another name for peanuts back then. The word penders is not in the dictionary but everybody knew what it meant. I grew up hearing it a lot. Another word for peanuts is "goobers", which is in the dictionary. It was used a lot too, but you never hear those words anymore.

Daddy was very lonesome for home and his family. I have the original letter from the War Department to Grandmama notifying her that he was "missing in action", and the original telegram from the War Department notifying her that he was "a prisoner of war". I have the original "note" from someone overseas (I can't make out his name) that reads: "I take pleasure in forwarding the attached note which has come to me through the lines", and attached to it is a small piece of paper that reads "Dear Mom, I am a prisoner of war, and I am feeling fine, so don't worry. Love Owen". I read in letters written later that he wasn't fine but he didn't want his family worrying. At that time they didn't know that he had been injured and he didn't want them to know yet. And he wasn't about to tell them that the POWs were starving for food and water, were very cold, very homesick, and not knowing whether they would make it out alive, much less back home. Reading these letters gave me a lot of insight as to what it was like for the soldiers and their families. I also have the original letter from Daddy to Mama telling her "I am a free man and coming home!"

Uncle Ernest told me about the first time he saw daddy after he came home from the war. He said daddy looked like a walking skeleton.

We didn't talk much about the war. My sisters and I knew not to ask questions. We heard enough to know it was a bad time with a lot of sad and terrible memories. Over the years, we picked up more details here and there. We knew Daddy saw a lot of death in the war. We knew he was scared, as all the other soldiers were, but they had a job to do and did it. I knew he was proud to be part of the D-Day invasion and the rest of the war that helped turn history around for the world.

Daddy talked a little about being a POW. We knew he almost starved to death and did anything to get something to eat. The men in his camp were fed thin grass soup. As often as possible he and another POW would sneak over into the adjoining camp and get in their line for thin potato soup. The POWs in Daddy camp were all injured and in bad shape, but the POWs in the adjoining camp were healthier and worked every day and were fed a little better. He said he wouldn't have survived if it hadn't been for some potato soup every now and then. He was a survivor. It was bitterly cold and they weren't allowed heat. The bugs were bad. He said he was interrogated by the Germans after they captured him. They let him know they knew all about his family, wife and daughter back home. This concerned him very much. He wondered how they knew so much about his personal life. He worried about his family but he never gave any information to the Germans.

Daddy was our hero, and even though he lived through a terrible experience, he came home and went back to living like before. He had a wife and daughter now. He was a hundred percent disabled but helped his father farm. They had to make a living. Times were very hard back then because of the war. Farming was hard too. Eventually he started taking odd jobs, whatever was available, to make a living. He never complained.

I want to tell you a little about Daddy's older brother, Major, mentioned above. He and Daddy were very close. Uncle Major joined the Army Air Corps from high school. He served in the Pacific Isles during WWII. Before he was shipped overseas before the war, Daddy wanted so bad to see Major, but that opportunity never happened. Daddy finally came home from the war in May of 1945 and the family knew that Major would be coming home soon too. They were all excited with anticipation because this would be the first time the entire family would be together again since 1942. However, the family received a telegram from the War Department that Uncle Major had been killed in a plane crash on December 7, 1945. He and a few other soldiers were on their way home from the Pacific Isles. They had to land in Honolulu because of engine problems with the plane. On take-off from Honolulu, the plane crashed and seven of the eight people on the plane were killed. I have the original letter from Uncle Major to Grandmama telling her about the problems with the plane and having to lay over in Honolulu, but hopefully he would be home soon and was looking forward to seeing all the family, especially Owen. Unfortunately the family didn't get this letter until after they got the telegram that he had been killed.

The reason I mention this story is because it was another part of history that was ingrained into our lives. My sisters and I grew up hearing about Uncle Major, but again, we knew not to ask too many questions and we knew it was a very sad and painful time for the family. Even though I never knew Uncle Major personally, I knew him from hearing about him and I have always loved him. From what I heard and read about him, he was a tall, gentle, quiet, respectful, considerate, fine young man and loved by all.

My younger sister, Laura Jo, was born February 12, 1948. My sisters and I are "baby boomers". Our family lived in different places in Leon and Wakulla Counties, wherever work was to be found. I don't remember living in Tallahassee because I was too young, but I was told daddy worked at a dairy just south of Tallahassee. I have a vague memory of being on a porch and seeing a lot of cows. I think that was the only time we lived in Tallahassee. I know we lived in a two story house on the second story, because I had a rocky horse that I rode all the time, and the family that lived on the first story knew when I was on my rocky horse. I had very curly hair as a child and Daddy loved to tell the story about me eating grits with my hand, then running my hand through my hair. He said I had to have my hair washed every day.

I went to school from the first grade through the 12th grade at Crawfordville School. However, I remember going to school in the old Courthouse during the first grade. I don't know why. It wasn't for very long. Mrs. Libert was our teacher. I can remember us playing under the hickory nut trees just back of the courthouse. The Wakulla County Medical Clinic was across the hall and the reason I remember this is because one day while outside during recess I injured myself, not bad but enough Mrs. Libert thought the county nurse, Mrs.C , should take a look. All the other kids teased me about having to get a shot and I was scared because I believed them. Fortunately, I didn't have to get a shot. I can remember being in the first grade at Crawfordville School too. The only thing I can figure is we had to go somewhere else temporarily for some reason and we went to the old Courthouse, which I thought was neat

My sister Laura and I had our tonsils removed at Crawfordville School. There were several other patients in the room with us. I think we were in Mrs. Taff's classroom. I remember eating ice-cream after surgery.

Mama and Daddy built a Jim Walter house just south of Crawfordville. We lived there longer than anywhere else. Daddy built us a fine playhouse there. It actually had a floor and a roof. The front and sides were open but that didn't matter. We spent a lot of time playing in it.

Because Mama and Daddy didn't have any sons, my sisters and I had to fill in and do boys work a lot. I chopped wood, sawed wood and loaded wood on our back porch. A fireplace was the only means of heat we had until we finally got a gas heater. We had to help cook, wash dishes, clean house, pick vegetables out of the garden, whatever needed to be done.

We had a washing machine but had to hang the clothes outside on a "clothes line" to dry. The clothes that we wore had to be starched, so after they dried on the clothes line, we would dip them in starch, wring them out and hang them out to dry again. Then after they dried the second time, we had to sprinkle them with water, roll them up, put them in a plastic bag and then in the refrigerator to let them set a while. Then we had to iron them. It seemed like a lot of work, but I realize now how fortunate we were. At least we didn't have to use a wash board and ringer washer like Grandmama did for years!

We found simple things to play with, like jacks and pick-up sticks, color, paper dolls, etc. inside. Outside we played hop scotch and other games. We would try to see how long we could walk on empty 50 gallon drums (barrels) turned on their sides, see how fast we could fill cola bottles with sand, see how fast we could run, play on our swing set or in our playhouse. We watched Tom & Jerry, Tarzan, Popeye, Roy Rogers and Dale Evans, etc. on TV. We always found something to do.

Cokes were 5 cents then and we thought it terrible when they went up to a dime! I'm sure we bought cokes at other stores, but I remember always buying them at the "ice plant" just north of where we lived at the time. The ice plant was always cool inside because there was always a big chuck of ice in it. Whenever someone wanted ice, they would cut a small piece off the big piece. Adjacent to the ice plant was a store and that is where we bought our cokes, snacks, and other things. My sisters and I used to collect cola bottles and take them to the ice plant store and get a refund. We could spend the money we made in the store. One day I bought a piggy bank with my money. Over time I filled this piggy bank with every penny, nickel, dime and quarter got, until I couldn't put another coin in it. I had to bust it with a hammer to get the money out, I can't remember the exact amount that was in it but it was over six dollars. I took that money to the Rehwinkel Store in Crawfordville, on the corner of Crawfordville Hwy. and Arran Rd., and bought a pair of tennis shoes and a notebook for school. I had enough money left for my family and I to go the drive-in theater that used to be down in Medart.

Our main church was the old Beulah Primitive Baptist Church in Crawfordville where Brother Emmet Whaley preached, but we went to a lot of other churches in the county, especially if they were having a revival, and we went to some tent revivals, which are very rare today.

We would go to downtown Tallahassee occasionally to see a movie at the Florida Theater or the State Theater. It cost a quarter to get in then. Sometimes we would go downtown to McCrory's Dime Store and a drug store at the corner, Bennetts. Mama and Daddy would always give us a dollar each to spend. I felt like I had a thousand dollars and I shopped very carefully for just the right thing. Sears & Roebuck was downtown then too and we did most of our shopping there.

We went swimming in every body of water around this area. We had a lot of fish-fries; made a lot of homemade ice-cream, the kind you had to turn by hand in a churn. We went to a lot of political rallies. The kids played while the adults visited and listened to politicians. We went to a lot of peanut boilings and on a lot of hay rides. We didn't realize it then, but it was the good old days! No drugs, very little crime. You treated everybody with respect and were treated with respect.

Daddy tried growing corn, peanuts, hogs and chickens. I didn't care for the chicken business. There were rows and rows of chickens, long rows. The chickens were kept in little wire cages which I didn't like. I felt sorry for them. We had to feed the chickens by pouring chicken feed in the feed troughs in front of the cages. Daddy instructed us after we poured the feed in the troughs to take our index finger and run it down the middle of the feed to even it out. We didn't like to do this because the chickens wanted to peck our hands. I would quickly stick my finger in the feed and run down the troughs. They still pecked my hand. Years later I realized all I needed to do was get a stick to use in place of my finger!

We had to pick the eggs, clean them, weigh them and then pack them in a box by small, medium and large sizes. It was a nasty, stinky job but we had to do it. Then we would take the packed eggs to Tallahassee to sell them. Fortunately for us, the chicken business didn't last long.

Mama sewed clothes for other people to make some extra money. She made a lot of our clothes. She always made our Easter dresses. We were always decked out on Easter with our hats, shoes, gloves and beautiful dresses that Mama made. She worked at the TB hospital in Tallahassee back in 1956 for $140 a month. My first job out of high school was $21 a week working at the Suwannee Store in Crawfordville. I thought I was somebody when I got a job in Tallahassee making $50 a week!

She worked at Wakulla Springs at the outside concession stand one summer when I was around 16. My sister Laura and I went to Wakulla Springs every day with her. A friend of ours would sometimes go with us and later in the day his father would pick us up and take us to Cherokee Sink to swim. Cherokee Sink felt so good and warm after swimming in the cold Wakulla Springs water.

When I was around three years old, my granddaddy's half sister, Georgianne Vickers, moved in with Grandmama and Granddaddy because she was getting on up in age and couldn't stay by herself any more. But before they could do that, they had to add on to their house. Before they added on, their house consisted of two small bedrooms, a big room that was the living and dining area, and a very small kitchen and very small back porch. They added on a living room, two more bedrooms, extended the kitchen and back porch and added a bathroom off the back porch. Before the bathroom they used an outhouse. I can only imagine what that was like for them. They must have felt like they had moved from a shack to a mansion.

Aunt Georgianne was a character. She could be feisty. I can remember my sisters and I sitting on the floor in front of the fire place in the living room, with a fire going, the lights out, and her telling us ghost stories. One day I saw her kicking at a snake that had crawled up on the front porch off the living room and she kept yelling "get outta here, get outta here" at it. It decided it had better "get outta here"! She had to have been in her late-nineties then. When she turned 100 years old in October 1955, the family had a big birthday party for her, at my grandparents' house. Family members came from everywhere. We had a huge crowd, around 200. However, Aunt Georgianne was in the hospital on the day of the party. A big birthday cake had been made with 100 on it. I always thought it so sad that she wasn't able to be at her 100th birthday party. After that, the Council family members decided to start meeting every year in October and that is when the Council Family Reunion started and we still meet today.

Eleanor, Owen, Beverly, Laura, & Judy Council

When I was in the eighth grade, my family and I moved to Augusta, Georgia. Daddy and Mama couldn't pay the mortgage on our Jim Walter house and we lost it. It was a sad time. I didn't want to leave home. I'll never forget pulling up in front of the house we were to live in Augusta. It was on Hicks St., which I felt was appropriately named because I felt like a country hick moving to a big city. The house seemed dark and dreary. All the houses on that block were just a few feet away from each other, just enough room to walk between them. The front of our house couldn't have been more than 15 ft. from the street, which was very busy with cars coming and going almost constantly. Our dog, Fiddlesticks, was hit by a car our first night there, but fortunately he wasn't hurt bad and survived. We were all use to living in the country, including Fiddlesticks, with big yards to run and play in, not much traffic on the highway, peace and quiet, and a lot of fresh air. I had to walk eight blocks to my new school which was three stories high. It was a junior high school with hundreds of students. I felt like I had landed on Mars, coming from a class of around 20 to a class of hundreds. It was a different world. Thank the Good Lord we lived there only six months and moved back HOME!

We lived in downtown Crawfordville when we moved back. Crawfordville became our playground for my sister, Laura, and our friends. We were all over the place, from Bream Fountain to Rock Hole, playing and exploring. The new courthouse was our playhouse. Back then in the late 50's and early 60s people didn't lock their doors and the doors to the Courthouse were never locked, so whenever the Courthouse was closed for business in the evenings and on the weekends and holidays, we would play inside. We played in the courtroom of course. We held court. We played judge, attorney and jury. We even had jail cells to send our prisoners to. It was air-conditioned in the summer, heated in the winter and we had bathrooms and water fountains. We had some good times there. We also played in the Crawfordville School. They kept the classrooms locked but we played in the halls, the auditorium and outside in the playground. The school house was not air-conditioned but we did have bathrooms and water fountains. Now when I think about us playing in the courthouse and school house, I shake my head with disbelief that we were even able to. Other people knew we did this, but I guess back then they felt it was okay. We didn't vandalize anything, didn't even think about it. Our parents taught us to respect other people's property.

All of my grandparents, parents, uncles and aunts are gone now. Daddy, bless his patriotic heart, was the last one in his family to go. He passed away March 20, 2011. My sisters and I are now the next generation. I feel so blessed to have grown up in Wakulla County during the 40s, 50s and 60s. Things are so different now. We worked hard and played hard, knew everybody, helped each other out. I'm a better person today for living here and Wakulla County will always be my home.
Submitted by: Beverly Council, 3575 Crawfordville, Hwy. Crawfordville, FL 32327

Crum Family

Nicholas Zorn emigrated with his family and a group of Lutherans from the Palatines and entered America via Charleston Harbor, South Carolina in 1735. They left behind the Zorn Castle in the Rhine Valley and members of the Zorn family. Not far from the castle is the Zorn River by which there is held Rose Festivals. Little did they know that two hundred years later Zorns would be growing roses in Tyler, Texas or that a beautiful Rose Festival would be held there annually.

Nicholas and Catherina Zorn's daughter, Magdalene, was born in Germany. Magdalene Zorn married Henry Herman Crummy who was also born in Germany and thought to be the first of his family to migrate to America. They were married on Tuesday June 9, 1752 in Orangeburg Church, in South Carolina, by Rev. John Giessendanner. The name Crummy was later changed to Crum.

Henry Herman and Magdalene Zorn Crummy had a son named David Crum. David Crum and Ann Berry Crum had a son named James Harmon Crum. James Harmon Sr. and Mary Ann Porter Crum had a son named James Harmon Crum Jr. James Jr. with (wife unknown) moved to Leon County Florida after

1828. He died in Leon County in 1832. (Wakulla did not become a County until 1843 when it was cut out of Leon County.) Their son was Andrew James Crum.

Andrew James Crum married Francis Minzah Levy. She was the daughter of Almond Levy and Henrietta Robeson. She was born in Florida. They are both buried in the Roberts Cemetery (near Cow Creek) in Franklin County, Florida. They had seven children.

James H Crum (1850)

Andrew Jackson Crum (1852)

Henry H. Crum (1855)

Perry Crum (1860)

Hardy H. Crum (1861)

Fannie C. Crum (1869)

Mary A. Crum (1871)

Andrew Jackson Crum married Minnie Lee Kelly. They had nine children; Mamie Crum, Mary Henrietta Crum, Minnie Susanna Crum, Maggie Jane Crum, William Jackson Crum, Rosa Lee Crum, Barbara Hall Crum, Samuel Saunders Crum, and Roy Ugene Crum.

This is how the Crum family and its' descendants came to be in Wakulla County, Florida. The Crum family is one of the largest families in Wakulla County. In the Bible, God says, "Go forth and multiply," and they did.

Mamie Crum (died at 9 years old and was twin sister to Mary Henrietta)

Mary Henrietta Crum

She was the daughter of Andrew Jackson Crum and Minnie Lee Kelly Crum. Her twin sister Mamie died when she was nine years old. Her nickname was Pickey. She married Edward Richard Hartsfield. They had the following eight children.

Mamie Hartsfield married Tieutus (Totts) Goss. They had two children: Fred Goss and Mandy Goss.

Minnie Hartsfield married Charles Benjamin Metcalf. They had three boys: Carl, Charles, and Clark Metcalf.

Frankie Hartsfield married Milton Kelly. They had two children: Sheila and David Kelly.

Edmond Hartsfield married Ruby Lee Boykin. They had one son: Robert (Bo) Hartsfield married Betty Jean Nichols.

Will Hartsfield married Jewell McCallister. They had five children: Mary Freda, Halene, Ethel, Jewell Ethel, and Billy Hartsfield.

Ford Hartsfield married Mary Nell Boykin. They had one daughter: Shirley Hartsfield who married James Ad Taylor.

Geneva Hartsfield married Joseph Lee (J.L.) Thomas. They had nine children: Delma, Bessie Nell, Marvis, Odell, Linda, Hixon, Eva, Isaac, and Joseph Lee (Junior) Thomas. *{Ford and Geneva were twins)*

Minnie Susanna Crum

She was the daughter of Andrew Jackson Crum and Minnie Lee Kelly Crum. She was known to everybody as "Aunt Tex". She was a midwife and delivered most of the babies in the area. She married Jonas Raiford Porter. They had eight children.

Gracie Lee Porter married 1st German Whaley/ 2nd Gordon Nichols. She had ten children: Lucille Whaley, Betty Jean Nichols, Ada Nichols, Nadine Nichols, Emily Nichols, Eloise Nichols, Ester Nichols, Alex Nichols, Clark Nichols and Joe Nichols.

Jessie Porter married Jessie Louise Harrell and they had nine children. J.R. Porter, Raymond Jacob (Scrunch) Porter, Willie Faye Porter, Alton Porter, Samp Porter, Linda Porter, Diane Porter, Don Porter and Cassie Porter. *{Don and Cassie are twins)*

Minnie Lou Porter married Rev. Monroe Taylor and they had nine Children. Rochelle Taylor, Amos Taylor, Robert Taylor, Steve Taylor, Dorothy Nell Taylor, Wanda Pearl

Taylor, Guy William Taylor, Mitchell Taylor, and Ricky Taylor.

Russell Porter married Blonza Lee and they had five sons. Fred, Jonas, Eddie Jack, Cort Lee, and Burt Porter.

Stephen Jackson Porter married Delphia Syvelle Robinson and they had twelve children. Shirley, Minnie Sue, Cynthia, Dellie, Essie, Shelia, Polly, Darlene, Dorlene, William W. (Buddy), William J., and Samuel Lee Porter. *{Darlene and Dorlene are twins)*

William Jackson Crum & Sally Ethel Moats Crum

Dellie Porter married Robert Barwick and they had one daughter Tammy Barwick.

Elizabeth Porter married Charles Barwick and they had six children. Mildred, Charles Jr., Ronnie, Louise, Norman and Margaret Barwick.

Darkas Porter married Ander Otto Revell and they had six children; Roland, Bobby, Pauline, Buck, Yvonne, and Joann Revell.

Maggie Jane Crum

She was the daughter of Andrew Jackson Crum and Minnie Lee Kelly Crum. She married John Adam Whetstone. They had eight children.

Andrew Jacob Whetstone married Ester and they had one child; Anita Carol Whetstone.

John Albert Whetstone married Juanita Harrell and they had two children; Carolyn Whetstone and Walter Whetstone.

Mary Bell Whetstone married George Metcalf and they had four children; Jerrell, Edgar, Morris and Lacy Metcalf.

Idell Whetstone married Wolford McCallister and they had four children; Norman, Edith, Wilson, and Archie McCallister.

Woodrow Whetstone married Katie Tucker and they had two children; Kathy Whetstone and Danny Whetstone.

Ester Whetstone married Curtis Kindell.

Macon Wayne Whetstone married Sarah Metcalf and they had two children; Sharon Whetstone and Phillip Whetstone.

Lona Whetstone married;

1st James Kindell. They had one child; Judy Kindell

2nd Roland Strickland. They had two children; Roland Strickland Jr. and Glenn Strickland.

3rd Cecil Nichols.

William Jackson Crum

He was the son of Andrew Jackson Crum and Minnie Lee Kelly Crum. He was a farmer and also worked as a maintenance man in the Wakulla County Court House. He married Sally Ethel Moats and they had fourteen children. One little girl died at birth.

Jack Crum married Jewell Kilgore and they had two children; Gary Crum and Gail Crum.

George Crum married Jeanette Harvell and they had four children; George Eddie, James, Shirley and Mike Crum.

Maggie Lee Crum married Andrew Sylvester (Pullback) Simmons. They had one son; Jerry Simmons.

Henry Crum married Rosa Lee Tucker and they had six children; Glynwood, Warren, Mec, Kenny, Ronald Fred and Donnie Crum.

Walter Crum married Marlene Tucker and they had one son; Robert Crum.

James Crum married Rena Mae Dalton and they had two sons; Clayton Crum and David Crum.

Louise Crum married Nathan Thompson and they had three children; Helen Thompson, Nathan Thompson and Larry Thompson.

Luther Crum married Olive and they had two daughters; Carol Crum and Debbie Crum.

Paul Crum married Patricia Anne Keaton and they had two children; Ricky Crum and Robby Crum.

Silas Crum married Barbara Ann Barron and they had five children; Kendall, Lisa, Bill, Harold and Kim Crum.

R.J. Crum married;

1st Eloise Edwards and they had five children; Danny, Donna, Dennis, Randy, & Kim Crum.

2nd Mary and they had two children; Denise and Jay Crum.

Amos Jackson Crum married Carolyn Willis and they had three children; Kaye Lynn Crum, Amos Jeffery Crum and Alan Jackson Crum.

Leonard Crum married;

1st Linda Stribling.

2nd Gladys Russ and they had four children; Douglas, Danny, David, & Denise.

3rd Mary Anderson and they had two children; Gregory and Sally.

4th Kathy Butler.

5th Barbara Warren.

Rosa Lee Crum

She was the daughter of Andrew Jackson Crum and Minnie Lee Kelly Crum. She married;

1st Alexander Metcalf and they had three children; Charles Ander Metcalf, Ernest Jefferson Metcalf, and Eddie Lee Metcalf

2nd Bill Brimner and they had one child; Samuel Jackson Brimner

Barbara Hall Crum

She was the youngest daughter of Andrew Jackson Crum and Minnie Lee Kelly Crum. She was only about 4ft 7 inches tall. She was known as "Aunt Dump." She married;

1st Azor Gaff and their daughter was Azor Rebecca Gaff who married Native Thompson.

2nd Henry Franklin Wells. They had two children; Bobby Wells married Grace Harrell, and Minnie Ada Wells died at five years old.

Samuel Saunders Crum

He was the son of Andrew Jackson Crum and Minnie Lee Kelly Crum. He married Ruby Lois Carter. They had four children; Julia Lee Crum, Alexander Crum, Houston Crum, and Martha Lee Crum.

Roy Ugene Crum

He was the son of Andrew Jackson Crum and Minnie Lee Kelly Crum. He married Maggie Nichols. They had seven children; Leon, Emmett, David, Rosco, Minnie, Ralph and Linda Crum.

Submitted and written by, Louise Thomas, 419 Buckhorn Creek Rd. Sopchoppy, Fl 32358

Josie Daniel-Our Move to Crawfordville

Our daddy was a turpentine man, and this is what led our family to Crawfordville. You would turpentine out crops or boxes. A box was 10,000 trees or cat faces on the trees where you got turpentine. You have to put streaks, taking a chip of wood out so the turpentine will run, every week for the summer. You could only turpentine a tree about five to seven years. After the trees were done, they usually cut them down into timber. Usually wherever there was a turpentine still there was a saw mill close by.

Our daddy planted the first pine trees that were ever planted in Wakulla County, in 1936, down where the Wakulla Public Library is right now. The trees were cut when they built the library there. Brother Emmett Whaley drove truck for us; in fact he drove the truck that moved us to Crawfordville. There may be a few of those trees left, but most have been cut. For years there was a sign down there that said the pines were planted in 1936.

Our family moved here from Sylvester, Georgia on May 24th, 1935 to begin a new turpentining operation. We remember that first day quite well! I was thirteen years old, in ninth grade; and my brother DP turned nine years old four days after we got here. We moved to a house that has since been moved over on Bream Fountain Rd. Sarah Beth Morrison lives there now. Her last name is not Morrison now, it's Sutton. Sarah Beth Sutton. They moved the house and we always called it the old Babe Raker house.

The school had just been built over here, made out of stones. When we got here in 1935 the first school year had just finished. We'd left when our school was out in Sylvester and drove right on down here. I even know what we had for supper that night! We had already put the wood stove up, and we had grits, canned salmon scrambled with eggs, and fried sweet potatoes. That was the best supper that night, we were really hungry. The first thing that my daddy did was to add a bathroom onto that house and put in plumbing to the kitchen and the bathroom. Then they put in electricity and got a refrigerator. It had a big old dome sitting on the top. It took four men to lift it, it was so heavy! It was a GE, one of the first ones.

In Crawfordville at that time there was no electricity, no running water; in fact it was almost unheard of. Our mama had bought an electric sewing machine and when we moved down here she had to trade it in to get a pedal one! When we moved down here we thought we'd come to the end of the world, I can tell you that!

We lived on Lower Bridge Rd, just a little ways down. The Wakulla News used to sit right behind where the bail bonds place is, right at the light. There's a two-story apartment house, vacant; that's where the Wakulla News used to be. It was an old tin building. L.S. Patton was the owner. His name was Luther but everybody called him L.S.

There were seven children in our family. All were born at home except one, with doctors and midwives. Doctors would come to the house!

Crawfordville's changed a lot. The goats and the cows and the hogs all ran wild, were in and out of the courthouse and the church. There were no fences. If you farmed, you had to put up a fence to protect your crops. In 1948 that was changed. Fuller Warren was governor and he got the no-fence law passed, where people had to keep all their cows and hogs penned up. They had marks in their ears or brands so people would know who owned them.

The cows could come after you sometimes. It wasn't anything for a horse to jump out in front of you in your car. High Road, where I live now, was just two little deep sand ruts. You couldn't pass anybody on it; you had to find a place to pull off the road if you met someone. In 1949 DP went to work for the State Road Department, later called the Department of Transportation, and they started paving 319 from here in Crawfordville up to Munson Slough. It already had a little narrow road out from Munson Slough but they constructed and paved it. Then they changed 319 from Wakulla and Woodville over to this area. High Road was one of the first streets that was paved in Crawfordville, in 1957 or '58.

The road from the Wakulla County line to Tallahassee was originally panels of concrete. When you drove across it, it would make a whup-whup-whup sound and make you think you had a flat tire. In Leon County you'd see people stopped on the side of the road to see if they had a flat tire.

Where the bail bonds place is right now they had one of probably two or three telephones that were in Crawfordville. One was in the courthouse, and JD Duggar who had a Gulf station had one, and Gladys Adams (Gladys Moore at that time) had one. It was done so somebody had some communication. If you needed to talk to anybody you'd call one of those telephones and they'd get a message to them to come and call or whatever.

When we came to Crawfordville there were other kids around. Clarence Morrison lived right next door. The house we rented was from his grandmother. We all went to school together. Mr. Roy Rewhinkel's store was where Talquin Electric just moved from, up to their new business.

Everything was personalized back then, everybody knew everybody. We had a safe growing up time, a good life. When we first came down here, we were invited to a house party down at Wakulla Beach. They had put all these boards down on the floor so we could put pallets down to sleep on. We carried our own food. The girls had cucumbers and onions for their sandwiches. I had never seen a cucumber sandwich, we always had meat sandwiches!

The old wooden courthouse was sitting right there where the present courthouse sits. And they had a big water tank. In the wintertime it would freeze and the water would overflow and there would be icicles hanging down. It would be frozen from the top of the tank, all running down to the ground, it was a pretty sight.

During the Depression in the early 30s we never felt it because we had all our own vegetables. Mama canned. She had a lot of black ladies who would come and help her can. We put up all our vegetables, and then we had our hogs, our cows to eat, chickens, milk and butter, pigeons, rabbits, geese, ducks, and turkeys. My daddy grew just about everything. We never had to worry about food.

We shared with the blacks who worked for us; we always took care of them. Old Uncle Henry Parrish, down between here and Medart, was a kid during slavery. We knew him, but he was getting to be old when we came along. He talked about it some, but most of the time it wasn't all that bad. My Dad grew up in North Carolina during slavery and they had slaves on their tobacco farm, but whoever worked for him, they took care of them. I remember them taking them to the doctor if the doctor couldn't come right there. He didn't let them suffer. My daddy was appointed to the rationing and draft boards during the war, very active in church. He was a deacon in church ever since I can remember. We've always been active in church.

There was a commodity warehouse during the Depression. You'd see women with four and five children walking behind. There was a sewing room where they could go and make fifty cents or a dollar. They made mattresses and gave them away. They gave away potatoes, onions, meal, sugar, flour -- the staples. One year my daddy planted two acres of potatoes and two of onions. We thought we could sell them, you know. But it was still that time when they were giving them away, and we could not sell them. Two of my brothers had to boil, in wash pots, every one of those onions and potatoes so the hogs would eat them, because hogs won't eat them raw!

Times aren't as hard right now as they were back in the Depression, but they're getting close. Now everyone has things that we didn't use to have, like electricity and running water, but you have to pay for them, and lots of people have no job and can't pay. Hardly anybody had a car. I bet there weren't but a dozen cars in Crawfordville.

Daddy had big trucks with high sides that were used in turpentining. They had a lot of pine gum in the beds. My brothers would go out and rake up pine straw and line the beds thickly and put a tarp on top of that and over the top, then go out in the woods and camp and hunt.

There were all kinds of remedies. There was a medicine called Black Draught, and there was syrup of Pepsin, Calomel, and Quinine. When we started school we had to take a dose of Calomel and then we kept Epsom salts to work that Calomel out of you. We stayed well. Calomel is something that if you eat anything sweet after you take it, you'd say it would salivate you, make your teeth fall out. We wouldn't eat anything sweet for a day or two after that! At Christmas time we'd take another dose of it to clean us out. It's a pink powdery stuff. It's in a lot of medicine today. You got it at the drug store or grocery store. Then there was Castoria, which was a laxative for babies, and a small amount would soothe their stomach, like a teaspoon of it. It wasn't that strong.

There were salespeople who traveled in horse-pulled wagons. They sold Raleigh products, black pepper, Watkins treatments, anything that would keep. Some of it was good, like Watkins. Hadacol had lots of alcohol in it. "You know why they called it Hadacol, don't you? Well, they hadda call it something!" You hear people refer to it still; it's supposed to be something like a vitamin. And Geritol was supposed to give you more energy.

Dr. Harper was here in Crawfordville. His house was where the funeral home is now. In the springtime we took sulfur and cream of tartar tablets. It kept our blood clean. You can still buy it. But it smells bad. It keeps away Beachworm (Ringworm or Impetigo). Dr. Hicks in Tallahassee recommended it. We just weren't sick much. The sulfur and cream of tartar will keep redbugs and ticks off you too, if you take it before you go in the woods. You can get powdered sulfur and dust it on your socks too.

We were not allowed to go barefoot until the middle of May, and then by the first of September we had to put our shoes on again.

We had different weather back then. We have so much hot weather now during the winter, and we didn't use to have that. Used to be, your first frost would come along in the latter part of September.

The first sunburn I ever saw anybody get was two of my brothers. It was July 4, 1935. (That was the first day I ever shot a pistol, too!) We all went to Shell Point and cooked fish, swam, and they got so burned, they couldn't wear shirts for three weeks! James even went into sun poisoning. They used cornstarch on sunburn. One of the best things you can use today on any burn is to cut up a potato, scrape the juice from it and put it on there and it won't blister. One time we were at Shell Point and DP burned himself on hot grease, and Miss Ruby Rehwinkel said, "Somebody get me a potato!" She sliced it and got all that milk stuff and put that on it, and it never even blistered up.

In school we had first grade through twelve. Our class was one of the largest classes and at some points in time we had 28, 29 or 30 people in it. But back then there were people in there who were four or five years older. They had not had a school to go to, and they stayed in the little community schools until 6th or 8th grade. We were fortunate to have had good schools. I was 16 when I graduated, and entered college in September -- Andrew College for Women in Cuthbert, GA. I was going to be a Home Economics teacher, and then I met John Daniel. He and I married in 1941 and were married until last year when he passed away, 68 years.

Submitted by: Josie L. Daniel, P.O. Box 172, Crawfordville, FL 32326November, 2010, as told to Linda Sheldon

My History; Lonnie Alfred Dispennette

I believe that this should begin with as much as I can remember about my Daddy, who was known as Dis by his friends in Wakulla County. He was born on Sand Mountain, which is outside of Guntersville, Alabama. His Daddy was a Saw Mill machinery mechanic. I understand he moved to Guntersville to help build a large Saw Mill outside of Guntersville. He liked the area and purchased a small farm on Sand Mountain. My grandfather raised cotton and other farm items there when he was not working at the mill. His name being John A. Dispennette married to Martha Bell Skinner. Daddy had 5 brothers and 4 sisters, one of which was his twin .They believed in large families in 1878.

Daddy, along with his brothers and sisters helped do the work on the farm. That is until one day when Daddy was 17 or 18 years old. They were picking cotton, the story goes that he worked a while, then went to his Daddy and gave him his cotton bag and told him that, this was not what he wanted to do, that he did not like to farm, particular picking cotton. He asked for his blessing to go find another means of work.

Daddy left and traveled to Texas where he had family. He soon went to work with a company that was putting up electric power lines in that area. Somewhere along the line he started working with a road construction company.

This is what brought him to Crawfordville, Fl. He was working for Malone Construction Co. out of Jacksonville who had the contract to build highway 90 East into Tallahassee, then build highway 98 south through Woodville, Wakulla Station into Crawfordville and down to the Medart, Sopchoppy, Carrabelle and along the coast. His job was to clear the right away of trees and stumps, then grade up the road ready for paving. This was accomplished in that day (early 1920s) with mules pulling sleds to move the dirt. With saws, axes, shovels and a bunch of sweat, men were able to prepare the road for paving. He was the Supervisor in charge of this group. He had a small army of workmen who followed the job and they made camp as they moved along with the road construction. There were many local workmen who also worked on this job with Daddy. Jobs were scarce, and the people were happy to have a chance to earn money that was also scarce. The year was 1925 or '26 and in this part of Florida, the Depression had already hit. This construction project put food on lots of tables.

They were working near the upper Wakulla River Bridge at this time and the camp where the traveling workers and mules stayed was located about one mile south of the river. Daddy usually found a room to rent in a nearby town when it was possible. He stopped at the Post Office in Crawfordville and the first person he saw was my mother Ruby Raker. She took the mail to the Arran Train Station twice each day and brought mail back from the train to the Post Office in Crawfordville.

Daddy asked her if she knew of anyone in town that might have a room to rent. To quote my Mama, she said he was the best looking man she had ever seen, and she sure wanted to see more of him. So she said yes, my mama has a room to rent. Well the fact was, she had a extra room but never rented it. But Mama said let me run to the house and make sure its available and I will be back here in about 30 minutes, that is if that is ok with you. He said sure, that would be fine.

She flew down to the house and told my grandmother who we all called Old Moma, what had happen and could she clean out one of the bedrooms and offer it to him for rent. She agreed and Mama got the room ready, then she went back to bring him down for a look. He rented the room and needless to say, a courting they started and after a while they got married. When the job was completed in this area he took Mama with him on his new assignments. I was born November 9, 1927 in the same house that contained the room he rented, a house we called home when Dad was not on a job somewhere away from Wakulla County. After I was old enough I was taken with them on his road building jobs.

On one of these jobs I got real sick and they brought me home. I was taken to Dr. Harper who said I had Malaria Fever. I was about age 3 or 4 at the time and it almost killed me. I can remember even after I started to school having the chills and fevers. Dr. Harper only had Quinine and aspirin to treat me with.

I was down at Uncle JD Duggar's Gulf Station with Mama one morning after school and Dr. Harper stopped by for gas and he had a visiting Doctor friend with him. The doctor saw me there with my mama and said to her, "That boy of yours has Malaria fever." Mama said, yes and the Quinine is not helping him at all. He told her to bring me to Dr. Harper's office the next morning. When we got there he told us about a new medicine called Atabrin, that would rid me of Malaria. He gave Mama enough of the little yellow pills to do the job.

He said my skin would turn as yellow as the pills, then clear up when the Malaria was gone. In 3 weeks I was back to my natural color, and the Malaria was gone. This is the man who saved my young life. I regret that I failed to get his name.

We were back at Uncle J.D's Gulf Station one day in August 1932. The School Superintendent stopped by and asked Mama how old I was. She said I would be 5 in November. He said: we need one more student in our school to qualify for State money, and would she object to him letting me start school this September. She said no, and I started school one year early. I graduated in June 1944 from Crawfordville High School, at the age of 16.

My first grade teacher was Mrs. Etta Maude Kirkland and it was in the original school house built years before with wood frame only. The old school house was torn down the summer of 1933 and the rock building that still standing was started and built where the old building had stood. School was to continue the next year in the local churches in Crawfordville while the new School was being finished.

The first and second grades were in the Primitive Baptist Church located then across the highway from the present First Baptist Church, first grade on one side, second grade on the other side of the Church. This was quite an experience. I remember in the fall of that year a circus setup in the field that was at that time behind the church. We kids had a ball watching the set-up and all the animals. In fact we each used up several pencils each day. The pencil sharpener was located next to the window looking towards the circus being setup, so we had to keep those pencils sharp so as to see the goings on outside.

By this time Daddy was working for the county road dept. and was home all the time. We were still living in the old home place with Old Mama, when Mama and Daddy decided to build a house on the back side of the Raker land. This was somewhere around 1930. The house faced what was then the main highway into Crawfordville, just north of the Cemetery. It was then state road 98 from Tallahassee on south down to Carrabelle. It took a long time to finish the house. We lived in one side of it for a long time before the other side had the flooring nailed down. No mortgage money in that depression time. My folks completed the house as they earned the money. We had an outdoor privy just like everyone else. No electricity was available to anyone, oil lamps made our light at night. We had a fire place in the living room, no heat in the other side even after it was finished. I can remember when Mr. Chapman finished wiring the house for electricity. We were a happy bunch. Mama turned the front porch light on and it was never turned off.

This went on for years as each house was wired and the electricity was turned on, they also left theirs on, it was sort of a celebration to celebrate that they at last had electricity.

Next big day was when the bath room was completed and we could tear down the outhouse. I was a teen ager when this was completed.

Daddy began to build a front porch on the house the last month of 1935, and with the help of several men he was able to complete it before Christmas of that year. The following year Daddy got real sick and being a Veteran of WWI, Mama was able to get him in the VA Hospital in Lake City. The Doctors said he had kidney poison, which was causing the fevers and pain. There was very little that they could do since there were medicines in that day like we now have to kill such poison. We went over each weekend to see him, and each time he was a little weaker than before. He passed away 6 weeks after he was admitted.

Needless to say, that was the worst day and time of my young life, I was 8 years old and had lost the best friend and Daddy anyone could have. I still have a letter Mama had received from Daddy while he was there in the Hospital. He was telling us that he had accepted Jesus as his Lord and Savior, and wanted us to know that he would meet us in Heaven one day if he failed to get over his illness.

At age 8 this didn't mean much at that time, but as I learned about the Lord and his saving Grace, this letter was a real treasure and I still treasure it. I was about 12 years old then at a Revival meeting at the Crawfordville First Baptist Church, I walked to the front and accepted Jesus as my personal Savior. I remember being Baptized in Brim Sink along with Carlton Tucker and several others. Having lost my Daddy at such a young age, my one favorite prayer was that God would let me live to see our three sons grown, married and have grandchildren for me to love.

God has blessed Ann and me with 8 grandchildren and 15 great-grandchildren! I thank him every day that these children are also being raised in a Christian Home like their father and grandfather.

Daddy loved to go to the different churches in Wakulla County especially when it was dinner on the grounds and all day singing. He would load me up and away we would go in his 1933 Chevrolet. Mama would beg off, but that didn't slow us down. I have enjoyed many a day on that front porch with Mama and Mama's sister Mary Duggar and her son Kendall was there on that porch nearly every afternoon. Kendall was only a few months younger than I, so we

Old Fashioned Corn Bread

1/2 cup butter
3 tablespoons white sugar
2 eggs
1 cup buttermilk
1/2 teaspoon baking soda
1 cup cornmeal
1 cup all-purpose flour
1/2 teaspoon salt

You can substitute 2 cups cornmeal mix in place of 1 C. cornmeal, 1 C. flour, and ½ teaspoon baking soda.

To make Crackling Cornbread, fry 1 C. cracklings and stir into mixture before baking.

Directions:
Preheat oven to 375 degrees F (175 degrees C).
Melt butter in large iron skillet.
Mix dry ingredients with eggs, and buttermilk, and stir until well blended.
Pour mixture on top of melted butter in iron skillet.
Bake in the preheated oven for 30 to 40 minutes, or until a toothpick inserted in the center comes out clean.
By Bill Frank 215 Stanley, Crawfordville, FL 32327

were like brothers. We spent many a day playing in the fields that are now covered with houses, Ace Hardware, Winn Dixie and all the places built north of town.

There was a bunch of us boys who ruled the roost in Crawfordville, Clarence Morrison, Dillard Dawkins, James (Haddock) Posey and all of his brothers and sisters, George Harper, Carlton Tucker, Calvin Cooper, Howard Andrews, Reginal Carraway, just to name a few. We had friends our age in Arran, Edsel and Jessie Nazworth, Smith Laws, Clayton Taff, H. D. Lawhon, and others. We had enough in C-ville and Arran to play each other in baseball nearly every weekend. Our transportation was our feet, we walked over to Arran, played ball and walked back afterwards.

I had kin folks all over the place, there was Mama's Sister, Mary Duggar; her husband J.D. Duggar, Aunt Gladys Moore, & husband Ralph Moore. She is my Mama's first cousin, but she was still our Aunt! Uncle J.D. ran the Gulf Service Station on the North East corner of Hwy 319 & Lower Bridge Rd. Aunt Gladys who remarried after Uncle Ralph died, remarried several years later to Bubba Adams, ran the Standard Service Station. My first job was at Aunt Gladys' Station when I was about 13 years old. I worked before school, and after school. There was also a cafe there where she fed me breakfast, lunch and dinner before I went home. She told Mama she was going to fatten me up. I was a very skinny boy, due in part to my bout with the Malaria fever. I was one of those that eating larger amounts of food had little effect on putting weight on me. But I made enough to buy a pair of lace up boots & my first bicycle. We lived in a small town. The entire student body 1st to 12th was about 225 back in those days. With students bused in from Newport, St. Marks & Wakulla Station.

In those days we did not have a lot of anything except love for each other and of where we were. We all got along together just like one big family. We were all poor...but you know we still had fun and enjoyed ourselves. Mr. Phil Carraway always invited the town to his place when it was hog killing time. It was usually at the first winters freeze. That was one day we all missed school and what a time we all had. Valda, Reginal and whole Carraway clan. We all loved Mr. & Mrs. Carraway and their Family.

Then we also had Cane Grindings. The Duggars up in Ivan had a big one every year. This was Uncle JD Duggar's Daddy's place. We drank cane juice, helped make syrup, played and had a fine time.

I remember one day Clarence Morrison & I was playing Cops & Robbers chasing one another on our bicycles. You could do that back then on the highway, only had a car drive through town every hour or so. Then, they did not speed at all. Clarence was the cop and he was chasing me south through town. The First Baptist Church was a wood frame building on blocks about two feet off the ground. The parking area between the church and roadway was gravel. Well as I approached the church at a high rate of bike speed, I decided to hide behind the big Oak in front of the church. When I hit that gravel I did not stop until I was 20 feet up under the church. Clarence was on his knees hollering, are you all right? I crawled out dragging my tore up bike. I skinned my arms and legs but survived to ride again.

We had many things like this, like the time we saw a Tarzan Movie, and we were out climbing trees trying to do what Tarzan had done. A limb broke with me and I hit the ground on my back. It knocked the wind out of me and I thought I was going to die, but soon the air came back. That stopped this kid from climbing trees to this day. Mama always planted a garden with vegetables of all kinds. My job was to hoe it, keep the weeds out and water it when it was dry. My buddies knew that I could not be free to play until the work in the garden was done each day. To speed up the games, they would come in with a hoe and help get the work completed.

Daddy worked on a road building project that I want to mention. At that time there were no road from Arran west to the Smith Creek area. He supervised a crew of men who built the present road over to Smith Creek. This consisted of cutting down the trees on the right away, digging up the stumps and grading up a road bed for travel. There were a large number of men from Wakulla County Area. J.B. Kyle, Emmett Whaley and others that my feeble mind cannot remember.

Mr. J.B. Kyle told me this story a few years ago. He said that Dis, (That is what they called Daddy, much easier than Dispennette.) would tell them that when they had dug a stump out of the ground, they was finished for the day. They could sit in the shade until quitting time. Well one day they had just got a huge stump out of the ground and was beginning to rest in the shade when the big boss man came riding up. They all jumped up, he said Dis told them to sit back down, which they did.

Well the Big Boss wanted to know what was going on and Daddy told him the deal he had with the men and if he wanted the road finished anytime soon he had better not have any problem with it. They shook hands and he left Daddy to do his job the way he thought best. Needless to say Mr. J.B. said after that they would do about anything for him.

The truck driver for this project was One-Eye Jack Pelt and when the road was finished he and Daddy were the first people to ride a vehicle over the new road from Arran to Smith Creek. When I was courting Ann Mccall, she lived at Smith Creek, her step-daddy was Major Langston. Daddy did me and her a real favor with that road, I had about worn it out from Crawfordville over there about twice a week until we married. December 6, 1947.

Mama married Jack Pelt several years after Daddy passed away. They had a daughter, Mary Francis, who I, to this day love a great amount. She married Tracy Haire, and lives in Tallahassee. She as well as my older sister, Edith, each graduated from Crawfordville High Schools. I graduated in June of 1944 from there also.

Growing up in Wakulla Country was a happy time. We weathered the hurricanes, the Great Depression, & World War II. We boys in high school worked for Mr. Jim Kirkland, who was the Forest Service Ranger, fighting forest fires throughout the county. He would pull up to the school, we would load up and off we went for as long as it took to put out the woods fire. One summer several of us boys worked at Camp Gordon Johnson while it was going strong training the soldiers for the impending invasion of France at Normandy. I was able to meet several of them, who later we found out, never survived the battles.

My step-dad, Pa-Jack, worked down there in the German POW camp that was located on the base. He struck up a friendship with one POW, who was a painter of pictures in his home town in Germany. He told Pa-Jack if he would get him some paint, brushes and canvas to paint on he would paint him some pictures. This he did and some of the finest pictures were painted with the supplies he furnished. Family members still have many of them on their walls. We had several different GI families living with us during that time so they could be together before going overseas to war.

After graduating in June of 44, I enrolled at Lively Voc. Tech in Tallahassee to study Radio repair. I finished the training and got a job at Sears Roebuck with the Radio Shop. Mr. Andy Wilder hired me and was my first boss there. I was living at a Boarding House on Gaines Street operated by my future wife's Aunt Faye. I did know Ann from school but did not know her family connection until after we were married.

The war was still going on and there were only 4 or 5 men working at Sears, all were in service somewhere. The next June I joined the Navy and went to boot camp at Bainbridge, Maryland. I was sworn in on the day Germany surrendered and got out of boot camp the day Japan surrendered. After a 10 day leave at home I was shipped to San Jose, Calif, (just outside of San Francisco). From there 75 of us were sent by a transport ship to Saipan Island Navy Base to relieve men who were eligible to go home for discharge. I could write a book on the experiences I had while there on that large Rock.

I did get up with Haddock Posey, who was in the army there, through mine and his mothers. Only person from home I ever ran into while in the Navy. By August of 1946 things had wound down and they cut my orders to go back to the discharge.

Well back to Sears, soon I had the opportunity to manage the Parts Department and soon I was made Manager of the whole Service Dept. I put together a fine group of men to do service work on Sears Merchandise. Louie Huggins, who retired a few years ago from Sears. Joe Thaggard, who retired from Talquin Elec. Billy Henderson, now deceased who went on to work for Channel 6 TV. There were many others who helped us to have an outstanding Service Dept. Standard operating procedure was a break morning and PM. To McCrorys 5 & 10 lunch counter. That is where I got to know Ann McCall since she worked near the front. After numerous attempts to get a date with her, one day she asked me to go with her to a birthday party. Well that started our courtship that ended in our marriage in Thomasville, Ga. Dec. 6, 1947. Some said it was a shot gun wedding. Our first son was born 18 months later. We named him Lonnie Jr., our next child was another boy we named John William, Then 13 years later we had another boy & named him James, he has been Jimmy until he grew up; now it's Jim. All of our daughters turned out to be boys.

I was offered a promotion in 1954 to move to Knoxville, Tenn., As Mechanical Supervisor of their Service Dept. Instead of about 7 servicemen I had over 20 men and 7 office employees. This old Wakulla County boy was in high cotton. I was fortunate enough to work for a real Store Manager, who at the time had over 30 years time with Sears. He was from the old school where their slogan, "Your Satisfaction Guaranteed or Your Money Back" was definitely a reality. He told me to satisfy the customer that was sent to my department with a complaint, regardless of the expense. I am sorry to say that over the years this policy was tossed out the window.

I accepted promotion to Customer Service Manager in Montgomery, Alabama in Feb. of 1960. I left Knoxville, TN. which had 9-10 inches of snow on the ground to travel to my new job with Sears. I left Ann and our two Sons, Lonnie Jr. & John behind to arrange to sell our house and make arrangements to move. With good luck and the Lord's help we were able to find a house in Montgomery to buy and sold the one we had in Knoxville.

Pay was not so good back in that period of time my salary the last year at Sears was less than $8000 for Managing the Customer Service Dept. with over 40 people. In 1963 I lost my desire to continue with Sears. A new generation of people had taken control of the Company and was doing everything they could do to run off the employees with many years employment. I was training people to do my job and they were paid over $10,000 per year, not counting bonus pay. The week I left Sears I knew of 11 other men who left at the same time, each with 15 to 20 years with Sears. Management accomplished their goal of getting rid of the "old timers". Most went directly to work for Sears's major competitors, at the time K-Mart got many of them

I found a job with Liberty National Life Insurance Company and resigned in June, 1963. A close friend from our church recommended me for the job, helped with my training. I was able to be the Top Sales Agent out of the 23 men in our office the first full year with LNLI. I continued in the Insurance business for the next 7 years, until the retail business won the battle and I went to work with Munford Inc. Supervising Convenience Stores. I worked for four different C-Store Companies over a period of 20 years before retiring and moving back to Florida in 1986.

Now for some of My Son's and their Wives History:

Lonnie Jr. married a sweet girl, Rena in Montgomery, where they still reside. Their daughter who is a graduate of Auburn Vet School has her own practice in Montgomery. She has a son and daughter; Anna and Jacob.

John married another sweet girl, Sara who had 2 children from a previous marriage whom he adopted into our family as Dispennettes. John and Sandy are their names. They also have another daughter named Jennifer. John and Sara recently built a beautiful home in Helen Ga. on the side of a mountain. Two daughters & a son and, 11 grandchildren at this writing, Sandy, Jennifer & John (our little John).

Jim Followed us back to Florida in 1987, he had stayed in Jonesboro, Ark, where we were living prior to coming back home to Florida. He met and fell in love with another sweet girl, Kathy, and he adopted her son from a previous marriage named Brandon and they have a daughter, Stacy. Jim has a son from a previous marriage named Denny Dispennette. Denny lives in Jonesboro, Ark and is a freshman at Arkansas State University in Jonesboro. Brandon is now a proud Marine stationed in Okinawa in the Pacific near Japan. I trust you have enjoyed my history!

Submitted by:Lonnie Henry Dispennette Wakulla AKA Lonnie Alfred Dispennette, 1161 Poplar, Dr., Tallahassee, FL 32301

We Are All Connected; Donaldson Family

It has been said that "all men are brothers", and that we are connected to such a degree, through so many generations and common experiences, that we can call each other 'family'. Wakulla County, no matter how widesprea d it is, or will become, will always maintain a familial existence for me. This is due, in part, to the efforts of my father's parents, Annie Lizzie and Columbus Theodore Donald-son.

Christopher "Theo", Annie, and Jeffrey Donaldson

Annie and 'Theo' were married on July 14th (the 2nd Sunday) of 1940, when she was sixteen, and he was eighteen. They would go on to have a family of eleven children: Clarence (1941), Charles ('43), Anne Catherine ('45), Herbert ('47), Alice Jean ('49), Hilly ('51), Eunice Luevater ('52), Allen Nelson ('54), Rosa Lee ('56), Robert Theodore ('58), and Jeffrey O'Neill ('60).

Theo had six siblings, all of whom could play instruments, from piano to guitar, and then some; the guitar being Theo's instrument of choice. He was also the only one in his family with a car, and would travel his brothers and sisters throughout the states of Florida and Georgia. In doing so, he would take along his guitar and sit-in on jam sessions with others from these states that he'd just met, or had come to know through his travels.

Annie had thirteen siblings, mainly girls. Before the boys came along, she and her sisters would help their father lumber trees for money. She would also buy baby chicks, raise them, and once grown, butcher them for money, to keep the family fed.

Eventually, Theo would join the Army (becoming a United States Veteran), as Annie walked from Crawfordville to Panacea, working as a cook in restaurants. She was one of the first African-American workers employed at the Oaks Restaurant and even worked at the King Fish Lodge. She also worked as a nanny for many families in the Wakulla County area. In this employ, she would cook, clean and help raise their children, many who have fond memories of

Annie and Theo Donaldson

her to this day. They include the Barwick, White, Pelt, and High families. Notables, such as the Harvey family also employed her. And, yes, Sheriff David Harvey was one of the children she helped to rear, along with the family of Mr. C.L. and Anita Townsend. In later years, after the passing of their husbands, Annie and Anita would become close friends, sitting for hours at each other's homes and traveling throughout the state together, 'antiquing' for items that to this day remain in the homes of them and their children.

Theo would become the first African-American boat captain in Panacea, Florida. As caretaker for Mr. C.I. Owen's property, he would man the yacht for fishing tours and the like. Each holiday, Mr. Owen and his wife would shower the Donaldson children with gifts and sweets from their trips abroad. As a mechanic, Theo worked for Capital Lincoln Mercury, along with other odd jobs such as tour guide on the boats at Wakulla Springs, and with the Taft family, loading timber, or "puck woodin", as is it was then called.

Their children were expected to work hard for their supper. The boys worked picking peanuts, and beans for crop owners, or as cooks in restaurants, or as mechanics. The girls often worked in the seafood industry, picking crabs at the local plants, or cleaning houses for white families in the community. This often meant leaving their home on

Sundays to travel as far as St. George Island to work throughout the week, returning late Friday to spend time at home, only to depart again on Sunday for another week's work. Their daughter, Eunice, later became one of the first African-American students to attend the all-white Crawfordville Elementary School, during the country's integration period, while two of their sons Alan, and Jeffrey would follow their father's example of joining the U.S. Armed Forces. Another son, Herbert, Sr. (my father), and his wife Rachel, were among the first custodians at the Wakulla Middle School when it opened its doors, and have touched the lives of, literally, thousands of young adults, instructors, and administrators, during their almost 30 years of service within the Wakulla County School system.

My grandfather Theo was killed in an automobile accident in August of 1983, and Grandmother Annie would survive him until August of 2008. I remember her celebrating May 20th (the target date for when the Emancipation Proclamation was signed), with family, friends, and much food. Her yard was filled with so many flowers that one often spent a great deal of time in plant conversation before they ever stepped onto the porch. I am sure there are plants all over this county that began as a 'break-off' from my grannies' front yard.

She couldn't help but nurture and spread love like this. I myself had been living in Atlanta, Georgia for about 5 years when I auditioned for the American Academy of Dramatic Arts and was, miraculously, accepted. This meant I had to move and find a place to stay in the Big Apple. My grandmother got wind of this, and one day, in her many sit-downs with Anita Townsend, she mentioned it. As it turns out, Anita's grandson, David, all the way up there in Maine had auditioned and was accepted into the Academy as well. These two grandmothers put their heads together, burned up their phone lines, and by the time I arrived in New York, October 10th, 1996, I not only had a roommate (David), but a piece of my historical 'family' by my side. Through no true effort of our own, other than what we perceived, at the time, to be our 'talent', he and I were connected; were, in actuality, a part of larger family tree whose roots go deeper than can ever be imagined.

Submitted by: Herb Donaldson, Palaver Tree Theater Company, Artistic Director, 232 MLK Blvd. Crawfordville, FL 32327

Memories of Purvis Preston Green and Mattie Lee (Reeves) Green

Purvis & Mattie Lee Green 1940s

For me as a young kid, life was great at "The Store "as we called it. The Store was the P.P. Green Grocery Store located at the corner of Whiddon Lake Road and Crawfordville Hwy. The store and the house of Purvis and Mattie is still there, it has fond memories for me because I was born there in January of 1942. Granddaddy and Grandmama ran the store with help from my mom (Bernice Green Strickland) and my aunt Hilda Green Stewart who married Ned Stewart. Mom and I lived there because my dad was lost in WWII. But for me those were the days, milk cows, chicken and all the farm raised things you want to eat. Granddaddy was taxi cab owner and driver back in the forties. I can remember the "Ice Man" bringing blocks of ice to the house for the ice box to keep things cold. I recall lots of family and other people trading (as they called it back then). The store had lots things that I still love to think about and eat. One of those was sweet cookies back then it was Johnny Cakes and strong cheese and a big old R.C. Boy was that good stuff. Back during the war (WWII) Mama and Grandma would make sandwiches for service boys.

Granddaddy on the hand did all sorts of things, like growing a garden, raising milk cows, milking those same cows for family use. Purvis and Mattie also raised egg laying chicken (free range type that ate everything in the yard?). We had eggs to eat and chicken to fry for supper. Customers would bring things in that they had grown or raised and trade for other things, but mostly that was a thing of the past. Most of their sales were for cash in those days. Some of it was on a credit and that was not a credit card. They had a little book or pad that they used to write down what you bought. And at the end of the week or month you would pay the bill. (This was called running a credit). Most all the stores did this type of business; stores back then were really competitive. I remember back when Purvis and Mattie were running the store, they would stay open late in the evening. Granddaddy

Mattie Reeves Green & Purvis Green

would go out in the middle of the dirt road (Hwy 319) and look down to Rossie Linzy's store, to see if his outside light was still on. He would not close the store until Mr. Rossie's light was off. Life was good back then; we went to the coast to fry fish and to have family picnics at Rock Landing in Panacea. We also got ice cream on the way back home.

The Purvis and Mattie Green family consisted of James Kenneth Green (Cora Lee Morris), Bernice Lee Green (J.M. Strickland), Joe Harper Green (Annie Kate Posey), Hilda Green (Ned Stewart). And there are tons of cousins to many to name. These are some of my cherished memories of P.P. Green and Mattie Lee (Reeves) Green. Both of these dear people have gone on to be with the Lord.

Submitted by: John Preston Strickland. PO Box 745, Crawfordville, FL 32326

Flavey Jackson Langston

Flavey Langston was born December 6, 1900, the second son of Jacob Irvin and Mary Ida (Strickland) Langston. He probably was born in the Smith Creek area, but grew up in Pigott. He helped on his parents' farm and, when he wasn't helping, he loved to play baseball. During World War I, he served as a corporal in the Army.

He and Yvonne Council married January 7, 1923 in Wakulla County. In late 1923, they bought property, next to Yvonne's mother, Missouri Council Benton, from Paris Allen.

Her step-father, Laurie Americus "Lollie" Benton, renovated the Allen home, living there after Misssouri died. Flavey and Yvonne built a house on the southern end of the property which burned down in the late 1930s. They then moved to Tallahassee. Flavey and his brother Roscoe started gillnetting mullet in 1924 and he would peddle fish from the back of his truck. He would travel from Wakulla County, going into Leon County and even into South Georgia. In the late 1920s he opened a market in what is called "Frenchtown" in Tallahassee. From there, he and his adopted son, Maurice Council, moved the market uptown within two blocks of the Capitol. Everyone knew that, if they wanted fresh seafood from a clean market, they could count on "Langston's Seafood".

In the 1950s and '60s, Flavey would farm land that he had bought in Wakulla County as well as the Council land belonging to Yvonne and Maurice. He grew peas, butterbeans, corn, watermelon and cantaloupe. He raised cattle on "the plantation" and pigs on the Council land. The pigs were fed the entrails of the fish from the seafood market along with the corn, watermelons and cantaloupes. A lot of people thought that he was just pouring money down the sand and sinkholes with his farming, but he had a good time doing it, and we enjoyed the benefits of his hard labor.

Working for Flavey were some Wakulla Countians that had started from the very beginning of the markets. They were; H.B. "Bee" and Fred Gavin, Cephus Donaldson, Charlie Johnson and later Bo Donaldson, Bee's son. They were faithful workers and could always be counted on. Bee and Fred were sons of Huel and Ola Gavin who used to work for the Council's in Wakulla County. They considered Flavey as family and when Flavey died, someone asked Fred how many sons did Flavey have? Fred replied,"Three: Maurice, Bee, and me." After Flavey died in 1972, Bee would call Yvonne every week to check up on her. He referred to her as "Momma". Fred died in 1982 and Bee in 1998, but they are still remembered by those of us who loved them. If everyone could love each other the way these people loved each other, the world would be a better place by far.

Submitted by: Gloria C. Dowden and Marcia C. Pearson, 3227 Tanager Trail, Tallahassee, Florida 32303. Sources: Family stories, Tallahassee City Directories, Newspaper articles, Census Records, marriage records, death certificates

Recipe for Good Living

Take 2 heaping cups of Patience
1 Heartful of love
2 handsful of Generosity
Dash Laughter
1 headful of Understanding
Sprinkle generously with kindness.
Add plenty of faith and mix well.
Spread over a lifetime and serve to everyone you meet.

Submitted by Cathy Gray Frank, 215 Stanley, Crawfordville, FL 32327

Laura Langston of Smith Creek

As though her life in its 82 years hadn't been eventful enough, Mrs. Laura Langston of Smith Creek had to add a few dividends after most people would have given up. And none would have taken the honor away from her. At the age of 74 she broke her right arm falling by the garden fence where she tripped over some lighter wood. The next year she broke her leg when she went out to feed some hogs and tripped over a piece of wire. It took four months for the leg to mend. But since "trouble comes not as single spies, but in entire battalions," at 79 she broke her left arm while shucking some corn to cook, and stumbled when she started up the back steps. After that everything went blank until she came to in a car going to the doctor in Quincy, and Mrs.

Langston feels that of all the men who tried to re-set her bones, none were able to get her back together again any better than "Humpty Dumpty" when he fell off the wall.

Laura Langston was both a Langston before she married and after her marriage and was born in Smith Creek in 1882 at the place where Hamp Langston now lives, though not in the same house. Her father was Robert "Shoat" Langston and her mother was Lizzie Colvin. (See Langston genealogy at the end of this article.) She had three brothers and four sisters.

Smith Creek is in the bee territory and Miss Laura says people had bees there as far back and she can remember, starting them from bee trees. She wore homespun clothes of cotton and wool that the girls in her family wove on a spinning wheel and loom. She still remembers the hours they spent knocking the shuttles together. The wool was dyed with indigo or Red Oak bark. The indigo reed was put in a barrel of water where was stirred with a hoe till the dye settled at the bottom.

Indigo, which was a chief southern export before the cotton gin was invented and thus increased cotton production. Cotton was first found growing wild and latter planted and cultivated. Underclothes were woven cotton. There was no elastic available and underwear had to be held up with buttons.

Smith Creek, in Mrs. Langston's childhood, was a world apart and still is the most isolated community in Wakulla County. The people who live there are nearer to Quincy than Tallahassee, and still without telephones. The people are very industrious with farming and bee keeping and have a better than average income.

In her childhood Mrs. Langston's parents went to town two or three times a year. That meant going to Quincy or Bristol and those trips included a treat of peppermint sticks.

The crops raised in north Florida then were much different than now. Before the big freeze of 1899 she remembers there were plenty of oranges, lemons, figs, grapes, and quinces. Even with such fruit that can no longer be raised in this area, Miss Laura thinks that cold weather in her time stayed cold longer.

Church was held once a month on Saturday and Sunday. On the weekends in warm weather, the men and boys went bathing. (It was improper for a woman to go bathing, though the bathing dresses of that time covered her from wrist to ankle and some.) Some of the early preachers Mrs. Langston remembers were Steve Revell, a Rev. Bostic and Jack Langston. The first Smith Creek Baptist Church was a log house where the cemetery is now located. A frame church was then built across the road and was destroyed by high wind. The present Smith Creek Baptist Church was built when Miss Laura was a small girl.

Mrs. Langston knew her husband, Jacob Jonathan Richard "Jake" Langston, all her life. They went to school together in a log building with half a pine log for a bench. The building had one window, with no glass or shutters and only one door. The Langstons' were married on December 17, 1899 when she was 17 and have been married 64 years. They were probably one of the oldest married couples in the county at that time. In that day, a girl of 25 was considered an old maid. She remembers at least 3 old maids in her community at the time she got married

She and Jake stayed in his father's home for 2 or 3 years until he built a house on the Branch (a stream running through Smith Creek and empties into the Ochlocknee) on the land given him by his father who in turn had bought it from a man named John Grant.

They raised chuffers (a hog feed), pinders, cane, sweet potatoes, velvet beans, and livestock. They smoked their hams with pine sap. In the summer they drank milk, made clabber, and gave the rest to the hogs. - "After we got a refrigerator," recalls Mrs. Langston, "We never had good cream because it was too cold to rise."

The Langston's had four children, Annie, Elma, Mary and Opal. Opal was born when her mother was 41 years old. She remembers that Jake went to get a doctor and the truck broke down and when he got back the baby had already arrived.

Mrs. Langston made diapers out of homespun cotton and boiled them in a kettle. Many of the children had Malaria and died either from that or complications arising from the Malaria. The next worst ailment was Pneumonia. The Langston's didn't have screens on the doors and windows until they were 50 years old and their water was poor until they had a deep well. Only occasionally did they have spring water. They made soap out of Oak ashes with spring water poured through it. All the children, both white and colored, were delivered by midwives. No colored people live in Smith Creek area today.

Memories of the horrors if World War I are still vivid to Miss Laura. Ira Langston and John Mercer, one of their hired men, both served in France. Another Smith Creek man, Troy Langston, went into the service but had served only two weeks when he died from the flu. Columbus Kyle, who went the same time as Troy, brought his body home. Columbus had the flu also, but he recovered. During the depression, the Langston's had enough food but no flour and no money because, "there wasn't much money astirin'."

Later in life the Langston's lived with their daughter Opal whose husband, Adron Anderson, was killed in a tractor accident in 1959. Mrs. Langston still cooks and makes beds. Her favorite TV program is "Love of Life" which might be a good description of herself.

Langston Genealogy

This is not a complete genealogy of the Langston family and is open for revision.

The first Langston in the area was John Langston who came from South Carolina to Liberty County sometime before the Civil War, (possibly in the 1840s which saw the largest influx of settlers in both counties,) to farm. He had one family of Negroes, looked after them well, and both the slaves and their owners worked hard from daylight to well after sundown. He raised cotton, cane, corn and everything they ate and used for the next three generations. Another lure for these early settlers was good hunting and fishing. The wild game and fish provided food pretty much year round.

John Langston's sons were:

I. Ervin, married Mary McMillan

1. Mack, married Carrie Strickland and then Mattie Cox. They had 3 girls and 3 boys.

2Judson died at age 25.

1. Mandy, never married.

2. Jake, married Laura Langston. They had 4 daughters, 1 died young.

3. Johnny died as a child.

II. Jack married Ceely McMillan, sister of his brother's wife.

1. Jimpse, married Laura Anderson

2. Bill married Sally Roberts. Bill died of smallpox about 2 weeks after coming home from the Civil War. They had 5 girls and 2 boys.

3. Ervin married Ida Strickland. They had 4 boys and 2 girls.

4. Ely married Clara Hartsfield.

5. Albert died as a baby.

6. Sally married Oliver Strickland. They had 5 girls and 3 boys. One died young.

7. Lizzie, Married Newton Kyle. They had 1 girl and 5 boys. His 5th son was Quintus is Latin for the number 5.

8. Mae married Lorenzo Cox. They had 3 boys and 3 girls.

9. Lila married Horace Tully and then Lon Maxwell. They had 3 boys and 2 girls.

III. Morgan died during the Civil War near Ringgold, Ga.

IV. Jake, married Mary Mobley, no children.

V. Caleb married Jane Collins. They had one child, Charles.

VI. Sally, married to a man named Grant. They had one girl, Sarah.

The above genealogy is that of Jake Langston's grandfather, Laura Langston's paternal grandfather was Jesse Langston who probably came from South Carolina to Liberty County along with John Langston. This makes Jake and Laura distant cousins. Laura's paternal grandmother, Mary Smith, had an uncle, Edwin Smith, who also came south with the Langston's. Laura's maternal grandfather was Henry Colvin who came south before the Civil War but returned north during the hostilities and his son served in the Union Army.

Laura Langston's father was Robert Bunyan "Shoat" Langston. Shoat married Elizabeth "Lizzie" Colvin. They had 8 children.

1. Laura Lawson Langston married Jake Langston. They had 4 children, Annie, Elma, Mary and Opal.

2. Leah married John Coleman Reynolds. They had 7 children. Willie, Earnest, Nina, Nellie, Albert, Tommy and W.D.

3. Mary Frances "Fannie" married Charlie Langston. They had 5 children, Mittie, Hamp, Major, Barney and Dolly Mae.

4. Bunyan married Abigail "Abbie" Creech. They had 6 children, Howard, Blanch, Arthur, Drew, Lucille and Thelma.

5. Noah married Florida Colvin, One son, Earl.

6. Ross married Clara Langston. They had 4 children, Paul, Robert, Donald and Betty.

7. Jessie married Sam Howard.

8. Edna married Almer Chester. One son, Woodrow.

Jake and Laura Langston's children are:

1. Annie died at age 28.

2. Elma married J.B. Kyle, whose children are Clyde, Mavis and Katherine.

3. Mary married Herschel Anderson, whose children are Addie Dora, Irving, Betty and Annette.

4. Opal, married Adron Anderson, whose children are Dottie, Randy, Adronna and Tony.

Jake Langston, born July 20, 1880, died December 17, 1972

Laura Langston, born February 27, 1882, died February 15, 1983.

This article printed in the Magnolia Monthly 1964. Written by; Elizabeth Smith. Permission to reprint given by: Elizabeth F. Smith Estate. Photo submitted by: Annette Roberts, 8674 D L Crosby Lane, Tallahassee, FL 32305

Yvonne Council Langston

Yvonne was the youngest child of John Cecil Council and Nancy Missouri Smith, his second wife. She was born June 19, 1906 and married Flavey Jackson Langston in 1923 in Crawfordville. They moved to Tallahassee when their adopted son, Maurice Council, graduated from high school in 1937.

Her life-long friend was Rosa Mae (Moore) Duggar. Rosa Mae was born in October of 1906, the daughter of May W. and Nellie Moore. Yvonne's first outing was to visit them. When they were growing up and going to school, Yvonne would walk to the Moore home. Once during the winter, she arrived there barefooted. Mr. Moore told her to come on in and warm her feet because her

Yvonne Council & Flavey Jackson Langston

toes looked like turkey necks. The girls would also take eggs to school so they could trade them at the store for candy at recess. After they were grown and married, they still stayed friends, calling and checking on each other when they grew too old to get together. During the Depression, she worked for the WPA in Crawfordville and in Perry transcribing court records. After World War II, she worked in the family seafood market when she wanted to. She also worked during the Legislative sessions and her final job was with Tillman's Gift Shop on South Adams in Tallahassee. She and Flavey were members of First Baptist Church in Tallahassee. She had been a member of the Beulah Primitive Baptist Church in Crawfordville and had been baptized in Brim Fountain. She and Flavey loved baseball, even going to the "Subway World Series" in the 1950s when the Yankees (Flavey's team) and the Dodgers (Bonne's team) were playing. They went with Jim and Etta Maude (Rouse) Kirkland. Years later, they still talked about New York City and the subway rides. Maurice's children called her, "Bonnie", and Flavey, "Tata". They considered them as their grandparents as Maurice's mother, Sue, had died when they were too small to remember. When they were growing up, it was always "Santa Claus" at Bonnie and Tata's. No matter what had been left under the tree at home, they could always count on the biggest haul being at their house. In 1953, Santa brought Bonnie a "J. Fred Muggs" monkey. She kept the old and well-worn fellow in the same spot in her bedroom so that any of her grandchildren and great-grand-children would know right where to find him. It has always been a well-known fact that Bonnie was a great cook. Her recipes for cornbread dressing and sweet potato soufflé are still being used at Thanksgiving and Christmas by her grandchildren. When the grandchildren were growing up, she would keep them overnight and serve the most elegant breakfast with her best china and silver, complete with cantaloupe filled with lime sherbet. When her great-grandchildren came along, Bonnie would keep them for what came to be known as "fun days". Each of the boys had their own special and individual time with her. She would take them to the store for a treat and to the grocery store to buy whatever they wanted her to fix for their lunch. They played games, colored, listened to her tell stories, watched baseball together and built memories.

Submitted by: Gloria C. Dowden and Marcia C. Pearson, 3227 Tanager Trail, Tallahassee, Florida, 32301

John Mills Sr.; The 'Black Mayor' Of Buckhorn

As I glance through the history of Wakulla County, I find myself hard-pressed to find anything that speaks to the contributions of the African-Americans, the blacks (or whatever description is popular at the moment), who were integral in the development of the place I call my home. One of those people was my grandfather, John Mills, Sr.

Many were the days that my parents (Rachel and Herbert Donald-son, Sr.), my brother (Kevin), my sister (Jennifer), and I, would travel through Crawford-ville, past Medart, to where the road splits to either Panacea, or Sop-choppy.

John Mills, Sr.

We would veer right,

and just before we came into Sopchoppy proper, there stood a small community known as Buckhorn. My grandfather was Buckhorn. He was known there as the 'Black Mayor'.

When he was approximately 13 years old, he planted a tree not far from the roadside. Through the years this tree would grow to be quite large in stature; so large, in fact, that he built a wooden table around it. People would gather beneath it to play cards, hang out and talk, meet for dates, have fish-fries after church, and sometimes, fight.

Grandaddy built a small store for the local folk to purchase general items. He offered a decent price as well as credit. Eventually, he would build over 30 small houses, renting to black and white people who were hard on their luck, but needed a break from a man they could trust. Later, he built the Buckhorn Café, and a small community center, where he showed black and white 'westerns' on Friday nights. During an election season, candidates, no matter their party affiliation were given an honorary fish fry where they could meet and greet with those in Buckhorn. Once the eating was done, the candidate would address the com-munity at large with a speech delivered from the foot of the large tree. This was a time for all to ask questions and vent on issues surrounding the election, as well as its process.

Buckhorn Café

In 1969, I arrived and became the firstborn grandson of the 'Black Mayor'. And as I grew, the many varied people and faces of that one community would become my second family. All who came into the store would pick me up, play with me, or bring their own children (my partners in crime) to roam out back, behind the store, as they shopped inside. At nights, when the store closed, Grandaddy would lay the pennies, nickels and dimes out on my little folding table by the fireplace. My job was to count the change properly and place the coins into small paper packets that read Pennies: 50 cents, Nickels $2, etc. I would have to wait a few more years before he moved me up to quarters.

The Mills Grocery Store

My brother and I (and my little sister, to some degree) have never forgotten those days at the café with the men in their bellbottoms and their wicked platform shoes; the stunningly made-up women with Afros at least one whole yard wide; the New Year's Eve parties where the big boys, years older than us, would do the unbelievable: hold 'Roman Candles' in their bare hands as the candle, spitting fire, would sling forth a color-filled brilliance that lit up the midnight sky; or the days when CB radios were the big thing, and the 'good buddies', all dressed in t-shirts with their 'handles' written across their backs, would fry chicken, shrimp, and mullet, while flipping burgers and blasting the funkiest of soul music, all in an effort to forget they'd ever grown up, or had children of their own.

How my Grandaddy made these things possible in an era where race relations in the county were not the best, and how he managed, somehow to make sure his mother, brothers, and most specifically his sisters, would never in their lifetimes be without a house of their own, will forever be something of a magical mystery to me. However, a bit of that magic begins to fade as I remember, with astounding vividness, sitting at the foot of the hospital bed we'd installed in his room as he lay dying, in June of 1980. I remember my mother's face, my father's, and my grandmother's, who, as she held my hand, stared into Grandaddy's eyes, and he into hers, as he drifted from this life. It was then that the house began to hum, and eventually to weep, for the people – my second family – stretched from his room, into the living room, onto the front porch, and out into the yard.

The day of the funeral, the hearse silently pulled up in front of his general store, and stopped. I stepped out from our house to the edge of the chain-link fence, across the street from his store, staring at the long dark car, knowing Grandaddy was inside. When I looked around, I noticed that those in the community had come outside of their doors, the homes he built for them, to gather and watch also. There we stood, united for that one, brief moment, in absolute silence. We all seemed to know, through no words that could have been spoken, what was passing; and what would never come this way again.

Many years later, I started the Palaver Tree Theater Company. The Palaver Tree is based on an old African tradition in which all members of the community would gather under the shade of a huge tree and discuss their lives and futures as a group, or solid unit. Whenever one of them was uncomfortable in their expression, or felt they could not fully articulate their concerns to the others, a 'griot','storyteller', or poet, in essence: an artist, would speak on their behalf. It was this tradition, shown to me as a child in how my grandfather lived his life, which remains to this day, my true inspiration.

Submitted by: Herb Donaldson, Palaver Tree Theater Company, Artistic Director, 232 MLK Blvd. Crawfordville, FL 32327

Building Roads; William and Dot Oaks

My father, William Wakulla Oaks, and my mother, Gertrude "Dot" Dannelley Oaks spent eighteen years of their married life's journey traveling through Florida before returning to the place of his birth to live.

Willie, as he was known as a boy in Wakulla County where he was born in 1907, was the son of William Harrison Oaks and Sally Thomas Oaks. Like so many southerners in the late 19th century, they sought to support their family by farming and they knew extreme hardships and grief. Poor health, poor soil and poor crops often took fearsome tribute

William Wakulla Oaks, and Gertrude "Dot" Dannelley Oaks

from these struggling, but God-fearing families, and so it was with the Oaks family. Willie's father died at the age of 35 leaving his mother, Sally, with three young children, having already lost two young sons to sickness. The youngest son was born two months after his father's death.

Sally, having been orphaned as a small child and raised in different homes as a servant, never attended school and could not read nor write. Therefore, to support her family she did manual labor, farming, housekeeping, washing, ironing, sewing, whatever she could to earn meager rations to support her family. Willie, like most boys of his day, attended school as a young child but when he got old enough to be a help on a farm he would take any job he could find. When he was a young teen, he worked at a turpentine still which was located just to the south of Wakulla Springs. He often told of helping load the barrels of turpentine and remembering the time a barrel was rolled over one of his big toes. He had no shoes. The toe gave him trouble the rest of his life.

When the State Road Department came to Wakulla County in the mid 1920s to complete clearing and providing a hard service for the road bed from Crawfordville to Wakulla Station (today's Hwy. 61) Willie and several local men were hired for the work of clearing the roadway. His salary was 50 cents per day for which he was thankful! Willie continued to work with the road crew doing whatever job he was given and in the late '20s the SRD was working to pave Highway 90, the main artery from Jacksonville to Pensacola, Willie left Crawfordville to travel with the road crew where he was known as "Bill". The crew, working from Tallahassee to Pensacola at that time lived along the way. The men would rent rooms, or beds, in "boarding houses" where they were supplied a bed and perhaps, two meals a day for a set amount to be paid each month when they received their SRD pay. This was a common method for a family to make a little extra money for their own needs. Many years later, Bill showed his family the house where he boarded in Caryville, their first stop after coming to Highway 90.

It was an ordinary little house facing the highway out in the country.

The SRD crew kept working and moving westward toward Pensacola. By 1930 they were between Defuniak Springs and Crestview and as they moved, the men were surveying the area of Crestview for a place to stay. Several of the crew found a hotel in Crestview located downtown near the railroad and business section. The Crescent Hotel was a large, two-storied frame building facing the railroad and town from the south side and had a large front porch where the guests could sit and "watch the world go by."

Manager of the hotel was Mrs. Maxie Bowers Dannelley Dozier, from Elba, Alabama, who had much experience managing boarding houses and hotels following the sudden death of her first husband and father of her four children, Ace W. Dannelley. Her youngest son, also named Ace, was born a few weeks after his father's death. Maxie and her second husband, Andrew M. Dozier, came to Florida in the mid-twenties to manage hotels from Seagrove Beach to Bonifay and Chipley before taking the Crescent Hotel in Crestview.

In 1930, Mrs. Dozier, with two teenage daughters and two younger sons, took in boarders and overnight guests at the well-known hotel. Bill Oaks, George Shores and several other road workers registered as "guests" of the hotel. Little did Bill and George know their world would soon change!

Mrs. Dozier's family were all involved in the operations of the hotel as well as going on with school, playing sports, etc. The girls did the housework, making beds, sweeping and packing lunches in the mornings. The boys stacked and brought in wood for the kitchen as well as outdoor chores.

1930-31 were pivotal years for Willie aka Bill Oaks as that was when he met his life partner, "Dot" Dannelley. His co-worker, George Shores, married Dot's sister, Mary Jane, and in April of 1931, Bill and Dot were married.

Bill remained with the State Road Department and they continued the nomadic life of moving as the road was built. Dot was not thrilled at the prospect of packing and moving as the job progressed and she asked a cabinet maker if he could build them a house on wheels that they could pull behind their car. When he replied in the affirmative, she told him to get busy and soon, there was a little two room frame building on wheels ready to go! It could be pulled from one stop to another behind the family vehicle and set up on blocks of wood. Of course, there had been trailers built before this time, but Dot liked to say she "helped start the mobile home business." Other road crew members had similar trailers built and as the team moved, so moved the families, sometimes to trailer parks, sometimes to unoccupied woods along the way.

Bill and Dot's first child, a son, died at birth in Enzor Hospital in Crestview where each of the following Oaks children, Betty Jo, Dannelley and Sally would be born regardless of where the family lived at the time.

They lived along the Gulf coast between Pensacola and Panama City while working on Highway 98. The story was always told of the crew chief advising the men to buy beach property as it was being sold for $5.00 per acre but at that time, there was nothing there but sand, salt, sea and sun! The men laughed and scoffed that they would have to be paid to take the land. Oh, little did they know!

After the stint on Highway 98, the crew was sent back to improve Highway 98 on the way to Jacksonville. By this time, the two-room trailer was not adequate for the growing family. Their son, Dannelley, had been born in 1938 and they were living in Live Oak in a large, older rental house where Betty Jo attended first grade. The following year the crew moved to Lake City and after a year or so there, they were sent to Mims where they were working on Highway 1. Here again, the family found rental housing and Betty Jo was enrolled in school. There were many fun things for the family to do...fish for bream in the many canals, go to the beaches and visit many of the central Florida tourist oriented towns.

December 7, 1941. Radio's evening news report changed the world for Americans. We had been attacked! We were at war! Everyone became involved. Bill registered for the draft but was some older than the required ages and he was also considered useful on the home front as a road builder. Dot signed up for Red Cross first aid courses and used Bill and Betty Jo as practice patients for learning different bandages, splints and slings. She also took on the volunteer job of airplane spotter where the volunteers were stationed in a tower constructed to watch for aircraft in the area. They were given charts to help identify the planes and given a guide to directions, etc. with instructions to call particular numbers to report. Keep in mind, there were relatively few aircraft in the skies in those days and you could hear and see them rather easily. Headlights of all cars in the area along the coast were painted black over the top half to cut the amount of light that could be seen from the air. Rationing coupons were issued and became a way of life. You were limited in the purchase of sugar, butter, gas and tires and other items which were needed for the war effort. Children were organized at school to collect cans, toothpaste tubes (thin metal, at that time) and all kinds of metal to be turned in for government recycling. Everyone was aware of the war effort as millions reported for military duty or jobs creating weapons, warships, aircraft and support supplies.

Bill and Dot moved next to Merritt Island just across the Indian River from Titusville. Here they lived in an apartment set up in a large two-story brick building that looked like it had been a fine mansion in former years. We were on the second floor but had a wonderful porch looking over a beautiful garden of tropical fruit trees and flowers. Bill went to work building runways for Patrick Air Force Base located just south of Cocoa Beach and Cape Canaveral.

At the close of the school year in 1943, Bill and Dot moved their family back to Crestview returning to where their lives together had begun. They rented a new log house in Crestview and he went to work building runways for Eglin Air Force Base. Dot gave birth to her second daughter, Sally, at Enzor Hospital.

In late 1944, the family moved to Panama City where Bill and Dot bought a house and five acres of land near where the airport was to be built. His first job there was clearing and leveling runways for the new airport. He then worked for Bay County Road Department keeping the county roads graded.

In 1949, Bill's mother was in declining health and he felt the need to return to Wakulla County. Dot and Betty Jo preferred to remain in Panama City but knew it was the right thing to do what he felt was needed. During the summer of 1949, the travels of Willie aka Bill Oaks brought him back to the place of his birth where he continued building roads. He worked as the county road superintendent before retiring. His early job with the State Road Department led to his career of traveling and building roads!

Submitted by Betty Green, PO Box 969, Crawfordville, FL 32327

Reflections of Granny and Granddaddy; Robert & Willodean Oliver

Home for me was down a dusty country road now known as Page-Oliver Road in Wakulla County, Florida. Looking back, I realize how much of an impact my grandparents had in my up-bringing. Grandparents fill a special place in the lives of their grandchildren. Every child needs the wisdom understanding, and unconditional love that grandparents can give. Parents tend to be too caught up in the day-to-day stresses of life. However, grandparents have the luxury of time and time is a precious commodity in the life of a child. My Granny Willodean and Granddaddy Robert Oliver gave me their time and they will always hold a special place in my heart because of this gift they heaped on me daily.

I don't believe I ever heard my grandparents speak a cross word in anger to each other not even when Granny killed Granddaddy's favorite turkey. One day my Granny and Granddaddy were building a new pen to put their turkeys in and Granny had a run-in with one of them. The only gobbler they had was old Tom. I don't know why, but Granddaddy loved that turkey as though it were a puppy that followed him nipping at his heels. But, Tom had a major problem! Whenever Granny fed the turkeys and gathered their eggs to put in the incubator, Tom would spur the calves on Granny's legs, drawing blood. He was a mean old cuss, but Granddaddy never saw that side of Tom until THAT DAY!

As Granny was using the square shovel to take up the grass, Tom came up behind her and spurred her. Without even thinking, Granny took the shovel and dinged old Tom upside the head! When Granddaddy got back from Woodville Lumber Company with the fence posts, Granny had to tell him what she had done. Tom was still staggering around in a daze. Granddaddy asked Granny,

"Willow, what have you done to my Tom?"

Granny replied, "I'm sorry Robert, but that turkey has spurred me for the last time!"

An hour later, Tom died and became Granny's contribution to the Thanksgiving meal.

Granddaddy often let me tag along to help him feed the animals and gather the eggs. Besides turkeys, they had chickens, cows, and hunting dogs. During those times, Granddaddy would bring a smile or a jolt of laughter from the pranks he'd play on me. He'd often tell me if I didn't behave, he'd cut my belly button out and blow smoke in it! He'd also pretend he had grabbed my nose, put his thumb between his fingers, and say, "I got your nose. See?"

Granny in her wisdom knew it was good to keep us kids out of trouble by giving us things to do. Usually, this meant helping her plant the vegetable garden. My sisters Gail, Jan, Lisa, and me along with our cousins Ray and Dennis would get up at dawn and head to the garden patch to help Granny, Aunt Dannie, and Mama plant row upon row of vegetables. The garden provided the three families with an abundance of vegetables and fellowship during the spring and fall harvest. We'd plant watermelon, squash, potatoes, lima beans, white acre peas, okra and sweet yellow corn. When harvest time came, all of us kids would help pick the vegetables in the garden so they could be preserved for winter.

Often, we would sit under the shed of my Uncle Pat's shop to shuck corn, and shell peas. There was a lot of family fellowship there with lively conversation between the three generations, and singing from us kids. We spent a lot of afternoons practicing hymns for church on Sunday. One of our favorite hymns to practice was "Amazing Grace."

Coming home from school was a special time for my sister Lisa, Ray, Dennis, and myself. At times it would sound a lot like the Walton's because Granny had to call us in for snack. She'd yell as loud as she could:

"Dennis, Ray, Lisa, Teresa, come here!"

Granny always had something good to eat. If we couldn't smell the sweetness of her chocolate cake when we came home from school, we knew we'd get some of those marshmallow pinwheel cookies she bought at Bo Lynn's grocery in St. Marks.

One time we went to the dock in St. Marks to pick Granddaddy up from the tugboat named the Janet and my cousin Donna (from my Daddy's side of the family) came along. She seemed kind of sad, so I asked her,

"Donna, what's wrong?" Feeling left out of the hello greetings she replied, "I don't have a granddaddy." I told her, "That's OK, I'll share my granddaddy with you, he won't mind."

Granddaddy took Lisa, Donna, and me to the wheelhouse and let us pretend we were steering the Janet.

Even in death, my Granny took care of us. She was having abdominal problems and eventually was diagnosed with Liver Cancer.

Mamaw's Cornbread Dressing (Louise Miller 1912-1991)

1 to 2 large skillets of baked cornbread, cooled
1 whole package celery, chopped
4 large bell peppers, chopped
4 large onions, chopped
4 to 5 boiled eggs chopped
4 to 5 raw eggs
2 qts chicken broth (may not use it all or may need more)
1 stick butter
Garlic, salt, pepper, basil, oregano, Italian seasoning, and celery seed to taste.
Put spices in vegetables while sautéing.
Sauté chopped vegetables in small amount of chicken broth until tender, add butter so it will melt. Crumble cornbread in a large bowl and add vegetables, and some chicken broth. Stir and add chicken broth until it's the consistency of making cornbread. (Sort of thick). Pour into a 9 x 13 pan, sprayed with Pam.
Bake at 350 until brown, 45 minutes to 1 hour.
Submitted by; Tanya Lynn, 165 Deepwood Dr. Crawfordville, FL 32327

She went in and out of the hospital during a six-month period. She led everyone in the family (including Granddaddy) to believe she was going for chemotherapy. All of us should have known better when we were seeing her get weaker each day. When she died, the oncologist told Granddaddy he had done all he could three months prior. Granny was going to the hospital for counseling to deal with her prognosis. Granny always thought of everybody else and dealing with death wasn't any different.

Granddaddy mourned the loss of Granny until his death eleven years later from a pulmonary blood clot after surgery to remove an aneurism of the stomach. Granddaddy never remarried. He continued to live in the two-bedroom house he and Granny shared for their 52 years of marriage. I have fond memories of Granddaddy's visits when Lisa and I got an air-hockey game for Christmas. You wouldn't believe someone his age would understand air-hockey, let alone actually play it! It didn't take long for Granddaddy to get the hang of the game. He became the champion! He would beat Lisa and me mercilessly by laying his forearm in front of his goal when either of us were about to score a goal. When we did manage to somehow get some goals and it looked like we were winning, he'd all of a sudden tell us, "I got to go home. You know my show is coming on and I can't miss it!" Granddaddy had to go home to catch Lonnie Anderson on *W.K.R.P. in Cincinnati*. Lonnie Anderson was the only love in his life after Granny.

As I look back I realize that my Granny and Granddaddy helped shape me into the woman I am. I see reflections of them each time I drive down Page-Oliver road and pass the old homestead they shared with my Aunt Dannie's family and mine. I cherish those times I shared with Granny and Granddaddy. Someday I hope to give my future grandchildren reflections of Granny and Granddaddy as I give them my most valuable commodity; time.

Submitted by: Teresa Skinner , 107 W. College St. Boston, GA.,31626

Debra and Etta Mae Council Pelt

Debra Juanita and Etta Mae were born into one of the pioneering families of Wakulla County, the Council family. They were born to Noah Columbus Council and Sarah Louvina (Green) Council. Noah was the son of John Cecil Council and Frances DeLaura (Posey) Council of Crawfordville. Louvina was the daughter of Thomas J. Green and Sarah A. (Reeves) Green of Ivan.

Debra was born in 1917 and Etta Mae in 1918 at the homestead on Arran Road. The sisters were eighteen months apart and were very close throughout their lives. In times past, women often died from disease or in childbirth and men would remarry and have second families; as was the case of Noah who had (5) children by his first wife and two with his second wife. Louvina was considered an "old maid" in her forties when she married Noah Columbus.

The family attended Old Beulah Primitive Baptist Church, at the Sink of Lost Creek. Their grandfather was a deacon and one of the founding fathers of the church. The sisters walked to school in Crawfordville which was a mile or so from their home. They didn't like to get wet and would cry if they had to walk in the rain. Debra was made to wait until Etta Mae was old enough to go to school so they could go together and she would not have to walk the distance by herself.

Once when their father was teaching Debra to plow at age nine, Etta Mae would not get out of the way. Their father jokingly told Debra to cut her toes off and when Debra let the plow fall, it accidentally cut two of Etta Mae's toes almost off. Debra was screaming and crying and they thought she was hurt but she was crying for her sister. Their mother stuck spider web in the cuts to stop the bleeding and wrapped her foot and her toes grew back together.

Their father died from complications of asthma when Debra was nine years old and Etta Mae was seven years old. It was hard for widow women with children. Many had no way of making a living and were at the mercy of family and neighbors. They grew what they could in the garden and picked blackberries and huckleberries to sell to the store in Crawfordville in exchange for groceries. They also would sell eggs when they would have them. During the Great Depression it was hard for everyone but more so for women who did not have a man in the house. At one point during this time, the three did not have anything much to eat and their mother started praying for the Lord to supply them with some food. That afternoon a thunder storm came and after the rain stopped there was a big turtle in the front yard. Their mother started rejoicing because God had answered her prayers and they ate turtle that night. On another occasion when they were without food and prayed, some birds were caught in an old fish net that hung on the fence. At Christmas one year, they had gone out to visit neighbors and when they got home, a big box was sitting on the porch full of food and clothes for the girls.

When weather permitted, they would walk to Ivan to visit with the Greens, their mother's side of the family, staying a week or two with their aunt and uncles. After their father died they no longer had a horse and wagon.

When the train came through Arran and by their home, sometimes the sparks from the train's engine would cause brush fires and they would have to run and put the fire out if the ground was dry.

They told of bad weather spun from the 1928 Storm that blew their house down with them in it. The wind picked the house up and set it down off the blocks. They got up in the bed with their mother shielding them with her body as rafters fell down around them. They were bruised and battered but not badly hurt and tried desperately to get to a neighboring house with trees falling down all around them. They both feared bad weather all their lives.

When Debra and Cager were courting, their mother insisted that Etta Mae go with them to chaperone. Debra got married at 15 to George Cajer Pelt and they had four children; Janice Pelt Brown (Ed), Maxine Pelt Lambeth (Ray), Randall Pelt (Ava) and Sharol Pelt Brown (Edwin) and two babies that died in childbirth. Etta Mae married Carmel Willie Pelt at age 18 and they had six children; Berlin Carmel Pelt (Ellen), Etta Jo Pelt Oliver (Ralph), Willie Bostic Pelt (Janis), Vera Pelt Wirick, Brenda Pelt McCarthy (Gene) and Carmen Pelt Sapp (Broward).

The two Council sisters married two brothers of the Pelt family and lived within shouting distance of each other all their married lives in Peltville. They were avid fishermen well up into their early eighties. Debra died in 2005 at age 88 and Etta Mae died in 2008 at 90 years of age. They are buried in the Pelt Family Cemetery on Bostic Pelt Road. They were women who had strong faith, character, endurance, hardworking, loyal to their husbands and loving mothers to their children.

Submitted by: Brenda Pelt McCarthy, Brenda Pelt McCarthy, 116 Carmel Lane, Crawfordville, FL

Oscar C. Peters

Oscar C. Peters lived in the Sopchoppy, FL area in the 1930s, and was well known in the area as a Skin Cancer Doctor. He was born

Oscar C Peters Rolling Store

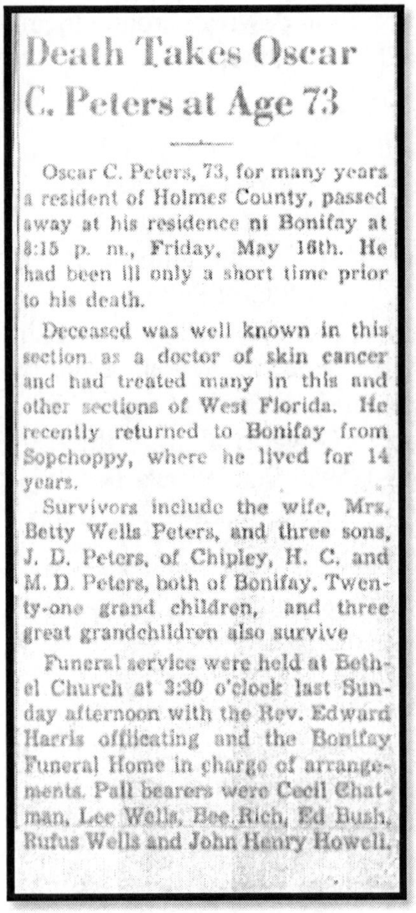

Death Takes Oscar C. Peters at Age 73

Oscar C. Peters, 73, for many years a resident of Holmes County, passed away at his residence ni Bonifay at 8:15 p. m., Friday, May 16th. He had been ill only a short time prior to his death.

Deceased was well known in this section as a doctor of skin cancer and had treated many in this and other sections of West Florida. He recently returned to Bonifay from Sopchoppy, where he lived for 14 years.

Survivors include the wife, Mrs. Betty Wells Peters, and three sons, J. D. Peters, of Chipley, H. C. and M. D. Peters, both of Bonifay. Twenty-one grand children, and three great grandchildren also survive

Funeral service were held at Bethel Church at 3:30 o'clock last Sunday afternoon with the Rev. Edward Harris officiating and the Bonifay Funeral Home in charge of arrangements. Pall bearers were Cecil Chatman, Lee Wells, Bee Rich, Ed Bush, Rufus Wells and John Henry Howell.

January 28, 1874, in Coffee County, Alabama. He was married to a lady named Sarah and they lived in Geneva, AL. Their son was named Jessie D. Peters.

Oscar's second marriage to my grandmother, Mary Elizabeth Wells, took place March 30, 1902. She was always called Betty and she and Oscar had two sons, Henry C. Peters and Med D. Peters.

Oscar and Betty made their living as farmers during the time they lived in Holmes County prior to moving to Sopchoppy. Their farm was called the Wells Place as my grandmothers' parents homesteaded there, and after Mr. Wells passed they took over running the farm. Along with farming, Granddaddy (Oscar) also had what was known as a Rolling Store. He would go throughout the county to remote farms and homes selling his wares (see photo). He was very enterprising, always looking for a better way of doing things.

He developed a medication that successfully removed and cured skin cancers. I was told this was what took him to the Sopchoppy area. My grandmother would tell of people coming to their home on Blossom Street in Sopchoppy from all over the state seeking treatment. They would stay until their skin cancers were healed.

Granddaddy became ill himself in the early part of 1947, from complications of diabetes. He wanted to get my grandmother back to Holmes County before he died so she would be near her family.

They returned to Bonifay and very shortly he passed away on May 16, 1947. See enclosed obituary.

As a child I recall my grandmother always spoke fondly of the time she and my grandfather lived in Sopchoppy. He loved fishing in the Sopchoppy River and being near Apalachicola where he could buy one of his favorite foods, oysters, by the bushel.

Much of my grandfather's life is a mystery to me, and I would love to know more about the man, because the little I do know is so fascinating to me.

Submitted by Lillian Peters Pittman, 9254 Terri's Landing, Calabash, N.C. 28467

The Family of Hobson Leo Raker and Beulah Council Raker

Daddy was born in 1898 and Beulah Council was born in 1902, in Wakulla County. Daddy was a fisherman most of his life and died of cancer at the age of 49. Momma did sewing and worked at Camp Gordon Johnston during World War II. Later she worked at the Department of Motor Vehicles until she retired. After my Dad died in 1947, we moved to Tallahassee where Momma lived until 1986 when she passed away at the age of 83. Daddy loved fishing. I remember, as a young boy, he carried me along with him for one week. In those days, they used a motorized launch where they slept, cooked and ate. They towed three skiffs with nets on them, out into the Bay. The skiffs did not have motors and my two uncles, M. D. Raker and Julius Duggar, and my father would row the skiffs around looking for fish. When they saw a group of mullet, two of them threw their nets across each other. Each net had a spear-like shaft on the end and they would thrust them into the bottom of the bay. Then they rowed their boats as hard as they could, and the nets would drag off the back of the skiffs, to circle the fish. The third one would zig-zag his net inside the circle. Then they would hang around and bang on their boats, giving the mullet time to swim into the nets and gill themselves. After the mullet gilled themselves, the men would retrieve their nets, gather the mullet, and put them in the skiff to take them back to the launch to put them on ice. This would go on for several days.

One day, when we were away from the launch looking for mullet, a sudden storm came up and we were unable to get back to the launch. We headed for the nearest little island. I remember getting out of the boat and kneeling down. Daddy covered me with a raincoat until the storm passed.

During our fishing trip, I remember we would have mullet and grits for breakfast, and for a change, we would have grits and mullet for supper. After several days of fishing, they would return to shore to sell their catch.

Like most folks in Wakulla County, Daddy had never been farther from home than South Georgia. After he developed cancer, he travelled alone to Rochester, Minnesota for treatment. I still have some of the letters he wrote to my mother during that time.

I remember Momma used to love to sew and do craft work. She hardly ever sat down without having something to work on in her hands.

Momma and Daddy had five children, 20 grandchildren and numerous great-grandchildren. The oldest child, Eldred, passed away in 2008 at the age of 86. Marjorie and (Warren) Council currently live in Tallahassee and retired from state government. Linda, the youngest, lives in Tennessee where she has spent most of her adult life. I retired from the Florida Highway Patrol after 29 years. Then I spent 15 years working part-time with the Wakulla County Sheriff's Office. I currently live in Leesburg, Florida and spend the summers in Western North Carolina.

I was born in Crawfordville near the location of the present Courthouse. Before I was born, my brother, Council told everyone he was going to have a baby brother named "Jimmy." However, when I was born I was named Oscar Montgomery, after my grandfather. As far as Council was concerned, though, he had a baby brother named "Jimmy" and to this day, I am known as "Jimmy" or "Jim." When we moved to Tallahassee and the school sent for my records, the school in Crawfordville had no record of "Oscar Montgomery" and we had to explain that the records were in the name of "Jimmy."

When I was 18 months old, my family moved into the house my father built on the corner of what is now Arran Road and Fulton Harvey Road, just west of the old Crawfordville School. The lumber for the house came from my grandparents' house in Ivan. We had wooden shutters to cover the window openings. There was no running water in the house and we used an outhouse for many years. I can remember getting up in the morning and breaking ice on top of the water in the water bucket in the kitchen.

During World War II, Steve and Laura Simmons would pick up several of us boys and take us down to Camp Gordon Johnston, to sell newspapers. The German prisoners working in the Mess Hall would occasionally buy newspapers and offered me fruit and cake.

Every year in November, family and friends gathered at Uncle Riley Harvey and Aunt Clara's house at cane grinding time. This was a good time of fellowship and fun. We would sit around and drink cane juice. The adults would visit and gossip; the kids had a great time playing.

For those who are not familiar with cane grinding, the cane was ground to squeeze the juice into a big vat. As it was cooking, the men would use a big strainer scoop to skim off the impurities that came to the top. The skimmings were dumped into a big hole they had dug in the ground, called the "buck hole." The remains of the stalks were thrown in a pile called the pumming pile and we kids all enjoyed playing on the pumming pile.

One night, Uncle Riley warned us kids be careful to stay away from the buck hole. I started to ask him where it was, when I found it the hard way. I fell into it! After they pulled me out, they hosed me down, trying to get all the mess off of me, but it was so sticky, that it didn't come off very well. I rode to the cane grinding with my sister, Marjorie. When it was time to go home, I was so dirty she wouldn't let me ride inside her car. I ended up having to ride home in the trunk.

My father and mother are both buried in the Crawfordville Cemetery.

Submitted & Written by: Jimmy Raker, 11316 Cuckoo Dr., Leesburg, FL 34788

B.K. Roberts

Remembering Justice B. K. Roberts from Sopchoppy, FL

This story about Justice Roberts does not include his journey to the community of his birth and development but his notable journey from that community to the Supreme Court of Florida!

Born in the small, isolated village of Sopchoppy, Florida in south-western Wakulla County on February 5, 1907 to Thomas and Florida Roberts, B. K., given the unlikely name of Bonny Kaslo by his Scottish mother was a serious, determined student from his earliest years.

We see him pictured on the front row of the entire Sopchoppy School about 1914 and in another school picture he is shown wearing dark-rimmed glasses, a trait defining him in many pictures.

When B. K. was thirteen years of age, he completed the eight years of schooling then offered in Wakulla County. His parents, hard-working farmers, "got the pennies together" for him to ride the train from Sopchoppy to Carrabelle, 19 miles away, to take the state teacher exam qualifying him to teach in Wakulla County schools. He had a strong appetite for knowledge and at the age of sixteen, he went to the then all-male University of Florida in Gainesville with the grand total of $16 in his pocket!

Although he had a succession of jobs including busing tables in The University cafeteria, he soon found himself living in a pup tent where a group of fellow students came to him one morning advising him to drop out, saying he was "not college material and his clothes were embarrassing."

The incident was formative and enduring. He remained in college and for the rest of his life, B. K. Roberts presented a formal, scholarly demeanor while always pursuing education. He dressed impeccably, and suggested others do the same as witnessed by Tallahassee Attorney Dexter Douglas who told of his early law practice in 1955. He asked the Judge for advice on improving his career and as Douglas

related, "He told me to go to Turner's Dept. Store and buy myself two or three nice suits, keep my shoes shined and my hair cut. I've followed that advice ever since."

In 1928, B. K. graduated from the University of Florida and began practicing law in Tallahassee. He said he only knew five people in Tallahassee and he worked 16 to 18 hours a day, representing people who sought his services whether they could pay or not. The Great Depression was in progress but when the economy began to improve those people he had helped became ambassadors of good will for him and between 1935 and 1942 he built a healthy practice. He and Mary Newman were married in 1937 and became parents of two children, Mary Jane (Miller) and Thomas.

When war was declared in 1942, B. K. entered the U. S. Coast Guard, serving for three years as shipping commissioner at the Port of Jacksonville where he controlled the movement of more than six million tons of munitions and implements of war without a casualty or a strike.

Following the war, B. K. returned to Tallahassee and rebuilt his law practice enlarging to include four young lawyers and five secretaries. He instituted an unprecedented policy: one third of his clients were non-fee paying.

On July 7, 1949, Gov. Fuller Warren appointed him as a justice to the Supreme Court of Florida. In 1953, he was elected as Chief Justice where he served three terms in that position.

He created the Florida Judicial Council, which led to the Public Defender Act and in 1965-66, he served on the Florida Constitutional Revision Commission and spear-headed the creation of the Florida State University Law School where he is honored by the main building being named for him. The Law School was one of his two pet projects. The second project reflected his love for his native county. He set upon a course to have Wakulla Springs made into a wildlife foundation in an endowed perpetual trust so that its natural beauty and educational benefits would be available to all.

BK Roberts at 92

In 1977, Justice Roberts retired from the Supreme Court and in 1978, a volume containing 36 of his appellate opinions, more than anyone including

U. S. Supreme Court Justices, was published by *American Law Reports.* In 1990, he was honored as a Great Floridian and awarded the Distinguished-Service Medal of Florida.

August 4, 1999, Justice B. K. Roberts died at age 92 in Tallahassee, Florida, where he is buried. His life's journey was monumental!

Submitted By: Betty Green, PO Box 969, Crawfordville, FL 32326. Based on information published by the Tallahassee Democrat, August 6, 1999, compiled by Gerald Ensley and an earlier article by Martha Taschereau in Florida State Reports, November, 1974

May you Live Forever

Dorothy and Lsyle Holden of Sopchoppy 1983

Love is born in every soul,
And made to multiply,
God's love surrounds us all,
In the trees, the earth, the sky.
Who are we to ever complain,
Or feel the earth owes us one day,
Or to be the sinner of our choice
And place the wrath of evil on display?
God gave us all the things we have,
And only evil can take away
The gifts we've cherished all our lives,
And still enjoy day after day.
And now that we are growing old,
Our lives will richer be,
If we look back at the gifts of God,
In a land we helped keep free.
Freedom is not free,
But has a long enduring plight
Freedom comes only when you feel
You are free to do only what is right.
It's not your age
On which life depends,
It's the way you live your life
Among your friends.
So, thank God that you have lived
A life so rich and free,
And enjoyed the gifts of God and man,
In a land of liberty.

Submitted By: Betty Green, PO Box 969, Crawfordville, FL 32326. Written by: Lysle Holden, for the Senior Citizens of Sopchoppy - September 10,1983

"Memories of Mama"; A Tribute to Delma Raker Roberts by Her Children

"Her children arise up, and call her blessed." Proverbs 31:28

When we were little, Daddy would bring home little Baby Ruth candy bars for us kids and a big one for Mama. We would quickly eat ours and look at Mama; she would divide hers with us. She would always share with her kids.

When I was in the 7th grade at Crawfordville High School, I was in a play one night. I didn't have a pair of shoes to wear but Mama had a pair that looked like today's loafers, so I wore them!

At age 16 I joined the Merchant Marines and went to Liverpool, England, on the hospital ship Wisteria to pick up troops who were wounded in the invasion at Normandy, France. This was the only trip I made in the Merchant Marines, and it was also the only time I have ever been homesick. It was good to get back home, but shortly afterwards at age 17, I enlisted in the Navy. When it came time to re-enlist I wrote Mama that I was thinking about staying in. She wrote me back and said that it was my life, but she really wished I would come home, so I did!

When my first wife and I got a divorce in Texas, I called Mama and told her I had to get my son Gene through school. She said: "Come home, and I will help you" so we moved in with Mama in Sopchoppy and Gene graduated from Wakulla High School.

In 1974 when we were building a new house for Mama, my brother-in-law Huck, my brother Ed, and I met one Sunday morning at the house, and Mama wanted to know what we were doing. Ed told her that we were going to wire the house, and she said, "I wish you would not do that on Sunday." End of that workday! As kids growing up on the farm, Daddy wanted us to work on Sunday, but Mama said, "No!"

I never heard Mama say anything bad about anyone. What a wonderful Mother we had! I loved her and still miss her.

Submitted By Laveda Roberts Hodge Raker;

Mama's lot in life was not an easy one, but she never complained and always looked on the bright side. She trusted in her Lord to take care of her and her family in all circumstances.

Proverbs 17:22 was Mama's philosophy: "A merry heart doeth good like a medicine."

Proverbs 31:10, 26 says, "Who can find a virtuous woman for her price is far above rubies." "She openeth her mouth with wisdom and in her tongue is the law of kindness."

Mama taught her children to know right from wrong, and trusted us to abide by that teaching. Her trust meant everything to me. She only saw good in, and always spoke well of and loved, everyone. Even in the nursing home, to people she had never seen before, she would say, "I love you." And to her children she always said, "I love you, always have and always will."

Mama enjoyed her children and often joined in games with us, sometimes staying up late at night to play with us.

After I married and had children of my own, we always took her with us on vacation. One vacation that stands out in my mind is a two-week camping trip at what is now known as Roberts Landing. Mama and I both like to fish and one day just we two went fishing from the bank in an old "slough" not far from the camp. We had been told that we wouldn't catch anything, but we went anyway. Well, we filled our fish string 'til it wouldn't hold another fish, left the fish biting and had to carry the string between us, each holding an end. That was just one of the "fun highlights" of that vacation, and many others.

Mama has always been a wonderful, sweet and loving Mother, and I thank God for giving her to us. Proverbs 31:28 says, "Her children arise up and call her blessed."

Mama, I love you, always have, and always will.

Submitted By Richard Randolph Roberts (Eulogy delivered at Mama's funeral service);

Thank you, Mama, for always looking on the bright side of life no matter how hard the times, and for keeping a positive outlook and realizing things would turn out well.

Thank you, Mama, for the values you taught by your words and deeds – values such as honor and trust and to know right from wrong.

Thank you, Mama, for being our provider and our security. No job was too menial for her and all hard work was respectable.

Thank you, Mama, for teaching us to smile and face adversity with hope and dignity as you had done at the age of 15 when your parents died and you and your sisters were orphaned.

Thank you, Mama, for being such a wonderful storyteller as you so frequently gathered us at your knee and built those bonds of love that have sustained us through the years.

Thank you, Mama, for showing us daily the meaning of hard work as you cooked 40 biscuits on the old wood stove at 4:00 a.m. and then led us to the fields to help us plow the corn and hoe the peanuts from dawn to dusk.

Thank you, Mama, for teaching us that cleanliness is next to godliness" as you toiled over the old iron pot boiling our clothes and then rubbing them clean on the old scrub board until many times your fingers got so sore they bled.

Thank you, Mama, for always participating with us in all of our activities; whether playing childhood games or going fishing or even camping. You added meaning to our growing up.

And finally, thank you, Mama, for teaching us that Sunday is a special day and that we must not work nor profit on Sunday. All she had to say was, "I wish you wouldn't."

Yes, Mama, as Proverbs 31:28 says: "Your children arise up and call [you] blessed."

Submitted By Eddie Earl Roberts (Written when spending the night with Mama while she was hospitalized;:

It's not the hard times and difficult events in her life that I remember. It's the way she faced adversity, always with a smile, dignity, and a sense of knowing all things would work out for the best.

She told me of being 15 years old, the oldest of three girls, when her mother and father died and being raised by her Uncle and Aunt who kept her from being put in an orphanage. Her formal education ended after the 8th grade due to there being no high school in Wakulla County. She went back to school later in life, attaining 10th grade.

I remember as a small boy how pretty she was even in the old work clothes. And of the times she would play ball with us kids and how I would marvel that a lady as old as she was could even walk much less run. She was in her early forties!

I remember her being a great storyteller. She would read stories to us as we sat on the floor at her feet as close as we could get too scared to go to bed by ourselves!

I remember the biscuits she would cook every morning (about 40) in the wood stove, before going to the field to plow or hoe. And how the plow would get caught in a root and she would unhitch the horse and hook it to the back of the plow to pull it loose, then continue to plow until time to fix dinner. All the children old enough would help her any way we could.

I remember on wash days she would boil our clothes in a cast iron pot in the yard and scrub them on a scrub board and rinse them in a tub and hang them out to dry on the clothes line.

I remember how important it was that I did things to please her and not cause her any problems, not out of fear, but out of respect for her. I remember when I thought I was going fishing on a Sunday. All she said was, "Son, I wish you wouldn't fish on Sundays." Those fish got a reprieve that day! And the time Brother Bill and I were doing some electrical wiring on her new house on a Sunday, and got caught by Mama. All she said was, "Boys, I wish you wouldn't work on Sundays." Bill said, "Ed, we will do this tomorrow."

I remember when she bought her first house with money she earned working at Sopchoppy School. And later, how proud she was when her children built her the only new house she ever owned and which she enjoyed until she entered the nursing home.

Mama had a hard and difficult life in raising nine children, but not once have I ever heard her complain. I never heard her say anything bad to or about any person. To me, she was the greatest person I have ever known, and everything I am or hope to be is due to the love she had for me. I will always remember Mama as that small boy did some fifty years ago as a pretty young lady who grew old and more beautiful, but never changed her values, love and devotion for her children, which was exceeded only by her love and devotion to her Lord.

Submitted By Callie Roberts Colvin Quigg;

I have a lot of precious memories of Mama, and I'm so thankful they can't be taken away from me. Following are just a few of those memories and thoughts I want to share.

God must have looked down through the pages of time and had my Mama in mind when He inspired the writing of the Book of Proverbs for she truly was a Proverbs mother!

Mama was my provider and security. "She looketh well to the ways of her household, and eateth not the bread of idleness." *(Proverbs 31:27)* She did all kinds of work to earn money for us to live on. No job was too menial as long as it was respectable. I remember, when I was in elementary school, Mama even washed the school's football uniforms which brought in about 25 cents per item of clothing, all done on a "ringer" washing machine!

Many, many times over the years I've heard her say that even though she had 9 children, she never had one to give away! Never did I worry that Mama would abandon or abuse me!

She was my sustainer. "She riseth also while it is yet night and giveth meat to her household." *(Proverbs 31:15)* Mama always made sure I had nourishment. At times when I thought there was no food in the house, miraculously Mama always found something to cook for us to eat. Even though it might be just grits and tomato gravy, it satisfied my hunger. And one thing for sure, she always saw to it that I ate a hearty breakfast before sending me off to school each day. Not until later years after I had married did I learn that my breakfast of tomato gravy, grits, and an over-light egg, all mixed together, made Mama gag at the sight of it! Only a Mother's deep love, devotion and patience would endure that in silence for years and years.

She was my strengthener. "She girdeth her loins with strength and strengtheneth her arms. Strength and honour are her clothing." *(Proverbs 31:17, 25)* Mama was an endless source of strength and energy. I know there were times when she felt bad or grew weary, but she never complained about not feeling well or being tired. Like the energizer rabbit, Mama just kept "going and going."

Even years later after I was married, Mama was still my source of strength. Before and after my first husband's death in 1969, Mama was the one I depended on. I called on her to come spend one night with me and my two babies until I could make some decisions on how to care for my sick husband and for them. Mama not only came for that one night, she ended up staying with me for the next three years! She took care of my son and daughter while I worked to provide for them. Even though Mama had just retired from working in the Sopchoppy High School's lunchroom and should have been enjoying her own leisure time, she never once complained about her sacrifice for me.

She was a Godly woman with a big loving heart, and she gave me a wonderful heritage. "She openeth her mouth with wisdom; and in her tongue is the law of kindness. Her children arise up, and call her blessed." *(Proverbs 31:26, 28)* Mama never spoke unkindly about anyone. Not only did she love her children, she loved everyone and didn't fail to let them know it. I can still hear her exact words: "I love you, always have, and always will!"

When I was a child, Mama didn't send me to church; she went with me. How vividly I remember our walking to church, over a mile one way! And as we walked, we would search the Scriptures, and I would memorize a Bible verse to share during Sunday morning worship. Mama not only professed to be a Christian, she lived it. She truly realized that her joy and strength came from the Lord, not from her circumstances. Her faith and devotion to God and to her family have made a difference in my own life, giving me values I can carry with me for the rest of my days. My prayer is that I can be half the Mother my Mama was.

The following poem, written by me, was read at Mama's home going service on September 27, 1996.

"Mama's Love"

Most mothers' love is so precious
And my Mama's love was no exception.
No matter who you were,
She always showed kindness, love and affection.

There never was a time in my life
When I doubted Mama loved me.
Through many good and hard times
She always provided and gave unselfishly.

Mama had many wonderful attributes
And caring for others was only one.
She also loved the Lord with all her heart
And trusted in Him for her life's race to run.

I've seen her kneel by her bed at night
And call out her children's names in prayer.
Oh, how precious my Mama was
And wonderful her love and care.

I know Mama's in a better place
Where she has often longed to be.
And one day when my life is over,
Once again, my Mama I will see.

Submitted By Callie Roberts Colvin Quigg:60 Mathers Farm road, Crawfordville, #L 32327

Thelma Gladys Roberts Sanders

Nathaniel Walker I and Gladys Thelma Roberts Sanders

Gladys was born on December 26, 1899. Her parents were Martha Louise Sunday Roberts and William Thomas Roberts of Curtis Mills. Her maternal grandparents were Mollie Roberts Sunday and Jim Sunday. They lived at Huckleberry Creek near Apalachicola, Florida. When Gladys was born her parents were living in Franklin County, between Crooked River and Womack Creek. It was a small settlement without a name. The town nearest to them where they went to the store and got their mail was called McEntyre.

When Gladys was six years old, they moved from there to the banks of Cow Creek. They lived in a three room house. Back then everybody used the living room as a bedroom too. Gladys was the elder of six children.

When Gladys was seven years old she started to school in Curtis Mills. This was the first year the school was built in 1907. The school was also used as a church. The school was moved years later, and is now located at the

Sopchoppy City Park. Gladys walked four miles round trip to school. She said, "Back then, it didn't bother us, we used to walk all the time." Gladys wore her dresses to her knees and wore cotton stockings. She carried her lunch in a tin bucket. Some of her teachers were Ethel Willis, Annie Braswell, Annette Allen, May Coggins, Mattle L. Willis, Viola Revell, Mahaley Brown, Betty Funderburk. Edith Helms, and Clarice McKenzie.

Gladys's mother played an accordion. Her mother's sister, Bashiba Sunday Sanders, who was married to Andrew Sanders, played the harp real good. Bashiba was a good actress in school plays too. That is where her son Clarence Sanders and his children got all their musical talent.

Gladys had several boyfriends. Their dates consisted of going to church and walking the roads. Nat Sanders walked her home for the first time when she was 16 years old. The Goodman boys used to write her notes in church all the time asking her to marry them. She always told them no. One day in church, Nat wrote her a note and asked her to marry him, he said he was not like those Goodman boys, he really meant it. She wrote him a note back and told him, Yes, that she cared more about him than anybody else, and she would marry him. This was before Nat went to the war in 1917. He came back from the war in 1919. They were married on January 16, 1920, at the court house in Apalachicola, by the Judge.

Back then people did not give each other wedding showers and she didn't have a hope chest either. Her mother-in-law, Mary Jane Sanders, gave Gladys a rooster and a hen. She told them if they always kept chickens, they would never go hungry. *Grandma Gladys gave me this information in a tape recorded conversation. In the background you can hear baby chicks chirping.*

Gladys stayed busy having babies and trying to take care of them. She never had time to be bored or very lonesome, she was to busy washing up the clothes, (usually took two full days a week), cooking (on a wood stove), cleaning and raising kids.

Gladys and Nat had eleven children. One little boy was born dead and one little girl Dorothy Mae died when she was five months old. Their children are: Mildred Sanders married Griffin Willis, Marjorie Sanders married Rev. Floyd Gray, Madelyn Sanders married Oscar Crowson, Marcia Inez Sanders married Willard Raker and then Henry Vause, Nathaniel Sanders Jr. married Tillie Thompson, Mahaley Ruth Sanders married J.W. Hurley and then James Smith, Bobby Sanders married Juanita Uffer and then Jane Williams, Janelle Sanders married Johnny Gray and then Jerry Crawford, and Donna Gail Sanders married Odell Dees.

The following "A Tribute To Grandma" was written by another granddaughter, Brenda Crowson Wilson.

I remember when we were growing up how much we loved going to "Grandma's house." You've heard the old saying, "Children should be seen and not heard", not at Grandma's house. Children came first with Grandma and Granddaddy. There was always something delicious on the stove and Granddaddy always managed to find a bag of candy.

There were always interesting things to see and do at Grandma's house, whether it was a new litter of calico kittens in the rag box under Grandma's feather bed or a box of fuzzy yellow biddies hatching out in the kitchen.

Grandma's chickens were near and dear to her heart. What a treat it was to go to the chicken yard and scatter scratch fed and collect chicken eggs. Now Granddaddy loved his hunting dogs but didn't share her love for chickens and cats. In fact, when the chickens would get into the garden, Granddaddy would sometimes threaten to shoot them. And even though Grandma loved Granddaddy better than anything in the world, that's when she would put her foot down. She was very protective of her chickens.

When she was in her late eighties, she still had her chicken yard. One evening about dusk dark, she took her walking stick and went out to the pen to check on her biddies. When she got there, there was no sign of them. All she saw was the paste board box they had been hatched in. She thought they might be hiding in the box so she reached down and picked up the box. When she did, all of a sudden a big rattlesnake slid out of the box on the ground with a biddy in his mouth. Grandma, without a second thought, whacked that snake over the head with her walking stick until he was dead. She was very protective of her chickens.

Oh, how we loved to spend the night with Grandma and Granddaddy. Not only did we get spoiled and petted, we could just about do anything we wanted as long as we didn't hurt ourselves or someone else. I remember waking up early in the morning with the smell of freshly perked coffee and frying bacon drifting from the kitchen. Grandma would be half humming, half whistling and old hymn as she cooked breakfast for the men who were getting ready to go hunting. In their deep voices, I could hear them talk about the deer hunt as they sat around the kitchen table drinking coffee. I remember laying in bed looking at the rough brown rafters as the shadows played over them from the yellow light in the kitchen. As those comforting blends of smells and sounds enveloped me, I would snuggle down into that warm feather bed and drift back into the blissful, secure sleep of childhood.

Thank you Grandma for all those wonderful memories, for your love, and most of all for the spiritual heritage you passed on to us. You taught us by example, to love God, to love our families, and to be thankful for our blessings. Thank you for the times when we came to you licking our wounds and complaining about the unfairness of life and you gently but firmly refused to join in our pity party. Instead, you showed us how to pick up the pieces and rebuild. Thank you for loving us when we were right and when we were wrong. Thank you for showing us that we can overcome every obstacle through faith in Jesus Christ. Grandma you have overcome this last obstacle with a victorious homecoming and that is the greatest example of all. Well done, good and faithful servant and wonderful grandmother.

Grandma Gladys died on December 10, 1997 at the age of 98, and is buried in the Sanders Cemetery in Curtis Mills, Florida. She will live forever in our hearts.

Submitted and written by, Louise Thomas and Brenda Wilson; 419 Buckhorn Creek Road, Sopchoppy, FL 32358-1609

Memories Of My Parents Calvin C. and Bertie L. Scarbrough

I am Clarice Scarbrough Wilks, the oldest of their five children. The other children are: Kenneth (deceased), Theresa Moore, John Calvin and Claudette Vaughan. Even though we live in Leon County, we have many ties to Wakulla County.

My parents met in 1923 when my Dad drove a delegation of members from the Beulah Primitive Baptist Association to Corinth Church in Holmes County, FL, which is near Ponce de Leon, FL, to attend the West Florida Primitive Baptist Association of which Mom was a member. She was the daughter of Rev. Manulous Carroll and Nancy Carroll of Westville, FL. It was LOVE at first sight and after two months of correspondence they were married on December 16, 1923 and came to make Leon County their home. Their marriage lasted 56 years, the Lord called Dad home July 2, 1979

The Beulah Primitive Baptist Association and the West Florida Primitive Baptist Association enjoyed a close relationship in the work of our Lord. In addition to my Grandfather Carroll being a Primitive Baptist preacher, three of his sons were called into the ministry and preached revivals in many of the Wakulla Primitive Baptist Churches. They were Noah Carroll, Lloyd Carroll and Elzie Carroll, all of Pensacola, FL.

My Dad was a carpenter by trade and built many homes in Leon and Wakulla County before going to work for Jack Simmons, he was hired as a Mill Wright at Elberto Crate and Box Company, but Mr. Simmons had other jobs for him to do including building a Mill in Cottondale, FL and one in Sumatra, FL and a Lodge for his family's use in Leon County and in 1941 he built another Lodge and Marina at Old Field on Ochlocknee Bay near Panacea, FL.

Bro. Emmett Whaley and my husband to be at that time, Malcolm Wilks, whom had just gotten out of the CCC Camp at Helen on Springhill Road, were hired by Dad as helpers. Since that time, every time we had the pleasure to be with Bro. Whaley, up until the time of my husband's death on December 16, 2002, Bro. Whaley would say, "Bro. Malcolm, I bet there are no other two men living who built a Marina with picks and shovels like we did." He never forgot it. Bro. Whaley also brought this out at Malcolm's funeral service that we were honored to have him preach.

It was about this same time period (1940) that Dad surrendered to the calling to preach the gospel. I'm sure Dad did a lot of practice preaching on this work crew. It was soon afterwards that Bro. Whaley was called to the Ministry and Dad had the pleasure of helping to ordain him. Dad and Bro. Whaley remained very close friends and worked together in the Ministry until Dad's death.

Dad served as Pastor of several Wakulla County Churches including: Friendship, Beulah, New Home, Spring Creek and Whiddon Lake.

Malcolm and I were married in 1942 and I don't remember attending many of the services in Wakulla County Churches with my parents, but I do remember Mom and Dad talking about the wonderful people in his churches. Dad was not a salaried preacher, but was given a free-will offering and the members were very generous with their home grown vegetables, meats, fish and eggs. Mom and the children who were still at home always went with Dad and because of the distance to travel on dirt roads (there were no paved roads) they would be welcomed in a member's home to spend the night after a night service or during revival services. Of course, they always were welcome to have dinner and sometimes supper in a member's home.

In addition to Dad's Pastorship in Wakulla County Churches, he also served as Pastor to White Primitive Baptist Church in Woodville, FL and New Hope Primitive Baptist Church, Springhill Road, in Leon County. Dad conducted many funeral services and married many couples in Wakulla & Leon County.

Mom never worked outside the home, but she was a helpmate to Dad and was a fine example of what a Preacher's wife should be. Mom was a good seamstress and made most of the clothes worn by her children. I remember Mom making skirts and dresses from printed feed sacks. I proudly wore them to school and no one ever knew I was wearing feed sacks.

Mom went to her heavenly home on September 2, 1998.

We have many friends in Wakulla County and Malcolm and I were fortunate enough to own a vacation (fishing) home on Ochlocknee River in Wakulla County. Our granddaughter, Kim Tucker, and three great-granddaughters, Locklyn, Blair and Tatum, reside in Wakulla County. Their Dad, Delwyn Tucker is the son of the late Carlton and Louise White Tucker, also from Wakulla County. Locklyn graduated from Wakulla High in 2008, Blair graduated from Wakulla High in 2011 and Tatum is in the 7th grade at Wakulla Middle School. We love Wakulla County.

Submitted By: Clarice Scarbrough Wilks, 7000 Springhill Rd, Tallahassee, FL 32305

Forrest and Roy Simmons

Forrest and Roy Simmons were important members of the community here in the 1940s. Roy & his wife Forrest worked for Gladys Griener Moore Adams. Gladys ran a restaurant in Crawfordville. This would have been difficult to do without the help of the Simmons couple.

Forrest helped cook and run the kitchen. She is shown here in the restaurant garden behind the store in Crawfordville in July of 1942.

Roy was like a prep cook, cleaning vegetables and doing background work. He was also the general handyman when needed. Roy is shown here with Jean Moore Dykes in the yard at the home of Gladys Adams.

Helen Adams Strickland, the daughter of Gladys Griener Moore Adams heard her mother speak fondly of this couple frequently.

Submitted by: Helen Adams Strckland. Story as told to Terri Gerrell

"My Pappa; Ralph Lowell Strickland"

A man of many great qualities! A husband, father, grandfather. A man of God, good character, upstanding citizen, survivor, hard worker, & a great since of humor. The list could go on & on. A man to be admired to say the least, & as my Pappa; I highly admired him.

Born September 5, 1910 - as a young man he attended school in the one room school house located where the present 7th precinct voting house is now. He helped his family with farming & continued to farm in his older years after retirement. I remember as a little girl, we used to pick peas in the gardens of our family field & sit on the front porch shelling them; then we'd load up the old green truck with the shells & take them back to the field to throw out to the cows.

He met my mamma as they both lived in the close knit community of Ivan & both their families were farmers. March 10, 1934, he became a husband to my mamma, Alma Green, & they were married for 50 amazing years. Together they had 6 children. Durwood Strickland, Imogene Whaley, Rod Strickland, Phyllis Lynn, Lila Strickland, & Larry Strickland. They were the grandparents to 12 grandchildren, myself being the youngest.

In the Great Depression, Pappa worked in during the WPA days helping to build bridges, railroads, & camps, one being Camp Gordon Johnson. At the age of 35 on June 8, 1949; he lost his right leg in a tractor accident while working for Mr. A.T. Raker cutting timber. Even though he only had one leg, I never knew my Pappa to be

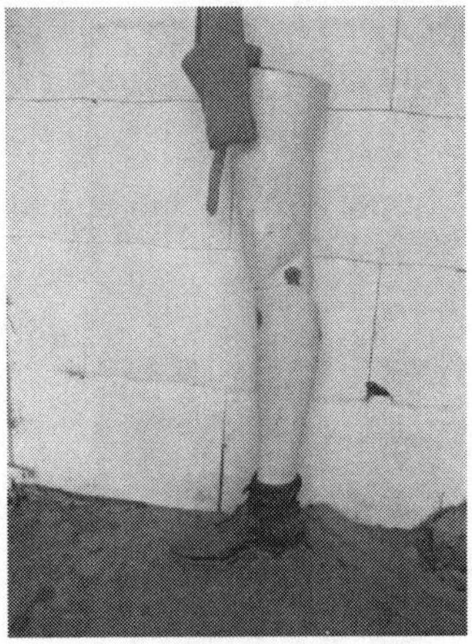

Layla McMillan and Ralph Strickland

handicapped. He could still pull fence line & hop a ladder to lay shingles on the roof. He had an old wooden leg that he never wore because he said, "It hurts my toes". He walked with his crutches.

After losing his leg, he did bookwork for "Tucker & Sons" for 15 years. 12 of those 15 years, he was county commissioner. That's two terms, for those who don't know. As a commissioner, he was one to vote on expanding our Wakulla County Extension Office for community services, such as the swine shows. From "Tucker & Sons", he went to work for Sunland Hospital where he painted & did general maintenance. From there, he went to work for Mr. Jewell Hudson planting pines & working with Mr. Henry Vause building houses in Hudson Heights. After that, he worked with the county road & bridge department, from which he retired. While working there, he was the one who got them to put the side trenches on the dirt roads so the water could run off.

After retirement, he went back to farming & enjoying his time as a pappa. His old green truck & the old tractor are still in the family & running today. He was my Pappa; Ralph Lowell Strickland.

Submitted by: 508-2742, Layla McMillan, 606 Whiddon Lake Rd, Crawfordville, FL 32327

Wakulla County Historical Society Founded 1991
•Collect
•Interpret
•Preserve
•Exhibit
1949-72
"Old Wakulla County Jail"

Smith's & Bradshaw's; Life at Spring Creek Florida; 1930s, 40s and 50s

Toilet Tissue Was A Luxury

"We went full circle, from eating indoors and going outdoors to the outhouse, to eating outdoors and going indoors to the bathroom." Dennis C. J. Smith is the fifth child born to William C. (Bill) and Hazel J. (Bradshaw) Smith. Bill Smith was born near Wright's Creek in northern Holmes County, Florida and Hazel (Bradshaw) Smith was born in Telogia, Florida. They met and married in Fort Myers, Florida and, after a hurricane completely destroyed their home there in 1928, they settled in Spring Creek, Florida. Hazel lived to be 84, and Bill died at 96 years of age.

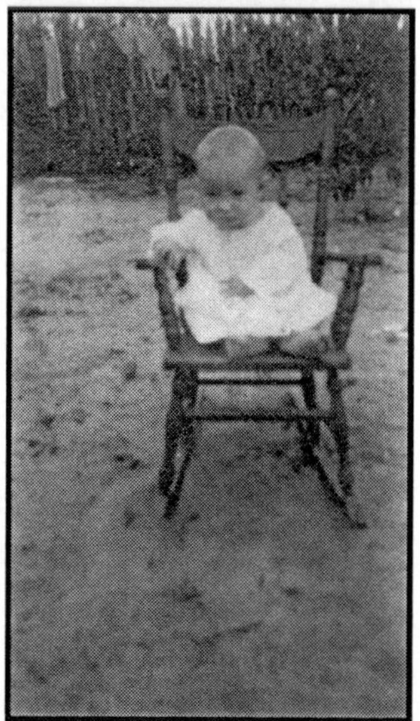

Dennis C. J. Smith

They had 12 children, seven of whom are still living. They raised four boys and six girls to adulthood. One son died from a fever when he was only a few months old and one girl was stillborn.

This article is compiled from over seventy years of memories. Dates, ages, and spelling of names may not be 100 percent correct. The country was recovering from the Great Depression and was at war (WWII and Korean) during my early years in Wakulla County. Many foods were rationed and each family was issued a ration card. Much of the food went to the war effort. None of my relatives had a telephone and only a few owned radios. Newspapers and radios were our only source of information about the war and that was several weeks old before we received it. We had no electricity until I was about ten years old. I remember friends and relatives walking to our house on Saturday nights to hear the Grand Ole Opry on a battery radio. The battery was almost as large as the radio and to preserve the battery, we only played the radio for special programs like news and The Opry. Also, we had so many chores to do we didn't have much time to listen to the radio.

Most of the residents of Spring Creek farmed, worked in the seafood industry, or both. My grandfather, Isham Bradshaw, was a farmer and also worked in the turpentine business. Isham had a female donkey called a Jenny to help till the fields. One day he was plowing with the little Jenny when he needed to back her up a few feet, but no matter what Granddad did, she would not go into reverse. So he walked around and bit her right on the nose to get her attention. After that, she gave him no more problems. My mother said one time her father sent some of the kids to the field to plant cottonseed. They came across a large rotten stump and they were tired, so they poured some of the seed in the cavity of the stump and covered the seed with sand. Weeks later, she and the other kids were at home when their dad walked in. He had found the sprouted seed and spliced several of the plants together. They knew what was coming, so they lined up for their punish-ment.

In 1920, Isham and Nancy (Nanny) Bradshaw bought about fifty acres of land near the intersection of the Spring Creek and Shell Point highways. Tragically, later that year Isham died just a few days before Thanksgiving. Then, less than five weeks afterwards, Mom's oldest brother, Judd and his close friend, Willie Womack, went hunting on Christmas Day, not long after Judd turned 20 years old. When they had returned home and were unloading their guns, someone called Willie's name and as he turned, his gun fired accidentally and the pellets hit Judd in the chest. As Judd was dying, he said, "Willie, you shot me but it was an accident." Willie moved away after that, and no one knew where he went. About twenty years later, Willie and his wife walked into the Fish House at West Goose Creek where we were working. He visited for a little while, then left and was never heard from again by any of the Bradshaw family.

Isham Bradshaw

Isham Bradshaw (far right) and first Spring Creek Grocery Store

Jud & C.K. Bradshaw

Mullet Fishing

A few years later, Nanny moved the family south to Ft. Myers where, in 1928, a hurricane destroyed their home, causing the family to have to return to the property in Wakulla county. Mom and Grandma had gone to a shelter before the storm, but Dad decided to stay at the house. When he saw the house could not withstand the wind, he started working his way to the front porch, dived into the yard and grabbed onto some clumps of grass. He looked up in time to see a car rolling toward him. It came right up to him and stopped just short of crushing him.

Our family worked a twelve acre farm in the summer and harvested seafood during the winter. We raised corn, velvet beans and chufas to feed the animals, and vegetables to feed the family. When I was a baby, Mom said she'd lay me on a quilt under a tree nearby while she worked in the field, and we kids spent many hours playing under a quilting frame while our grandmothers, mothers and aunts spent time together sewing colorful quilts by hand for their families.

Jud and C.K. Bradshaw

For meat, we raised cows, hogs, turkeys, chickens, rabbits, ducks and guineas. We worked the seine yards at West Goose Creek and Shell Point, getting three cents a pound for the mullet we caught. One special day we caught 22,000 pounds of mullet. It was my job to hold the lead line of the seine on the ground while the seine was being pulled ashore. I was too small and lightweight to stand with my foot on the lead line, so I had to get down on my hands and knees in the icy waters and hold the line with both hands. Ever had a mullet hit your ankle at full speed, or a stingray bounce off your foot? We picked up the mullet, washed the sand off of them, and iced them down to have them ready to load on the truck the next morning. We couldn't afford boots or slicker suits to keep our clothes dry, so we kept a bonfire going to help dry our clothes and keep us warm. Most of the fish were sold to restaurants and retail seafood businesses in north Florida and south Georgia. Mr. George Nesmith leased the West Goose Creek seine yard from the government. Dalton and Brother Raker oversaw the operation and hauled the fish to the markets.

Mullet Fishing

Dad and I were gathering oysters one day with Aunt Amy and Uncle Ade Trull when Lamar Braswell, known as the hermit of Shell Point, approached us and said he needed a hand. He'd stopped Walker Creek with a net and penned in more mullet than he could handle. We had two boats and Lamar had two boats and two nets, so my Dad and Uncle Ade went with Lamar to 'boat' the mullet, while Aunt Amy and I continued to collect oysters. When stopping a creek the fisherman would string one net across the creek at high tide then wait for the tide to fall. The second net was used to drag the deep holes and put the mullet on the bank. As the tide rose and the boat could be maneuvered in the shallow water, the fish were loaded in the boat. When we finished, we had four boats loaded to capacity with mullet and oysters, and a very good payday. We picked up oysters in the winter for $1.50 a bushel. During the summer we used #2 wash tubs to gather plentiful scallops when they were in season. On one of our trips, we were motoring in shallow water when a shark about six feet long surfaced within a few feet of our boat, made a 180 degree turn, and disappeared. A while after that, Aunt Amy had waded further out, using her large apron to hold more scallops before she headed back to dump them in the tub. We heard a loud scream and looked up just in time to see her scattering all her scallops into the water. A scallop had pinched her through the apron, and she thought the shark had come back for her. It reminded me of the time my Aunt Juddy caught one of her boobs in the washing machine wringer.

Lamar Braswell was a native of Wakulla County and lived most of his life here, except

Waiting On Sunrise And Mullet

for the short time he worked in Jacksonville. He carried only what belongings he could fit in a fourteen foot boat with his fish net and a pair of oars. He led a quiet solitary existence and slept on the beach wherever nightfall might find him. He had no family in the area that I am aware of. He'd catch a load of fish and sell them to one of the fish camps. If someone he knew happened to be at the camp, he'd give them a pan full of mullet. He bought enough groceries to last several days, then he'd go up one of the creeks until his food ran out. He had no need for money except for food, or maintenance on his boat and net. He never went to town or shopped for clothes. Friends he'd see at the fish camps often gave him some clean clothes. Not long after he became a hermit, a cyst began growing on his wrist. My Aunt Amy and Uncle Ade thought it was cancer. They took him to their house, cleaned him up and got him some medical attention. He began attending church and after a few weeks, the cyst dried up and fell off leaving only a slight scar. Lamar returned once more to the life he loved, living on the bays of Wakulla County for many more years. One winter's morning at Stuart Cove I found Lamar asleep on the ground, curled up around a lantern for warmth. He had nothing on but a slicker suit, and during the night his head had rolled against the lantern globe, raising a large blister on his forehead. That old man probably knew the habits of mullet better than any other fisherman in the area. One day, he and I were standing on the shore at West Goose Creek when a small school of mullet approached, and Lamar said, "Look at that school of mullet. There should be about forty-five of them." He struck the mullet with his net and I think he caught forty-three fish. He figured the other two went through or under the net. He liked his coffee strong and black and brewed it over a small fire in a pot. Lamar was a familiar sight until his death at 73, and was well known by the local people and many tourists who frequented the area.

Some years later, while serving in the United States Air Force, I spent a year, seventeen days, and three hours on the northern part of the Greenland Ice Cap. Temperatures ranged from 35 degrees above down to 45 degrees below zero with chill factors reaching 90 to 100 degrees below zero, and winds of 150

Wild Boar Tusks

miles per hour. However, the closest I ever came to freezing to death was working on an oyster bar at Grass Inlet. I'd gotten wet and was so cold I had to go ashore, wrap myself in burlap bags and lay down in some tall grass so the sun could shine on me. When I thawed out enough, I went back to the oyster bar. The money I made that day was used to buy my school clothes.

Cattle farmers hauled truckloads of cattle into the Spring Creek area and turned them loose to graze on the open land. Usually, once a year, the cattle farmers would bring in a load of quarter horses and hire the local men to round up the cattle. They ran the cattle through a tick dip, hauled some to the market and left some behind as breeding stock. The riders were not accustomed to riding horses that made sudden turns and stops, so the men usually got bruised up from being hit by tree limbs or thrown from their horses. A schoolmate of mine was in an accident late one night when he ran into a group of these cattle lying in the roadway. He killed five cows and totaled his vehicle.

Wild hogs, known as "piney woods rooters" were plentiful and played a key role in the survival of my family. Each hog farmer had their own earmark, registered at the courthouse, so they could mark their hogs and release them in the woods to eat acorns and other foodstuff provided by nature. When we wanted a hog to butcher or sell, we used a trap to catch it, but most of the time we took a dog with us to catch the hog and hold it until we could tie it up. Hog buyers would stop by our house about once a month and give $5-15 per hog depending on size. Some hogs were very poor and we fed them corn for a few weeks to fatten them up before we sold them. We released some as breeding stock into the wild to fend for themselves. Every few days we went back to the area we released the hogs and scatter some corn on the ground. The hogs tended to stay there rather than roaming and scattering to other areas. Sometimes this custom led to cases of hog stealing. My Dad took a poacher to court one time, but wasn't able to prove his claim. On one of our hog hunting trips, Dad and I had walked about a mile from our truck when our dog Butch caught a wild boar with long tusks that weighed more than I did. When Dad reached into his pocket for string to tie the hog with, he realized that he had left the string in the car. We pulled the hog underneath a tree that I could easily climb if I had to. He instructed me to hold the hog by the back legs, and to keep him on his back so he couldn't use his front feet to dig into the ground and pull away from me. Dad left Butch with me for protection should I lose my grip on the hog, until I could climb the tree. I was able to hold the back legs, but I just couldn't hold them still. The hog kept jerking his back feet back and forth,

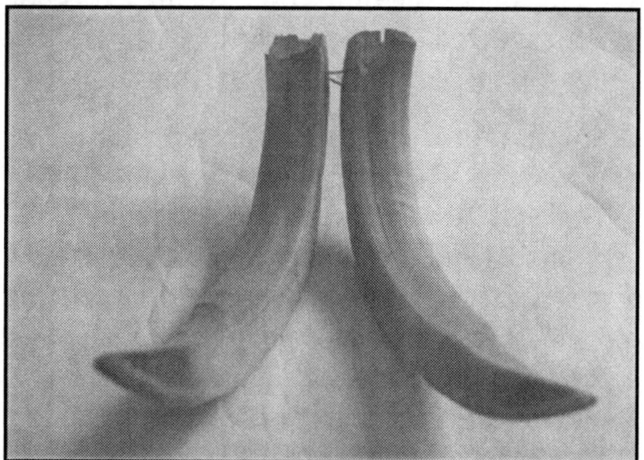

Wild Boar Tusks

rubbing my knuckles together. When Dad returned a half hour later with the string, I was still holding the hog, but my knuckles were skinned up and bleeding, We did not want a $15.00 hog to get away from us. I was about thirteen years of age at that time. To this day, I still have two sets of wild boar tusks hanging on our fireplace. Since our property adjoined the wildlife refuge, we could see hogs feeding just across the fence from our house. One night, Dad and Butch went into the refuge and caught a pig that weighed a good hundred pounds. Dad tied it up with some string and lifted it up over the fence. But when he put his foot into the fence to climb over, he stuck his foot straight into the hog's mouth. There he is on one side of the fence with the hog on the other side chomping down on his foot. He finally freed his foot and penned up the hog, but his foot swelled so bad it was difficult for him to get his shoe on for several days.

While in our front yard one afternoon we saw a huge rattlesnake coming toward us out of the refuge. Mom grabbed a long stick to kill it with, but the snake never coiled up, it just raised its head higher off the ground and kept coming. When the snake decided it was time to escape back into the woods, Mom went after it to make sure it was dead.

A "hot bath" for us was a #2 washtub full of water that had been sitting in the sun for a couple of hours. However, we had to keep an eye on the tub while the water was warming to keep the ducks out of it. If the weather was not too cold, we could take a shower with rain water running off the roof of the house.

A "rolling" grocery store stopped by our house once a week. That is how we were introduced to Hadacol. It was marketed as a vitamin supplement and it was very popular in the dry southern states because it contained 12 percent alcohol. The Watkins Company came by selling non-prescription drugs. Watkins Liniment was very popular at that time and is still on the market, although some of the ingredients may have changed over the years. Cloverine Salve was also popular. A person could order a case of it and sell the individual tins for a share of the profit. Fruits, vegetables and fresh fish were sold house to house, when in season. James Nazareth drove the ice truck and delivered a block of ice to our house every couple of days. He would load the ice on the truck in Crawfordville. In the summertime, a fifty pound block of ice may only weigh forty or forty-five pounds by the time it arrived at our house. James had red hair and he was accused of being the father of every red-haired baby born on his route.

Willard K. Durrance, the insurance salesman stopped by our house weekly to collect our insurance premiums. We did not have a checking account and three cent postage stamps were too expensive. Before I left home to begin my military career some fifty-five years ago, Mom bought a $250.00 burial insurance policy on me. The premiums are twelve cents a week and I am still paying premiums on that policy. When I die, I will need to add a few dollars to the policy to cover the burial expenses. The policy is with the Western and Southern Life Insurance Company. One day, Willard stopped by and told us that he had just saved a woman's life. She had waded out into a pond and was fishing with a cane pole. As Willard was driving by, he saw the woman desperately trying to get out of the water and an alligator was gaining on her. He shot the alligator with a pistol and the lady was able to escape.

In a similar incident, I was squirrel hunting with my dog along the shore of Long Pond when an alligator spotted my dog and started chasing it. The dog ran to me for help and just as the gator was approaching the shore, I realized the gator was dead-set on having my dog for lunch. I shot the gator with a 12 gauge shotgun, using number eight shot, and the gator disappeared under the water. When my dad came home from work that afternoon, I explained all the events to him and told him I thought I had killed the gator but couldn't find him. He assured me that I had not killed that gator. That night, Dad, Uncle Ade and I took his boat and a carbide light to the pond. We had only paddled a few yards when we saw the eyes of the gator. As we got closer to it, Uncle Ade shot the gator with a 22-caliber rifle and it bellied up and started churning up the water. Dad told me to grab the gator by the hind leg and pull it up on the side of the boat. I was hesitant at first, but finally grabbed the leg and pulled the gator out of the water enough that Dad cut the gator's backbone into with a hatchet and the fight was over. The gator was seven feet long and we sold the hide for $2.25 a foot. That bought enough groceries to feed us and Uncle Ade's family for a week.

Uncle Bryce & Aunt Lorlie Vickers

A gentleman by the name of Wade H. Swilley owned an acre of land with a grist mill on it. His property joined the St Marks Refuge on one side and my grandparents' property on three sides. Mr. Swilley had no family in that area. He asked my parents to bury him in the grist mill when he died. My parents knew the mill would rot and fall-down one day, so they buried him on what they thought was his land. After his death on March 2, 1925, my parents bought the acre of land for the taxes owed on it which I understand was less than three dollars. When they surveyed the land, my parents discovered that they had buried him on my grandparents' property. Many years later, Mom and I were in our front yard about a hundred yards from the grave when we saw what looked like a large ball of fire rise from the grave and slowly travel just above tree-top level over the wildlife refuge and settled out of sight behind the trees. In a few moments, it rose up above the trees and traveled back to the grave. The fireball made several of these trips before it settled on the grave and disappeared. Mom thought Mr. Swilley's spirit had returned to haunt her family for not burying him in his grist mill.

My Great-Uncle Bryce and Aunt Lovie Vickers lived near my grandmother. Their daughter Lottie Mae, husband George Baker and son Talmadge also lived close by. According to Lottie Mae, one day George picked up his rusty old shotgun and walked down to a nearby pond. She heard a gunshot but thought nothing about it. When he did not return to the house, she went to investigate. She found him dead from a gunshot wound to the head. She never knew if his death was an accident or suicide.

Ade Trull and Parents

Nanny Bradshaw babysat Talmadge while Aunt Lovie and Lottie walked five miles one way to work in the sewing factory in Crawfordville. On the way home, Lottie would jog so she would have more daylight time to spend with Talmadge before he went to sleep for the night. They'd buy small amounts of groceries from Mr. Roy Rehwinkel's store, and put them in two separate bags, making it easier to carry them. When the school bus driver, Rob Green, stopped to pick up the kids, Aunt Lovie would bag up any excess vegetables she had from her garden and ask

Mr. Green to drop them off to families in need when he picked up their kids. Occasionally, the Vickers family, friends and neighbors took a net and dragged it across Long Pond. Then everyone enjoyed a fish-fry on the banks of the pond.

Aunt Amy and Uncle Ade owned the property around Long Pond and for years there was no fish in the pond. Dad was walking by the pond one day with a string of fish he had caught nearby, and on a whim he just dumped the fish in the water. After few years, he decided to see how well his idea had worked and was surprised when he made a great catch of warmouth. After that, we frequently took our cane poles to the pond and always went home with a fine mess of fish. Aunt Amy grew curious about the fish and asked where we caught them. We knew she would drag the pond with a net, so we told her we caught them in the "Molly Hole." This went on for some time and one day when I stopped in for a visit she told me she had figured out that we were catching the fish in Long Pond, which was on her property. She told me to get some earthworms and take her fishing with me, so I did. We fished for a good while but never even got a bite. She was happy after that and Dad and I continued to fish in Long Pond (or should I say "Molly Hole?")

Uncle Ade would weave large grass ropes that were strung alongside tug boats to protect them from damage when they bumped into the barges. The diameter of each bumper was small at each end and thick in the middle. I loved to hang out with him and talk to him while he was working. I don't know where he got it, but he gave me the nickname "Bentine, Dentine, Kerosene." I guess that is better than Dennis The Menace.

Many of the country songs during that period of time were real tear-jerkers, such as: Red Sovine's "Little Rosa", "Giddyup-Go" and "Dear John"; Hank Williams' "Blue Eyes Crying in the Rain", "Cold Cold Heart", and Roy Acuff (King of the Grand Ole Opry) had several sad songs like "Low and Lonely" and "Precious Jewel". One weekend, after putting on a show at Crawfordville High School, Roy and his band decided to visit Shell Point for some seafood. They stopped at our house and asked for directions. We only lived a couple of hundred yards from the fork of the Shell Point and Spring Creek roads, and it was a thrill to meet them and tell them how to get there. Most radio country musical programs started with a fast paced instrumental like "Orange Blossom Special," one of my all time favorites, and ended with a gospel song.

We did not own a car until I was about ten years old. Mr. Henry Smith, Dad's employer, gave him a 1931 Ford Model A to drive to work. The rumble seat had been removed and a wooden truck bed had been built in its place. The car had a full turn and a half of loose motion in the steering column. Gasoline was about 20 cents a gallon and the pumps worked by manually filling a measured glass container at the top of the pump with fuel to be gravity fed into the automobile. Since we depended on wood for cooking and heating, the car was a real time-saver. Before, we had been using a mule and a two wheel cart to haul firewood and fence posts. Firewood was cut with a crosscut saw and an axe. Blisters were taken for granted. I often helped Granddad Coley Smith cut firewood and I was horsing round on a trip back to the house, and took a wild swing at a stump with my axe. The axe glanced off the stump, slicing through my boot and cutting the leader to my little toe. The cut was about two inches long, but I got an infection and had to borrow some crutches to be able to get around. The cut was very swollen and not healing well at all. One night I arrived home after dark, and my dog ran out to greet me knocking one of my crutches out of my hand. It fell across my sore foot and ruptured the cut. The fluid drained out of the wound and in a few days I could walk on the foot again. Sometimes nature has its ways of healing our wounds. One of the best treatments for a wound I always heard was to let the dog lick it then go wade in saltwater. I'm sure some modern doctors will take issue with me about this.

There are sixty-seven counties in the state of Florida. For some time, each county was ranked from one to sixty-seven based on the population. Wakulla County was number sixty-five or the third least populated county in the state. These numbers would be the first numbers to appear on your vehicle license plates. The 1930 census reported 5,468 and the 1950 census reported 5,258 people in Wakulla County, Florida. Not until 1970 did the population exceed 6,000. A large portion of the land in Wakulla County is owned by the US Government and is known as the St. Marks Wildlife Refuge. Large companies like St. Joe Paper owned large portions of the land as well. That leaves only a small portion of the land that can be developed to promote growth.

As far back as I can remember, a black gentleman named Joe Gavin, lived with my Aunt Corrine and Uncle Isadore Porter. The way I remember the story is that a local man was walking home from work one afternoon and as he was passing some hog pens, he heard a baby crying. He went to investigate and found that someone had dropped a newborn baby in the hog pen. He carried the baby home with him and since he and his wife had a newborn baby, she nursed Joe until he could eat solid foods. I'm not sure what age he was when he began staying with my aunt and uncle, but he lived with them until he died. Joe never married, and all of the kids loved to be around Joe because he would play with us. Joe had a pretty bad stutter when he talked. On weekends Joe would walk about six miles to Shadeville, a black community, and party with them. He was deathly afraid of the dark and on his way home about midnight, he always walked real fast and whistled as loud as he could. One night, Dad was walking home when he heard Joe coming. They were near John Gray's house so Dad hid beside the road and scared Joe so badly that Joe ran up on John's porch, knocking the front door open and falling inside the house. John and his wife had been in bed, and there was John was trying to light a kerosene lamp while Joe was rolling around on the floor. Afterwards, Joe said John asked him who scared him, but he didn't see who it was. Isadore, Corrine and Joe ran a boat building business. They mostly built 14 foot plywood boats that were popular with the commercial and sports fishermen.

Lacey & Corine Bradshaw

Many of the kids our age experimented with smoking Rabbit Tobacco, also known as Everlasting or Catfoot. We'd go behind the barn, take the dry leaves, roll them in brown paper and smoke it like a cigarette. Dad never caught me smoking but some of my sisters were not so lucky. I was lucky they did not squeal on me. Dad was afraid we'd burn the barn down along with all the animal feed stored in it.

In his later years, Dad still always maintained a garden about an acre in size. Much of his gardening was done with a hand push plow, until his son-in-law, Billy Hartsfield, gave him a small gas-powered garden tractor. One time, the tractor would not start and Dad felt he just had to plow the garden, so he used the push plow and made my sister Inez help him. It was very embarrassing to her since the garden was located right beside the busy highway. Even after he entered a nursing home at the age of 93, he got his son Ronnie to bring him some cloves of garlic from the garden at home, which he planted in the flower boxes at the nursing home where it was gathered and enjoyed by the staff working there.

In 1940, when I was two years old a sudden storm came up and blew the back half of our house down. We were all in the front room and no one was injured. My parents boarded up the open end of the house until they could purchase a house from my Uncle C. K. Bradshaw. They paid him about $40.00 for the house and one acre of land.

My Mom and her brother C. K. were going somewhere in a horse-drawn wagon when a sudden storm came up and lightning struck a tree near them, rendering them both unconscious. After the horse managed to recover from the shock, it was able to get them safely back home. Uncle C. K. also told about walking through some thick brush and stepping on a coiled rattlesnake. He slipped and fell on the snake but managed to get away without being bitten. For a long time after that, though, he said each step he took felt like his feet were slipping out from under him.

One of my earliest memories was some of us going with my cousin Raymond Stephens to pick persimmons at the Council Field, an abandoned farm near our house. After getting our persimmons, he had put me on his shoulders and we were walking back down the dirt road when we heard a vehicle approaching, and everyone climbed over a three foot embankment of sand to let the car pass. Henry Hodge was driving the car and as it came even with us, he swerved the car into the bank of sand. The car jumped the bank and almost knocked Raymond's legs out from under him. Since Raymond was well over 6 feet tall, I was able to see all the action. Henry offered no reason for almost running us down. My Mom was very upset about the incident, but Henry's wife, Dosha, explained that he had been drinking and did not realize what he had done. Some years later, Raymond had picked me up in his little Ford and we were headed to Spring Creek. We came up behind a slow moving truck with several kids in the back. Raymond sped up to pass the truck when a huge wild boar came out of some tall grass and attempted to cross the road between the truck and us. Our car hit the hog broadside, killing it, and knocked it across the road and up on the other bank. When Raymond hit the brakes, the car almost flipped end over end into the truck. That was many years before we learned about seat belts.

Dad and I were hunting squirrels early one morning when someone fired a shotgun from close by. Some of the pellets hit me but bounced off the thick coat I was wearing. My dad let out a yell but we never saw who fired the shot.

Dad, my brother-in-law Leroy Miley and I set out one day armed with a crosscut saw and an axe to rob a wild bee tree. We used rolled up rags that we set on fire to create a smokescreen that kept the bees at bay most of the time. Leroy was deathly afraid of bees. If a bee lit on him, he'd start running, leaving smoke trailing off behind him. He couldn't keep from swatting the bees, and of course the bees would sting him. We'd put the queen bee into a homemade hive and all the other bees would gather around her. We left the beehive near the tree we robbed for several days until the bees settled in, then at dusk, we could move the bees and hive to our small farm.

During a party at Spring Creek, an unidentified man walked up behind a deputy sheriff standing on the porch of a house and snatched his 45-calibeer pistol from its holster and shot three men standing in the yard-wounding them, but they all survived. My Dad removed the two remaining live rounds from the gun and kept them in the hat box of our chifferobe at home until he died, but no one's seen them since.

The roof of our house was made of cypress shingles. Sometimes the stove pipes got so hot that the shingles would catch fire. We kept a ladder against the house and a foot tub full of water nearby. The first one to spot the fire had to climb the ladder and pour water on the fire. Then we had shingles to replace before the next rain.

We did not wash clothes on New Year's day, walk with one shoe on and one off, sit in a chair with only one leg touching the floor, sweep the floor after dark, sing in bed, walk under a ladder, open an umbrella in the house or let a black cat cross our path if we could help it. We never told where we caught our last mess of fresh fish or where we found an oyster bar with large oysters on it. These superstitions and others like them were taken very seriously by people back then and many are still followed today.

Sand gnats or "no-see-ums," were so abundant that you couldn't sit outside and rest without building a smoldering fire to keep them away. Then your clothes smelled like smoke. I believe Wakulla County had all the biting flies that were ever created to plague mankind: gnats, mosquitoes, yellow flies, dog flies, cow flies and horse flies. The sting of yellow jackets, wasps, bees, hornets, bumblebees, and centipedes could also be very painful. One day I got stung thirteen times by yellow jackets…not a pleasant memory. We had seed ticks (tiny), gopher ticks (medium) and bear ticks (large). Every time we ventured into the woods, we had to check ourselves (and each other) for ticks. Sandworms caused what we knew as 'ground itch'. One of the causes was going barefoot around farm animals. In severe cases, it felt like your feet were going to rot off. We also had to check the animals for any injuries because flies laid their eggs in any open wound. The eggs hatched into worms that would eat the flesh away until the animal died. We always kept a can of Smear-62 (we called it Smear-X) on hand to treat any wounds we saw on the livestock.

Lacey Bradshaw Metcalf

When I was about five years old, my sister Lena Pearl was dating a guy with only one arm. I don't remember his name or how he lost his arm, but he and Lena told me that if they had some fish bait they would take me fishing. I knew where a dead pine log lay near our house, so I grabbed a can, ran to the log, peeled the bark off, picked out several fat juicy worms and headed home. They took a look at the worms and said they needed more. I ran to collect more worms and this time when I got back, they had left without me.

My brother R. P. was sitting in the Spring Creek Café when a young lady walked in and asked if she could join him for a drink. After a while, two large young men came in and one of them asked the girl why she stood him up. An argument started and one of the men slapped the lady across the face and R. P. decked him. The two men grabbed R. P. by each arm, got a running start toward the screen door and sent him flying through it. Then they took the lady and left. The good guy does not always win.

B. F. Paige was our mail carrier for 42 years. When Mom needed stamps or a money order, all she had to do was leave the cash in the mail box. Mr. Page would fill the order and put the change in the box. Mr. Page was a very civic-minded man who dedicated his life to serving the people of his city, county and state in various ways for many years.

The day before I started first grade, I was

playing with a car tire, running and pushing the tire as fast as I could. As it slowed down, I laid my hand on the tire and a piece of glass in the tread ripped my right thumb to the bone from the base to the nail. When my thumb healed, it was drawn up at an angle. Sometime later however, I cut the same thumb again and was able to straighten it out. During that time, it was difficult learning to write and keeping up with my school work.

On weekends, we'd get up before daylight, feed and water the livestock, then head to the refuge to grunt for night crawlers. This consisted of driving a wooden stake in the ground and rubbing an axe head or rusty piece of flat iron across the stake. The vibrations caused the worms to come to the surface of the ground where we gathered them for bait. With our cans full of worms, we'd take our cane poles and walk to some of the local ponds, wade out into the pond and fish for warmouth. Sometimes there would be four or five large alligators in view. We didn't bother them and they didn't bother us. A couple of times little two foot gators would snap at my fishing cork. I'd jerk the line and snag them in the side. Even a small gator can get pretty mad when you try to remove a hook from its side. Occasionally, a water moccasin swam out to check us out. One smack on the head with a cane pole and it would change its area of surveillance.

I remember one time Dad invited Pete Joyner and his son Charles to go fishing with us. After we had grubbed enough worms to fill our cans, we pulled the stakes out of the ground. However, mine did not want to come out so I gave the stake a hard jerk and when I did, my right hand struck the sharp hatchet I was holding in my left hand. I split my hand down the right side and shaved the skin off the top of two fingers. I got sent home and they went fishing with my worms. About every two months, Dad loaded my brothers and I in the car and drove us to Mr. Joyner's house, unannounced, for haircuts. Pete spent most of his morning cutting our hair at no charge. He had six boys of his own and he cut their hair. Albert Moore, the barber in town charged 75 cents for a haircut and we could not afford it.

My oldest sister, Lena Pearl, lived in Leonardtown, Maryland and was scheduled for major surgery. Mom took a Greyhound bus to be with Lena during her recovery, leaving me in charge of four small kids while Dad worked. When Mom returned home, all five of us were in bed with the measles and I was too weak to walk. My first cousins, Anita and Selva Jean Lynn, came to help me prepare meals and take care of the other kids, but my recovery time was very slow. Measles, mumps, whooping cough and chicken pox were a sure thing in those days. There were three different types of measles that made the rounds. We only knew them as big red, little red and three day measles. Years later, during my military career, I had worked hard to get leave approval and go home for a few days. When I arrived home, my Mom informed me that I had the three day measles and she put me to bed.

My older brother, R. P. had a cyst on his shin and it was getting quite large. Our sister Lena Pearl wanted to lance it, but he wanted no part of that. One day as she was feeding the animals and R. P. was following close behind her, Lena swung the feed bucket and hit the cyst. It ruptured and R. P. thought he was going to die, but the cyst actually got better and he recovered.

Dennis and R.P. Smith

When I was about nine or ten, my Mom often sent me to my grandfather

Coley Smith's house a little over a mile away to pick up a gallon of milk when our cows were 'dry.' It was usually at dusk and I had to cross Coggins Branch, a favorite panther hideout. My dog went with me, and often times we were chased by a small herd of ornery cows. I knew Dad would kill me if I spilled the milk, so I'd run to a tree with plenty of low limbs in case I had to climb it before the cows got bored and left the area. That is why I learned to throw 'lighter' knots and pine cones at such an early age. By the time I arrived home, butter would be forming at the top of the milk jug. That was about the time I thought pasteurized milk came from cows that had been milked 'in the pasture.' We skimmed the rich cream from the top of the milk and saved it until we had a quart of cream. Then we'd put the cream in a half gallon jug and shake it until it turned to butter. One of the men that delivered ice to our house loved sour milk. On ice delivery days, if we set a quart of milk on top of the ice box to sour, he'd drink the whole bottle and leave it behind for a refill. We kept our milk cows in a pen at night, but let them graze in the pasture during the day. At milking time, when I called the cows all of them came to me except one hornless ol' muley cow. I'd have to take a rope and lead her to the barn to be milked. One day, my brother R.P. decided he'd bring the cow to the barn for me. She got up close behind R. P. and butted him in the backside every step he took all the way to the barn.

As we did not have grass in our yard, we had no need for a lawnmower. We hoed the weeds, keeping the yard swept clean with a broom made from gallberry bushes tied together with string. The only air conditioning we had was to open the doors and windows and let the air circulate if there was any kind of breeze blowing. Otherwise, we depended on fanning ourselves with the end of a turkey wing or piece of cardboard stapled to a stick, which usually had a funeral home advertisement on it.

I was attending Jimmy Sarvis' birthday party one night when we saw some vehicles stop about 200 yards from us. A few minutes later, we saw a fire and as we ran to check it out, the vehicles sped away. There was a cross burning in front of the driveway to my cousin Wilburn Vickers' house. We figured the KKK had set the cross on fire because Wilburn made moonshine for a living. Some "shady" things went on in our part of Wakulla County. As my Dad was hunting in the woods near our house, he heard someone coming through the brush, so he squatted down to wait and see what was going on. He saw a man reach into some palmettos and pull out a keg of moonshine. He put the keg on a stump and started siphoning some of the moonshine into a jug. About that time, Dad hollered and the man took off, leaving everything behind. Dad finished filling the jug, put the keg back into the palmetto, took the jug and went home.

Dad let me start hunting when I was about thirteen years old but I had to hunt by myself. That eliminated the possibility of me shooting a hunting partner or a partner shooting me. His only exception to that rule was to let me hunt rabbits with the Green brothers. The gun I got to use was an old 12 gauge shotgun that belonged to him. It was so worn that each time I fired it, the forearm came off, and if I wasn't careful the barrel would separate from the stock. I had to put it back together sometimes before I could

Grandma Penny Clemons Vickers
(Grandma Nannie Bradshaw's Mother)

fire the next shot.

The first dogs I remember we owned were named Frank and Floor. Frank was R. P.'s dog and Floor was mine. Frank died of old age. Dad loaned Floor to a friend to do some squirrel hunting and he told my Dad that he had lost Floor during the hunt. Several days later Dad was in Crawfordville talking to some ladies at the beauty shop door when he felt something rear up on him. When he turned around, he discovered it was Floor. About that time, a gentleman Dad knew said he liked the dog and wanted to know if he could have her. Floor was eight years old and getting too old to hunt wild hogs, so Dad gave her to him. I was really upset when Dad told me what he had done.

Many hunters lost their hunting dogs in our area and the dogs became wild. We trapped a beautiful female dog and had intentions of taming her, but we were not successful. We bred her with my grandfather's bulldog and trained one of her puppies, Butch, to hunt wild hogs and raccoons. Butch was a silent tracker, meaning he did not bark until he had the animal in sight. I only knew of two creatures he would not catch. One was an alligator and the other was a panther. Butch would track a panther until he got the panther in sight, then he'd then turn and come back to me. The hair on his back would be standing straight up, and he would growl a few times then go track the panther a little farther.

Another time, a wild female dog came to our house looking for food. With our dog's help Dad caught the wild dog and, looping a rope around its neck, took it to the house. When they got upon the porch he tried to hold onto the dog but the rope was old and the dog snapped the rope into. As it ran to the road, a flat bed truck was passing by. The dog was running so fast that it jumped on the bed of the truck and off on the other side of the road. We never saw that dog again.

Dad worked for Henry and Alma Smith of Crawfordville. Their son-in-law Fred Carlin and his Dad had one walker and two blue tick hounds. They liked to bring their dogs down to hunt with our dog Butch because he ran silently until he spied the raccoon. The walker tracked a few yards behind Butch and the blue ticks brought up the rear. One night, they treed a raccoon and when we shined the light on the coon, it started down the tree. When it got within ten feet of the ground, it jumped into the middle of the pack of dogs. The coon got a firm hold on one of the hounds and the other three dogs got a firm hold on the coon. What a fight: four men, four dogs and one raccoon. The raccoon lost.

My cousin Woodrow Porter had stopped by our house and began bragging about how good his coon dog was. Dad said he would put our dog Butch up against any coon dog in the county. Woodrow challenged Dad to a hunt and agreed to take Butch on the first hunt. They planned to hunt until midnight. Woodrow arrived at our house well before dark and said he was ready to go, but Dad kept delaying the start of the hunt until 8pm. Dad and I normally killed from one to three coons per hunt. That night we killed five and still had more time to hunt. We told Woodrow it was his turn and he could start earlier if he wished. Woodrow never showed up for his hunt and we heard no more bragging about his dog.

Grandpa Isham Bradshaw and Judson Bradshaw

Raccoons were bad to raid our corn field at night. Butch would go hunting by himself, tree a coon or two, and sit at the base of the tree barking until Dad or I got out of bed and killed them. One night Butch treed two adult, and three half grown coons in two trees near each other. Dad got all five of them. One night, I killed two coons that Butch had treed in separate trees. However, raccoons are very smart. When a dog picks up the coon's trail and starts barking, the coon will climb up a tree a few feet then jump down, marking several trees that way. Often when a dog gets to the marked tree, it will sit and bark until the hunter arrives. By that time, the coon is long gone and the dog is wondering what happened. When Butch got to the first tree, he'd bark twice then make a wide circle around the tree. If the coon had only marked the tree, Butch could pick up its trail and continue the chase. If the dog circled the tree, then went back to the tree and barked again, we were 99 percent sure the coon was still up the tree. When we shot a coon out of a tree, Butch would grab it by the throat and shake it a couple of times and lay it down. If the coon lay still Butch knew it was dead and began looking for another trail. If the coon moved, Butch grabbed the throat again and held on until he knew he'd finished the job.

Otter pelts brought a very good price but they are very smart and difficult to trap. We discovered an otter was hanging out in a pond near Grass Inlet, but before we could get close enough to shoot, the otter would disappear beneath the water and we'd never see him surface. We made a thorough search of the waterline, and discovered a narrow path in some thick grass. The otter was leaving that pond and traveling over land to another body of water. The next time we were at the pond, Dad worked his way around the pond and I headed for its exit spot. When the otter saw me waiting at his escape route, he turned and swam to the center of the pond and Dad shot it. You guessed it; I drew the short straw and had to retrieve the otter, carrying the cold, wet, limp animal to the car. We made enough money from the pelt to feed us for two weeks though.

Cousins Albert and Pap Porter told me about going to check their traps and discovering they had bagged a bobcat. Deciding to have a little fun, they took some long sticks and poked at the cat, causing it snarl and lunge at them. After they killed the cat and were removing it from the trap, they were very surprised to find that the trap was only holding the cat by one toe, and it was about stretched to its limit.

I always wondered what I would do if I was out hunting and walked up on a moonshine still. One day, I did just that, but I saw no sign of current activity. Much of the equipment was still onsite, but it appeared the owner was in the process of moving the still. I told Dad about it, and we decided to 'help' him move. The drums were great to store corn in. The jugs were used for canning and the troughs made good hog feeders. I never knew who it belonged to. I should have asked the Internal Revenue Service for a reward.

One day, my cousin Wilburn Vickers was walking to his still with a fifty pound sack of corn on his shoulders. He spotted some IRS agents approaching and decided to make a run for it, but the bag of corn was slowing him down, so he dropped it. He knew the area much better than the agents did and he was able to lose them in the thick brush. Somehow, it seemed Wilburn always had inside information and knew when the IRS agents were close to raiding one of his stills, because he'd move it during the night. He never served any prison time for his illegal moonshine activities. My great-uncle, Fate Vickers, also made moonshine, and was well known for his ability to make corks from the wood of ash trees for fishing nets and seines, using a foot-powered lathe. His brother Rile farmed to raise food for his family and animals, then made moonshine to pay his bills. The IRS agents surprised him at his still one time and he had to make a run for it. The agents however, knew about where he lived. When they arrived at Uncle Rile's house, though, they found him calmly sitting on his front porch steps fanning himself.

Seines, gill nets and pocket nets strung between two trees or posts were common sights in peoples' front yard. My parents and my Aunt Amy and Uncle Ade Trull would hang nets for local fishermen. I learned this trade at an early age. The keys were to have the correct number of leads and corks properly spaced on the lines. The spacing of each knot tied on the lines was critical to keep the net/seine hanging straight between the lead and cork lines. For various reasons, holes would appear in the nets/seines and would require patching.

I especially enjoyed hunting Wood ducks because they landed in the pond, but came out on the hill to eat acorns. That way, when we shot the ducks we did not have to wade or swim out in the cold water to pick them up. We always saved the duck feathers to stuff pillows with. Canadian geese used to come to this area by the thousands in the winter time. The geese spent the daylight hours feeding around the bay, then headed inland to the corn fields to feed at night. The government planted a large field of corn in the refuge. It was known as the 'Ade Trull' field. One morning while I was waiting for the school bus to arrive, I heard a flock of geese coming over our house. I grabbed my shotgun and fired one shot. A large goose spread its wings and sailed to the ground near my Aunt Amy's house. She heard the shot and caught the goose when it landed. The school bus was due any time so I checked the goose to see where the pellets had hit. I could not find any blood on the bird so I pulled the feathers from one wing and put the goose in the chicken yard. When I got home the goose had settled in and was eating corn with the chickens. Months later, I sold it for five dollars to a man that wanted it for breeding purposes. One hunting guide was arrested for using an airplane to herd some geese to the area where hunters were waiting for a good shot at them. My cousin, Ella Margaret Stevens, reportedly fired at a goose in flight with a 22- caliber rifle and broke its neck.

While my parents were away at work one day, I was standing in our front yard feeding some of our home-grown turkeys when a car passed by. The driver turned the car around, drove into our yard and said, "Hey, Buddy, are those turkeys for sale?" "They sure are," I replied. He said he was from Tallahassee and had told his wife he was going hunting over the weekend, but instead of hunting, he got drunk and spent the weekend partying at Shell Point. He needed proof that he had been hunting, so I told him to pick out the turkey he wanted and I would catch it for him. He felt that he should shoot it with his shotgun and asked for my permission. I told him to go ahead. He loaded his gun and as the turkeys were moving around in the yard, he tried to take aim but was not too steady. He asked me if I'd catch the turkey and tie it to a post so he could shoot it in the head. I caught the turkey and tied its feet over the clothes line so its head would hang down and allow for a clean shot. He tried to take aim again but was still weaving pretty badly. When he fired his gun, the pellets did hit the turkey but only broke its wing. He gave up, so I killed the bird for him, he paid me and went on his way. I wish I could have heard the story he told his wife when he arrived home. Who knows; the turkey may have prevented a divorce.

Rats were always a problem in the barn where we stored our corn for feeding the animals. If a rat ran up your pants leg, the only way to get it out without it biting you was to squeeze it to death. Each fall, we'd fill the barn with ears of corn, shucked and stored in 55 gallon drums to protect it from the rats. We fed whole ears of corn to the horse or mule and the hogs. We had to hand-shell the corn we fed to the chickens and turkeys. Also, the chickens and hogs got fresh wild clover from the field. Free range chickens and turkeys were very clever at hiding their nests, and there could be several eggs in a nest before we found it. Therefore, Mom had to break each egg in a saucer or cup to make sure it was still good before she put it in the frying pan.

A Rat snake fell through a crack in the ceiling and landed on Nanny's kitchen table while she was eating lunch one day. Snakes were useful in keeping the rat population down, but hungry snakes often got into our chicken coop for a meal of fresh eggs. Of course, this highly upset the chickens and their squawking alerted us that something was wrong in the henhouse. After the snake swallowed the eggs, it could not move very fast, and I'd crush the eggs before I killed the snake. Jay birds also raised a ruckus when a snake got in their nest of eggs or hatchlings.

Nannie Bradshaw

A friend arrived to visit Nanny one day; bringing her two pet spider monkeys along, perched on her shoulders. Nanny would not let her come inside the house with the monkeys, so she tied them to a limb of a chinaberry tree in the yard. The monkeys ate some of the chinaberries, and when their owner started to leave one monkey was dead and the other one was very sick. She took the sick monkey with her and left the dead one behind. The monkey's skull made a good play toy and it was free.

When one of Nanny's elderly neighbors passed away, several friends and neighbors gathered to take part in the long-standing tradition of "sitting up with the body." During the night all of them had dozed off to sleep except for one gentleman. He got bored because he had no one to talk to, so he propped the body up in the casket and put a potato in its hand. He then went outside and threw a potato through the window, and suddenly no one was sleepy anymore.

There were no nursing homes back then and when a family member got ill, their family took care of them. My grandmother Nanny was a diabetic, and at the age of 64 she went into a coma. When she awoke, she asked to speak to all of the grandchildren that were playing in the yard. We all gathered around the bed and she talked to us for a few minutes before she died. I can't remember what we talked about as I was only eight years old at the time, but I was very surprised and upset that she was gone so quickly. My grandfather Isham, and my paternal grandmother Ida Smith, died before I was born, so I know very little about them.

A typical day for me began at 5am. In the wintertime, I had to build a fire in the wood heater to heat some water and thaw out the water pump. I then fed and watered a horse, a couple of pens of chickens, several pens of hogs, turkeys, ducks and sometimes rabbits. If any animals got out of their pen overnight, I mended the fence, chased them down and put them back in their pen. While Mom cooked breakfast, I washed as much animal feed off me as possible before going to school. When carrying buckets of feed to the trough, animals were very good at making you spill some of it on your shoes and clothes. After school, I'd work in the fields until almost dark, then feed and water all the animals. Daylight savings time had not been invented at that time.

Periodically, we ordered baby chicks by the hundred from a company in Ohio and received them by mail. We could specify that we wanted a meat producing chicken, but many times, the company would substitute and send us some white leghorns. The leghorns were good layers, but came up short on the meat side.

My brother R.P. was five years older than me and Dad often made him stay home from school and work on the farm. At the end of each school day, his teacher gave me his lesson assignments for him to complete at home. He'd do them and I'd take them to his teacher the next day. School work was not easy to complete with six to eight kids in a small room and one kerosene lamp for lighting. There were not enough chairs for everyone to sit down at the same time.

L to R - Hazel Bradshaw, Maude Metcalf, and Amie Bradshaw

While R.P. was plowing a field with a mule, a red fox come out of some underbrush and started chasing him around the mule. He could tell that the fox was rabid so he ran to the house, got his shotgun and killed the animal. After work, when he went to feed his puppy that was tied in the backyard, it snapped at him, and he realized it had gotten the disease too. In the summer time, we were always watchful for animals behaving strangely.

We always made our own toys. A syrup bucket filled with sand, with a metal rod thru the middle, and a string tied to each end of the rod made a great toy. We'd run and pull the syrup bucket, making turns to see how sharp a turn we could make without flipping the bucket of sand over. An old axe handle for a bat and an empty Pet Milk can for a ball and you could play a game of 'soft ball' or should I say 'hard ball.' When the can became so smashed up that sharp edges might cut our hands, it was time for a new milk can. If we could find about a twelve inch metal rim and a stiff piece of wire we were lucky indeed. We'd bend one end of the wire into a U-shape then throw the wheel, starting a rolling motion. By using the U-shaped end of the wire to guide the rim we tried to see just how long we could run with it and keep it going. The wire had to stay just below the center of the rim to maintain control. Boys carried pockets full of marbles to school so they could play 'for keeps' games during recess. I made various styles of slingshots to play with. I was never much good at hitting anything but had fun trying. Hopscotch was a good game for a bunch of kids to play. Ball and jacks were popular among the girls. We also spent many hours playing hide-and-seek.

Peanut boils were always a well-attended event, and frequently included a snipe hunt. We'd give a youngster or newcomer a burlap bag or 'croaker' sack, take them out into the woods and tell them to hold the bag while we went to round up a snipe and drive it their way. Then we left them in the dark and went back to the peanut boil.

Uncle Tate and Aunt Maggie (Revell) Vickers
Children: Wilburn and Eunice (L to R)

We went barefoot most of the time but when we did get a pair of shoes, we wore them until they had holes in the soles. We cut up old inner tubes and made inserts for our shoes. The inserts didn't stop sandspurs, though. I'd try to run the few yards from my house to my grandmother's without shoes on, but the sand was so hot that I couldn't make it all the way. I had to stop, scratch out a small hole and stand in it until my feet cooled down before I could make another run for it. Although we did not give or receive presents at Christmas, there was always lots of special holiday foods to feast on. We'd have a ham or perhaps a turkey or hen with oyster dressing. Our sweet potatoes were stored underground, so we always had plenty of fragrant yams to eat as well as collard greens and hot 'cathead' biscuits. For dessert we'd have a banana pudding, using bread instead of vanilla wafers; a pineapple cake and a jelly or chocolate 15 layer cake.

Mom would make us egg and biscuit sandwiches for lunch at school. My classmates made fun of me so I seldom took them to school. Terry Crum, a close friend of mine, loved egg sandwiches, so when I did take them to school, I'd trade Terry my sandwiches for his cafeteria lunch. This was before free school lunches were introduced. Terry didn't care if someone made fun of him. When we could find a couple of nickels, we bought a coke or RC cola and a bag of salted peanuts; we'd pour the peanuts into the coke and munch away. Several years later, while serving in the Air Force, Terry and I were both stationed on the Greenland ice cap at the same time.

When the kids started getting a little grumpy and hard to get along with, Mom thought we were 'bilious' and needed a good cleaning out. She'd gather everyone up and give us a large dose of fever grass or regulator tea, ex-lax or some other nasty laxative. On one such occasion, Aunt Juddy happened to stop by the house. She had been drinking and Mom thought she needed a good 'cleaning out' too, so she was included. It almost killed her but her system was squeaky clean for awhile. I'm sure a little trip 'behind the woodshed' would have done us better than the laxative, but it still served its purpose because after a round of laxative, we were too weak to get up to any mischief.

After Uncle Ade's death, a gentleman began keeping company with Aunt Amy. One night while he was visiting her, Aunt Juddy and my sister Inez decided to peek through her window. While they were at the window, a cat scared them to death when it ran out from under the house causing Juddy to screech, and Aunt Amy to catch the girls spying on them.

Greens

2 lbs desired type of greens
3 cups of water (or until greens are covered)
½ lb of hog jowls or favorite smoked pork
Salt and Pepper to taste
Directions:
Wash and cut up desired type of greens into small pieces.

Place in a large soup pot, cover with water, and bring to a boil.

While the greens cook, in a large iron skillet, cook ½ pound of hog jowls or your favorite pork. Cook until tender then add to the greens.

Bring the greens to a second boil and cook until water is reduced to one-half. Lower the temperature and cook until tender.

Submitted by: By Bill Frank, 15 Stanley, Crawfordville, FL. 32327

Aunt Juddy often came home tipsy, and one night she set a can of beer under her bed and went to sleep. When she woke the next morning, she reached for the can and took a big swig. Something didn't feel quite right and she found that a cockroach had crawled in the can and drowned during the night.

Mom and us kids had walked down the road one afternoon to visit some relatives, and while we were there, a severe thunder storm came up. When we returned home, we noticed the front door of the house was standing wide open. We had locked it with a dead bolt before we left home. We found that a bolt of lightning had hit an oak tree about 100 feet from the house. The lightning had followed a wire fence that was nailed to the tree until it got to a heavy wooden gate in our front yard. The power of the strike shook the house so violently it opened the door to the house and threw the splinters from the gate into our living room. Had we been home, it's most likely that we would have been sitting in the living room. Who says we didn't have electric fences in those days?

I remember fighter pilots from Tyndall Air Force Base, in Panama City training over the bay at West Goose Creek. They came off the bay so low they'd have to gain altitude to clear the roof of the fish house. One plane would 'tow' a target while other pilots shot at it. One day a pilot shot the target's tow cable, causing the target to fall to the ground. The target was made of screen wire, so when Dad found it he carried it home to put screens in our windows. We even had enough screen left over to make hoods to use when we robbed wild bee hives. Flying at such low altitudes and firing at the targets sometimes put fishermen in harm's way. I believe it was Clyde Gray that had a close encounter like that and filed a report with the Tyndall AFB officials.

On one occasion, we heard the engine of a fighter plane sputtering and saw it crash in the woods behind our house. The pilot bailed out and my family went to help him. He was taken to Crawfordville where he could get transportation back to Tyndall AFB. Another time, the pilot was not as lucky and died in the crash. The plane was partially buried in the ground and my parents had to use some old tin cans to dig the pilot out.

Shell Point was owned by the Taff family. Helen (Taff) Roberts and her husband G.D. Roberts managed the Shell Point Restaurant and rented boats to tourists. R.P. worked for them. In September 1950, Hurricane Easy blew many of their plywood boats away and scattered them out in the marsh. Helen's brother Charles and R. P. were about the same age and were good friends. Charles got a plane from Tallahassee to fly down and locate the boats so R. P. could tow them back in. On their way down from Tallahassee, Charles and the pilot flew over our house just above tree top level. R. P. was waiting just off shore for them to arrive. When the plane flew over him, it suddenly took a nosedive into the water. The pilot died instantly but Charles was still alive. He took Charles to shore and went back to the plane to recover the pilot. We were told that Charles died as the ambulance was passing our house on the way to the hospital. It took R. P. a long time to recover from that incident. During that hurricane, I remember our little frame house shaking violently, but it withstood the winds.

We had an English teacher at Crawfordville High School named Etta Mae Whitton. I thought she was one of the best looking teachers I'd ever seen. One day she caught us all talking about Marilyn Monroe instead of doing our schoolwork. She stood up and asked what Marilyn Monroe had that she didn't, and all I could think of was blonde hair. Later that day Mrs. Whitton had left the room for a few minutes and a student stepped out in the hall and threw an orange at Bill Moore's classroom across the hall, smashing it into a poster taped to the door. When Mrs. Whitton returned, Mr. Moore told her no one would tell him who had ruined the poster, but after she talked to the class the guilty party did report to the principal's office for punishment.

Our shop class was the last class of the day at school. We had to rush around to clean the shop before heading to the school bus. The teacher usually walked around the class with a yardstick in his hand. If we were moving too slowly, he'd pop us on the backside. One day, he reached out to swat Walter Forbes and Walter jumped aside so fast he split the seat of his pants. Walter told his Mom, Ms. Elzie, that the teacher had hit him so hard that it split his pants. The next day, Ms. Elzie arrived at the class threatening to spank the shop teacher. The students thought they were going to get to referee, but the teacher talked her out of the idea.

If we got sick at school, we had to suffer through the whole day. We didn't have a phone and our parents couldn't pick us up. Mrs. C.L. Townsend served as the county nurse, but there was no doctor or dentist in Wakulla County. I remember neighbors with a toothache often came to see my Dad. He had inherited a pair of tooth extractors from my Granny Bradshaw. Dad would seat them in a chair on the back porch and after a couple of shots of whiskey or moonshine; he'd extract the problem teeth. Many people had false teeth by the time they were forty years of age. Mom always frayed the ends of a small green tree limb and used it to clean her teeth.

Dad drove a school bus for several years. He carried a cane on the bus and if the kids started any trouble, he'd stop the bus, take them off the bus and spank them in front of the other kids…me included. We had "mud hole" days off from school. After a heavy rain, the school bus could not cross some of the mud holes and the driver would take the kids back home. Dad was driving the bus one day when the engine stalled out in the middle of a mud hole and he couldn't restart it. When he raised the hood of the bus, he realized that the battery was missing. While Dad stayed with the bus and kids, I believe Daniel Green and another one of the older kids started walking back toward the school. They found the battery in the road, and returned it to the bus. Dad reinstalled the battery and we continued our trip home. We arrived a little late, but we made it.

A girl named Patsy Hodge got mad with her bus driver on the way home one day, so she threw one of her shoes out the bus window. She then demanded that the driver turn the bus around and pick up her shoe, but he refused. The next morning Mrs. Dosha Hodge met the school bus and threatened the driver because her daughter only had one shoe to wear to school.

Most of the families had several kids in school at the same time and many of the families were related. If one family started a feud with another, the relatives invariably took sides. On the way to school one morning, all the families except the Rob Green and Bill Smith families started a feud. Bill Smith was the driver that day, and Rob Green was a former bus driver. Mr. Rob was a religious man and I have heard stories of him pulling the school bus off on the side of the road to pray for the kids. The principal, Mr. Blanton, didn't figure he had the strength to spank all of us at once, so he had all of the kids assemble in the school auditorium for a stern lecture.

Keeping pests from destroying our garden was always a problem. Three of the Green boys, Robert, Pasco, Charles, and I devised a plan using their car, to reduce the rabbit population. Our plan was to drive down the dirt roads with two of us sitting on the front fenders, shooting rabbits when we'd see their eyes shining in the dark. One night, I took a shot at a rabbit sitting in my neighbor's front yard and missed. Just as the neighbor opened the front door to his house, I fired another round and he slammed the door shut. We did not stop to pick up that rabbit. The next day I should have told him that we were out protecting his garden for him, but I was afraid to. That same night, we were doing about 30 miles per hour when a rabbit starting running down the middle of the road ahead of us. Charles shot it through the head with a 22-caliber rifle. The boys never let me live that down.

I kept steel traps set in our garden to catch rabbits. One morning just before the school bus arrived, I went out to check the traps and found a skunk in one of the traps. I made a decision to shoot the skunk and leave it in the trap until I got home from school, but I did not realize that the wind was blowing my way. In my first class of the day Mrs. Whitton sniffed a couple of times and I knew I was in trouble. She asked who had the 'run-in' with the skunk. Jimmy Sarvis spoke up and said, "Dennis did." I had to sit in the back of the classroom the rest of the day.

When making cane syrup, I had the job of feeding the cane stalks into the grinding mill. With cane juice all over me and a yellow jacket stuck in my gummy hair, it was difficult to remember to duck when the mule pulling the pole on the grinder came around. The kids liked to hide a small jar of cane skimmings and let it ferment. Mom and Dad always kept a beady-eye on us if we took a few sips.

The crows, blue jays, and cardinals were assisting the rabbits in destroying our garden, and I got pretty good at building bird traps. However, crows and jays were also pretty good at avoiding the traps. One day I did catch a cardinal, and when I got home, several people were standing in our yard talking. I was holding the bird down by my side and didn't notice that my dog had walked up to check out the bird. The bird clamped down on the dog's ear, and the dog started running around the house with the bird holding on for dear life. After circling the house a couple of times, the bird finally let go and flew away.

My Dad, Uncle C. K., a friend named Alonzo Burnette and I were gathering oysters near Stuart Cove when we overloaded our boat. As we approached an island, the boat began to take on water and was in danger of sinking. Dad yelled for all of us to jump overboard. Dad said I looked at him and hesitated for a few seconds before I jumped into the cold water. Since Uncle C.K. was the smallest of the four, he was selected to climb back in the boat and bail the water out. Later, after we had climbed back in the boat, we slowly made our way up to the island. While Uncle C.K. ran the boat in shallow water along its shore, Dad, Alonzo and I walked around the island until we got in calmer water on the other side and made our way safely back to the landing, saving the boat, motor and oysters. We could not afford rubber boots and the best oysters were still underwater at low tide. Alonzo did not like to wade and gather oysters so he'd always stay along the waterline and pick up scissor-bill oysters. My great uncle Rile Vickers was at the landing when we arrived, and seeing us all soaking wet and cold, he yelled out: "By Golly, did Lonzo finally get his tootsies wet?"

To make money to buy school clothes, I'd set steel traps in Coggins Branch. At daybreak each morning, I grabbed my gun and walked a mile to check my traps. I usually caught from one to three raccoons a night. I sold the hides for fifty cents each and the meat for dollar. One morning, as I approached the branch, I saw a large panther standing in the middle of the road looking back at me. We stared at each other for what seemed to be several minutes. I walked slowly toward the panther and he began walking down the road in front of me. After several yards, he jumped into some brush beside the road. When I got within a few feet of that spot, he jumped back into the road in front of me. We stared at each other a little bit longer and I followed him down the road again. The second time he left the road so did I, and headed in the opposite direction. I respected him but was not afraid of him. I could have shot the cat, but it was almost as if

Maxine Conley and Hazel Smith

he wanted to be my friend, so I let him go and I went on my way. Fortunately, I did not catch a coon that night. A coon in a trap would have been an easy breakfast for the panther. If I had been carrying a raccoon, the panther may have been tempted to attack me. I told my dad about the incident and taking him to the spot where it happened, showed him the large tracks in the middle of the road.

I was squirrel hunting one morning at Long Pond when some mallard ducks flew in and landed on the water near me. I was sitting with my back against an oak tree in an open area. I did not have time to hide or reload my twelve gauge shot-gun with a larger shot.

So, I lay flat on the ground and fired one number six shot at the ducks hitting three of them. As I was wading out in the waist deep cold water, one of the ducks started swimming away, so I shot it again. I picked up all three ducks by their necks and ran the half mile to the house, there was no one home as I entered the front door, so I leaned my gun against the wall and went out the back door, dropping the ducks on the back porch. Much to my surprise, one duck jumped to its feet and ran into the house and another one flew away. It was flying bout eight feet off the ground, but try as I might, I could not reach it. After running several yards, I gave up the fight and returned to the house where I recaptured the one duck that was still walking around in the kitchen and killed it. Instead of a three duck dinner, I had to settle for two.

Every Saturday morning I had to jump out of bed, feed and water all the animals and then hand pump enough water to fill the wash pot, and build a fire around it to heat water to wash clothes. Then I filled two #2 wash tubs with cold water to rinse the clothes in. We made our own soap by rendering cracklins', and adding the hog lard to water and lye crystals, cooking it down until it was a creamy consistency. We poured the mixture into a bucket and cooled it until it was solid, then it was divided into bars of soap that we could cut up and dissolve in hot water.

Hog killing time - Ronnie Smith, Bill Smith, and Earl Smith

On Sunday mornings we killed, cleaned and cut up three chickens for dinner. It was nothing for several people to stop by just when it was about time to eat. My favorite mid-morning snack was to grab a large leftover biscuit, punch a hole in it with my finger and fill it with honey or syrup on my way out the back door and back to work. Another snack was to eat peanut butter by the spoonful and wash it down with a glass of sugar water. Supplying food for ourselves meant spending many hours over a hot wood stove canning vegetables. We'd haul cart loads of lighter logs and stack them near the house. I had to make sure that there was plenty of firewood cut for the stove, heater and wash pot. I wore out a lot of axe handles. My grandfather Coley cut hickory logs in the length of an axe handle then split them. When they were dry enough, he used a drawing knife to shape the axe handle. It was very important that the grain of the wood ran straight or the handle would break easily. Also if the wood was not dry, the handle would shrink and the axe would come off the handle. We used a lot of wedges to make sure that didn't happen.

We killed about five or six hogs a year. We smoked some of the meat and salted the rest with rock salt. We kept the smoke in the smokehouse going 24-hours a day until the meat was cured. Sometimes, we had problems with intruders stealing food from us. One year, our salted and smoked meat started disappearing. Dad spread the word to our neighbors that all of us would be going to church one Sunday night. He planned to leave the house with us but return to wait for the intruder, but by the time he got back to the house he found the man already in the house helping himself to some salt meat. Dad grabbed his trusty old shotgun but had forgotten to load it before he left the house. As the thief is running across the field, Dad is chasing him and trying to load the gun. When the man slowed to climb the fence, Dad took one shot at his backside. It did not knock him down, but it did stop him from stealing our meat. Late one night a few weeks later a car drove up to our house and the driver blew the horn. Dad got out of bed and went to see what he wanted. My sister Inez awoke went to the kitchen to get a drink of water and found a man in the kitchen stealing food. She screamed, and Dad ran back in the house in time to see the thief run out the back door, get into the car with the driver and take off down the road.

At the age of thirteen, I got a job at Live Oak Island. I worked six days a week for $15.00 and was provided a place to sleep and three meals a day. I rented fourteen foot plywood boats for $3.00 a day and sold ice and fish bait. Fishermen rented the boats to go speckled trout fishing and many of them came in at the end of the day loaded with up to 100 fish. During that summer a storm came up suddenly and sank one of our rented boats with three men from Georgia on board. They clung to the overturned boat for about two hours before being rescued by other fishermen. One of the men told me he was exhausted and about to give up the fight when he was rescued. A week later, another fisherman found the capsized boat and towed it back to the fish camp, but he refused to release the boat and motor until he was paid a towing fee.

Live Oak Island was owned by a man named Redfern. A couple named Turner leased the island and I worked for them. Mrs. Turner ran the restaurant and Aunt Amy worked for her there as a cook. Mr. Turner just stayed in his room most of the time. Mr. Redfern did not believe in paying income tax. Mr. Turner would come to the ice house at closing time and count the money I had collected that day. I'd give him the receipts, which he tore into tiny strips and dropped into the water. After a couple of seasons, the Internal Revenue paid us a visit and gave the owner three months to close the business and vacate the island. He was allowed to take the portable equipment with him, but had to leave all fixed equipment behind. Mr. Lewis, a banker from Tallahassee bought the island. When it came time for my day off, Mr. Lewis took me home and never came back to pick me up for work.

Earl Smith and Bill Smith - Hog Killing

After losing my job at Live Oak Island, I went to work for the Moore family at Stuart Cove. I rented boats, sold fish bait, snacks and soft drinks, washed the family dishes that accumulated during the day, and chased squirrels out of the kitchen. The squirrels would chew through the screen wire, get into the flour and spread it all over the kitchen. That took hours to clean up. After a few months, Mrs. Moore had all she could take from the squirrels. She asked me to kill some of the squirrels but not to do it close to the house where she could see them. I think I killed about eighty squirrels that winter, thinning them out pretty well. I mentioned to Jimmy Sarvis at school one day that I was killing the squirrels and what my agreement was with Mrs. Moore. Jimmy wanted my job, so he told Mrs. Moore that I said I had killed some squirrels in her yard when she was not home. She fired me and hired Jimmy before I discovered what he had done. That was okay though, because our family was getting tired of squirrel stew anyway.

A local commercial fisherman struck some fish with his net near a spring across the creek from Stuart Cove. He caught a 150 pound jewfish and Mrs. Moore asked him to hang it up under the shelter. Mrs. Moore got her fishing rod and camera and had someone take a picture of her and the fish. She had the picture published in the Tallahassee Democrat with the caption: "This 150lb jewfish was caught at Stuart Cove."

In 1953, Mom, Dad and eight of us kids were still living in a one bedroom house. We had one bed in the living room and two in the bedroom. We had bought sixty acres of land where the Spring Creek highway crosses state road 30A. Dad was working at the Raker sawmill then and was able to bring home lots of odd boards of green lumber. We cut fat lighter logs for the under penning of the house. With a crosscut saw, a handsaw, an axe, 2 hammers, a hatchet and a bucket of crooked nails, we launched an effort to build a four bedroom house. We had the framework almost completed when we saw a survey team marking the route for the construction of the new state road. The line was slated to go through one corner of our land and out the other corner. This route would cut our sixty acres into two triangles and take the house out completely. We stopped work and Dad made a fast trip to Judge Porter's office. The Judge persuaded the developers to change the survey so that it took a 68' strip down the side of our property, which spared the house. The state did not offer to pay us anything for the land, but Dad did talk them into putting up a hog wire fence along our new property line.

While building the house, I always sat on top of the stud plate. Dad cut the boards to length and nailed the bottom of the board, while I nailed the top. But if Dad got sidetracked for some reason, I got bored very quickly. Once, I saw my younger brother Earl walking by with a big roll of caps from a cap gun, so I talked him into pitching them up to me and was hitting the caps with the hammer. Of course I dropped the hammer, which caught Dad on the side of the head just before it smashed his thumb. His thumb swelled so bad he had to quit work for the rest of the day. I was sure he would kill me when I came down, but he was hurting too bad. In the weeks to come the house was quickly becoming a reality, so I had to take a grubbing hoe and clear a one acre and a three acre garden plot for our new home. When I'd finished and was burning the brush pile, my youngest sister Carlene walked through some of the hot ashes and badly burned her feet.

I believe it was the summer of 1954; a couple of families were grubbing for earth worms near Arran, Florida. Their kids were playing with matches and set the forest on fire. The fire was so hot that it damaged some of the old growth pine trees and the trees became infested with beetles. I worked with 4 cousins that summer, J.A., Bill and Wilburn Vickers and Melvin Martin, cutting the trees and hauling the logs to Raker's Sawmill. We were pressed for time because if the trees were left long enough the damage would discolor the wood. We were on the way home from work one evening when the log truck met a jeep coming toward us on a dirt road with deep ditches on either side. In trying to avoid the jeep, J.A. steered the truck loaded with logs too close to the edge of the road and it caved in. As the truck was rolling on its side, Melvin opened the door, intending to jump out. Fortunately, the truck door hit the ditch bank and pushed Melvin back inside the truck. If he had gotten his hand or head outside the door he could have been seriously injured or killed. When the truck stopped, it was leaning about 45 degrees on its right side with all the logs still intact. The owner of the jeep hooked his tow chain to the front of the truck, and with the combined power of both vehicles we were able to free the truck, continuing our journey to the sawmill, then on home.

In the mid '50s, Dad began work as a chauffeur for a Mr. Thurston Smith and his mother, "Aunt" Marie from Bradenton, Florida. A few years later, the Smiths moved to Panacea, Florida, and Dad began working for them as a handyman. Mr. Thurston was a master watch repairman, and was paralyzed except for his arms. He reclined on a rolling lounge bed and traveled everywhere he went in a hearse. Mr. Thurston loved to hunt and fish, so one cool fall day Dad and I took him squirrel hunting. We positioned him near Culpert sink, a favorite hunting spot of mine, and left him for about two hours. Dad and I did not kill a single squirrel. When we returned, Mr. Thurston pointed and said, "There is a squirrel over there, one over there, and one over there." He had killed three squirrels while laying in one place, and we had none. That made his day and gave him some bragging rights.

On Fridays, Mom wrote our grocery list on a postcard and mailed it to the Charley Rehwinkel Grocery Store about two miles from where we lived. Mom was limited to $10.00 a week for groceries but she almost always included ten cents for candy at the bottom of the list. If Mom forgot to add candy to the list, Mr. or Mrs. Rehwinkel included it anyway. They normally put in ten packets of Kits candy because that could easily be divided among the eight kids living at home. On Saturday mornings, Mr. Charley would deliver the groceries to our house on credit. When we sold a hog, caught some mullet or gathered some oysters or scallops, we'd pay our grocery bill. Mr. Charley had about an acre of land in front of his store and he hired me to use a grubbing hoe to clear the piece of property of all underbrush. He paid me a dollar a day, fed me lunch and gave me one coke each day. I could not drink the coke until after I'd eaten so it would not spoil my lunch.

My nieces and nephews tell me that some of their fondest childhood memories were the times spent sitting on my parents' front porch 'batting the breeze.' When in season, watermelons and homemade ice cream were always great crowd pleasers. The younger kids would play softball in the cow pasture, while carefully dodging cow patties.

There were twenty-one graduates in the Class of 1956 at Crawfordville High School. This was the largest graduating class the school had ever had. At graduation, I was selected as the student most likely to succeed as a farmer. I had a reputation for raising hot peppers, and I enjoyed gardening, but saw no future for me in farming. For the ceremony we were required to wear a suit, so I raised enough money to buy a pair of black pants, a white shirt and a tie. I had borrowed a suit coat from Dalbert Strange, who was about twice my size. When we arrived at the school, I draped the coat over my arm and complained that the weather was too hot to wear a coat and put my gown on. After the graduation ceremony, I again draped the coat over my arm and departed. No one but my family knew the coat didn't fit me.

C. K. Bradshaw

After graduation, the best paying jobs were in Tallahassee. To get a job I needed a car and to buy a car, I needed a job, a catch 22 situation. I knew there was no future for me in farming or the seafood industry. I wanted to serve my country and on July 2, 1956, I joined the United States Air Force. I served 26 years and two months on active duty and 17 years and two month with Civil Service. My wife, Jannefier Lee Grizzard and I were married on June 14, 1960, in El Paso, Texas. We have three outstanding children and the oldest also made the Air Force a career. We have three grandchildren and five grand-dogs. We now do artistic woodturning under the name of Smithworks in Panama City. Some of our turned pieces have been given as gifts on the NBC Today Show and some turnings have been used in a skit on Saturday Night Live. The American Association of Woodturners published a profile on us and we have appeared on local TV shows, also writing a couple of articles for a national woodturning magazine. We have donated a lot of our work to charity and we are presently making ball point pens (Freedom Pens) and shipping them to our military in Iraq and Afghanistan. This effort is non-profit for us and we sell just enough pens to buy more pen kits. Mrs. Betty Green, the Wakulla county historian asked us to write this article. This is a rewrite of an article published in the Wakulla Times in September 2003. We still own property in Wakulla County and call it home.

Submitted By: Dennis C. J. Smith, sawdustmkr@knology.net,, 5225 Park St, Panama City, Florida 32404.

Memories of Aaron and Lola Strickland

Let's start this memory with a family history as I know it. My dad and mom were John Mathew and Bernice Lee (Green) Strickland. His dad and mom was Aaron Benjamin and Lola (Eubanks) Strickland, Aaron's dad and mom was Benjamin and Annie Ida (Mathis) Strickland and his dad and mom was Isom and Permelia (Hall) Strickland.

Aaron B Strickland Lola Eubanks Strickland

Granddaddy and Grandmama Strickland were to me the sweetest people in the world and I have such fond memories of them. From the time I was a small child I made visits to their little farm and had the time of my life. Granddaddy most of the time had a few animals which was a mule for sure, and a bull, plus the cow. He had hogs of all types, male, female, black, white, red and mixtures of those colors. In the winter time they and the family would have hog killings and the processing of that meat. Boy was that a lesson in life, where the pork came from, how it was processed (the smoking of the meat) the different cuts of the meat and so on. We had a time, good food and plenty of cousins and all the love you needed as a kid. And not to forget outhouses, boy was that something. My favorite cousin was James Strickland and we knew him as "Ballzee" he was the son Bud and X.V. Strickland and his sister was Janette Strickland. I also spent lots of time with them and we had fun. Ballzee and I chopped wood for the wood stove in the winter time that was my Christmas vacation. But that was not work for me I was having fun. In the summer time Grandmama would let us go swimming at Whiddon Lake which I always thought was a pond. Grandmama would ask if my mom would mind if I went swimming, and I would say to her, “oh no she would not mind". Granddaddy would let us ride whatever he had at the time, horse, mule or bull. Granddaddy Strickland was an animal whisper, he could handle any animal. He did it from birth with them by touching and talking to them. Grandmama was the best cook; we ate very well all the time, all country cooking. Most of it was home grown food and very plentiful. I never heard them say a bad word or ever get mad. We also went to church at the Ivan Assembly of God with Grandmama and I got the basis of my beliefs. In the summer my cousin and I would make bows and arrows to play with, and other types of homemade toys. Mom would give me $ 10.00 for the month to spend and we would walk down to Rossy Linzys' store. We went through the woods not on the Highway. We got one drink (soda) a day and peanuts to go in that drink. Sometimes it would be a Moon Pie we got, not to go in the drink. This was the life at Grandma Stricklands' house. I will say it was some of the best times of my life. There was no TV, no walkman, no computer, and no cell phone. Thank God for those days. These are the things I remember about my time there at Ben Haden, Wakulla, Florida.

Submitted By; John Preston Strickland, PO Box 745, Crawfordville, FL 32326

My Clans Stories of Taffs and Pelts

My dad was William Reginald Taff (1900-1983,) youngest of four other brothers; my uncles Tully, (b. 1883) Calhoun, (b.1892) Beatty, (b.1895) and Commodore Oliver Hazard Perry Taff (b.1897) I've shown uncle C's full name to indicate my granny Taff's propensity and appreciation of lengthy names. There were five sisters: aunts Sina, (b.1885) Nellie, (b.1889) Mary, (b.1891) Clara and Alma, twins born 1903. Their parents were George Washington and Mary Cada Carraway Taff, and all these named have passed on. Without proof positive, I will say they were of good Irish, Welch and English Stock. Granny Taff's father, Labon Carraway, was in a Confederate cavalry outfit, captured at Mash's Island and imprisoned at Ship Island, Miss. An older Carraway cousin told that the Carraway family boiled and ate shoes, bridles and the like trying to survive during his imprisonment. My great-grandfather William T. Taff, served a year in the 10th Fla. (CSA) regiment. Legend has it, that he returned home and was shot and killed on his front porch. His brother Joseph D. Taff was in the 5th Fla. Regiment, apparently survived the battle of Gettysburg, and was captured during the battle of the

Mary C. Carraway Taff 1865 – 1958; George Washington Taff 1860 - 1942

Wilderness. He was imprisoned at Elmira, N.Y., exchanged in Oct. 1864 and died a month later. He was cited for distinguished service.

Granny Taff, hallowed be her name, was a near saint. She raised other people's kids. The hoboes that rode the rails of the G.F.& A. railroad knew where the Taff house was and would go begging for food. If she had at least flour & lard on hand, she would prepare biscuits and flour gravy. Two of the family houses were adjacent to the railroad below Arran, the last maybe a mile southwest of Arran. One of the homes caught fire and thankfully, the family got out; but my dad, very small, could not be found and there was much wailing. However, he was found in a bundle of blankets that made it out. He had gone to sleep in the blankets behind a door and was thrown out with them. In her later years, well after the death of her husband, Granny would stay around with her sons and daughters. She loved to listen to *Garner Ted Armstrong and the World Tomorrow*, and snot-nosed children best stay away. Houston Taff, son of Uncle Commodore and my youngest Taff first cousin and I were once apprehended by Granny. We were bare footed, sun tanned and hair bleached white by the sun. Granny chewed us out, describing our appearance as that of "heathens." Yet, like her daughters and grizzled sons, we worshiped the ground she walked upon.

My Dad would tell me about their living conditions; they were pioneers in every sense of the word; no electricity or indoor plumbing. Lying in his bed, he would hear panthers screaming in the bay galls and ponds near the home. One of his duties as a child was to round up their cows every evening and head them toward home. Dad said the cows would be running ahead of him and he would begin to hear the sand that he kicked up hitting the leaves behind him; he would get more and more apprehensive of the sound until he was fearfully running full tilt. One of their wild cows got after Dad one evening and he dove, unfortunately, into a bed of "Spanish bayonets," and lost forever the vision in his right eye. Granny decided she would send him to a doctor in Tallahassee, a journey of around 25 miles and requiring him to stay perhaps several days at the doctor's home. With Dad's oldest brother Tully driving the mule and wagon, they departed, arriving in Tallahassee about dark. Dad got out of the wagon and approached the doctor's home while Tully and the wagon began the journey back to Arran. Dad decided rather quickly that he wasn't about to stay and quickly pursued Tully, silently slipping onto the back of the wagon. Tully looked over his shoulder, smiled a bit and saying not a word, headed south to Arran.

Somewhere during this time, Dad and his brother, Uncle Commodore, caught themselves a mess of head lice. Granny mixed up a concoction of lard and sulphur and judiciously applied it to the boy's heads and scalps, and locked them in the smokehouse. Both survived. Uncle Commodore was about 3 yrs. older than Dad. He had two good eyes while Dad had one. In those days many children wore homemade cotton gowns with persimmon seed buttons on the front. These two were each other's nemesis, with Uncle Commodore generally holding the advantage. Once Uncle Commodore who was quick and agile, provoked his younger brother, who then chased him about the yard. There was a nearby two wheeled ox cart with the back on the ground and the tongue up. Uncle Commodore ran up the cart, out on the tongue and tried to leap to the ground. Unfortunately for him, his gown caught on the tongue, leaving him suspended, swinging and twisting in the air. Dad, praying "Thank you Lord, for the blessings I am about to receive," found himself a seasoned sassafras limb and proceeded to thrash his older brother severely.

I have failed to mention that Arran was my Ancestral home. It lies about 3 miles west of

Crawfordville (the county seat) and on the G.F. & A railroad, now long abandoned. My grandfather George W. Taff and family were there along with my great-grandfather Columbus Crawford Pelt, known to most as "Uncle Monk." My dad would tell people that

(Right) George Washington Taff 1860 - 1942
(Left) Half Brother Boykin

"nobody lived behind them," which was literally the truth. great-grandfather C. C. Pelt and great-grandmother, Mary Elizabeth Lawhon Pelt had one child, my grandfather Barnwell Rhett, I am sure named after "fire eating" secessionists in South Carolina. My mother, Estelle Pelt Taff, who taught school in the state of Florida about 40 years, and in her latter years, ashamedly told me that "Uncle Monk" made and sold a little moon shine. I assured her that, in his time, people had to do what was necessary to survive, and I personally felt no shame. Like my Taff grandmother, they fed and raised the children of others.

George S. Taff, USMC 1943

One year, Granddad Taff had got his corn planted and coming up. I suppose it was his custom to go "the bay," probably with others, net and salt down mullet for his family. He gathered up his sons, advising them in the strongest terms that, when he returned, there had best not be a weed showing amongst the corn. Days later upon his return, the corn patch was laden with weeds. Again, he assembled his sons and demanded to know why the corn had not been weeded. Uncle Beatty, third eldest brother, self appointed spokesman and future businessman declared: "Pa, every since you left, Commodore and Willie (the 2 youngest) have done nothing but play, and Pa, if you do your duty, you will whip the two of them." His dad replied: "Beatty you are exactly right. Go get me a stout switch and I will do my duty." When Beatty returned with the switch, his dad proceeded to thoroughly thrash him.

Some few years later, my dad and some other Arran boys decided to walk north up the railroad to the community of Ivan to attend a revival, which is somewhat laughable. The whole idea was to meet some of the young ladies in attendance. In his pocket Dad had an old owl-head pistol in which was one bullet. The Ivan boys were not averse to fighting, had the Arran boys outnumbered, and advised them that, after services there would be hell to play. Sure enough, they were waiting outside for the Arranites to exit the church. Dad pulled out the old pistol and advised them: "Fellows, I have one bullet in this thing, but if this goes any further, one of you will wear the bullet home," thus ending said confrontation.

In spite of his impoverished background, Dad "got around." My mother even told me that he had dated Miss Ruby Diamond, a lady in Tallahassee, a philanthropist to and for Florida State College for Women, and for whom Ruby

Diamond auditorium was named. Yet, there was an incident involving a good friend of Dad and his family, one Mr. Jim Kirkland, who would marry Miss Etta Maude Rouse of Sopchoppy, south of Arran. Jim could only be described as a "character" or a "scamp," and I say this with affection. I assume it was in the village of Panacea that my dad sat with two proper young ladies, along with their chaperone, waiting on Jim, who would provide transportation. The young ladies had not met Jim and began questioning Dad, inquiring about his "character," and so on. Dad assured them that Jim was refined, educated and every bit the gentleman. In other words Dad was lying through his teeth. Momentarily, with his one good eye, Dad noticed a huge cloud of dust to the north, headed for Panacea at a high rate of speed. It was Jim in his roadster. As he approached, Dad could see that Jim had on a pair of bib overalls, maybe a white shirt, and wearing a Mexican sombrero with cotton balls dangling. Jim slammed on brakes in front of Dad and the young ladies, and proceeded to do a "hook slide" before them, unfortunately turning his roadster up on one side. The end of this story is not known by this writer, but obviously ended in disaster, and in my Dad's case, embarrassment.

Dad's brother, Uncle Beatty purchased Shell Point, year unknown. Dad worked in the seine yard, etc., but his main job was to take the fish, which were salted down in barrels, to Georgia and sell them. At some point, one of the men involved decided that Dad had defrauded him. (Names deleted to protect the guilty and innocent.) Dad was a man of medium to small stature, while his accuser was huge. It turned out that they met in some beer joint, location unknown, probably Panacea, Dad at a table alone, his accuser and his friend at another. Dad's adversary began talking about him in a loud, accusatory voice. (When my Dad told me about this, he said he didn't even have a pocket knife on him.) Dad was dressed to the "nines," wearing a "claw hammer coat." One word led to another, with a challenge being made to carry the argument outside. Dad walked by his tormentor, who, with his knife cut off a tail of Dad's coat. Dad led the way out, not knowing what to do, and when the other man came through the door, he, as Dad said, shut off the light from a 60 watt bulb inside the establishment. The man proceeded; knife and all, while Dad kept backing up until his hand brushed something. He had backed into a pile of scrap iron. What his hand had brushed was the clutch pedal of a Model "A" or a Model "T" and this he came up with, and struck the man down. The gentleman arose to continue the fight and was again struck down. The fight was over at this point and they became the best of friends afterwards.

Uncle Calhoun, second eldest brother, was a man of few words and not one to be trifled with. He was slow to anger, but trouble followed when he reached his limit. I remember him as being one of the larger of the brothers. He wound up running a meat market, later a Sinclair filling station and a cafe at "four points," basically a road intersection on the south end of Tallahassee. In the early years, and here again, we must protect the names of the guilty, two Wakulla County gentlemen, about three sheets to the wind and needing a way home, knowing Uncle Calhoun, walked up and requested to borrow his vehicle. Uncle Calhoun, cutting up a beef with a meat cleaver, denied them. One persisted, cursing Calhoun, removing his flat brimmed straw hat and sailed that, striking Calhoun and bloodying

Broward Taff, WWII, USAF

his nose and finally, utterly frustrated, leaned over the counter and gritted his teeth. That did it. With meat cleaver in hand, Calhoun leaped over the counter, advising that he "could not stand an SB gritting his teeth at him," and chased the fellows down the road. I was a 1 7 yr. old Marine recruit at Parris Island, SC and was called to the Chaplain when he died, July 4, 1957. His antagonist was a best friend of my father and our family. In his restaurant, Uncle Calhoun's pork-pig barbecue sandwich was the best I ever had.

If great-grandfather William T. Taff had any remorse that he and his brother Joseph D., were in the Confederate Army, and probably

Front: Left to right: Aunt Nellie Taff Vause, Granny Taff, William Reginald (Dad), Clara Alice Taff Vause; Back left to right: Commodore, Tully Beatty, Calhoun

he didn't, about all his great-grandsons served the U.S. during WWII, there being nine or ten of them. G. W., (uncle Tully's son,) me, and Houston, (the youngest, son of Uncle Commodore,) were far too young. Clayton, U.S.N., eldest son of Uncle Commodore, served on Okinawa. Broward, eldest son of uncle Beatty, was a bomber pilot. He saw serious combat in Europe; piloted transports in Korea and old C-47 "spookies" in Vietnam. He was the "dare-devil" of the lot. He retired a Lt. Colonel, USAF. His younger brother, George was with the Second Marine Division in a machine gun section on the Pacific Islands of Tarawa and Saipan. A close friend of Broward and George was Jack Yaeger, Jr. of Tallahassee, as were Broward and George. Yaeger was a fighter pilot and flew bombing and strafing missions in support of Marines on the ground in Saipan, supposedly not knowing one of his best friends was on the ground beneath him. George and Yaeger would eventually run into each other, as Yaeger would relate in his book Smiling Jack Yaeger, (c) 1997, an excellent memoir. As related by my cousin Clayton, after the surrender of Germany, the Eighth Air Force, to which Broward belonged, landed their bombers on the Island of Hiroshima, off Okinawa. Clayton said there were planes on the ground as far as one could see. I suppose Broward continued bombing missions over Japan and knew where Yaeger and the fighter pilot's tents were. He and his four engine bomber were coming in one day, maybe from a mission; he cut the engines of the big B-24 and came lumbering in low over Yaeger's tent, and at once revved up the engines, full throttle, causing a horrendous disturbance. Yaeger, fully awake, came boiling out of his tent, shaking his fist at the big bomber, yelling "Damn you, Broward Taff, you.

At other times, some of which I barely remember, Broward would be home; he would rent a plane, and I have a vague memory of him doing aerobatics over Arran. Once, he with our cousin

William Reginald Taff, Sheriff Wakulla County 1957 - 1977

Clayton managed to land near the Lost Creek Bridge, near Arran, and taxied the plane up to Uncle Commodore's house. It was necessary to get the plane turned around, and this Clayton did, lifting the tail up, heading the thing back east. Our granny Taff was in my Uncles home and came out of the house, a broom in one hand, shaking a fist with the other, advising her grandsons to get that plane away from there. It is ironic that Broward's younger brother Charles died in a plane crash near Shell Point, searching for their dad's rental skiff boats after a storm. Years later, one of Broward's younger sons, Stan, a "bush pilot" working with Native Indian tribes in Alaska, crashed his plane into a mountain and did not survive.

I barely remember the trains coming through Arran. Once, I recall a train headed north, leaving Camp Gordon Johnson. The troops on it were throwing out fruit, candy bars and change, while we kids, black and white scrambled in the dirt picking up what we could. I have often wondered how many of those fellows got home alive from World War II. Uncle Evander Vause, married to Dad's sister, Aunt Alice, ran a small store at the intersection of Arran Road and the G.F.& A railroad. He and his family would eventually move to Quincy, Fl., where he would again run a small store. He would be robbed and killed there over $25 or $30, in a crime never solved.

My great-great-grandfather on the maternal side was Durant J. Pelt, born in 1818, married to Melvina Posey. He served in a Confederate reserve outfit, Co. E., 1st Fl. He and Melvina were parents of Shelton, Henry Ellis, Columbus C. (my great-Grandfather,) Andrew Jackson, Virginia, Noah, Peter, Melvina, George W., and Durant, Jr., a WWI veteran. Their homestead was about a mile or two Southeast of Arran. I always smile when I think about their children's nicknames: Aunt Puss, Uncle Pig, Uncle Tobe, Uncle Bostic, Uncle Monk (my great-grandfather) and Aunt Gennie. I have previously told a little about "Monk," well known in his neck of the woods. Some fellows from Arran, probably already a little bit "loaded," went to Uncle "Monk's" place, to re-fortify. It was necessary to cross a small branch, or creek. As they came away, approaching this branch, there was a small limb, protruding from the water, and upon which was a small turtle. One passenger in the car exclaimed "My God would you look at the cooters on that limb."

One of the fiercest Pelts was Uncle Tobe (Henry Ellis, died 1931.) Once, he was on a bear hunt with some of the Lawhon clan (my great-grandmother was a Lawhon,) and the dogs had bayed up a bear close to a pond. Uncle Tobe rushed in to kill the bear; which, crazed by the dogs, charged Uncle Tobe, got him down and tried to maul him. Fortunately, one of the Lawhons came and shot the bear off him. Some days later, some of the Lawhons came to Uncle Tobe, wanting him and his dogs to join in another bear hunt. Supposedly, he said "I have told you once, and I am telling you again, I am not interested in no damn bear."

When Dad was a kid, he helped Uncle Tobe put new hand riven wooden shingles on a corn crib. Things proceeded well, but Uncle Tobes eyes were failing him. He hit his fingers with a hammer, stood up cursing and threw his hammer into a nearby bed of palmettos; said to my Dad, "Boy, get up and go get my

Columbus Crawford (Monk) Pelt and Mary Elizabeth Lawhon Pelt

(Left) Phillip Lawhon;(Right) Barnwell Rhett Pelt

hammer." Naturally, my Dad obeyed him. It was not long before he struck his fingers again; stood up and hurled the hammer, exclaiming "Damn these blind eyes of mine, I wish they would fly out of my head like rifle balls, bouncing off those pines. Boy, go get my hammer." Again, Dad obeyed, but he claimed he told Uncle Tobe that he would not do this again. I don't think I believe my Dad.

My grandfather tied up around 1,100 acres of land near Purify Bay, and moved his family there. This was done with the assistance of a relative down state. A storm hit the Purify area in 1928 and pretty well wiped out the possessions of my grandparents. In the meantime, the relative down state was severely injured, no longer able to hold up his part of the business arrangement. My grandfather Barnwell Rhett Pelt, who had rowed his boat over to Spring Creek to visit friends and relatives, and leaving on a freezing night, died in the bay he loved in 1932. Like so many families in the South during the Great Depression, hundreds of acres of family property, live stock and so on were lost.

One of my best friends, a cousin and classmate was Berlin Pelt, son of Carmel Pelt, a close friend of the family who served in North Africa and in Europe in Gen. Patton's Third Army. I was also close to Randall and Donald Pelt and all were descendants of Uncle Bostic. We would run Little Creek and Lost Creek like a bunch of coons hunting and fishing, legal and otherwise. Living close by was cousin "Jibb" Pelt, a state Game Warden and son of Uncle Tobe. For some reason, Cousin Jibb would use his personal vehicle, an old Chevrolet truck. Once, he almost caught Berlin and me coming out to a road, carrying our gigs, which we were using illegally in Lost Creek. Fortunately, we managed to throw them in the bushes before cousin Jibb, aka "Hootchiepap,"saw them. He accosted us, knowing what we had been doing. I could see Uncle Tobe in his eyes while he advised us that he would eventually catch us, two young violators, scared straight, at least temporarily.

Submitted by Wm. Rhett Taff P.0. Box 1657 Crawfordville, Fl. 32326

Joseph Lee Thomas

Joseph Lee Thomas was born in Bell, Florida on October 23, 1915. His parents were Joseph Ernest and Emeline Kinsey Thomas.

His ancestors have been traced back to Holmestrand, Norway. Christopher Galschit (born 1681) married Anne Margarethe Thue (born 1683) and they had two sons Neils and Lars. Neils and Lars went to sea as sailors. Lars was born in 1683. Lars migrated to Cecil County, Maryland. He married and they had two daughters. One of the daughters, Anne Gailshott married John Thomas who migrated to Cecil, Maryland from Wales. They migrated to South Carolina and then on to Screven County, Georgia. They named their son Gilshott Ransom Thomas. He married Helen Williams and they had a son named James Ransom Thomas who married Sallie Sarah Banner. Both James and his father Gilshott fought in the Revolutionary War. James Ransom Thomas Sr. is buried in the Cemetery of Shiloh Primitive Baptist Church in Blackshear, Georgia. James and Sallie Sarah had seven children. Their son Lewis Thomas was born in 1789. Lewis married Elizabeth Mixon and they had nine children. Their son Joseph Thomas was born in 1815. Joseph married Rhoda Waldron. They had thirteen children. Their son Lewis Rance Thomas was born in 1841.

Lewis Rance Thomas married Martha Nettles in 1860. *This is the Grand Parents of Joseph Lee Thomas.* On March 4, 1862 he enlisted in the Confederate Army. He was wounded at Boonsboro, Md. on September 14, 1862. He was promoted 4th Sgt. In December 1862 and promoted again to 1st Sgt. On March 23, 1864. After the war he moved to Bell, Gilchrest County, Florida. Lewis and Martha had eight children. After Martha's death he married Rachel Townsend. He and Rachel had two children. After her death Lewis married Osceola Long and they had ten children. He was the father of twenty children. Joseph Ernest Thomas was born on January 30, 1868. He was the son of Lewis Rance and Martha.

Joseph Ernest Thomas married Emeline Kinsey on December 28, 1898. They had four children. Joseph Lee (J.L.) was only four years old when his father died from the flu. J.L.'s mother remarried and had a daughter. His mother died from the flu in 1920.

J.L. went to live with his Aunt Minnie and Uncle Clarence. He completed the eighth grade which was a high as you could go in Bell.

When he was 15 years old his brother Levi came to get him. He lived with Levi and his wife Lula Belle in Shadeville, near Wakulla Springs. He went to work helping Levi sell moonshine. They also planted pine trees for the WPA.

He became friends with Charlie Barwick, who was Lula Belle's nephew. He wound up going to Panacea where he met Geneva Hartsfield at the Panacea Mineral Springs. They starting courting and went to Apalachicola where they got married in 1940.

They had nine children. Delma Thomas married Patsy Sanders, Bessie Nell Thomas married Cecil Gilbert, Marvis Thomas married Louise Willis, Odell Thomas married Gracie Golden, Linda Thomas married Buddy Camp, Hixon Thomas married Bashby Sanders, Eva Thomas married and Early Duggar, Isaac Thomas married Debbie Chitty and then Elizabeth Floyd , Joseph Lee(Junior) Thomas got killed in an automobile accident when he was just 15 years old in 1970. They raised their children in Panacea where they spent most of their life making a living in the bay. He was a commercial fisherman, taught by his father-in-law Ed Hartsfield. He started J.L. Thomas and Son's Seafood which later developed into one of the largest seafood companies in the state of Florida.

J. L. died on November 18, 1968 and is buried in the Panacea Cemetery.

Submitted and written by, Louise Thomas, 419 Buckhorn Creek Rd. Sopchoppy, Fl 32358

Janie Ruth Ward Thurmond

Wakulla County Native- Janie's Life Story

"Dr. Harper, I need you to come to my house because my wife Eunice is ready to deliver," Nathaniel "Nat" Walker Ward, Sr. excitedly exclaimed when he arrived at the doctor's house. This was very early in the morning on Thursday March 8, 1934 and Dr. Joseph Harper hurried to Nat's home and helped to bring a baby girl named Janie Ruth Ward into this world. Janie arrived at the Ward home on "Mail Road", now named Lawhon Mill Road in the "suburbs" of Medart, Wakulla County, Florida. Eunice Green Ward (born in Live Oak community near Crawfordville on June 25, 1904) and Nat (born in Crawfordville

Young Janie Ward Thurmond

January 23, 1900) had built their first house, a four room wood frame home, in 1930 near my Grandmother Ruth Gwaltney Green (born April 1887 in Wakulla County near Arran where her father Lewis Gwaltney had a general store). Eunice wanted to live nearby and be of assistance to her mother Ruth and younger siblings. Grandma Ruth Green had been left a widow with six young children when my Grandpa Willie T. Green (born in 1880 in the Live Oak community near Crawfordville, Wakulla County) died in 1923 from typhoid fever. In fact Grandma Ruth suffered three tragedies within one month in 1923, all from typhoid fever. She not only lost her husband, but her father Lewis Gwaltney, and a sister Bessie Gwaltney Roberts. When Eunice's father Willie T. died, she was 18 years old and was encouraged by the Superintendent of Schools in Wakulla County, Mr. Jake Pigott to teach school in the nearby one room school house at Live Oak, only about a mile from where the Green family lived. So Eunice began teaching on a temporary certificate in 1923 and then took the state teacher's test in 1924 and received her certificate. I am privileged to have her original temporary certificate and also her three other certificates she received by taking the State teacher's tests. Interestingly enough these certificates have her test scores on them. During her teaching years she taught in one room school houses in St. Marks, Crawfordville, and Otter Creek, as well as her first school at Live Oak. In December 1924 Eunice and Nat got married so Teacher Eunice Green became Teacher Eunice Green Ward. Since Eunice was the oldest child in her family, she taught her brothers and sisters at Live Oak school. One interesting story her brother Homer Green told me was that he urinated in his pants at school one day so teacher Eunice whipped him. He got mad and went home and his mother Ruth whipped him. Also to compound his troubles, she sent him back to school and teacher Eunice whipped him for leaving school without permission. My Uncle Homer laughingly told me that he couldn't win either way that day.

Ruth Gwaltney Green

I do not remember a lot of things that happened during my pre-school years. But one of the things I want to do in this story is give glory to God who has blessed me in so many wonderful ways all throughout my life. As a young girl of 14, I dedicated my life to Jesus Christ and started a personal relationship with Him that has grown sweeter and sweeter as I have grown and matured. Accepting Jesus Christ as my Lord and Savior was the most important decision I have ever made in my whole life and I suggest that it should be the most important decision anyone can make with his or her life. When I was born my sister Clarice Irene was eight years old and my brother, Nathaniel Walker "N.W." Ward, Jr.

Nathaniel Walker Ward Sr. & Eunice Green Ward

was 6 ½ years old. We had a loving family who loved Jesus and had a daily devotion time each evening where we read the Bible and prayed together. My Dad was not raised in a Christian family so in his early years he knew nothing about being a Christian. On Mom and Dad's wedding night Mom knelt down beside the bed to pray. Dad asked her what she was doing and she replied that she was doing what she had always done before going to bed, she was praying. Dad said he wanted to do that too so he accepted Jesus as his personal Savior on his wedding night. Nat remained a dedicated Christian all his life and later became a minister of the Gospel of Jesus Christ, pastoring White Church in Woodville, Beulah

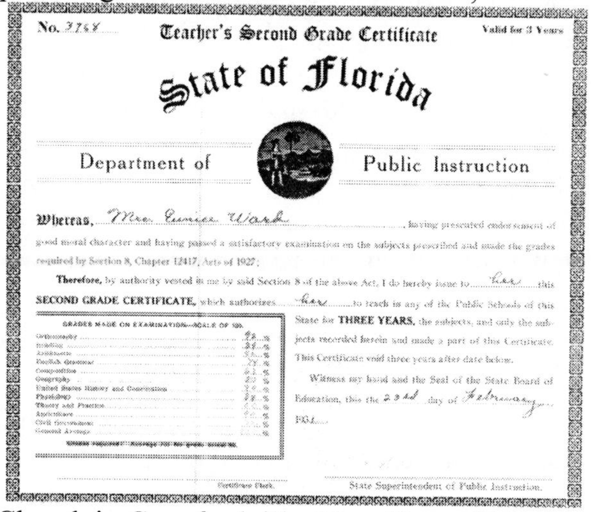
No. 3768 Teacher's Second Grade Certificate Valid for 3 Years

State of Florida

Department of Public Instruction

Whereas, Mrs. Eunice Ward, having presented endorsement of good moral character and having passed a satisfactory examination on the subjects prescribed and made the grades required by Section 8, Chapter 12417, Acts of 1927;

Therefore, by authority vested in me by said Section 8 of the above Act, I do hereby issue to her this SECOND GRADE CERTIFICATE, which authorizes her to teach in any of the Public Schools of this State for THREE YEARS, the subjects, and only the subjects recorded herein and made a part of this Certificate. This Certificate void three years after date below.

Witness my hand and the Seal of the State Board of Education, this the 23rd day of February 193...

GRADES MADE ON EXAMINATION—SCALE OF 100.

State Superintendent of Public Instruction.

Church in Crawfordville, New Home Church in Otter Creek, and preaching many other places. He with God's help, was always a good provider for our family so we had all our needs met. My mother came from a Godly family - her mother Ruth was a saint, her father Willie T. was a minister of the gospel of Jesus Christ pastoring at Friendship Primitive Baptist Church in the early 1900s. Grandma Ruth had a number of ministers among her pioneer ancestors that I will tell you about later. Grandma Ruth was so very faithful to our Lord Jesus Christ and her church, Friendship. I remember as a little girl how she loved Jesus and talked about Him to family and friends. I also remember she had a plaque hanging in her living room that stated, "Only one life will soon be past. Only what is done for Christ will last". This statement, although not understood at that time is so true.

An early memory of mine at age 4 or 5 is of a traveling evangelist by the name of Sister Cobb who came to Grandma Green's house asking if she could preach in Grandma's barn and invite the neighbors to attend. Grandma Ruth gave permission and the meetings began. Our family attended every night, however one night I got very sleepy, so Mom took me home (about one block from bam) and changed me into my pajamas and put me to bed. As soon as she left to go back to the meeting, I got wide awake, put my clothes back on and walked back to the barn. To say the least, Mom was very unhappy with me since she had gone to the trouble to carry me home and put me to bed. I also remember a few times when evangelists built brush arbors and had church in them a couple of places along the "Mail Road" where we lived.

As a young girl, I remember a couple of times when Mr. Luther Lovett came and taught a basic music school at Friendship Church which was attended by many in the Medart community. We learned some simple things about music notes and a few other basic musical rules. This same Mr. Lovett had several children who sang with him as a group -Mr. Lovett, Edna, John, James, Wendell, and Virgil - The Lovett Family. I

Eunice Green Ward, Willie T. & Ruth Green, Alice Green McKenzie

also have many other fond memories of Friendship Church which I attended into my teen years.

One of my fond memories as a little girl was the "Rolling Store", a covered, closed in panel truck with built in shelves along the sides filled with staple foods and other basic supplies. This truck would drive from home to home around the countryside selling to everyone. As a small child I really enjoyed helping Mom shop in the Rolling Store. Another memory was the "Ice Man", Mr. Cloyce Vause with young son Lee as his helper, who would deliver ice to our door for our "ice box" which was our early refrigerator (we had no electricity). Often I was given the gift of a small piece of broken ice to suck on. What a treat on a hot summer day.

Since we had no electricity, our drinking water came from a hand pump with a pipe driven about 10 -15 feet into the ground. By the way, it tasted very good and refreshing -I wish I had some now. Our toilet was a small outdoor building (outhouse) with two holes in the wooden seat and an old out of date catalog. That means that two people could possibly use the toilet at the same time even though I don't remember that ever happening.

In winter our only source of heat for our house came from a wood burning fireplace in the living room with a chimney built on the outside. One of my many chores in winter was to bring wood into the house. We had a woodpile where the wood was dumped when we hauled it from the forest. Sometimes if there was no wood in the woodpile, I had to go to the forest and gather it. Of course the fire always went out at night so as a young girl it was my lot to build the fire in the morning. Needless to say, I learned to build a fire very fast. We were always on the lookout for a mystery wood that helped to get a fire started very quickly that we called lightard (short for wood to light a fire). This was obtained from certain pine trees scattered throughout the forest that had died and had stored up a lot of resin thus making them very flammable. I still enjoy going into the woods and picking up lightard, especially knots, today. As a youngster another use of this wood was cooking our meals on a wood stove which did provide some extra heat in winter but unfortunately unwanted heat in summer. We later upgraded to an oil burning cook stove and felt we were almost like city folks.

One weekly chore was clothes washing. On one day each week we lined up 3 big wash tubs on tables outside and started our clothes washing. The first tub was used to wash the clothes along with a scrub board, and the other two were to rinse them. Pumping water for all these tubs was another chore. We also had a big wash pot with an open fire underneath which we used to boil the white clothes to keep them extra white. Of course after rinsing them twice, we hung them on our clothes lines (in earlier times some people who did not have clothes lines used the shrubbery and other plants in their yard to lay the clothes on for drying). Washing the clothes was always a big job which lasted a large portion of the day.

A spring and summer job was gardening. We always had a big garden with lots of vegetables so with no electricity and no freezer there was always canning going on in summer. We not only canned vegetables but also made jelly, jams, and preserves from berries, pears, figs, and any other fruit we could find or grow. In the fall or winter there was always a time for hog killing that took place at least once a year. We made our own bacon, sausage, pork chops, ham, and even hogshead cheese. The bacon, sausage, and ham were smoked in our little smoke house (we actually used real smoke not the liquid stuff they use today) and this took several days. The smoking process was not just for taste but was also a preservative element. You can see that we grew most of our own food which included vegetables, fruits, and meat. All this was lots of work but the food was very delicious.

A big change in our family took place in 1944 when my brother N.W. joined the Navy as a 17 year old boy (I was 10) to serve in World War II. Young men were being drafted into the military so N.W. wanted to choose his branch of service because most young men drafted were drafted into the army. My sister Clarice got married to Robert Calhoun Taff in 1945 when I was 11 years old. My younger sister Patsy was only 3 or 4 years old at that time so I was left as the only sibling to do much of the work around the house. I spent time each day caring for chickens, pigs, and cows that had to be fed, watered, and other care. We always had a milk cow which Mom and I took turns milking each morning. One week I would milk the cow and Mom would cook breakfast. The next week we switched those tasks. I did all of these things in AM before I could dress to meet the school bus driven by Mr. Troy Eubanks and head to Sopchoppy for school where I attended all my elementary and secondary years. When I returned home from school each day I fed the animals, gathered wood in winter (sometimes I had to go into the forest if no wood had been hauled to our woodpile), worked in the garden in spring and summer, milked the cow sometimes, before I studied. I did my homework mainly by the light of a kerosene or gas lamp. Despite all of this extra work I graduated in 1952 in my senior class of 18 as valedictorian. Several of my classmates still live in the area where we grew up. I now live less than 1/2 mile from where I was born and raised. Classmates Gracie Corley Roberts, Dan Strickland, Ronald Langston, and Claxton Vause all live in the Sopchoppy area.

Of course all was not work. One of my favorite things to do in fall was go over to Uncle Horace Mather's farm for the cane grinding and syrup making. We children always played on the pummy pile (the pummy was the cane stalks after the juice was removed by squeezing it to remove the juice). We also drank cane juice and enjoyed socializing with each other. Uncle Horace was half brother to my Grandpa Green. They shared the same mother Isabella "Bell" Sanders Green Mathers who owned hundreds of acres of land in the Live Oak area. The acres of land that Horace got from his mother "Bell" is still in the Mathers family today as Mather's Farm and our daughter-in-law Debbie, Duane's wife is part of that family. Most of the land Willie T. Green received from his mother "Bell" has been sold to other people but the Thurmond family has continued to own the 20 acres they received from the family back in the early 1970s and this is the only part of the Green family land that stayed in the family continually all the years since around 1905. The Thurmonds have acquired some of the other acreage that was in the Green family back in 1905 but had previously been sold to others.

On the "Mail Road", on the land adjoining us to the south, were our closest neighbors the Will and Sally White family. Interestingly enough presently, my closest neighbor on Frank Jones Road is Wilhemina White Morrison one of Will and Sally's daughters. Another of Will and Sally's daughters who is near my age, June White Purvis was one of my closest friends who played with me a lot when we were small. We would meet halfway between our two houses to play but I would stop closer to my house and June would stop closer to her house so we would yell from

Family of J. Harold & Janie Ward Thurmond. (All 18)

about 100 feet apart to each other to come on half way (this was part of our game). We were best friends and spent many wonderful hours playing together, building playhouses in the woods even at the Sasser Field just north of us. I don't get to see June very often now. She married Jerry Purvis, a doctor, and they have lived and he has practiced medicine for around 50 years in the Valdosta, GA. area.

My other playmates were my cousins who were mainly boys so we played boy games outside most of the time; games such as football with a tin can or whatever else we found that was suitable. My main playmate was my cousin who was only 1 year older than me and who also graduated with me in 1952, Gwynn Scarbrough, son of Sam and Trudie Scarbrough. Sam died when Gwynn was less than two years old so Gwynn and his Mom lived with Grandma Ruth about one block away. We were just like brother and sister while growing up and spent lots of time playing together during our young years. Just as with my friend June Purvis, Gwynn and I don't get to see each other much anymore because he moved to Valdosta, Ga. in the 1950s and has lived there ever since. My friend June gets to see him more often than I do. Gwynn was in his 50s when he felt called of the Lord to be a minister of the Gospel of Jesus Christ just as his father Sam had been. He pastored at the First Baptist Church in Morven, Ga. for about ten years in the 1990s and I found out recently that one of our great, great uncles, James Giles had pastored in the 1800's at the Methodist church in Morven, Ga. Another cousin playmate was Alvin Moore who was 2 or 3 years younger than I so he was that little kid that just bugged us and tagged along. Alvin and his mother Willie Ruth who lost her husband when Alvin was a little baby also lived with Grandma Green.

Other than my Mom, Grandma Green's children are Alice who married Wattie McKenzie at the age of 14. They had 12 children who all lived to be adults and have families of their own. Edith was the third member of the Willie T. and Ruth Green clan. She married Sam Ward who happened to be brother to my daddy, Nat. So I had four double first cousins from that union. The next member of that family to come into this world was a boy named Trammel. He married Doris Hagens whose father was a doctor and Dr. Hagens had married into the Taft family of Wakulla County. Trammel and Doris had 3 children, 2 boys to help carry on the Green name and one girl. Trudie was child number 5 in the Green family with her one son Gwynn that I have already talked about. Willie Ruth was next with her son Alvin that I just mentioned. The second son Homer joined the Green family and he married Dot Forehand who helped him raise one son and 2 daughters. His son also helped to carry on the Green family name. Next came Hyatt who had three sons to help keep the Green family name in existence. The baby who was born around the time that Grandpa Willie T. died was named Opal. Sadly, Opal only lived about one year.

A big surprise happened on December 7, 1941 when I was almost 8 years old. The Japanese bombed Pearl Harbour and our country was thrust into World War II. I remember hearing all the talk, concern, and confusion among the adults that day so I didn't think anything about it when I was sent to stay with Grandma Green on December 8. Before long, to my surprise, I was informed that I had a baby sister delivered at home by Dr. Joseph Harper who had also delivered me in 1934. My little sister, Eunice Patricia was named after our mother. For coming and delivering Patsy, Dr. Harper was paid with a coffee can full of pennies (approximately $25) that Dad had been saving for a long time. Of course Patsy was never old enough to help me with the daily chores because she was only 10 by the time I graduated from high school.

After graduation from high school in 1952, I moved to Tallahassee into an apartment on North Gadsden Street with two cousins, Hilda and Maxine McKenzie. I had a job in the State Capitol building for the Comptroller's office as a key punch operator. There were about 16 girls working in that office when I began working there. That number increased to 26 by the time I had been there almost seven years and had worked myself into the position of assistant supervisor of that section. I had a promising career ahead of me with the State of Florida but something else that was more important came along for me to do. I got married and quit work to stay home with Duane who was 19 months old when Jayce Harold Thurmond and I got married on November 26, 1958. Duane's mother, Thelma Barineau had become like a sister to me and was my best friend. She and I worked together, went to church together, and spent most of our time together. In June 1956 Thelma and Jayce Harold Thurmond got married. I was the maid of honor in their wedding. Ten months later on April 15, 1957 Harold Duane Thurmond came into this world. Three months after Duane was born, on July 16, 1957 Thelma was killed in an automobile accident in Oklahoma while they were on their way for Harold to interview for a teaching job in Madison County, Florida. Harold was in the army stationed at Ft. Riley Kansas.

Young Jayce Harold Thurmond

So that he could get out of the army to be able to take care of his baby, Duane, Harold took that teaching job in Madison County and moved to Florida. Needless to say I had an attachment to Duane. Well to make a long story short Harold and I got married 16 months later on November 26, 1958 while Harold was teaching in Moultrie, Ga. We were a readymade family of three to begin with. We lived in Moultrie the first 6 months of our married life then moved to Tallahassee, Florida where Harold began teaching at Augusta Raa in 1959, the first year Raa opened as a Junior High School. While Harold was teaching at Raa for seven years we lived at three different places in Tallahassee, with our last residence being 2404 Tupelo Terrace. Also while in Tallahassee we added two more members to our family. Brent was born June 25, 1960 which happened to be my mother's birthday. Mother Eunice Green Ward had been born just 56 years earlier in Wakulla County. Then on August 11, 1962 our baby girl Janna came into our home. Over the years, since 1978 we have had ten wonderful grandchildren added to the family. Duane and Debbie (Mathers) Thurmond have three; Michael born in 1978 is now married to Kari; Anthony born in 1979 is married to Miria, and Krista born in 1982 is married to Dale. Brent and Anne (McCoy) Thurmond have three; Meagan born in 1988, Sarah born in 1989, and Wesley born in 1994. Janna and Steve Currieo have four; Ashley born in 1986 and married to Matt, Alii born in 1988, Ariel born in 1991, and Andrew born in 1995. Our family enjoyed our time in Tallahassee.

Sgt. Jayce Harold Thurmond.
U.S. Army 1955-1957

But Tallahassee turned out not to continue to be our home because in August 1966 our family moved to Winter Garden, Florida where Harold became Assistant Principal of Lakeview High School. It is interesting how God works in all things, because the Principal, Bob Moore, who was a Christian, was hunting an Assistant Principal. Bob for some unknown reason went to the Social Studies applications when he didn't even need a Social Studies teacher and "accidentally" pulled from a whole drawer of applications the folder of J. Harold Thurmond who was certified in administration but had only applied for a teaching job thinking there would be no need to apply in a new school system for an administrative job. God continued to work. Bob Moore called Harold and invited him down to Winter Garden for an interview. Needless to say that interview and the ones with the school board went well (God has a way of seeing that those things happen when it is His will). One exciting thing that happened while in Winter Garden was I started to College. Everyone else in our family was in school so I decided to join them after being out of high school for 15 years. Valencia Junior College began in 1967 in Orlando so I became a part time student during their first year in operation. We greatly enjoyed our two years in Winter Garden but God had other plans for our family. In the summer of 1968, Bill Payne, who had just become Superintendent of Schools of Wakulla County, called Harold and offered him the position of General Supervisor of Wakulla Schools. Harold felt that would be a great opportunity for him so our family prayed about that and we felt this was the proper move at that time. It turned out to be one of the most important decisions our family ever made for several reasons. One reason - Wakulla County was a wonderful place to raise our family, but another reason was that Disney World had just bought the land just south of Winter Garden and after Disney World opened, the small town pleasant atmosphere of little Winter Garden completely changed. It was no longer the place to raise a family anymore. Another good thing about moving to Wakulla County - I got to attend Tallahassee Junior College, where I graduated and then moved on to Florida State University where I graduated Magna Cum Laude in 1972, exactly 20 years after high school graduation.

Our three children, Duane age 11, Brent age 8, and Janna age 6 all enjoyed Wakulla County and all did well in our very good school system here in Wakulla with Duane graduating from Wakulla High School in 1975, Brent in 1978, and Janna in 1980. Janna graduated as Valedictorian of her class of 1980 just as Mama Janie had done at Sopchoppy High back in 1952.

Young Jayce Harold and Janie Ward Thurmond Family. Tallahassee, FL

I mentioned earlier that my Mom became a one room school teacher at the age of 19. Her first teaching job was about a mile from where her family lived at Live Oak School (very near where Brother Emmitt Whaley lived most of his life and he was also one of her early students). She taught her brothers and sisters there and later taught her own older daughter and son. She not only taught at Live Oak School but also at St. Marks, Crawfordville, and Otter Creek, all these being one room school houses. She started something in her family because I became a teacher; I married a teacher J. Harold Thurmond; our daughter Janna became a teacher; and our granddaughter Alli became a teacher. There are several other teachers in our family; daughter-in-law Anne is a teacher, grandson-in-law Matt is a teacher, grandson Anthony plans to teach, and granddaughter-in-law Kari plans to teach. I taught at Crawfordville Elementary for 23 years beginning in 1972 at age 38. I retired from there in 1995 and we have fully enjoyed our retirement doing a lot of travelling with much of it being short term mission's trips.

It is wonderful that God has a plan for our lives and He has a way of working everything out for those plans. I would have never dreamed that God had a plan for my husband Harold to become Clerk of Court in Wakulla County. In fact when Harold first mentioned to me that he was thinking and praying about running for that job, I objected because I told him that politics was dirty and not a thing for a good man like him to get involved in. Harold asked me if I would pray about it, so I reluctantly agreed to pray. When I did really pray about it, the Lord changed my mind and my attitude about it, so because of God's guidance Harold was elected as Clerk of Court in 1988, the same year he retired from education after spending 31 years in that field. We felt that God had placed Harold in different positions in the school system so that the majority of the people in the county knew him by the time he ran for the position of Clerk of Court. To add to that blessing, when Harold decided to retire from the Clerk's job, our son Brent had become interested in that position. Brent decided to run for Clerk and with God's help the people of Wakulla elected him in 1996. Brent is still blessed to hold that position after 14 years on the job. My Dad, Nat Ward, Sr. would have been so proud of Harold and Brent being Clerk of Court of Wakulla County because he loved Wakulla County. When World War II ended my dad wanted to provide a job for my brother who was getting out of the Navy, so he bought a grocery store in Medart and named it N. W. Ward and Son. But to Dad's surprise my brother N.W. did not want to work in Wakulla County. He had his mind made up that he wanted to live in Tallahassee and work there. By this time I was about 12 years old so I started helping Dad at the store on some occasions. As time went on I learned to do all of the jobs at the store. I became the clerk (helping people find their items and bag them), the ice cream server (making ice cream cones), the butcher (I cut meat, even using the cleaver to cut bones), the cashier (taking the money and running the cash register, also giving some people credit and they would pay at the end of the month), the service station attendant (putting gas and oil in peoples car), and any other job that needed to be done around the store. At times I got off the school bus at the store in the afternoon to help Dad. Other times I kept the store while Dad ran errands and went to preach on some Saturdays. During the summer I helped when I was needed at the store. This store provided great work experience for me since I helped in it for most of my teen years. So the store should have been named N. W. Ward and Daughter. Dad kept this store until the early 1950s.

Lewis Gwaltney, Corporal Civil War; Present at Battle of Natural Bridge

I feel very fortunate and especially want to thank God that I was born and raised in Wakulla County. I also want to thank God for my relatives who were some of the early pioneers in this great county. Being raised in a Christian family, becoming a Christian myself at a young age, and having all the Christian ancestors does not make me any greater Christian than anyone else but I am thankful for all these blessings. Great-grandpa Lewis Gwaltney (Grandma Green's father) had a store in Arran, the town the railroad ran through. It was the main depot for the county. The train brought many items that people needed and my mom told me of meeting the train to get ice and other goods. Great-grandpa Lewis also served in the Civil War fighting in Florida (Natural Bridge being one of these), Tennessee, and North Carolina and becoming a Corporal. He was wounded in one of the battles. He is pictured along with a number of other veterans of the Civil War in a photo that was taken around 1900 and is displayed around Wakulla County.

Grandpa Willie T. Green, besides being a dedicated Christian and minister (he pastored at Friendship Primitive Baptist and filled in at many other churches), was also very active in the early 1900s in Wakulla County. According to some information in his diary that I have, he did a lot of farming, carpenter work, built chimneys, built boats, built fences, and helped put in the early phone lines in the Medart area. He also had one of the few phones in this area around 1911.

He was appointed by the Governor of the State of Florida, Sidney Catts to be the food conservation agent for the county during World War I. He was county agent around 1918 and is pictured as County Agent with the Corn Club (a group of young men displaying their corn).

Grandma Green's grandfather and my great, great-grandfather, William A. Giles served as county Judge in the 1860's, fought at the battle of Natural Bridge during the Civil War, but also served as a lay minister in the Methodist church. Great, great-grandpa William A. had at least three sons who were ministers. One of those three, Enoch H. Giles was the first pastor of the Sopchoppy Methodist Church in 1868-69. He also pastored Crawfordville Methodist at that same time and could have been the first pastor there but that is not documented. This same Enoch H. Giles served as a Chaplain during the Civil War from 1863-1865 and earned the rank of Captain. He served not only in Florida but in Finegan's Brigade in Bentonville, N.C. Enoch served as a circuit riding Methodist minister for 44 years beginning in 1854 when he was ordained and licensed in the State of Florida. I mentioned earlier that an ancestor of mine pastored at the Methodist Church in Morven, Ga. in the 1800s where my cousin Gwynn Scarbrough pastored the Baptist Church in the 1990's. That early ancestor was James Giles. Two of my great uncles helped in the battle of Natural Bridge as 16 (William W) and 14 (Samuel) year old young men and then served as county judges in the 1890s (these men were brothers of my Grandma Ruth's Mom (whose name was Martha "Mattie" Giles Gwaltney) - William Wesley Giles served from 1890 through 1894 and happened to be the Judge in 1892 when the courthouse burned to the ground. I have seen some of Uncle William's notes he wrote by hand in some of the record books in the courthouse. Then in 1895 Samuel Giles became the Judge and served until 1899. After William W. left the Judges office he moved to the Ashmore - Sopchoppy area and became a

Captain Enoch H. Giles. Chaplain in The Civil War 1863-1865

Sylvester Augustus "Bess" Ward 1861-1921

post master either at Ashmore or Sopchoppy. He also owned a general store in Ashmore which was one of the stops of the GF&A Railroad. Grandma Green's Mom died when she was very young and the 1900 census stated that Grandma Green at age 13 was living in Ashmore with her uncle William Wesley Giles. After Samuel's term as Judge, he moved to Carrabelle, became a postmaster, and later was elected to the State Legislature. Some Giles family members came to Wakulla County in the 1840's from South Carolina with the Crawfords (Crawfordville was named for the Crawfords). Some other Giles family men were deacons in the churches of our area.

All Eighteen of the Thurmond Family on a Dress Up Occasion

Not only were my Mom Eunice Green Ward's Giles and Gwaltney families very prominent in early Wakulla County, but my dad, Nathaniel "Nat" Walker Ward Sr. also had family who were very active in the lSOCs in our county. One was Sylvester Augustus "Bess" Ward (born in 1861). He married Sarah Jane Stephens (born in 1867 in Wakulla County) from the Spring Creek area. Bess and Sarah were living in Crawfordville in January 1900 when my dad was born there (Dad showed us the exact area where he was born in January 1900). During the late 1800s and early 1900s Grandpa Bess owned a Fish Camp in Spring Creek. Judge Donald McLeod was the County Judge from 1900 through 1928. His daughter Martha McLeod who was born in Crawfordville in June 1900 (the same year that my Dad was born in Crawfordville), told me this story.

Judge McLeod with his family would travel to Spring Creek sometimes on weekends and camp at Grandpa Bess's Fish Camp because the judge loved to fish. On one occasion Grandpa Bess told Martha's Mom that the mullet was not a fish but could be a bird because it had a gizzard. Later a court case came before Judge McLeod of some Wakulla fishermen being charged with catching fish (mullet) at the wrong time of year. This was very troubling to the Judge because he didn't want to convict these fine men. His wife told him what Bess Ward had said about the mullet so Judge McLeod used that argument to free the fishermen.

I feel blessed of God to be a Wakulla County resident and thank God for the many, many opportunities He has given me over my 77 years.

Submitted by: Janie Ward Thurmond, 307 Frank Jones Road, Crawfordville, Florida 32327

Brother Johnny Whaley

I am not exactly sure of the date but I believe it to be somewhere around 1943. The road going into Spring Creek at that time was a dirt road and each week Brother Johnny Whaley would get to the intersection of Jack Crum Rd. and Spring Creek Road and on those weeks it had been raining he would take his shoes off, roll up his pants leg and go the last mile into Spring Creek bare footed. When he reached Spring Creek he would clean his feet off put his shoes back on. He then would hold church services on my grandparents front porch. (Wilmer and Hannah Dykes) That is until my husband's grandfather Langston donated the property where the church now sits and of course a church was built. I have posted pictures of Brother Johnny and my great-grandparents Forney and Susie Stevens on the historical website.

Submitted By: Marlene Gray Harrison, 115 N Airport Rd. Perry, FL 32348

John Elias Whiddon, Jr.

I was born in Carrabelle and moved up here to Wakulla County at the age of two. I've been here off and on the rest of my life, 81 years.

As I grew up to where I could realize what was going on, my daddy and I did a lot of opussum hunting at night. We'd chase opussums up trees and my daddy would take an axe and cut them down; and when they'd fall the dog would chase the opussum. One night we were up the road, cutting down a pretty good sized tree and the axe came off of the handle. It hit me in the head and sliced it open pretty good. Daddy took me up to Mama at the house and got me doctored up and all. Back then when you got a deep gash they used spider webs on it to stop the blood. My Daddy got mad at the axe. He took the axe and laid it out across the anvil and busted it wide open. I thought to myself, "What good is that gonna do?"

Back then you just didn't go to the doctor for everything, you know. So I just went ahead and kept that spider web and all in my head till it started healing up. I've always been pretty good at healing. They put a bandage over it to keep trash from getting in it, kept it wrapped up awhile, probably about a week. It started healing back together and they took the spider webs and all out of it. So I got over that.

John Elias Whiddon, Jr

In the daytime, me and my dad would go out digging gophers. We'd find a gopher hole and stick a pole in there to find out how far down the hole went before it turned. My dad would take a shovel and dig down until he came to the tunnel the gopher had made in there. Then he'd take a hook and put it down into the back of his hole and pull him out. We'd bring the gophers home and skin them, clean them up, and my mama would cook them. You cook them like chicken, with rice, dumplings, stuff like that. We'd eat them.

My father was the kind of man who would do anything for anybody, anywhere; he'd be there to help them. Whatever he wanted to do could always come later. He never charged anyone for what he did. He was good, he was humble, a hard-working man. Whenever he was home he'd be out making a garden or something. Greens, turnips, rutabagas, tomatoes, cucumbers, sweet potatoes, beans, peas, a couple rows of corn; he'd plant all of that. We always had enough to eat. We had chickens, hogs, and I got a cow later on. We had grape vines on a big arbor. We mostly ate them, didn't make much wine or jelly from them. Daddy would bring home cut branches from fruit trees and stick them in the ground and they'd grow. We had more fruit than we could eat! We made good pies and jelly.

We had an old hen that hatched out ten or eleven biddies. But they kept going missing. One day we learned why, the snake that had been eating them ate so many that he got too big to get through the fence!

We grew cane too, and ground it up and made syrup out of it. We used our Model A Ford to run the cane mill. We tied the steering wheel over to the side so that it would keep going in a circle, then just let it go on its own in low gear.

My mother stayed busy. She'd keep up with the feed and the clothes and all. She'd sit down and patch overalls for me to wear, and I'd wear them like they were brand new.

She was a good cook. She made biscuits in a big old lard can lid, about two dozen at a time. There were biscuits at every meal. We liked to punch a hole in them and fill them with syrup, eat them that way. Sometimes for breakfast we'd get a bowl, crumble up a biscuit in it, pour coffee in there and add some syrup. It would mix up just right. We'd go out in the field and work till dinner time, then go sit in the shade, open a jar of syrup, make a hole in a biscuit and pour in the syrup, sit there and eat it. The biscuits were pretty big, about the size of a Hardee's biscuit now. I still like biscuits. You can take a good hot biscuit and sop up syrup with it, that's good too. You can make a meal on it. Mama always fixed something up for us to eat.

That's my sister Mary Lee in front, and my half brother sitting on the porch

For bacon, we had a smoke house across from the kitchen where we smoked meat, hams, or a side of bacon. If we didn't smoke it, we'd put it in salt to cure it. When you were ready to eat it later on, you'd take it out of the barrel and wash the salt out of it. We used to have mullet cured that way. You could clean them off and soak the salt out of them, fry them up and they tasted just like fresh fish. We could keep them eight or nine months when they were salted down.

My favorite thing my mother made was jelly cakes. They had five or six thin layers with jelly in between. That's the way all the cakes were made.

We'd buy flour from the store in 50lb. bags. We had corn meal made at the mill, to make cornbread from.

We lived in an old log house that my granddaddy had built. You could look up through the ceiling at night and see the stars and things. It had an old wooden shingle roof on it. They'd take and rive the shingles out, you know, split them up, and then cover the house in them. You could see the moon up through the roof, but when it rained, you might have one or two places in the house that would leak. We'd set a pot down on the floor to catch the water.

We had a fireplace in the south end of the house and it was made out of old wooden sticks with clay put over them. Every once in awhile we'd have a big fire in it and the clay would fall down and the sticks would start catching on fire. We'd have to pull all the fire out of it, stop it from burning, and the next day we'd get some more clay and wrap the sticks back up in the clay. This happened about every time we built a big fire in it during the wintertime. It got to where we got an old wood heater and put it in the middle of the living room and quit using the fireplace. The living room had an old wooden window with a stand built outside where we kept our wood. You'd open the window, get some wood and put it on the fire. When we'd get to running low on wood we'd have to get out there and tote two or three big armloads of wood to the stand. The heater worked better because it was one of these old potbellied heaters, you know. It would get red hot, heat up the whole living room. The living room was about 12 feet wide and about the same length. It would keep that room hot. When we'd go to bed at night, there was cover on the bed, but we wouldn't freeze, we'd stay warm the rest of the night.

This picture is the old house. That's my sister Mary Lee in front, and my half brother sitting on the porch. He had paralysis. He couldn't get up and walk because his feet were all turned over. He had paralysis at an early age, from Pellagra. He ended up going to Gainesville and they told him they thought they could get his feet straightened out so he could walk.

They told him it would be a 50/50 chance, and he was willing to take it, but he didn't get over it. I had a sister Estelle, she died on Christmas day. She was about 12, 13 years old. Ruby was my half sister and she had already died earlier. We never did know what Estelle died of. She'd been getting along alright a couple of days before. We'd gotten some apples and oranges for Christmas and we figured it was something in the fruit that went bad on her. Mama and Daddy adopted my cousin Bill when he was one hour old. His mama, Aunt Lizzie, was Daddy's sister. She died trying to give birth to Bill's twin.

We'd get up in the morning, go out and do all the chores. Daddy would get up and go to work. He worked for the WPA. That's a project that Roosevelt started to give people work so they could make enough money to live on. Crawfordville School down here, is made of lime rock. My daddy helped hew all the rocks, squared them up so they could make walls out of them. They cut the hole for the windows and all in them, and they built that school down there. That's what we used for a school until last year when they built a new elementary school on that Arran highway about 3/4 of a mile from the old school.

Where the voting house is, when you leave 319 coming in, the first little house on the left was a three room school house. That's where we started school. We'd get up in the morning, didn't have any shoes or anything, the ground would be frozen and we'd walk to school. The cold weather didn't seem to bother us too much. We'd get out from school in the evening, walk back home.

I quit school when I was beginning in the fifth grade and started helping my dad more to create a living. He was working on the national forest then, so they got me a job with him up there. I was a little fellow about 16 years old and I used a shovel on the dump trucks just like my daddy did. That's the only way we had of loading the dump trucks. We'd load them up with dirt for places where they were fixing the roads. Back then the trucks were smaller than they are now; they'd hold about four yards of dirt. Now they've got these big 10 or 12 yard trucks, it would take you all day to load one of them. It was usually about six people that were loading the dump truck, and we'd take about an hour or hour and a half to load it. Then we'd go back and get another load. We averaged three or four loads a day. You were pretty tired when it come knocking off time to come home. Then we'd get on the truck and ride about six miles up the road here where the forest station was, and then walk home about five miles. It was hard on people, but that's just how it was.

My daddy never would complain about

anything. I heard him talk a couple of times about his chest hurting, but he never slowed down going to work. He'd get up every morning and he'd catch the truck on 319, which was a dirt road then, and ride into town for work.

A guy had an old 1927 Buick truck with the back cut down and a truck body built on. It had 32" tires on it. The man wanted $75.00 for it. So the first payday I made, I bought that truck so we'd have a way of going. That's all the car we had for awhile, and then I got a chance to buy an old Model T truck. Daddy got out one day and was cranking it, and it kicked back on him and broke his arm. Where the funeral home is now in Crawfordville was a doctor's office, Dr. Harper. We took him down there and Dr. Harper put a cast on it. He was out of work for a couple of weeks until he could go back and be a water boy for them.

I went to town one day and I got stopped by a highway patrol. He wanted to know if I had a license. I had picked up a friend on the way to town.

Come to find out, the license that I had wasn't good unless I had a licensed driver with me. So he came in handy! When I went to get my license I was 16, I think. I drove my car down to Crawfordville, to the courthouse. It was a dirt road all the way down there, and there was a big water tank across from it. I went and met the sheriff, but he told me he didn't have time right then to give me my license. So he just sat down and wrote me a note to the circuit court to go ahead and give me my license! That way I didn't have to drive back without a license.

I took my mama and daddy uptown to Tallahassee whenever they needed to go. We'd go up there to buy shoes or clothes. They had some for sale in Crawfordville but they were awfully high. We also had a rolling store down here. He'd come around sometimes. We'd get our ice delivered to us too. We didn't have an ice box, so we'd dig a hole and keep it in there with whatever needed to be kept on ice. It was 20, 25 cents. When I got a little older I worked with the man that made the ice down here. He made it in 300lb. blocks. We'd break them up into 50lb. pieces using an ice pick. I delivered ice to people who came in there and bought it. He had a meal grinding outfit there too. His name was Woodberry, I think. He could make about 24 300-lb.blocks of ice at a time. He made it in big drums. When it was time to take it out, you hosed the drum down, and then turned it over on its side and the ice would slide out.

On Saturdays and Sundays, the people used to come out and pick flowers. honeysuckle, violets, wildflowers and all. Girls, boys, husbands and wives would all go out flower picking. We spent most Saturdays and Sundays doing that when they were in bloom.

They had a railroad track that went along back out here. There's a power line that goes along there now. But the train came out of Tallahassee and went to Carrabelle, turned around and came back. It had an old steam engine. I'd get ready to go to town and go out here and flag the train down. For 20 to 25 cents I could ride the train. I'd just take a rag

Carrie and Johnnie Whiddon. Carrie is holding Mary Ann (Johnson) Blackburn

and wave it, and the agent would know I wanted to ride. He'd stop to where I could get on. Coming back, they had a button in the car that you'd pull to let them know you wanted to get off. The engineer would know where he picked me up and he'd let me off near there. I'd walk though a little strip of woods there and come back to the house. I did that several times.

They finally quit running the old train and came down and took up the track. They also had turpentine stills and platforms where the barrels of turpentine would be loaded, at Springhill. Going up Springhill highway, the first place that you come to where there are houses on both sides of the road; they had a 30-foot dock out there for loading the turpentine barrels on the train. You'd load them by hand, with a dolly. I don't know what they did with it in Tallahassee.

I dipped turpentine. You've seen these trees with faces and grooves on them. They'd hang a cup on that, and the turpentine would run down into it. You'd set your bucket down, take the cup off the tree and pour the turpentine into the bucket. Then the bucketful would be poured into a barrel and loaded on the train. Lots of people did this, you didn't have to work for a company or anything, and if you were underage that was all right. I did this before I went to work loading the dump trucks.

When we went to work we'd take a lunch with us. When it was time to eat we'd go sit down in the shade by a tree and eat lunch. I had a first cousin who was killed out here on the road. He was out there digging gopher once day and stood up against a tree during a storm to keep from getting wet, and the lightning struck the tree. I was about 12 or 13.

There used to be a Gosset place, they called it, by the railroad track, where my Aunt Rosa and Uncle Elmer lived for awhile. There was a spring there that had some of the coldest, best drinking water coming out all the time. We brought a lot of the water back to the house to cook with and all.

We'd go out fighting fire a lot. One evening a fellow came by and picked my dad up in a marsh buggy which was used to fight the fires in the forest. My dad had stopped for a rest and they all got up and walked off. Mose Strickland looked around and said, "Johnnie's not with us." So they went back to where they'd been resting. He hadn't moved, he'd died there, had a heart attack. They put him on the big marsh buggy and brought him out to highway 20 and carried him to the hospital, but he was already gone.

In the Military

Before age 18 I'd never spent the night anywhere else except at my cousins' in Arran. I'd stay with them a day or two sometimes. When I signed up and went in the service I was sent to Camp Blanding, took my training at Ft. McClellan, Alabama and I shipped out of there to Camp Kilmer, New Jersey. I was to be sent overseas to Japan where the War was still going on. They came up with a deal where you could enlist for a year and when the end of the year came you were supposed to get out and you also got a 30 day furlough back home. I came back home, stayed 30 days with mama and daddy and all and had to go back to Ft. MacPherson, Georgia to report. So I went back and was transferred over and loaded on a troop ship to Le Havre, France.

We got out and stayed a few days, and then we went to, I believe, Hamburg, Germany. It was cold as the dickens there, with icicles hanging from the eaves of the barracks to the ground. We stayed there about a week, and then shipped to Munich, Germany. I was there two or three days and caught the German measles and had to go to the hospital for two weeks. They carried me over there in an ambulance. When they let me loose to come back I didn't know how to get to the barracks so I just took off walking from the hospital. I don't understand how I found my way, but when I got back to the barracks all the troops had shipped out. So I got with the next group, stayed there a few days and then shipped to Durlock, Germany where I stayed for eight or nine months.

I was in the half track division. A half track has a big rubber track like a caterpillar on the back, and the front has a hood and wheels with rubber tires like a truck. They were about 12 feet long and had 37 mm guns on them, and machine guns. The guns were on turntables. A half track would go about everywhere you put it, didn't hardly ever get stuck. You drove it just like a regular truck, with gears. They were really heavy. They trained us to drive them and I got a license.

Just before we left they told us to take the half tracks up somewhere in the northern part of Germany and just park them there in a vacant lot.

All that military equipment, parked out in a big open field. All you could see was just trucks and jeeps, half tracks, tanks, all parked there. The war was over with the Germans. We celebrated and marched all day long that day.

They used us as security police for the civilians. We'd go on duty night and day and carry people to jail if they didn't have a pass to be out on the street. We did this for eight months. We visited Hitler's mansion while we were in Durlock. We were riding around one night and decided to go see what it looked like. There were steps leading up to it, and I drove the jeep right up them. There wasn't anyone living there then, it was just a building, and we couldn't get inside because it was all locked up.

Home Again

When I came home from the war I had several years of GI Bill I could go to school on. I could go to a regular school, or some kind of a business school, or something that I liked to do. I decided that I'd take up flying. But I had to make a living and I couldn't get enough flying time to pass all my exams that I needed, so I had to quit flying. I wasn't getting paid for the school that I was going to for flying. So that knocked me out of it for several years. But I eventually went back, got my time in and got my pilot license and everything.

I had several hours in, of flying time. I had a log book; I kept a log of my time. I wasn't scared. I went up one day in the wintertime and it was kind of cold. Well, I got cold and I pulled on the lever that said "Heat" but when I pulled it on, the sound of the airplane engine changed, because the heat came off of the exhaust. I was afraid that was going to cause me to fall, so I pushed it back in. I finally got a hold of the instructor and asked him, and he told me that would give me the heat as long as I wasn't coming in for a landing. You're not supposed to pull that heater button at that time because the engine needs some heat to keep the carburetor from icing up. So I got through that flight and landed and all.

I was flying out of an airport on Route 27 outside Tallahassee during the training. I flew around the area and finally got enough hours of flying time to be able to go cross country by myself. So I went down to Panama City, flew around there a little and landed, refueled the plane, took off and headed back to Tallahassee.

I rented a plane one day and took one of the children. We flew down to Dog Island. I was going to land but I figured the airport was too short, so I didn't land. You had to take off going out over the water and land going in over the water of the bay down there. So we flew around a little, looking around, and came back. Then I flew down to Apalachicola and went in there. My sister and my wife met us down there at the hangar.

Me and my brother in law had a plane apiece. So we flew down there and I think that's where I took my oldest daughter up for a ride. She said she didn't like it.

When I soloed, it was all right. I went with a

guy to pick up one of the planes that we used for flying training in Augusta, GA. He got lost going up there, and it took longer than we thought. We had to come back into Tallahassee at night, but neither one of us had any time in night flying.

I set my course and headed on back, and that guy kept calling me and telling me I was too far over west. But I went ahead and stayed on my course and landed in Tallahassee and he came in and landed behind me. You can tell where you are at night by the lights of the cities. Actually, I enjoyed coming in after dark. You could see the rows of lights where you were to land, red on one side and white on the other. But I always sat down and wrote down my path and the things I'd pass along the way, so I could tell where I was at.

When I flew solo to Panama City I got off track and ended up in DeFuniak Springs. I landed and found out where I was at, and all I had to do then was to follow the coastline around until I came to Panama City.

It got to where you had to pay fifteen dollars an hour for the airplane, which was cheap in those days. Now it would cost you probably fifty or seventy-five dollars an hour. I had a chance to buy an airplane, a two passenger plane, a Tripacer. We would have had to have a lot of work done on it in order to make it air worthy. My brother in law wanted to buy it, but I wasn't making enough money to put my part in.

When I'd come flying down close to the yard, people would get out and wave, they knew it was me.

I developed an inner ear problem, though. Every time I'd go up I'd get dizzy. I got kind of scared to go up flying, afraid I'd black out and not be able to make it back. So I more or less let it go.

Riding motorcycles was another thing I liked to do. I'd go out riding at night with the boys when I was off work. My first motorcycle was an old '85 Indian. It was a big motorcycle like a Harley was, but the gear shift was backwards in it, and it had what they called a "suicide clutch." If you ran the motor up the clutch would let it go in gear and take off with you. I got thrown one time by doing that.

I also drag-raced. They had the drag races on Route 20 going out of Tallahassee. I had a 396 Chevrolet Biscayne, I forget what year it was. It was an ex-Highway Patrol car, heavy and made for speed. It had a pretty powerful motor in it, and I had some head work done on it, pulled the heads off of it, had the valves fixed and everything, to where it had more power. Put valve springs on it, built it up to where it was souped up pretty well. I raced it on Saturday nights. There was a 350 Camaro, a lady had had all kinds of souped-up work done on it. She outran me every time down the quarter track. I went up there one night and put a bag of ice on the intake manifold, cranked up, and outran the Camaro. She got mad, came back cussin' and left and went home! I don't know how many times she had outrun me.

I learned to work on motors starting with my first old truck. I just did it, and that's how I learned. I kept on until I fixed it, that's the way it was. The old Model T was the simplest one to fix. The first gear in it was the clutch, a peddle you mashed down. And reverse was a peddle you mashed down. High gear was a lever over on the left side. When you mashed that clutch down and got it up where you could drop the high gear down, you'd drop it down and go truckin' down the road. You'd have to pull those bands out when they'd get worn out. I pulled them out, took an old GI army belt and riveted it back to the bands, put it back in and ran it two or three months until it wore out and I had to change the bands again. I got gas for it at Fred Green's store.

"If man can make it, then man can fix it." My daddy taught me that, and that's what I tried to teach my kids. That's how they got the idea I could fix most anything. I always tried to teach them to do the job right. Most anybody you teach to do it right, won't do it right. I'd go back and fix it.

That's where they got the idea that nothing they did suited me. The kids would do what they could and I was always around. If they weren't doing it right I'd take over and do it. They'd watch while I did it.

I bought a chain saw and went around getting people to give me trees to cut down. I had an old '62 International truck and we started putting the pulp wood on it and hauling it to the mill. My son, Gary Ashburn, and any others who were big enough helped. They learned about hard work. I remember when we went down to Carrabelle to cut pulp wood down there. The guy was charging stumpage on that. I'd take it to Shadeville where they had the mill. Stumpage is what we paid for the trees we cut down. Mine went to a pulp mill to make paper out of.

I was also a crane operator for Jackson & Cook, putting up steel for buildings and the first Panama City crossover. I feel kind of good when we go by something I worked on. We did a lot of work on some of the FSU buildings in Panama City too. I learned how to work the crane by watching the crane operator and then just doing it, practicing. I was up to doing anything if I could learn something new.

As I was working at Jackson & Cook I learned about the job of operating the movie projector at the Capital Drive-In Theatre in Tallahassee at night. I ran the projectors at night while I worked all day at Jackson & Cook for two years.

The best job I had was operating the crane for Jackson & Cook. I worked that job for 18 1/2 years. I left because I needed to make money for retirement. I went to work then as a mechanic for the county for two years, and then Castoldi Dump trucks for a year and a half. Then I was hired as bus mechanic for the county schools.

I feel good about my life. I worked hard, did my best to treat others right and take care of my family. If the Lord will go with me and lead and guide throughout the rest of my life I will be happy.

The most important things I've done are getting a home built to raise my family in and getting it paid for, getting married and raising a family, and seeing my grandchildren grow up. I'm most proud of my children, grandchildren, great-grandchildren; and that most of my family lives next to me on the old home place.

Starting at Back Left to Right; 1.Ben Whiddon, 2.Stanley Whiddon, 3.Joyce Ashburn, 4.Linda Jo Davis, 5.Gary Ashburn, 6.Dennis Whiddon, 7.Eric Pfeufer, 8.John Casteneira, 9.Jennifer Casteneira, 10.Michelle Faircloth, 11.Norma Whiddon, 12.John Whiddon, J., 13.Gavin Pfeufer, 14.Angela Pfeufer, 15.Larry Burse, 16.Cindy Burse, 17.Molly Whiddon, 18.Kate Whiddon, 19.Seth Whiddon, 20.Daniel Burse, 21.Ian Burse, 22.Ginger Whiddon

I tried to teach my kids everything I knew and they still don't know nothing! I'd make them do it over until they got it right. I hope they respect me for that.

John, Jr. and Norma Whiddon dress up for dinner on a cruise to Cozumel in April, 2003

The most important people in my life have been my mother Carrie Lee Bratcher Whiddon and my father John Elias Whiddon, Sr. The things I care about the most are my wife Norma (we'll be married 53 years in July), my family, my Christian belief in the Lord Jesus Christ, my home, friends, neighbors, my sister and her family, and the fact that I am a self-made man. I am proud to be an American.

Life has been better for me since I accepted the Lord as my Savior. My belief in Him has helped me through troubled times and I'm proud that He provided me with a home place to live and die at. He has been good to me.

Submitted By: John Elias Whiddon, Jr.,265 Stokely Rd. Crawfordville, FL, 32327

Geneva Hartsfield Thomas Whisenant

Geneva's parents were Richard Edward Hartsfield and Mary Henrietta Crum. Geneva was the twin sister of Elmer Eugene (Ford) Hartsfield. No one would ever know they were twins by looking at them. He was very tall and she was short. Her brothers & sisters were Minnie Metcalf, Mamie Goss, Frankie Kelly, Edmond Hartsfield, Will Hartsfield, Mose Hartsfield and Ford Hartsfield. She was raised in Panacea. Her father made a living from the bay.

When Geneva was nine years old her mother died from Pneumonia. Her daddy never remarried. He raised his children with the help of his older daughter Mamie.

Geneva went to school in Panacea until the school shut down and the children were bused to the Sopchoppy School. Her father did not want his children to go to school in Sopchoppy. This suited Geneva find as she did not want to go anyway. She did not learn to read and write. Mamie, Minnie and Frankie all learned to read and write but none of her brothers did.

Geneva starting courting Joseph Lee (J.L.) Thomas and they went to Apalachicola and got married in 1940 when she was just 15 years old. They had nine children by the time she was 29 years old. Their children are: Delma , Bessie, Marvis, Odell, Linda, Hixon, Eva, Isaac and Junior.

She had a hard life while she was raising her children. She worked in the bay to help make a living. She might not have learned to read and write but nobody could our figure her when it came to arithmetic.

J.L. died in 1968 and she still had Delma, Isaac and Junior living at home with her. Marvis came back and took over the management of the seafood business. It became a family business with all the brothers and sisters involved.

Junior got killed in an automobile accident in 1970. Isaac got married in 1971 and Delma got married in 1978. This left her living alone. She did not like living alone. She would make one of her grandchildren stay with her at night. She eloped with Arthur Whisenant in 1978, which was a shock to the whole family.

He was a wonderful husband to her. He would do anything for her or take her anywhere she wanted to go. He would take her and her sisters to Tallahassee every Saturday to the flea market, shopping and out to eat.

They went to church together every Sunday.

After Arthur died in 1989, she started keeping

Geneva Hartsfield Thomas Whisenant

the nursery at the First Baptist Church. All the children in town loved her and called her "Big Mama."

She loved Christmas and would start her Christmas shopping in January. She always had a gift for everyone in the family and for the people at church. She was always bringing candy to church for the children.

She died on May 20, 1999 and is buried at the Panacea Cemetery. She was a very special person and loved by everyone who knew her.

Submitted and written by, Louise Thomas, 419 Buckhorn Creek Rd. Sopchoppy, Fl 32358

Griffin O'Neil Willis

Sometime in the year of 1893, there was a railroad built through Wakulla County. Soon after the completion of the railroad, there was a large turpentine still built close to the railroad tracks. People moved into the area to work the turpentine still, which resulted in the birth of a little town, called Ashmore, Florida. The town was named after the Ashmore family, which was one of the more prominent families and possibly the first family to move to this little community.

This turpentine still required lots of labor to gather the raw gum from the trees. There were thousands of acres of growing pines to be worked. The town of Ashmore grew to almost a hundred houses and buildings to house the labor and business of the town. There were four or five stores, stores, a post office, school, blacksmith shop and train station.

The main store was the company store, which was owned and operated by the turpentine company. At this store the workers could charge their merchandise until the crop of gum was harvested at the end of each year. Some received a little cash and others ended up still in debt to the company store all depending on how well the family tried to live that year.

The other stores sold groceries along with other merchandise. There was a good many people that worked someplace else or farmed giving the Ashmore stores a good list of customers.

The blacksmith shop was owned and operated by Mr. John Simmons. He made most anything from iron. He also made wagon wheels, and repaired wagons. He helped build caskets to bury the dead of the community.

On a very cold day, February 3, 1918, a baby boy was born to James Walter Willis and Ethel Griffin Willis in this little town of Ashmore. They named their first and only son Griffin O'Neil Willis. My father worked in turpentine for several years but at my birth he was having cross tyes cut for the railroad. My mother came to Wakulla County as a school teacher from Wewahitchka, Florida. She was teaching at Oak Park School when she and my dad met, fell in love and married.

As I was growing up I began to watch, look and listen to everything of interest to me. I spent many hours watching Mr. John Simmons, the blacksmith work. The worst job I ever knew of him doing was stopping by our house and pulling a couple of teeth for me.

My mother home schooled me until I was in the third grade. By then I was older and large enough to walk the two miles to the Sopchoppy School, as there was no such thing as a school bus.

The storm we had in 1928 blew most of the pine trees down finishing the turpentine business for Ashmore. People began leaving looking for work elsewhere. There was still business going on such as the cross tye business and a small sawmill hauled lumber to Ashmore to be shipped by train.

During the summer the kids in the neighborhood stayed in our favorite swimming hole side of the railroad where the water ran under the railroad bed causing a fairly large hole of water which we used very happily. When the fall of the year came around we had fun climbing the pecan trees and gathering pecans which was a specialty for goodies to eat.

My dad got the contract from Wakulla County to transport the kids to school. He owned and operated his bus for several years.

I trapped during the winter while going to high school. The fur I sold helped provide me with a little spending money. At one time the County Road Department had a real foreman in this part of the county. The labor was divided with men in the area that was being worked at that time. I was just old enough to be hired. The pay was 25 cents per hour. When we got our pay it was with a due bill on the county since the county was broke, we could trade the due bills to Mr. Lawhon or Mr. Ashmore for merchandise. They charged us 25% for holding them until such time the county got money to make them good.

Willis Family

I graduated from Sopchoppy High School in 1935. Our senior banquet was held in the hall just outside the home economics classroom. The meal was prepared by the home economics class.

The first time I saw Mildred was when she was in the seventh grade. After I graduated I decided to take the teachers exam to become a teacher. I went back to school to review the eighth grade as a booster for my exam and Mildred was in my eighth grade class.

I got my teaching certificate but all the teachers had been hired for the year and my certificate was good for only one year therefore my teaching career came to an end before it started.

I joined the C.C.C. for Civilian Construction Camp in Ocala National Forrest where I spent about 10 months. I came home to see my parents and my girl, Mildred, every time I could build up some leave time. I was down in the dumps thinking of Mildred and missing her. I went to the Captain's office to get him to write me a discharge. I told him I was going back on the mail truck. I was in love. He told me to get somebody to write a letter saying I had a job and I would get an honorable discharge. My Mama wrote a letter saying I had a job with my Daddy in the bee business.

Mildred and I got married. We later bought the house in Buckhorn. I hauled pulp wood and anything else I could find to do. We had three children and another one on the way, when I got my letter from Uncle Sam. I served my time during World War II. During that time my parents house in Ashmore caught fire and burned down. They moved in with Mildred and the babies.

When I got out of the Army, mydaddy and I bought property in Sopchoppy. We turned one old building into a store and built a house onto the store for my parents. I built a shop next door and started my business as an automobile mechanic. After my parents died we sold their store and built a store with a house on back next to the shop.

Mildred and I have had a wonderful life together. We raised five children.

Mary Ellen married T.D. Whaley; Carlton "Buddy", married Diane Broughton; Dale Story, & then Mary Boone; Carolyn married Amos Crum; Louise married Marvis Thomas; and Wayne married Rosa Winchester and then Sherry King.

Submittedby: Louise Thomas, 419 Buckhorn Creek Rd. Sopchoppy, Fl 32358. Written by, Griffin Willis

Remembered and Appreciated for Their Love Of Local History

Thomas C. "Buddy" Watson 03/01/1932-07/07, 2011

Allen R "Pete" Gerrell, 11/26/1932-8/3/2007

1st President of The Wakulla County Historical Society

Fred Lawhon, 3/29/1921-4/02/2009

Arlan "Ink" Bowen 10/14/1931-01/23/2010

WCHS Treasurer from 1997 until his death in 2010. He was a serious "keeper of the funds" which allowed the Society to fund three grants for the museum renovation

WATER STORIES AROUND THE COUNTY

A Trip to the Fishery

What it was like to take a trip to the fishery at Shell Point Beach around 1915. These trips were most always overnight, but never more than a two night stay. Housing was not conducive to a long stay. The only house on the beach was more of a storage or supply house than a home, although Mr. Bob Raker stayed there regularly during the height of the season.

The trips to Shell Point had to be scheduled somewhat by the tides! A mile or so from the beach, the road was underwater though the marshy areas. At periods of high tide, the horses had trouble staying on the featureless road and a misstep off the road could mean a wagon mired in the marsh. Upon arriving the adults began immediately to help the fisherman set up the fishing nets and gear. Further down toward the beach from the house was a large sand mound, an Indian mound, on which the kids would play. Along the side of the mound was a creek which one could wade across at low tide.

Over beside a cluster of trees the men folk would pull in the fire logs, ends pointing into the center spot, Indian style. Bricks could be picked up in the sand and placed in a manner that a very large tripod legs with an iron skillet could set securely. This skillet was certainly the center of what this was all about!

The cooking and eating of the three times a day feast was the "it" of the trip, cornbread hoecakes, grits and the freshest mullet was the meal. One was supposed to over eat on these trips each family would bring goodies, such as cakes, cookies or a dish of baked beans.

Another important part of the preparation was the smudge pots. These smudge pots were not actual pots. They were small pits in the sand dug on the windward side of the house near the windows. Fires were lit in the pits and allowed to burn down to glowing coals. On top of these coals were placed corn cobs or hard pine cones. These didn't flame up, but rather smoldered for a long time giving off a thick smoke which whiffed through the house. This kept away the pesky mosquitoes, gnats and biting files.

For the children, eating, wading, poking at creatures in the nets and running up and down the sand mound was a large part of their entertainment. The other was watching all the men folk as they set about with the nets. A lookout climbed a tree down the beach. He could spot a school of fish and identify them by the type of ripples they made on the surface of the water. The net was already anchored to a heavy stake onshore and a net pulling boat readied.

When the fish were spotted, the lookout would motion to the boat to go put. The net crew would go out pulling the net in a semi circle. The lead weighted bottom of the net sank and moved along the floor of the bay. The top of the net had cork floats to keep it at the top of the water.

When the lookout called "all aboard" he was telling the crew on the boat the fish where inside the area the net would include as it was pulled in. The boat crew would respond quickly to the lookouts command with "come ashore". As the boat reached the shore all hands joined in pulling the huge net on the beach with its load of trapped, but very lively fish! Adults running after some of these lively fish also add bits of laughter to the work. After the fish were contained the real work began, fish had to be cleaned right away. The nets had to be re-hung on their drying racks and threads had to be inspected for need repairs before the next run. "No taste to a fish, like a fresh fish caught!"

Written by: Franklin D. Howard© 1994. Permission to print by: Susan Sapronetti, Tallahassee, FL

Live Oak Island Scalloping

I grew up on the Old St. Augustine Road in Leon County. Our closest neighbors were Gordon and Mary Claire Pichard. Gordon was President of Talquin Electric Cooperative.

Jim, George, James W. Sr., and Aline Apthorp

The Pichards owned a cabin on the ease side of Live Oak Island and we were sometimes invited down to go scalloping. Gordon would take my family of four out on the flats in his airboat. We usually were able to pick up our

fill of scallops. It was on these outings that I learned one of life's little lessons. Scallops can swim!

Submitted by: George E. Apthorp, 2888 Spring Creek Hwy, Crawfordville, FL 32327

Shell Point Weekends; Circa 1948 – 1958

On fishing trips we would rent one of the 18 ft wooden skiffs which were plenty big enough for our family of four. My Dad's 5 horse Elgin motor got us anywhere we needed to go, albeit not too fast. In the cooler months we would scoop up fiddler crabs in the tidal creek, which was eliminated when the marina was dug out, and fish for sheeps head at the Glory Hole in Spring Creek. In warmer months we fished the flats for trout and trolled the oyster bars for reds. Since we couldn't afford gas, bait and ice, we kept our fish on a stringer. Occasionally, Dad would have to shoo off a shark trying for an easy meal. My mother always packed a lunch and we would picnic on one of the small islands in the western part of the bay. Dad, my mother, Aline, my brother, Jim and myself were living the good life!

Submitted by: George E. Apthorp, 2888 Spring Creek Hwy, Crawfordville, FL 32327

The Wild Goose

Of all the sounds of the wild, my favorite is the plaintive call of the wild goose. It floods my mind with warm and happy memories of home.

The call is first heard, almost imperceptibly, the memories are stirred, and as it grows louder, it draws your attention to the source, making it impossible to ignore as you look heavenward and see the flight of the majestic Canadian geese.

If they are flying high to some distant location, their "V" shaped formation is nearly perfect, with the dominant goose in the lead. If flying low, their formation may be ragged and irregular and their calls more insistent and boisterous.

In the 1930s my mother, Vera Gresham, who was living at the St. Marks Lighthouse, was given the honor of banding the first Canada goose when the St. Marks National Wildlife Refuge was created. And if you look closely at the signs marking the boundary to that refuge, and all other national refuges, I believe you'll see the wild goose honored by its image prominently displayed.

My daddy, E. W. Roberts, was unable to make a living and support his family the entire year with just his fishing business at St. Marks. In the winter months, when deep sea fishing was poor, he enclosed the sides of his 60 foot excursion boat, the Osprey, and used it for hunting the wild goose. He became a guide in the winter and took hunting parties of men, mostly from Georgia, "Down East" to goose hunt. I remember his fee was $100.00 a day, which back in those days, was a pretty good income. Sometimes they would stay on the Osprey and go inshore in small skiffs to hunt. There were times though, when they'd pull a houseboat down there and anchor it up in Cow Creek, using it as their base camp. I'm pretty sure that houseboat was owned by Mr. O. P. Shields of St. Marks. The anchorage for the Osprey was right off Rock Island, about

twenty or so miles east of the St. Marks Lighthouse.

When school didn't interfere, my daddy would take me with him and I loved those trips, especially when we stayed on the houseboat, what a life for a young fellow! What I remember most was those evenings after the men came in from the hunt. It was so much fun for me to just sit and listen to them laugh and talk, warm inside the Osprey or houseboat, as the cold wind whistled outside. Those were fine men and I know they must have enjoyed making me laugh with them at their stories, which were great. And I thought my daddy, who, after all, was their guide, was king of the world.

And always, in the distance, the call of the wild goose.

Submitted By John Y. Roberts, 958 Lonefeather Dr, Tallahassee, FL 32311

Story about Wakulla Springs

My grandparents Nelton and Thelma Jernigan moved from Alabama in the 1930s so my grandfather could take a job at Wakulla Springs working as a mechanic and carpenter. My great-grandparents Grady and Mary

Hagler (Thelma's parents) had already moved here from Alabama and had heard that Mr. Ed Ball was asking if anyone knew someone that could work on diesel motors. At that time, my grandmother said that Wakulla Springs generated their own electricity by these motors. My grandparents moved to Wakulla Springs and lived in the employee housing - individual small houses on the grounds of the Springs. In 1941 my mother, Mary Nelda Jernigan (Russ) was born at Tallahassee Memorial Hospital and joined the family at the little 2 story house at the Springs.

My grandmother shared with me that Mr. Ed Ball's wife thought that Mary Nelda was the prettiest baby she had ever seen. My grandmother would dress my mom up and take her down by the water where everyone would sit around and visit. Thelma said that Mrs. Ball confided that she wished she could live simply like her, because she did not feel like she had any friends other than people who liked her because of money and status.

On one occasion, a "rich" woman was visiting and staying in the hotel and brought a little dog with her. Mr. Ball came and asked Nelton if he could have some of the men build a dog house so he and Thelma could watch the dog overnight. The dog house was built - and when the lady brought the dog over, she gave Thelma strict instructions to not yell at the dog. The lady told her to just say "no, no" and that was it. Well....the dog barked all night, and over and over Thelma went to the door and said "no, no"...."no, no"...until Nelton went outside and finally yelled at it, explaining to her that you just "needed to talk to it like it was a dog". The next morning, when they came to get the dog, Mrs. Ball brought Thelma a present. It was a play pen for baby Mary Nelda. This was a rare item for most people to have at the time and Thelma shared that she would lend out the play pen for years and years to different friends and relatives. She also remembered, 60 years later, who finally broke it, but I won't say! Thelma washed diapers and hung them on a line. One day, Mary Nelda got ahold of an empty Clorox bottle and swallowed a few drops. Thelma ran to the Hotel to use the phone to call the Doctor. She was told to just have Mary Nelda drink some milkshake and they stayed in the Hotel all day drinking malts and shakes until Mary Nelda would not drink them ever again.

During World War II, soldiers would come to the Springs from Camp Gordon Johnson for recreation and training. If the soldiers were at Camp Johnson, they knew they were going to Germany. The soldiers would train at the Springs by jumping off the towers into the water that had been set on fire with gasoline. Thelma said she fed many yankees and introduced them to grits and eggs.

Tommy Lee Lewis (?) cooked at the Hotel. Nelton would stop by the kitchen to see what was on the menu, and Tommy would tell him what to get and what not to get. According to Thelma, horse meat was fed to guest during the war.

The first Wakulla Springs Hotel burned down. At the time of the fire, Nelton threw a blanket over him and went into the hotel to help put it out. Workers ran a water hose on him while he went in to turn off the gas. Furniture from the hotel was thrown out of the upstairs windows. Nelton was given a rocking chair that had one of the arms broken off from being thrown out. He then offered anyone $1.00 if they found the missing arm of the chair. The arm was found and repaired and Mary Nelda still has the rocking chair today.

After the fire, the hotel asked Thelma to use her stove to cook for the workers since the kitchen was gone. Mr. Ball furnished the groceries. One of the other ladies was worried about Mr. Ball having to eat outside in that condition and Thelma said "he can get a paper plate and back up against a tree just like the others". Also during this time, the Tarzan movies were being filmed at Wakulla Springs and several monkeys ran free and would steal the workers lunches.

Within the next 3-4 years Nelton and Thelma built their own house at Wakulla Station and Nelton opened his own garage.

Submitted By: Karen Thompson, 2872 Shadeville Hwy., Crawfordville, FL 32327 supkarent@gmail.com

Fishing Guide at the Breakaway Lodge

My daddy was a fisherman and hunter, so I grew up fishing and hunting from the time I was just a young boy. I started guiding fishing parties some while I was just a boy still in school. They had the Breakaway Lodge down on the Ochlocknee River off US 319 just over into Franklin County, just across the Ochlocknee Bridge and down to the left. It was a private lodge owned at that time by Fenton Jones and his wife Mildred. During World War II the Army took it over and used it as a retreat area for officers. They took over a lot of things on the Franklin County side of Ochlocknee River and Ochlocknee Bay. They had houses that the service people, mostly officers, could rent. They built Lanark Village for that purpose.

So anyway, after the War Fenton Jones bought the old lodge and fixed it back up and started it as a membership lodge. It had probably been a membership lodge before, but I was too young to know about it back then. Times were real hard for our family when I was growing up. If I needed some money to buy some clothes or go out of town playing sports, I'd borrow what I needed from Fenton Jones. I'd meet him at the Post Office in Sopchoppy, and back then he paid six dollars a day to guide a fishing party. So I'd borrow six dollars from him, and the next time he needed a guide, if there were more people than the regular fishing guides could handle he'd come and get me. I did that up until the time I finished high school.

After I got out of the service and worked in Port St. Joe for a few years, we moved back to Sopchoppy and I worked at the Breakaway Lodge from March, 1959 to September, 1960 when I started as the Police Chief here in Sopchoppy. I still would do some guiding after that, but mostly from that time on I was involved in law enforcement except for my time at Olin.

Mr. Jones had boats, motors, gas (Gulf marine gas, which was white gas), docks, and storage closets where members could keep their own motor if they had it. He charged them for whatever they used plus what he paid us as guides. The lodge furnished a lunch, and had a dining room where they fed them a good breakfast and supper. Most of the time the people would take the fish they'd caught back home with them. We had a freezer, and when we came in we'd take the gills and intestines out and just put the fish in there. We took out just the parts that would tend to spoil. A lot of times if the females had red roe in them I'd keep that and bring it home. Vonita and the girls really liked the red roe, and of course I did too.

We carried a lot of real nice people. Some whose names people might recognize would be Bobby Dodd, his son, wife and daughter. Bobby was a real famous football coach. At that time, one of the top coaches in the country, he was a good man. I also guided the man who used to be Bobby Dodd's assistant head coach and became the head coach at the University of Florida, Ray Graves.

They were super good people. Bobby Dodd would fish wherever he could, even up in Canada. Back then we had a bait they called a Yellow Sally or Silver Doctor. It was a bait that had a spinner on it, a Hildebrandt spinner, with a lead weight and feathers on it, and on the back of that you'd put a frog-colored pork chunk on it. It didn't matter where they were fishing, in North America that's what they'd fish with. They'd catch a lot of fish with it. They would buy those frog-colored pork chunks to put on it; the chunk would be green on one side like the belly of a frog. So where you had the skin side, they'd have a frog color on it. And then the other side was white, like the fat. So they would bring that stuff, they'd have cases of that. We didn't have any money and would fish all day on one piece, but they'd take one off and put a new one on every time the tannic acid in the water turned the color a little bit. They might use four or five jars of those pork chunks in one day! I think there were about five in each jar.

We fished mostly in the Ochlocknee, Sopchoppy and Crooked River, places you could get to off the Ochlocknee River. But then we'd go into the St. Marks Wildlife Refuge, where you had to take a boat on a trailer. Bobby Dodd had two new cars every year. He'd have a station wagon and his wife a Buick. And we'd just slip an aluminum boat in the back of that station wagon when we fished in the Refuge. We'd run into one of those little lakes and he'd want to go around it just one time, then we'd have to load the boat back up in the station wagon and go to the next one. We might fish fifteen or twenty lakes in a day! That was a lot of work, you'd be well tired. You'd start out before daylight and get home after dark at night. That was a long, long day for six dollars! But I had a lot of good times, really, fishing with people. Some didn't fish as hard as he did. He hardly took time for lunch, didn't want to miss a cast.

Back then some of the people you guided would tip you. Back when we were making six dollars a day, Bobby Dodd would tip you five dollars. He was very, very good to the people that fished with him. And if he brought fifteen people with him he'd tip every one of those guides that same amount, not just the ones that fished with him.

I had one man that I used to fish with, who was a doctor in, I believe, LaGrange, Georgia. By that time, Fenton Jones had gotten up to paying us nine dollars a day. This doctor would give me ten dollars a day for a tip. I remember one time I was fishing with him way up in the swift water in the Ochlocknee River, above the tide water. We saw a bunch of little gators, only six to nine inches long. And he was wanting one of those little gators for his young son. We got to going around and dipping them up in a net, and we ended up with about half a dozen of them. This was way back in the early '60s sometime. It would be illegal now, but wasn't then. After awhile I got to thinking about where the mama gator was!

Another time I was fishing with him and his little boy. The doctor was a very good fisherman, very good caster. But he cast left-handed. And so he put the little boy up in the front seat and he got in the back seat. Well, he was casting left-handed, and he cast right by my head. I was back there handling the boat and felt that bait come right by my head numerous times! One time he made a cast and hit me right upside the head. He had a Silver Doctor on, a Yellow Sally. Well that lead hit

Claxton with 8 lbs. 5 oz. bass he caught in a local lake.

me right up around the temple, and I felt all this stuff running down my cheek and thought I was bleeding all over, but it turned out it was water running out of all those feathers!

I had another man one time, he was a doctor also. We were fishing in New River, out from Carrabelle, and he cast and hung up in the bushes. Well, normally you'd have to scull up to the bushes and get the plug out. But he was snatching on it, snatch, snatch, and that plug came loose and shot right back like a sling shot, and buried up in his cheek. He opened up his kit and got out a pair of cutter pliers and told me to cut the hook off. I thought, "How in the world am I going to do that?" It was a treble hook and one of the hooks had caught him. But some way I got it cut off. Then he said, "Now take it and punch it on through." I thought, "My goodness, you want me to stick that hook in there further?" He said, "Do what I said!" Well I did, and of course the point came out. You know, that was the only way you could get it out without pulling back against the barb. He had some kind of antiseptic in his tackle box and he put a little bit of it on that cheek and the next morning you could hardly tell where the hook had gone in. That kind of thing didn't happen very often.

I had another man one time, his name was Ed Dodd. He was an artist and he would draw comics for the paper. He had bought a new Ambassador reel and rod, which was kind of the top of the line back then, real expensive. He was casting, and on that reel you had a little plunger that you'd mash, and that would release the spool to where you could make the cast. And then when you'd turn your handle it would re-engage that. So this was the first time he'd ever used it, and he forgot to mash that plunger. Well, he threw reel, rod and all over into Womack Creek! This creek had real deep holes in it, and the one we were over must have been at least twenty-five feet deep. I finally got out and cut a long pole and set some treble hooks on it and drug it around as best I could down in there, and I hooked that rod on one of the eyes and brought it up. The man reached in his pocket, got ten dollars and handed it to me right there.

I had another man one time who was the Clerk of the Supreme Court in Tennessee. He was a guest of one of the members, down here from Chattanooga. We were coming back about a mile and a half above the Ochlocknee River Bridge and I was overtaking a boat ahead of us, running faster than the other boat. But the boat was making kind of high waves. What I'd do when I was overtaking a boat like that was, I'd get my boat over and just get it to where I could just roll up over it longways, and then I could go on. Well, when I started up it made the boat kind of tilt. This man thought we were fixing to turn over, and he just rose up and dove right out of that boat! I had to turn around and go get him.

I had another man one time and it was his first time being at the Breakaway. He was wanting to join as a member. Fenton had me take him up the Ochlocknee River into the swift water. I didn't especially want to do it because I didn't know what kind of fisherman he was; you had to be a pretty good fisherman to know what to do in that swift water or you'd work your guide to death getting you out of the bushes.

Nolan Sanders and Claxton Vause Jr. holding fish caught by Georgia Tech head football coach Bobby Dodd and his son Bobby Jr. Standing in the background is William Evans and Fenton Jones.

But we went over on the Liberty County side of the Ochlocknee River, over to Whitehead Lake and put in there. It's a slough that runs off the river and comes all down through the woods and then some places it'll widen out a little bit, and we call that part a lake. It'll eventually go on back into the river. So we were fishing along there and an old brushy-topped oak tree had fallen in. I told him to cast up toward the hill and just work along the edge of that brushy top. On the way up there he kept telling me about all these big bass he'd caught in south Florida. I mean, you would have thought he was a world class fisherman the way he talked. Anyway, about halfway along that brushy top, a big bass hit it and he set the hook. And the first thing he did was, he stood straight up in the boat and leaned his legs back over against the side of the boat on the opposite side from where the fish was. And he had his rod stuck up there; I bet the tip of that rod was twelve, fourteen feet up in the air, almost. And he was a-reelin'. Of course that bass came up out of the water, about eight pounds, shaking his head, and as he did he threw the hooks out. And this fellow just went right over backwards into that swift water! He came up about ten feet ahead of the boat and he was still trying to reel like he had the fish on there! The water was cold, I tried to get him to go back to the lodge and change clothes, but he wouldn't do it. Well, I thought right quick he was telling me a story about all those big fish he'd caught. He sure did get excited over that one.

I had a lot of people who were very, very good fishermen. One old man was about eighty years old and he could be the contrariest old man that I ever saw. I asked somebody one time if he was that way to everybody, and they said, "Well, while he's home his wife rules the roost. She tells him what to do and what not to do. When he gets away from her, he takes advantage of it!" So I was fishing with him right down the river between the 319 bridge and where the Ochlocknee State Park is now. About halfway down there, there's a little old place over in the grass on the left that makes like a little lake on the Wakulla County side of the river. There were some lily pads up in there. He made a cast, fishing with a top water bait or Devil Horse, and he got a backlash in his reel. Well, he had the worst birds nest you ever saw in there, and he was a-fiddlin' with it and trying to get it out. A bass hit it. And him over here now, had his line all tied up to where he couldn't reel, he couldn't do anything. I told him, "Stick that rod back here and let me get a hold of that line." Well, he didn't do it, and I had to crawl up there and get a hold of the line. I took the line and actually drug that bass in, a seven pound bass. I got him close enough that I could dip him up. Normally, he would have torn loose, because the rod would have some give to it. Anyway, old man Sam, when he got back to the Breakaway he was talking about him catching that big old bass!

Another time I was fishing with him and we were in a little creek off Dead River. He made a cast and a small bass hit it, and when he reeled in, he had two!

Another time I had Mr. Ed Dodd up here in what we called Mack Slough. Just before we'd put in that morning it had rained real hard, so the banks were muddy and so was the water. Back then we fished a lot with Devil Horses. It's a top water bait with three sets of treble hooks on it and kind of small spinners. Before we started using those, we used something called a "Nippadiddy." It was a top water plug, but it had big spinners on it. It had three sets of hooks too, trebles. Anyway, I had a small tackle box and I had taken all my Nippadiddies out and didn't have anything but Devil Horses in the box. I told him, with that water muddy like it was, to put on a bait with bigger spinners. So we fished down about half a mile below where we'd put in, and he finally got a strike. He set the hook and he was a-reelin', reelin', reelin'; and of course there was no way to see the fish, with the water so muddy. I was just trying to go by the line from the tip of his rod to see if the fish was just under the water. I dipped my net down to see if I could dip the bass up, and it was a little bit deeper than what I'd thought. But when I got up, the tail of the fish got nearly right up to the top of the water. I told him, "I believe that fish had two tails!" He finally played around and got it back up there, and he had caught two on that one cast. One weighed four and a half pounds and the other weighed three and a half. Eight pounds of bass on that one cast, and that was the only strike we got all day! I think one hit it and the other one was trying to take it away from him and got hooked too.

How did we know where to take people each time? We didn't, really. It's a guess. In tide water, maybe you'd know that the tide would be more favorable in a certain place, or if you were going up the river above the tide water and the water level was down to a certain level you'd know to fish there. Just a lot of guessing, really, and relying on a lot of things that you'd done in the past. You'd just learn it yourself, by trial and error. When I first started, I asked my daddy sometimes because he was more familiar with that fishing down there than I was. He'd tell me places to go.

I remember one time when I was still just a boy in school and Bobby Dodd had a lot of his people down here. They all had a bet on who would catch the most fish. Well, I had one of them and we were fishing in what we called Bear Creek. It's got two ends to it in the Ochlocknee River; in other words it makes a big old loop over on the Franklin County side and then comes back out way down the river. But we were fishing there and had caught eight bass. He had a fairly nice string of bass.

Well, back then we didn't have ice chests to put them in; you'd just string them on a string and hang the string out behind the boat. You'd put the fish stringer up through the bottom lip of the bass, through kind of a hard section around the bottom of that lip, and then you'd put it up behind that through the skin and a little thin meat there. You'd bring it out of a thin place in the top lip. So anyway, we had eight bass on there. We were getting ready to come in, and I reached back there and cranked the outboard motor. And I looked back and there was just a string hanging there. I had cut the whole string of bass off with the propeller! When we got back he was telling all these others how many we had caught, and he'd just hold up that string! Everybody just said, "Yeah." He couldn't convince them!

One time I was fishing in Whiskey George Creek and I had the fish strung out behind the boat like that. I looked back and a moccasin had one of them over half swallowed. He'd chewed on it until he was halfway up that fish!

Another time I was fishing in a pond by myself, casting off the bank, and I had three or four fish on a stringer. I'd just stick the point of it down in the ground and let the string stay out in the water, to keep the fish alive. And I saw about a five foot gator trying to get the fish. So I dragged the fish out up on the bank twelve or fifteen feet, under a tree and started casting again. When I looked around again, there was that gator, coming up on that hill trying to get my fish!

Another time there in that same pond, there was a gator laying out about fifteen or twenty feet off the bank. I cast out about twenty feet past him and over six or eight feet to his right. A bass hit it and I was reeling him in, and when that bass got near where that gator was, I mean before you could bat your eye the gator had that fish. So for just a minute there, I had the fish and the gator! But then the gator ended up with the fish.

Another time my daddy and I were fishing over in what they used to call Tucker Lake, over on James' Island. He kept casting a plug out there to a gator, and he finally got it. He reeled it back around to me, and I just cut the line and let him go with the plug.

One time I was fishing with a man up above Silver Lake, off the Ochlocknee River, and there were moccasins swimming across it. The man put on an underwater plug with all those hooks on it, and he threw it across and snagged one. He came reeling back to me and I cut his line off. The snake swam off with the plug. The man looked at me like I was crazy. He'd thought I was going to take that moccasin off, but I wasn't going to!

Submitted By: Claxton Vause Jr., P.O. Box 145, Sopchoppy, FL 32358, as told to Linda Sheldon.

Little Jett, a Tarpon, and Me

I spent some of my formative years living the perfect boy's life in and around the little fishing village of St. Marks, Florida. For those of you who are unfamiliar with St. Marks, and don't have ready access to a state map, it is situated on the St. Marks river, near Apalachee Bay. It is in the "Big Bend" of Florida, in the panhandle, about 20 miles due south of Tallahassee. The episode I recount is factual, and occurred sometime about 1955.

Not far from the junction of the St. Marks and Wakulla rivers, at Fort San Marcos de Apalachee, about 1955, there was a great place to catch tarpon. The tarpon, or "Silver King" is one of the top game fish in the entire world. I'm going to let you in on a secret by telling you where those big fish may still be, and also about how it was that Little Jett and I got involved with one of them.

Little Jett was a young black boy, about my age, maybe twelve years old, and we became friends when he began helping his daddy clean fish at my daddy's fishing dock at St. Marks. We knew him as "Little Jett" because his older brother's name was Jett, and it was only later I learned his true name, Samuel G. Harper. Anyway, Little Jett was such a happy go lucky fellow, always full of fun, never without a smile on his face. I remember how we'd watch the gar fish rolling on the surface of the river near our dock, and how Little Jett made up a song which went something like..."there goes Mr. Gar-Fish, a courtin' up the river, just a courtin'. Can't you hear him a callin', where are you Miss GAR fish, where are you?" He had a talent for making up songs like that at the drop of a hat. We had lots of fun around the dock in the middle of the day before the boats would come in and we'd both have to start working.

When things were kind of slow during the day, I enjoyed fishing in both the St. Marks and Wakulla rivers. I spent lots of time fishing and hunting with another good friend from St. Marks, Sam Mock. There wasn't much about fishing and hunting that Sam didn't know, and that's how I came to find my "Tarpon Hole". Sam had showed it to me.

Tarpon are primarily salt-water fish, but for some reason, at a certain time of the year, I don't recall now exactly when, they'd venture from out in Apalachee Bay, up into the fresh water of the St. Marks and Wakulla rivers. From our dock, far enough up the St. Marks river that the water was always fresh, even on high tide, we'd see them rolling out in the river, their backs and tail fins breaking the surface of the water.

Now I know sports fishermen have different and varied methods of catching the mighty tarpon. But we were kids and not interested in using ultra light tackle or anything like that. What we wanted to do was land a big tarpon any way we could. We wanted to show off. I guess you could say we were unsophisticated. To minimize the fish's chances of getting away, we'd either use a strong hand line or a deep sea fishing rod and reel with at least 80 pound test line. Because the tarpon's mouth is so hard, when fishing for them, it is necessary to allow the fish to run at least thirty or forty feet with your bait, giving the fish no resistance, before setting the hook. If you try to set the hook too soon, old Mr. Tarpon will just spit it out and laugh at you. Although difficult to catch, the fisherman is very much rewarded when he or she is able to land a tarpon. They are a streamlined fish, bright silver in color, and often weigh from eighty to a hundred and fifty pounds or more. And finally, I don't think you'll get a better fight from any game fish. Irrespective of its size, the tarpon will always give you a real show and put up a hard fight, with strong runs and majestic leaps high out of the water.

Now to the Tarpon Hole, if you travel up the Wakulla River, maybe two miles from the fort, on your right you'll see a fairly large creek. That'll be Boggy Creek. That Tarpon Hole was out in the river, right off the mouth of that creek. At the right time of the year, that water would just be boiling with tarpon. I don't know why they congregated there, I just know for certain they were always there.

Little Jett knew about tarpon, and so did I, but neither of us had ever been lucky enough to catch one. We decided to try to do something about that, and I told him all about that Tarpon Hole off Boggy Creek. He got permission from his daddy to go with me, and off we went in my cypress skiff and 3 horse power Evinrude outboard motor. And sure enough, those tarpon were there waiting for us. I had rigged up a deep sea fishing rod and reel, plenty of leader wire at the end of my line so the fish wouldn't cut the line, a nice large, sharp hook, and half a mullet for bait. We dropped our anchor off Boggy Creek and I cast my bait out into the river, almost on the backs of those fish, which were rolling near the surface. I pulled off about thirty feet of line from my Penn reel, carefully coiling it in the bottom of the boat, set my drag just right, and locked the reel. Soon I detected some slight movement of my line, so slight that I attributed it to a blue crab. But soon enough, something very big ran that crab off and Little Jett and I had us some real action!

All of a sudden, I noticed my coiled line was running out real fast and I said, "Look, Little Jett, get ready, one's got it!" When the slack in the line ran out, I stood up and reared that rod back with all my strength, setting the hook. No question I had a very big tarpon on the line as the drag screamed as he pulled line off in a straight run away from our boat. Then, just as tarpon are known to do, the line went slack as he turned and began a run right straight back toward our boat, attempting to take the pressure off the hook so he could dislodge it. But I reeled in quickly and got some pressure back on him. I remember shouting, "Little Jett, we've got us a monster here!" Maybe not exactly the right words to put Little Jett at ease. His eyes were big and I saw fear and terror in his face as he hung onto our boat, up near the bow, for dear life. But I didn't have time to think about what Little Jett was thinking about as that big fish went under our boat then turned and headed back out toward the middle of the river, pulling line from my reel as he ran. He went deep and then I could tell he was heading for the surface. I swear when that tarpon made his first jump, it looked like I had a mule on my line. What a beautiful sight he made as he tail walked before splashing back down. He looked to be at least as large as the boat we were in, and it was fourteen feet. I was ecstatic!

I couldn't believe my ears when I heard Little Jett shouting, "Cut the line, cut the line! Let him go, let him go!" I glanced over at Little Jett and he was still as far up in the bow and away from me as he could get. I shouted back, "Are you crazy? I'm not about to cut this line, I'm going to catch this rascal. Little Jett, we've got ourselves a trophy!" All the while, I was in the fight of my life. That fish would run first at us, then away. Then I got a second beautiful jump out of him, and Little Jett and I could see him shaking his big head, trying to throw the hook. Little Jett was horrified and started back up, shouting as loud as he could about how I should cut the line. He was yelling something about how that fish was going to sink our boat and he didn't know how to swim. He was pleading, almost crying as he was saying he just knew we were both about to die. But there was no way I had any intention of letting that fish go.

Sadly for me, and wonderful for Little Jett, the tarpon came blasting out of the water right near our boat on his third jump. He had come running back toward me so fast, reel in as I may, there was no way I could keep the tension on the line. As he broke the water, I got some tension back on him, but not enough. He shook his head violently, throwing water on Little Jett and me. The line was too slack and that hook flew from his mouth as if shot from a gun. I had been fighting him for about thirty minutes, and now he was gone!

Looking back on it, how funny was the contrast in moods between Little Jett and me. I was exhausted and sick with disappointment, so sad I wanted to cry, and I've never seen Little Jett in higher sprits.You could just see the relief all over his face. At first I was kind of angry with him for being so happy about me losing my trophy fish. But as we headed for home, Little Jett's personality caused my demeanor to change, and we laughed and joked about that old fish all the way back. He was convinced that if I had tried to put that tarpon in the boat, we would have both surely drowned or the fish would have beat us to death with its tail.

Little Jett was cured of any desire to go any kind of fishing with me after that. I soon lost all contact with Little Jett, and didn't know what became of him. I was told not long ago by an elderly black gentleman, Sam Donaldson, who works part time at Shell Island Fish Camp on the Wakulla river, that Little Jett retired from the Army and makes his residence in Tallahassee. I'll bet you anything that among the stock of stories he tells his grandchildren, there's one near the top about that big fish, and how it almost did us in that day at Boggy Creek.

My good friend and childhood fishing and hunting partner, Sam Mock, who first showed me that Tarpon Hole when we were just boys, never gave up his love of fishing. You can find him today, working as a guide taking folks out fishing for speckled trout and redfish from the Shell Island Fish Camp in St. Marks. He's had over 50 years experience, and I would put him up against any guide in the state of Florida. Few can match his knowledge or experience, and none are better fishermen.

As for me, I left my beloved Florida many years ago to travel all around the world as a Special Agent with the Naval Criminal Investigative Service. But I always returned to the unspoiled beauty of north Florida in my dreams, and often relived that day at Boggy Creek on the Wakulla river. Finally, in my 60th year, I came back home to Florida. And maybe, just maybe, someday I'll put a boat in the river and take another shot at the "Silver King".

As a post script, not long after I submitted this story to Sport Fishing magazine, I was shocked and saddened to see in the March 18, 2005, obituary section of the Tallahassee Democrat, "Samuel G. Harper, 62, who retired from the U.S. Army, died Wednesday, March 16, 2005." A very hard lesson was learned by me, and I pass it along. Friends, never put off going to see those you care about or renewing old friendships. Another shock came to me when I learned that on January 18, 2009, Wakulla County lost a mighty fine man and lifelong professional fishing guide, and I lost a good friend of more than 50 years, Samuel E. Mock, Sr., who as a boy, showed me that Tarpon Hole off Boggy Creek. My consolation is that Little Jett, Samuel G. Harper, and Sam Mock may live on in my story, and I dedicate it to their memory.

Submitted By: John Y. Roberts 58 Lone Feather Dr., Tallahassee, Florida 32311 (850)656-2606 (home) (850)556-2362 (cell)

Terranova Fishing Trip at St. George Island

Back in the summer of 1983 my brother and I went on a fishing trip to St. George Island.

We were fishing for Redfish at the Bob Sykes Cut, on the west end of the island. We were anchored in our 16 foot boat in the 30 foot water at the middle of the cut. Suddenly the anchor rope shifted to the right and flipped the boat. We had the anchor tied off at the back corner cleat on the boat (big mistake as your anchor should be front secured). A huge man-a-ray, approximately12 foot wing span, had tangled up in our anchor rope. The boat submerged completely under water, leaving my brother and me treading water.

We lost the boat, tackle and all belongings. As we swam to the jetties, we lost sight of our boat going south. Although we did catch a glimpse of the ray airborne with the anchor rope tangled on the front of him. Believe it or not!

Submitted By: Mike and Mitch Terranova,2802 Plant St, Tallahassee, FL 32304; miketerranova@acousti.com

Wakulla River Ferry

The previous photo is a photo card that was mailed to; W.H. Smith in McIntern, FL.

The card says "For Greenie Roberts"

Wakulla River Ferry

Tuesday, Apr, 20th, 1926

It is believed that Greenie Roberts is the child and Edward A. Hill is the boatman.

Submitted by; Betty Green, PO Box 969, Crawfordville, FL

The Big Blow at Shell Point Beach

Early October, 1941:

The seine yard had opened as it usually did on the first Monday in October; there was nothing unusual about this day, just a normal day, sun shining and a little warm. As evening wore on and turned into night, the stars were shining, the moon was up, and the tide was rising. About 9:00pm my brother, "RC", arrived home from his visit with his future wife, Clarice Ward, and by 10pm we were all in bed asleep, (nothing unusual about this night). We were used to summer squalls, but they only lasted about twenty minutes before being gone. We had no way of knowing what the weather was doing in those days, no telephones or radios; we only had nature's signs. Only a few people in Wakulla County had radios, maybe there were 5 telephones and a few had electricity. The county was just coming out of the "Great Depression" of the twenties and thirties. Shell Point Beach was just one little strip of dry land about 300 feet wide and a mile long. The road then ran exactly where it does today, south to the new Coast Guard Station, then a sharp left down a 2-rut road just off the beach; just back of this little strip of land was a scrub oak and palmetto thicket, the rest was salt flats and marsh grass. This little strip of land was possibly about three feet higher than the bay or the marsh on the north side of the beach.

The Long Night:

At approximately 11:30pm, someone knocked on our door, my daddy went to the door and it was Joshua Harvey, my lifetime friend. He woke us up to tell us we needed to get ready to leave Shell Point, as a storm was already there. He had a truckload of seine yard hands in Mr. Ira Raker's truck. Mr. Raker was the yard boss and they were leaving. We got up and dressed as quickly as possible, Daddy asked RC to move the truck to higher ground; he did and returned to the house. My little sister, Mary Emma, was only eighteen days old; we wrapped her in a blanket and then an oilcloth to keep her dry. We started out the back door to the truck, and by this time the water was two feet deep under the house and the wind was blowing 80-90 miles per hour. (This is just a rough guess on my part.) We headed for the truck but we didn't quite make it, the wind got a hold on the truck and flipped it upside down in the Oak thicket. (I guess we were lucky we didn't make it to the truck or we would have been under it.)

If you believe in Miracles or Divine Intervention, I am going to tell you about two or three. I just told you about Number One - the truck incident. As we could not go down the beach road, there was only one thing to do, that was to walk through the Oak thicket. Therefore, we started out, by this time, the water was waist deep on us. My mother insisted on carrying the baby (this was her last child). Daddy was holding on to me and my sister, Carolyn. After a while walking, falling over stumps and roots, Mother fell with the baby and was completely submerged under the water! We got her and the baby back up and both were OK. We saw that this was not going to work, so my brother, RC, took the baby and had not gone too far when he fell, he got back up on his own and both were OK. Meanwhile, the water was getting deeper and the wind was blowing harder. After what seemed like an eternity, we made it to the main road.

Miracle #two: The Baby never even got damp from being submerged several times, or in fact, during the whole storm. So, now we are on the main road, all we have to do is to wade up the road until we get to dry land. What we did not know at that time was the storm surge was five miles ahead of us. We waded until we came to where the firehouse is today; there we ran into a roaring creek, and the small bridge had been washed away, the creek was impossible to cross. My daddy said there was only one thing left to do, that was to climb a tree. He sent my brother, RC, my mother and the baby to find the right tree. He left my sister, Carolyn, and me a little way behind, while he checked out the creek, making sure there was no way we could cross the creek. While standing there waiting, the wind picked up and the current took Carolyn away from me. She was kicking and floundering around. I hollered to Daddy to get Carolyn when she floated by him; he grabbed at her but missed, as a last desperate attempt he grabbed at her long hair, and at this time he was able to get a good hold on the hair and pulled her to where he was standing. That was miracle #three.

Not being able to cross the creek, we all moved to the tree that RC had selected; it was a small Water Oak about six or eight inches in diameter, with several limbs on each side, with the lowest being about eight feet off the ground. We helped my mother up first and then handed her the baby, then Carolyn and I went up. RC and Daddy came up last. I bet we would have been a remarkable sight to see all of us in that small Oak tree. Later I asked RC why he had selected that tree, he said only that it beat the one anyone else found. There we sat for the rest of the night while the wind blew and the water rose. The water was at least six to seven feet deep under our tree. Later we found out the storm surge reached almost the intersection of Shell Point and Spring Creek Road, approximately six miles inland. When daylight finally broke, what a sight! (You would have had to be there to appreciate it!) All around us, trees were uprooted and blown over but our little tree held fast. In one tree close to us was a little oopussum sitting in the fork of that tree out of the reach of the water. On another side in a small cedar tree were three little snakes, one would crawl up as far as it could then another snake would crawl up and knock him off, all trying to get out of the water, this went on for hours.

But the most amazing sight of all was a little ways away was a blown over tree with lots of limbs on it; a cow had gotten up in those limbs and was standing there with her calf, which had his front feet up on his mother's back, with his nose and head barely out of the water and it survived the storm this way. In those days cows roamed free in Wakulla County.

We had a few boats that we rented out for fishing parties and one that was larger than the rest belonged to the Gissendanner Family of Tallahassee (we called it "the gissendanner"). When daylight broke this boat was floating high and dry not more than seventy five feet from us! There you have two miracles: (1) our tree held fast, and (2) a boat was there for us. All our other boats were lost and never found. At any rate, it was several hours before we could leave that tree, we had to wait on the wind to slack and the water to recede.

You may ask, "Was I scared?" the answer is NO. I was used to stormy weather and could swim very well. In those days, an eleven year old boy in Wakulla County could take care of himself. If he got into trouble, he got himself out of it as best he could.

Well, the water finally receded and the wind slacked some, we were able to get out of the tree and return home. Our house was still intact but had no floor. It was built on stilts and the waves had knocked the entire floor out. When we got home, our dog, Sunny, was sitting on the beach with his ears flopping in the wind and looking out over the bay. I guess he thought his family was gone for good. He was really glad to see us and jumped with joy. We left Sunny in the house when we left; how he survived, we will never know.

At this time, Shell Point Beach was divided into two parts by a small creek that was very calm. My brother, RC, and I decided to see what had happened on the other side of the creek. This creek was full of water and running very swift, from the water that was returning to the bay. We took off our clothes, got way up stream, swam down with the current and crossed at the same time. We made it to the other side safely but my mother who could not see us, (but found our clothes) thought we were gone for sure. As I said, boys could take care of themselves in those days.

RC and I proceeded on up the beach. It was as if nothing had ever been built there, everything was gone. We found two survivors, Mr. Henry Hodge and Mr. Perry Gray. They had not made it out, and told us how they had survived. If you know anything about hurricanes, you know they do not blow continuously. It will blow for several minutes and then lull for a minute or two, this is how these two men survived. They were on the highest part of the beach and would run toward the wind when it lulled and be blown back when the wind (and water) rose again. They told us that they almost gave up several times, but self preservation took over (it will make you try the impossible).

I believe this was the worst hurricane to ever hit Wakulla County. It took three lives in Wakulla, a Mr. Raker and two black men, I do not know. I understand they were trying to recover a seine net from one of the seine yards when they drowned.

Well, the storm is over. The road has dried up so it is passable and here comes a school bus with several men in it looking for survivors. They found eight of us, my family and two more. The bus belonged to Mr. Robert Green (Mr. Rob), on it were three of my uncles: Cager Pelt, John Pelt and Willie Taff. Within a month, we moved to Tallahassee, my mother refused to live at Shell Point anymore, she never did live there again but did go back for short visits.

Mr. Rob Green, (the owner of the survivor bus) was my bus driver for my early years of school and the father of my best boyhood friend, Dan Green.

I was a little hesitant to write or tell this story, as some may not believe it. I assure you that every word is true. My cousin, Clayton Taff, and my friend, Council Raker, encouraged me to write this story, so thanks to them, here it is.

Submitted By: Carlos Taff, 291 Bostic Pelt Road, Crawfordville, FL 32327

Note: Thanks to Carolyn Olah for the typing, etc, for this story. My daddy: Robert Calhoun Taff - 11/9/1892-7/4/1957 Mother: Sena Pelt Taff - 3/8/1900-7/18/1983 Brother: Robert Calhoun Taff, Jr. - 4/20/1925-6/5/2002 (Self): Carlos Taff- 11/5/1930 Sister: Carolyn Taff-6/22/1933 Sister: Mary Emma Taff (Baby in story)-9/18/1941

George Washington Lynn

George Washington Lynn was born December 23, 1873 in Decatur County, GA to Francis Marion and Joannah (Norris) Lynn. He died August 28, 1956 in St. Marks, FL. He married June 4, 1884 in Decatur Co. GA, Dora Ann Barber who was born December 29, 1874 and died July 8, 1957 in St. Marks, FL and both are buried in Corinth Cemetery, Seminole Co. GA.

They moved to Tiger Hammock, Wakulla County, Florida about 1928 and were in the sawmill business. They eventually turned to the fishing business and moved to St. Marks.

They were the parents of 11 children.

1. Newton Jasper Lynn (b) August 2, 1895 (d) February 10, 1931 Never married.
2. Alva Gordon Lynn (b) April 30, 1898 (d) April 10, 1958 Married #1 Carmen Yvonne Adams (b) Sept. 26, 1905 (d) Oct. 1, 1931 Married #2 Lorene Taylor.
3. Ira Lynn (b) March 30, 1900 stillborn
4. Raymond Anderson Lynn (b) May 11, 1901 (d) December 16, 1923 Never married.
5. Rufus Atword Lynn (b) May 18, 1902 (d) May 22, 1956 Married Decatur Co. GA September 24, 1927 1st Thelma Lewis, 2nd Judy Bradshaw.
6. Lynnie Lynn (b) November 2, 1907 (d) October 20, 1911
7. James Releford Lynn (b) February 10, 1908 (d) April 9, 1983 Married Decatur Co. GA September 7, 1930 1st Rachel Nix, 2nd Married Decatur Co. GA, April 3, 1937 Lomie Chester (b) Oct. 20, 1919 (d) January 26, 1999 Buried Salem Baptist Church Cemetery, Decatur County, GA.
8. J. T. "Bo" Lynn (b) December 9, 1909 (d) December 9, 1957 Married Lillian Estelle Moore
9. Georgia Lee Lynn (b) May 30, 1912 (d) December 22, 1958 Married Walter C. Neal (d) December 22, 1958 Car Accident; NO CHILDREN

George Washington Lynn and Dora Barber Lynn

Catch of Grouper

10. William Albert "Heck" Lynn (b) September 6, 1914 (d) December 29, 2006 St. Marks, FL. Married May 19, 1939 Leon County, FL Jessie Vause (b) January 3, 1913 (d) Oct

11. Harvey Anderson Lynn (b) May 6, 1918 (d) January 6, 1947

William Albert Lynn, the 10th child of George Washington and Dora Ann (Barber) Lynn, was born in Bainbridge, Decatur County, Georgia on September 6, 1914. His family moved to Wakulla County about 1928 to Tiger Hammock to cut timber.

Gramps met Granny (Jesse Vause) at the square dances held around the county in private homes, mostly at Uncle Phil Carraway and Bill Council's home.

They went together for 6 years before they got married on May 19, 1939 in Leon County FL. Gramps bought a piece of land in St. Marks, Florida and built a house and moved his father and mother, George and Dora, to the new home. He and Granny moved in with them.

Gramps worked on a tugboat and would be gone for a month at a time. When he came home it would be for a few days and he'd be gone again.

The Greyhound

Later on, Gramps bought some more property on the river bank and began building his marina and started a commercial fishing business.

His first boat was called the Greyhound. He took parties out grouper and snapper fishing. He fished this boat for 7 or 8 years. He had built several cabins for the parties to stay in and Granny took care of cleaning and washing towels and sheets.

Next he built the Lucky Lady and commercial fished her for 16 years. He sold her and was planning to retire but couldn't stand being without a boat so he had the Princess built. He

The Lucky Lady

fished her for 3 years and sold her. He built a house boat to takeout on the flats to stay in at night so he could mullet fish. One summer he decided the house boat was too narrow, so he cut it right down the middle and added 3 feet to the boat so it would be wider.

Later on Gramps built a smaller boat The Mini Slab and rigged it to go shrimping. However, he didn't like shrimping so he used it to catch bait to sell in the marina.

Granny and Gramps had five boys, all who still work in St. Marks.

Back row: Richard, Johnnie, W.A.
Front row: Andy, Heck, and Allen Lynn (Lynn Brothers)

1. Walter Albert (WA) Lynn (b) Aug. 18, 1940 Married Aug 3, 1961 Judy Council

2. Derrell Eugene Lynn (b) Dec. 29, 1943 Married Sept. 12, 1964 Phyllis Ann Strickland (b) May 11, 1945. (d) August 16, 2005. Buried Whiddon Lake Cemetery, Wakulla County FL.

3. John Thomas Lynn (b) Sept. 5, 1946 Married April 8, 1970 Sharon Diane Strickland (b) July 19, 1946.

4. Chester Allen Lynn (b) July 3, 1953 Married Oct. 27, 1972 Wakulla Station, FL, Tanya Louise Watts (b) Nov. 24, 1952.

5. Marion Anderson Lynn (b) April 20, 1956 Married Aug. 21, 1985 Patsy McCullers (b) Feb. 1, 1956. (DIV 1993) Married 2nd August 5, 2004 Lynn Williams Roberts.

Submitted by: Tanya Lynn, 165 Deepwood Dr., Crawfordville, FL 32327

Living Along The Wakulla Coast In The 30s & 40s

This was a pristine area in those days, no smog, no pollution, no canals, just beautiful marsh grass, bays, creeks and salt flats. No amount of people from St. Marks River to Ochlocknee River. However there were a few permanent residents along the coast, mostly just fishing villages or single family residents. At the St. Marks Lighthouse were the Gresham Family, Mr. Gresham was the lighthouse keeper. My Daddy, Calhoun Taff, was given a job by Mr. Gresham to maintain the blinker light on Shell Point Reef and on Panacea Bay; entrance at Ozori, a basin in Panacea Bay. Mr. Gresham brought the supplies over to Shell Point where we lived. The supplies consisted of batteries and bulbs. In those days we did not have an outboard motor, so we would row a boat to Shell Point Reef, change any bulbs or batteries that needed to be changed, wash the bird droppings off the light, and row on to Panacea, do the same and then row back home to Shell Point. This was an all day chore and

St Marks Lighthouse

had to be done weekly. We were paid $25.00 monthly but in those days that was a lot of money. After his first pay check, Daddy bought an outboard motor; five horse power Johnson. It wasn't fast but it sure beat rowing. He bought it from Mr. Bo Lynn in St. Marks, in his life time he bought more motors but always from Mr. Lynn. He thought no one else sold motors, I guess, or else just liked to trade with Mr. Lynn.

Now, back to the coast moving west to Wakulla Beach or Walker Beach as it was known then. The Walker's owned it then and there were about five houses with a Hotel. The Hotel was owned by Senator Walker, the remains of the old Hotel can be seen to this day. This area was actually platted out as a town according to local records, known as East Goose Creek. This is separate from West Goose Creek by several creeks. The main creek being Goose Creek, there are also, Menslor Creek and Shepard Creek. Shepard Creek goes up stream to Shepard Spring.

Wakulla Beach was occasionally used as a seine yard during the Fall mullet run but mostly was used by Black Americans as a landing for gill netters. The name of some of the families that used it as a landing was the Farmers, Triplets, Rev. Mathews, Harveys, Davis, and Harguits. There are now three summer homes located there today.

Now, we move across Goose Creek Bay to West Goose Creek which was a seine yard for many years. Some of the operators of West Goose Creek seine yard were Mr. George Nesmith, Mr. Dalton Raker, Mr. Lee Spears and Mr. Maurice Raker. West Goose Creek had two permanent houses and a fish house. One house was totally destroyed by a

Mullet Stew

Slice sweet potatoes and onions.
Layer in order:
Sweet potatoes
Onions
Sprinkle with flour, salt & pepper.
Layer mullet fillets, mullet gizzards, mullet heads.
Sprinkle with flour, salt & pepper.
Repeat layers until pot is almost full.
Add enough water to keep bottom layer from scorching.
Cook on medium heat until done.
When eating, thank the Good Lord for Wakulla mullet fishermen.

Recipe submitted by Gloria Council Dowden in memory of her mother, Inez Council, who would never even taste it but would cook it for her daddy, Maurice Council and, his life-long best friend, John Ferrell.

hurricane but the other house and the fish house were rebuilt and used for many more years. The Refuge in 1968 closed West Goose Creek to use as a Bald Eagle nesting area. The last house fell into disrepair and was finally destroyed by a hurricane. This seine yard was used for many years for picnics, camping, fish-fries, celebrations or just to watch the mullet being seined out of the bay; this was an exciting thing to watch if you had never seen it before.

Let's move on west to Live Oak Island, it had two houses and a fish house. Mr. Council was the owner and sold fish and rented a few party boats. A small creek behind the beach had been dug out where boats were moored, the fish house backed up to this small creek. Mr. Council was the first person to have electric

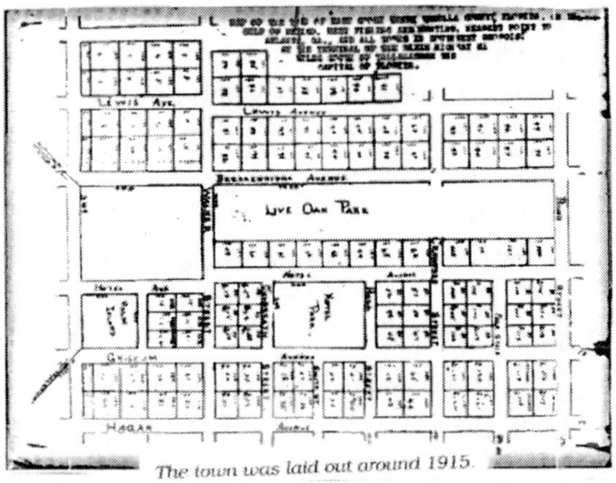
Live Oak Park
The town was laid out around 1915.

Platt of Wakulla Beach or Walker Beach as it was known then

lights I ever saw on the coast. He also ran a small store in part of his house. The electricity was supplied by a Delco Generator that ran on a gasoline engine that in turned charged a battery; the battery looked like a square glass cube with a few marbles in it. It would give you light for a few hours but they were so dim you could hardly see, an oil lamp would have given more light, but this was considered modern in those days. Mr. Council, in his store, sold most essentials such as; cornmeal, lard, salt and fishing supplies. People liked to cook their fish after fishing all day. A boat rented for $2.00 a day and you furnished your own motor or you could hire a Guide for about $7.00 a day with a motor but you still had to furnish your own bait and tackle; which consisted mostly of cut mullet and a 20 foot bamboo fishing pole. There were rods and reels in those days but few people owned them.

Our next stop, Shell Point Beach, I believe I know how it got its name, but I have no proof, just my thinking by putting two and two together. My family moved to Shell Point when I was just a small boy, so at first I just played, this was paradise to me. Later I became interested in my surrounding and began to explore like boys will do. I learned all of the trails through the woods and marsh grass. I found things I had never seen before like Indian Mounds and a few spear points made of flint rock.

Now this is how I think that Shell Point got it name. Going down Shell Point Road, when you get to where you make a left turn to go up the beach, looking to your right or to the west, this is a point of land that runs out to the bay. In the 1930s this whole point was a giant shell mount, at least 100 foot wide and the whole length of the point. It was at least 3 feet higher

Shell Point – Sam Acre and Unknown Male

than the ground with any kind of shells that grew in the bay on it; oysters, conch, scallops, clams, Pearl oyster and some kinds I don't know. All shells left there after being eaten by

Native Americans, so my belief is the first person who saw this shell pile named it Shell Point. This shell pile didn't last until the end of the 30s, they were sold and hauled away. The older peopled called this point, Old Point. What these shells were used for I never learned.

Let me tell you a little more about Shell Point. The road that leads to Shell Point is not the original road. The beginning of the road at the intersection of Spring Creek Road and Shell Point Road made many detours out through the woods in order to avoid ponds, creeks and continued to the present day Fire Station, then took a left, crossed a salt flat then came out east of the public beach; of course, this was before my time but you could still see the old road bed and ruts made by wagons. Living at Shell Point you never had to worry about going hungry, there was an abundance of sea food and in the fall thousands of Canadian geese and ducks. We feasted on them during the fall. My brother, R.C. Taff, and I kept the family supplied with them; the biggest problem for us was buying shot gun shells. Shells were cheap but money was scarce so we would save up our nickels and pennies. We could buy 6 shells for 25 cents, we treated them like gold. You only needed one shell to kill all the ducks you could carry home; they would be in rafts of thousands most any where you looked. My brother, R.C., and I started hunting when we were about 8 years old or big enough to carry the gun safely. We were told by our daddy, Calhoun Taff, to never point a gun at anything we did not intend to kill. We bought our shells at Mr. Roy Rehwinkel store in Crawfordville. To show you the price of things then a pair of overalls were $1.25 and if you bought $10.00 worth of groceries, you got a pair of overalls FREE. I'm sure that was Mr. Roy's way of helping his customers out, you didn't have to spend the $10.00 all at once, just save the sale ticket until you got to the $10.00 and Mr. Roy would honor them.

Back to the coast, moving a little further West to Cedar Creek Landing, most people do not know that it existed. Cedar Creek Landing was between Shell Point and Grass Inlet (now known as Oyster Bay). Cedar Creek Landing had three houses mostly for gill net fisherman to live in. One interesting thing is about all I knew about Cedar Creek at the mouth of the creek there was a salt kettle where salt was made by cooking out salt water during the Civil War like many other places along Wakulla's coast. The remains of which have been gone for many years but someone might be interested in knowing about this place one day and its purpose. Now let's go a little further west to Grass Inlet seine yard. This seine yard had two big houses built on stilts about seven to eight feet off of the ground, one house was for living in and the other was a fish house, where fish were weighed, iced and sold fresh. So far as I know fish were not split and salted there. If so, not in any great quantity like other seine yards. One reason being this yard was known as a dribble yard, mullet did not come through it in great bunches, only in smaller schools. Thus, the name Dribble yard. Some of the people who fished this yard were: Mr. Perry Gray, Mr. Henry Green, Mr. Jeff Green, Mr. Rob Green, Mr. George Ward and Mr. Henry Hodge. I am trying to leave myself out of this story as much as possible but since I was part of it, I can't leave myself out completely and still tell it like it was. These fishermen would get me to come help them fish on weekends and holidays when I was not in school. My job was to hold down the lead line so that the fish did not swim under the net. Holding down a lead line took a little know how, to let it slide under your foot and not be thrown into the net, something I learned at an early age by watching other people do it. My pay would be what change they had in their pocket at the time, sometimes fifty or sixty cent some time less, sometimes just a Thank You. But I was doing what I liked to do, which was the main thing.

Now, let's move a little further west to Stuart Cove, which was owned by Mr. John Gray and his family. Mr. Gray and his sons fished, he had a launch boat, which made a different sound while the motor was running from any other launch. You could tell it from anyone else's launch when you heard it coming. You already know what a launch was; I will explain it better later.

Now we will move over to the biggest fishing port in Wakulla County, in those days it was the community of Spring Creek. While writing this story I realized it would take three or four books to tell the complete story of Spring Creek, so here is a shorter version. Spring Creek has the largest group of fresh water springs in the U.S. or possibly in the World. There are at least twelve or maybe more, it was and is a natural harbor. It has been owned by the Spears Family for many years, my life time friend Mr. Lee Spears, and Spring Creek Historian, supplied me with most of the following information.

In the 20s, 30s and 40s, there were over one hundred fishermen working out of Spring Creek in small skiff boats, powered by oars. Let's talk more about launches; these boats were mostly flat bottom with car motors in them, twenty to twenty-five feet in length with a cab and sleeping bunks, a big box for icing fish in the middle. These boats had no transmission, when the motor was started it was moving, only way to stop was to shut the motor off. What these boats were used for was to pull skiff boats and to haul fish that were caught, these boats were iced up and went out fishing on Monday morning and came back on Thursday. This trip was called going "down shore". Some launches stopped off at Indian Pass, others went as far as Rock Island, all pulling skiff boats. When they reached their destination, each fisherman, fished individually in his own skiff but sometimes they worked together in order to have more net in the water. To make a bigger circle around the fish or to cut down the size of a circle to

Spring Creek-End of Pavement looking North

make the fish gill themselves in the net. The fish were brought back to the big boat (launch) and iced down until the boats returned to port. Each man received a share of the sale of the fish. Usually there were trucks waiting to take the fish to Florida and Georgia markets as soon as the launches returned. Fridays were about mending and dyeing nets in homemade dye made from Red Oak bark. The nets were made out of cotton twine or flax. If the nets were not mended and dyed weekly they would not last very long. You could not find a Red Oak tree anywhere close to the coast that had not been debarked as high as anyone could reach. Some of the people who owned and ran these launches, along with the boats' names were Mr. Wilmer Dykes (The Sondra); Mr. Roscoe Langston (Suit Us); Mr. Earl Warren (Laura C); Mr. Jesse Porter (Florida); Mr. Russell Porter (Newport); and Mr. William Lee Spears (Maryann). Mr. Willie owned the fish house in Spring Creek and bought 95% of all the fish that were caught, he in turn sold to other dealers. This way of life continued until the World War 2 draft started. Most all of the young fisherman and boat owners were drafted into the army, this effectively put a stop to most fishing on a scale of the size it was.

However, some fishing continued until the net limitation passed in 1994, then the rules and regulation of FWCC put most everyone out of the fishing business.

Taking up a Seine net in Panacea, Florida

Before I end this story, I just want to say there were a lot of fishermen in St. Marks, Newport and Panacea, I did not mean to slight them in any way. I just don't know enough about those areas to write about at this time, maybe later.

This story is dedicated to the fishing families who made and lived this story. Also to the Spears Family who are the oldest continuous fishing family in Wakulla County. This family still runs a small fishing operation at Spring Creek; Barbara and Lee Spears, and their two sons are the present operators of that business. Many thanks to my special friend and typist, Carolyn Olah.

Submitted By: Carlos Taff; 291 Bostic Pelt Road, Crawfordville, FL 32327 (2011)

WAKULLA COUNTY LANDMARKS

The Dry Cleaner

Together my parents, Max and Doris Davis, mastered the dry-cleaning business which was secondary to Daddy's full time airline job. During the first year in Crawfordville we lived behind the dry cleaner which was located directly across the street from Mrs. "Aunt Babe" Tucker's home and our church, First Baptist. Today, there is a log building on the property. The wooden structure which housed us and the dry cleaner was typical of several WWII buildings in town. It was long and narrow with about 50 feet of highway frontage. Around the corner was the Suwannee Store. Up the street across from the courthouse was Mr. Albert Moore's barbershop, Mr. Harold Smith's drug store, and beyond that was a coin laundry which Daddy later bought so that my younger brother, Glenn Neal "Buddy" Davis, had a chore.

The dry cleaner had a huge backyard with pear, fig and pecan trees, grape vines and all sorts of entertainment. Perched in the top of our favorite pecan tree we could see everything. One day Buddy and I watched a neighbor catch a chicken, chop its head off, catch the thing again, and pluck it clean. At the ages of six and four years, it was the most impressive sight we had ever seen. Once, Buddy and I launched our first business venture—a pear stand. It seemed much more logical than lemonade. After all, we had pears not lemons. It turned out the pears were, indeed, lemons. Much to our chagrin, Mama would not tolerate our money making scheme in front of the dry cleaner! We enjoyed walking to the air-conditioned drug store for a 10-cent cold drink, and walking through the air-conditioned courthouse to fetch the mail from the Post Office. One day Mama sent six-year-old Buddy to Mr. Roy Rehwinkel's General Store (at the corner across Arran Road from the courthouse) for a spool of thread. Mr. Rehwinkel told Buddy he needed another penny for tax. Buddy replied, "Mama didn't say tax, she told me to get thread." Mr. Rehwinkel just laughed. He and Buddy became fast friends and later he was one of Buddy's best clients. Buddy was often sighted around town steering his bicycle with one hand and pulling the lawnmower with the other.

Sandra Davis 1966

After we moved from the dry-cleaner to the pink house (which Mama quickly painted white) up the road beyond the cemetery, the living quarters of the dry cleaner became storage much like a huge attic with many cavernous rooms that could become anything imaginable. One room was used for hanging the fresh cleaned clothes to dry on rainy days. Clothesline wire zig-zagged from side to side in the entire room. This room was perfect for making a playhouse. Depending on how I hung old blankets from wire to wire I could make a stage for theatrical performances or a three-room apartment with furniture made from suitcases and boxes. I spent hours and hours playing there. The suitcases were full of dress up clothes and hats. Once when I was recovering from illness but feeling well enough to play, Mama caught me with a camera in my favorite dress up frock.

When they ran out of space at church, two more of the dry cleaner rooms were became Sunday school rooms for junior and intermediate boys whom Daddy and others taught Bible lessons. Daddy has always taught Sunday school. Having been a Sunday school student from the time he was born, he has always been faithful to attend and teach.

Dismissed was an era when they closed the dry cleaner and Daddy tore it down to salvage building material, but the memories shall always be delightful.

Submitted by, Sandra Davis Vidak, 396 J.K. Moore Rd., Crawfordville, FL 32327

Pigott's Store in Medart

This is the history as my Dad, John Pigott told me. John S. Pigott Jr. was born in the old store, August 23rd, 1922.

Great Uncle Bernard built the store, around the first of 1922. Granddad Steve Pigott & Great Uncle Jake sometimes ran the business together sometimes they ran it on their own. It was a general store with groceries & dry goods. I understand that the depression didn't affect them.

In May of 1958 Dad was still in the U.S. Navy & we were moving to his last duty station at NAS Sanford, FL. We had stopped in Crestview, FL., to visit dad's brother Virgil Pigott. After everyone when to bed, my Dad & Uncle stayed up to talk. Uncle Virgil told my Dad that the old store was up for sale from their Uncle Jake & Aunt Lucy. The idea was that when Dad retired they would take over the store, my Dad would run it and we would live in the back. I don't know when the wife's were told. It was not what my Mother ever had planned.

On Labor Day 1960 they took it over. Dad was not out of the Navy yet, but we moved to Medart to start the school year. Until Dad retired we lived next door with my Granddad & Granny. Uncle Jake & Aunt Lucy continued to live in the back of the store. Dad would come home on the weekends & during the week my Mother and Granddad ran the store. In the spring of 1961, Dad retired from the Navy.

Several things I remember about taking the store over. The day before Labor Day, the last day Uncle Jake & Aunt Lucy ran the store we were there and a customer bought a coke & my aunt proceed to give the money to my dad and Uncle Jake grunted about the money. It was funny; Aunt Lucy was just ready to turn things over. The front door faced highway. Out the front was a covered porch with the gas pumps, had an old hand crank kerosene pump sitting to the side & a loafers bench on each side of the door. The store's retail area was about 30ft by 30ft, had two wall shelves down both sides. Had two long counters that were 4ft out from wall shelves. A Coca-cola ice box that sit toward the front of the store. Off to the north of the store was an old garage about 20ft by 20ft with an apartment. Over the years small Model A and T parts would come to the top of the ground.

When we moved into the living quarters back of the store, dad had remodeled it for us to live in. There was a door between the store and our living room. At supper time the three kids had to take turns sitting at a little table at the door to eat & get up to wait on customers. That was Mother's way for us all to eat together.

Not long after retirement, Dad used his GI Bill to go to cabinet making school at Lively. He drove to school about every day. After customers realized that he was going to town & going by building material stores, they started asking him to pick up plywood & hardware. A lot of customers said they would rather pay extra than have to make a trip themselves. That was how we got into hardware & building supplies. We rented for quite a few years the Old Durance Store (Mike's Paint & Body Shop now); Wakulla High School was being built at that time. Dad borrowed $500.00 to buy hardware & nails for stock. For several years we would take orders, go to town buy the supplies & bring the order back an extra board or two for our stock. So at this time we had two stores a mile apart, one a grocery store, the other hardware & building supply. Dad kept the two stores a part for about a year before moving the hardware & building down to the Pigott's old store and used the old garage. Over the years we added storage buildings out back to store building supplies. We slowly over the years got out of selling groceries. We had a block wall built from old store across the front of old garage. A few years later tore the old garage down & finished off that to make a new store for the hardware & building supply.

During this time of starting the Lumber & building supply store I had graduated from Sopchoppy High School, just like my Dad before me. I was going to Chipola Jr. College. On the weekends & summers I work in the hardware & building supply store. I went in the U.S. Navy, in 1970, I knew where I was coming back to work.

Dad had been telling me that someday the business would be mine. The summer of 1974 Dad surprised all of us; he decided to run for county commissioner & won. When he left to campaign for office, he left the store with Mother & me. He would stick his head in the door & ask are you paying all the bills.

After his 4 years as Commissioner, he gave it up. He came back helping in the store. Later he took up working on locks. He loved working on locks, seeing people & enjoyed life.

I would say I ran the store up to 2003 but that would be wrong. Mother was right there. Over the years my wife, kids, sister, nephews, nieces work in the store. My children, nephews & nieces were raised in the store; we had a play pen in office. As they got older to walk they would pull nails out of the bins. It was for sure a family business. We had it for 42 years, made a living & supported Wakulla County. Over the years we had a lot of high school kid's work with us. It is great to see how many of them progressed in life. Some in law enforcement, medical, armed forces, school board member & County Commissioner.

It was hard to close the store, I felt like the Captain of a ship, having no choice but to let it sink. We are thankful for the years we had & the great support we had from our Wakulla Co. people.

Submitted and written By: Stephen E. Pigott, 2820 Coastal Hwy, Crawfordville, FL 32327

Little Town of Sopchoppy

Little town of Sopchoppy,
You will always be home to me,
No matter where I'd roam,
Your dirt roads always called me home.

With your dark river flowing past,
I'm gone and will swim there no more,
This time only death will bring me at last,
Never again to find love on your shore.

Some of my most cherished times,
Were spent on your worn streets,
My only barefoot worry was cactus spines,
And trying to beat summers' heat.

Eating chocolate cake on Mama's dish,
And running paths thru tall pines,
Me and Cousin Gary always got our wish,
When checking our trot lines.

You're where I met my first love, Vickie,
Walking down the street looking so pretty,
My cousin, Leanne and her husband, Joe,
Thoughts of ya'll make memories flow.

Part of my dearly beloved childhood,
Dirt roads, wood piles, and collard greens,
Never realizing I had it so good,
You're set with many beloved scenes.

The old party spot and big swamp,
Down 22, me and George would romp,
My old friends, Wayne, Carl and Davy,
Now those memories call to me.

Uncle Cecil giving chew to Uncle Pull,
The Jr. Store managed by Grandma Jewell,
Many of us are now long gone,
Some moved and some passed on.

They did you up in lights,
To be viewed on Christmas night,
In that old Mustang we would ride,
As they went by on the left side.

The old red building where I used to hang,
By the loafers bench caught in the rain,
Those places gone, like the dinosaur,
We will hang out there nevermore.

I long for those days gone by,
But now can only wish and sigh,
Sopchoppy, you're a grand old girl,
No finer place in all the world.

Submitted By: Glenn Wheeler, 7/13/11 Florida State Prison 7819 NW 228th St. Raiford, FL 32026-1210

Carraway's Meat Market; Meat Block and Scales

There is a meat block and a set of weighing scales that came from A. B. Carraway's meat market in Sopchoppy. They were recently donated to the Wakulla County Museum and Archives. These items were part of an ongoing meat market which was purchased in 1936 by Ausley Burl Carraway, Sr. The market was housed in a lean-to against the west wall of the old hotel which was located on the southwest corner of Rose Street and Second Avenue. In 1938, the market was moved diagonally across Rose Street where it remained in operation until the late 1940s when it finally closed.

Carraway's meat market in Sopchoppy, Burl Carraway and Sidney Hodge

Submitted by; Betty Green, PO Box 969, Crawfordville, FL

The Oaks Restaurant; At the Bridge in Panacea

I have so many good memories of growing up in Crawfordville. One of them is when Daddy treated us to supper at The Oaks at the bridge in Panacea, renowned for good seafood. Unique place mats cleverly featured the first names of the owner's children and grandchildren on Oak leaves. During the many times I dined at The Oaks the place mat always mesmerized me for several minutes and made me smile when it was updated with names of great-grandchildren. Sometimes on a busy evening we got to sit on the long yellow leather cushioned couches in the waiting area and watch folks come and go.

We rarely sat there very long before one of the ladies at the counter escorted us to the a booth that Mama preferred. The crackers and garlic butter arrived at our table in a little ceramic boat which delighted my brother and me. After

The Vidaks 1977

we consumed several crackers spread thick with butter Daddy reminded us not to eat too many and spoil our meal. We were never concerned with the menu, whatever Daddy ordered was just fine and always delicious.

On one particular evening in October 1977, unbeknownst to me I was to meet my future husband at The Oaks. The blind date was set up by his friend and my friend who were dating. The friends picked me up at my house and the fellow was to meet us at the restaurant. As we arrived in the parking lot, worried about adjusting my attire, I asked, is he here yet; do you see his car? My friend replied, "No, I don't see his moped anywhere." Did he say, *moped*(?) I thought and then; "this is going to be very bad." The three of us sat down on those familiar yellow couches in the waiting area looking toward the window. Suddenly the butterflies in my belly fluttered and conversation became difficult. Pretty soon a well-dressed tall and slender good-looking fellow walked quickly by the window toward the door. It didn't occur to me that this fellow was my date due to absence of an expected windblown look from a moped ride. Shortly thereafter, the fellow was standing before us and introduced to me. I caught his first name but not the last one I'd never heard before.

We enjoyed the usual good meal The Oaks provided though I was surprised not to be seated in a booth and then laughed to myself remembering that the booth was Mama's preference not necessarily mine. I considered for a moment this right of passage that I was grown and sitting at a table in that restaurant with three other adults not related to me. Conversation during the meal was lively in our attempts to discover what or whom we had in common. My girlfriend excused herself and asked me to join her. During the application of lipstick in the ladies' room she asked if I wanted the fellow to drive me home. I replied that it would be fine but riding on a moped would be interesting. I'm not sure what was the cue but when we returned to the table the guys stood and we made our way out of the restaurant. The fellow asked to drive me home and in the parking lot we bid our friends adieu. He didn't give me the moped helmet and instead opened a car door for me which to my delight was a sporty brown 1976 Datsun 280-Z! My friend winked at me as I realized his enjoyment in making me think this guy would arrive on a moped. The fellow followed the complicated directions to my house, see that tree, turn left on this dirt road. He admitted later thinking he would never find the way to a

The Vidak Family at The Oaks 1978

highway that evening. Indeed, he did find his way out and back to my house again, but there were a couple of dates before I learned to pronounce his last name correctly and its origin.

We dined many more times at The Oaks while dating and after we married in 1978. It is where we ate when both sets of parents met and where many in our family enjoyed supper following our wedding departure. The Oaks will always be a place of special memories for us and we were deeply saddened when it closed.

Submitted By: Sandra Davis Vidak, 396 J.K. Moore Rd., Crawfordville, FL 32327

Lonnie Alfred Dispennette's School-1932 forward

I was born at home in Crawfordville, Florida 11-09-27 delivered by Dr. Bond. My Father, Lonnie Dispennette came to this area working for Malone Construction Company as General Manager of a crew of workers clearing the right of way of trees and grading up the highway from Tallahassee to Wakulla Station and into Crawfordville with plans to continue to Sopchoppy and Carrabelle. After I was old enough my mother and I joined him on the road and during this time I contracted Malarial fever. At that time there was no cure for Malaria. Only Aspirin to ease the chills & fevers. I was about 3 years old when the fevers started. It continued even after I started to school in 1932.

My mother, Ruby Raker Dispennette at that time worked for the Post Office carrying the mail over to Arran (located 3 miles west) to meet the train going south in the AM and back when it came thru to Tallahassee in the P M. bringing and dropping the mail each trip. I rode with her every day, and one day after the morning trip we were at Uncle JD Duggers Gulf Station in Crawfordville, the Wakulla County School Director stopped by. He asked Mama how old I was, 4 and will be 5 the 9th of November. He told her that they needed one more new student to have enough to be qualified for the State School funds. With your permission he said that I could arrange for your son to start a year younger in September. I think she was glad to get me out from under her, so with her approval I started to school September of 1932. 4 yr old and 5 in November!

Mrs. Etta Maude Kirkland was my teacher in the original wood frame school building. I was sick with the Malarial fever and I really do not remember very much of what she taught me that year.

After the first of 1933 one Saturday we were at Uncle JD's Gulf Station at the corner of 319 & what is now ML King Blvd. Dr. Harper, our local Doctor stopped to introduced his visiting friend, who was also a Doctor. Today I wish I could remember his name. Here is why! He looked at me, then turned to Mama and asked, do you know he has Malarial. She replied, yes, but we cannot find a cure. He said, bring your son over to Dr. Harper's Office at 4 PM this afternoon, I believe we have an answer to that. She said thanks and we will see you at that time.

When we arrived, the Doctor showed us a bottle of small yellow pills. He told us that the cure for Malaria had been developed and these pills are the result of that work. They have just been made available for us to use.

The Doctor told Mama that I must take one pill each day. Also my skin would begin to turn as yellow as the pills and remain yellow until the pills had been all taken. Mama asked him what was the cost for this treatment. Nothing, the Doctor said, just let Dr. Harper know how this turns out so he can pass it on to me. We left the office hoping that this "Cure" would really work.

Mama gave me my first pill that day and continued each afternoon. My skin began to turn yellow as the pill I was taking. He had said when the last pill was taken, the yellow would begin to fade away and I would be free of the Malaria completely. He was not wrong! My fever began to stop and by the time my skin turned back to it normal color, I was cured!

I never had another fever! This Doctor saved my life and I do not know his name. He allowed me to enjoy my family and friends to a ripe old age. I was 83 November 9, 2010.

Back to my story of the schools in Wakulla County.

School was a joy to attend without the Malaria fevers that I had up to that time.

The first year I attended school, we were in the old wood frame building there in Crawfordville located where the Rock building now sets on the Arran Rd. When school was out at the end of my first year the WPA began to tear the old wood building down to make way for a new one built with rock. It meant we would have no school building for classes since it would take over 12 months to complete the new building.

The classes for 1933 were held in the various local churches while the construction of our new school building continued.

The Grade 1 & 2 were in a church building on a dirt road opposite the Dr. Harper's two story house in a small church building about 300 yards from the highway to the east.

The first grade was on one side of the room the 2nd grade was on the other side. We had a two hole John for the boys and another for the girls outside the rear of the church. The boys were on one side of the building and the girls on the other side. This was my 2nd grade and I cannot remember my teacher's name. Only the good times we all had together that year while our new rock school building was being built.

There was a large open field behind the church and a circus came into town and setup in this field. We all enjoyed seeing the people doing this in our back yard.

By the time for the new school term to start (my 3rd grade) our new building had been finished and ready to use.

The Rock School Building for all classes one thru twelve was for students as follows. Elementary for those from Crawfordville, Arran and the in Ivan area which is now up in the area of the Walmart Store

Middle and High students from Crawfordville, Arran, Ivan, Wakulla Station, St. Marks north to the county line attended the Crawfordville School. The areas outside of Crawfordville were brought in by school buses.

Sopchoppy also had a new building built by the WPA and served that end of the county one through 12th Grade. Their new building was a rock one like ours.

My 3rd grade classes were in the new Rock School Building. We had a nice library and I believe that during my years going to school there I read every book in it.

When the new building was open, the students going to the old school building in Arran were then able to attend the new school in Crawfordville.

A few years later it was decided to tear down the old school building in Arran and use materials out of it to build a lunch room building at our school in Crawfordville.

We had a very active FFA organization at our school and the members agreed to tear down the old Arran school building, haul the lumber to our new school and build a lunch room out of the materials. I remember working several days & weeks assisting in this project.

The lunch room building we built, still stands on the east side of the Rock School which is now used by the Wakulla County School administration as a Office Complex. Many new school buildings now take care of Wakulla County from one end to the other.

The schools are the very best in every respect. Many families have moved into the county due to the schools' reputation.

World War II began before I reached high school. We had a 6 man football team, baseball & basket ball when the War began.

Only buses that were allowed to run were to transport students to school. All sports activities between schools were cancelled until the War ended.

When I reached the 9th grade no sports were available. I never wore any kind of sports clothing during my time in school. No one did because there were none available until the war was ended and gas was available again.

In my school days there were no football fields, baseball fields, no gym for basket ball and other indoor sports.

Outdoor basketball courts on a packed down clay floor. Baseball in a grass field marked off with a strand of barb wire to mark a home run.

I do remember the time some those older Crawfordville boys lifted the Vo-Ag teacher's little car up about 5 feet on top of a pile of cross ties. Was he mad, and did those boys make him beg for them to put the car back on the ground.

The only sport we played was baseball between the boys in Arran & Crawfordville. We would walk the 3 miles to Arran play against the boys there on Saturday. The next Saturday they would walk over and play on our field. Uniforms? Blue overalls, I never had a sports uniform of any kind in the Wakulla County School. This was because of the war during my last 4 years in school.

I graduated from CHS June 1944, age 16. I was crazy about radio. I read everything I could find on it. Mama paid for a correspondence course on radio which I finished before finishing high school.

I went to Lively Vo-Tech in Tallahassee to study radio, my teacher was Mr. Devane who lived in Chattahoochee. His son owns the WGWD 93.3 FM Country Radio station in Quincy.

I completed my studies under Mr. Devane and was hired by Sears Roebuck & Co in September 1944 as a radio serviceman. The war was still going on, and there were only 4 male employees at Sears. I was 16 at that time and made the sum of 22.00 dollars for 44 hours each week.

All of my buddies had either been drafted or enlisted and when I made it to age 17 I enlisted in the US Navy. I was sworn in on the day Germany surrendered and got out of boot camp the day Japan surrendered and the war was ended. The training was much different for us than it was for those that were trained to go to war. I was sent to Saipan Island and served there until most of the men and women that were over there in the Pacific Area had been processed thru our base and sent back to the States.

I went back to Sears and stayed with them for 20 Years. 10 years in The Tallahassee Store, 7 years in the Knoxville Sears Store and 3 years in the Montgomery, AL. Sears Store. These were my real schools. I had some of the people who helped make Sears Roebuck & Company to become number one store in the world at that time. These old timers taught me more than any college could have. I have used that training in the life insurance business and in the C-Store business.

And my last working years was in the Convenience Store business in 6 different areas of the USA, FL, GA, SC, MO & ARK.

We moved back home to Tallahassee in 1986 and stay in touch with Wakulla County and the fine people there.

Submitted by: Lonnie Henry Dispennette AKA Lonnie Alfred, 1161 Poplar Dr., Tallahassee, FL 32301 11/09/1927.....05/16/2011

What Is A Seine Yard?

In writing this I am trying to preserve some of Wakulla County's history as I knew it in my time, from 1930 until present.

In my early years, I was raised at Shell Point Beach, so what is a seine yard? A seine yard was a place along Wakulla and Franklin County Beaches which was fairly level with the channel running close to the beach where mullet ran or swam during the fall mullet run. To seine means to make a half circle with a net from the beach out to a point, then back to the beach where fish are trapped then seined out by pulling the net from both ends. These yards had to be clean with no rocks, no shells, and no grass; otherwise, you would tear up the net or let the fish swim under, if it came off the bottom. Thus the name seine yard. Clearing of objects and the cutting of grass was an annual affair at some seine yards, others stayed fairly clean all year long. Shell Point had two seine yards, one was called the Big yard (located where the county park is today), the other was called the Small yard (located where the canal goes into the Shell Point yacht basin). The large yard was fished on the rising tide and the small yard was fished on the falling tide. Remember, the object was to catch as many fish as possible during the fall run. Shell Point seine yard opened the first Monday in October and closed the 1st of December. The fall mullet run actually begins in Louisiana and east Texas and continues east to south Florida. Some of the other seine yards were located at St. Marks, West Goose Creek, Grass Inlet (now Oyster Bay), Skipper Bay, Bottoms, Levy Bay, in Franklin County; Sunday Reel, Mud Cove, and several smaller ones strewed in-between along the coast.

I am concentrating on the ones at Shell Point because those are the ones I know the most about. The month of October was usually about cleaning and repairing the equipment used in fishing and trying to catch enough fish to feed all the people who helped fish, they were referred to as hands, they were usually from small farms who were through with their crops and needed a little income to get though the winter months or turpentine workers who worked in turpentine stills and woods, gum or turpentine does not flow much in the winter. The first two weeks are busy times at seine yards, there were a lot of repairs and cleaning to be made to the boats which had been turned up all summer, they had to be chinked and tarred, This means that the bottoms where the boards were nailed on crossways had to be stuffed with cotton and cold tarred. These old time boats were made of cypress boards, the sides were of a solid cypress board and the bottom was many cypress boards nailed cross ways, after the cotton was stuffed into the cracks between the boards and tarred the boats were put into the water. It took several days for the boat to absorbed water in the boards so as not to sink. There were many other chores to be tended.

The house where the hands slept had to be cleaned; this was just a house with no floor, other than the ground, with a rack on the sides for the hands to sleep. Each man brought his own mattress, usually made out of Spanish Moss. Close to this shack was a fire scaffold with sides and sand on it, as not to burn it down, this was where all of the cooking was done. Big frying pans with legs on them sat over an open fire, these pans were called spiders (on account of the legs), each pan had an iron lid, and fire could be placed on top of it when cooking bread. The main meal consisted of fish and fish bread (part flour, part meal and fish grease), also with some meals they had cane syrup brought from the farms and some sweet potatoes which was roasted in the fire.

Some of the other equipment used was a fish scaffold built at the water's edge, also a fish house with ice boxes, another shed with no floor. Two net reels similar to a ferris wheel, only smaller, made from timbers and post put into the ground, a dipping box, a rectangular box with handles on both ends and a screen bottom for washing split fish. Two seine boats, two seines, one lookout tower and two sets of oars. Now, let me explain what all of this equipment was used for.

Fish scaffold used to split fish on as it was impossible to ice all of the fish that were caught. They had to be split and salted in order to preserve them. They were then sold to Georgia and Florida Fish Markets. The fish were mostly split to recover the Red Roe, which is actually yellow and the most valuable part of the mullet, it was worth more than the whole fish (which it is today, in the twenty-first century).

(1) A Fish House—as many fish as possible were iced in fish boxes and sold as fresh fish.

(2) Two net reels— these reels were used to roll the seines up on, as the nets were made of cotton twine and had to be dried in the sun when they were through being fished with, otherwise they would rot and come apart. These reels were an ideal place for youngsters to play, so we thought but caused a lot of us to get spankings when we got caught, which was often.

(3) Dipping Box-when fish were split for salting they had to be washed in order to remove the blood from them, so they were put in this box and two men would wade out to hip deep water and slosh the box up and down a couple of times, then the fish were ready to be salted and packed into barrels. One concern was sharks which were attracted to the blood, so usually someone was holding a shotgun and could shoot at the sharks to scare them away (as they were big and many of them).

(4)The seine boats—These boats were big and cumbersome, in fact not much more than a rectangular box, with a sharp end on one end and a net table on the other end. Two seats about middle ways, it took five men to handle one of these boats. It had four oars, two on each side with one man manning each oar. These oars were seventeen feet long and very heavy (the size of these oars was told to me by my lifetime friend a Black American, and a gentle man, Mr. Joshua Harvey, deceased). So, it took five men to handle a boat twenty-eight feet long and eight to ten feet wide. Four men just to row it out to the buoy which was in the channel and one to tie it off when it reached the buoy.

The boat was loaded with a net on the stern which was trailing off as the boat was rowed out to the buoy. They were rowing against the current and the wind. The current is very strong in the Shell Point channel on the rising tide. When they reached the buoy, they had made one half circle with the net bagging out behind the boat. The fifth man on the boat was in the bow and hooked a rope on a hook, when the bow of the boat reached the buoy. The rowers could not leave their oars, thus, the five men. Remember, the canal which runs in front of Shell Point is a modern addition of the nineteen-fifties and was not there in the thirties and forties.

Now, let me tell you a little about the buoy. A buoy can be used for many things, it can be used to tie something to or it can tell you where to go or not to go, depending on its color and what it is used for. This buoy at Shell Point was used for tying a boat to only, and was made out of a keg or a malt barrel originally used to hold Coca-Cola syrup, as was most barrels used at the seine yard. This buoy was held in place by a rectangular frame about eight feet long and four feet wide, made of oak wood timbers with long iron spikes stuck through the timbers to hold it in place. Oak wood will sink when in a single board form but is used to make boat parts and in this form will float. Usually this buoy was destroyed in the summer by summer squalls or maybe by a hurricane and had to be replaced each year. A highlight of opening week of the season was retrieving the rope which was tied to the harrow or attaching a new rope to it. The young men would attempt to dive down into the channel at low tide and retrieve the end of the rope or attach a new one to it. The swimmer who was able to dive down an do this was paid an extra dollar. This was a fun time watching these young men try out there manhood and diving ability. This was enjoyed by all, there was great laughter as each man tried and a lot of kidding that went on until one of the men was successful, then he was everyone's Hero for a few days.

OK, now we have the boat to the buoy and tied off, but, how do we get it back to shore to complete the circle and trap the fish. I know you might be asking this question; if these boats were this big and cumbersome, how? This is where good old American ingenuity came into play. The operators of the seine yard realized that this boat could not be rowed fast enough to trap mullet before they escaped, as they are very fast fish, and will do a turnaround or hundred-eighty degree in a moment's notice, if anything or any noise disturbs them or they see anything unusual in their path. They have very good eye sight as any fisherman can tell you. The owner came up with a plan, it was called a head rope, (what is a head rope?). It was a one and a half inch thick rope that was tied to the front of the boat and trailed along side of the boat until it reached the buoy, and was tied off. The trailing end of the rope reached the shore and beyond where it was run through a pulley on a tower. This pulley hung vertically. The rope then continued to a lower pulley stand that hung horizontally, and then the rope went to a tie post with a peg in the side of it. When the boat was secured to the buoy this rope was tightened by hand by the men on the shore so that it was completely out of the water and would not scare the fish, it was half hitched to the tie post. This rope left the boat close to the water but by the time it reached the beach it was high above the water, thus it did not frighten the fish. This is why the first pulley was on a high tower. This rope then continued parallel to the beach to a bench where eight or ten of the hands (men) sat. When the man on the lookout tower yelled "come ashore", the fifth man in the boat turned the buoy loose from the boat, the eight or ten men sitting on the bench grabbed the rope and ran with it as fast as possible down the beach pulling the boat to shore and trapping the fish in the circle, actually it was a half circle. The net was pulled onto the beach from both ends. This seine yard was fished this way until someone thought about hooking a truck or car to the head rope and pulling the boat in that way, which was faster and a whole lot less work. Later I will go through with a strike or a lick as it is called. But, for now more about the man on the lookout tower. This tower was a two or three leg tower built like a ladder with a seat and back rest on the top of it. The man on the tower was known as the yard boss, he was the absolute boss of the whole operation, he told everyone when to fish, not to fish, to cook, to eat and when to sleep. In those days people respected one another and no one went on the beach or up ahead of a seine yard, absolutely no one. In case a dolphin went ahead of a seine yard, they were scared off with a high powered rifle, which was kept on the lookout tower. Some of the yard bosses in those days were: Mr. Ira Raker, owner of Shell Point; Mr. Beaty Taff, who bought Shell Point from Mr. Raker in the late thirty's; others I knew were: Mr. Isadore Porter; Mr Alford Vickers; Mr. R.C. Taff; and Mr. B.B. Stevens, and some I can't remember.

The second boat was much smaller as was the second seine and could be oared around fish and used at the small yard.

More about the big seine. This seine was about one thousand feet long and was a pocket seine, it was made with one and one-half inch meshes which means one and one-half inch square. Around all four sides of the mesh or three inches stretched. Each end of this net started off with fewer meshes which made it shallow on both ends, as the beach would be close to shore, then much deeper in the middle, otherwise it was made to fit the depth of the water where it was fished. It started off about seven feet deep on both ends and was about twenty-five feet deep in the middle. This was the pocket which was in the channel when it was deployed but it was not stretched tight but had slack in the pocket so that it bagged out in the current. As the tide rose it had a heavy lead line on the bottom and a line on top with a big seine cork about every two feet on the top line. The lead line kept it on the bottom which the cork line kept the net floating on the top above the water. This is about the best I can explain a seine to you but believe you can get the idea from this description of a seine. There are two types of seines, one hung straight the same depth all along its length and one with a pocket as described above.

Most of the hands were Black Americans who did most of the work with White Americans scattered among them. The Whites slept in another shack a little distance away but mostly they always ate and associated together. The owner had a big house for him and his family. There was also a Commissary (store), where the owner sold essentials, tobacco and etc. This way of fishing continued until 1941, when an early October hurricane wiped Shell Point out, everything was destroyed; boats, and houses. Several lives were lost in Wakulla and Franklin Counties. The seine yard and boats were replaced and the seine yard was fished for many more years but never in its original fashion.

Well, I told you I would go through a strike or a lick, as it was called then. So, here goes, let's go back to the middle thirties. Shell Point was only a little small spit of land with no houses except one which was a three part house with the three being located side by side. The first being the kitchen and dining room, the second was the commissary, where essentials was sold, and the third was the sleeping quarters. These three were built about four feet off the ground on stilts and with a front porch connecting all three, which was screened in. There was three shacks with no floors except the ground, where the hands slept and a fish house. This is just a little background on what Shell Point looked like. Remember, there were no other houses or canals at this time.

So, let's do a lick. The seine boat is tied to the buoy, the seine is ballooned out in a half circle in the rising tide, there is a light breeze blowing out of the northwest, a north western is breaking out but not there yet. This is the time for mullet to run as they move mostly ahead of or in weather. It's around the first of November when the roe (eggs) is almost grown in the mullet. The yard boss is on the lookout tower, the hands are sitting on a bench with the head rope across their knees. Everyone is being very quiet; no one is walking anywhere close to or on the beach.

Remember, earlier I told you mullet can see a long way from under the water. Suddenly, the yard boss sees a stirring in the water down the beach to the east, mullet in this area always runs to the west, the old saying is "right eye to the bank". There are several ways to see fish but you need to have a trained eye to see them. One way is if it's a big bunch, the water will rise up one to two inches above the surface in a circle, another way is a shake, if you hold your hand out in front of you, palm down and barely shake it from side to side, this is how a small bunch will look. Sometimes you see a string of mullet that looks this way, you might also see them jump, this depends on the wind and depth of the water. Other times if the water is deep you will only see a flash in the water. This is an art most people never acquire, it takes many years of perfecting.

Now, back to the lookout tower, the stirring the lookout boss saw has moved closer to the net. This is where he must know what he is doing, what he saw was a string of mullet. He has to have a lot of patience at this point, he must let the string of fish get under the headline but he can't wait until the fish hit the back of the net or they will turn and run out of the net before the seine boat can get to the beach. Suddenly you hear "come ashore", the hands sitting on the bench jump up and pull the rope out of its half hitch on the hitching post and run with all there might down the beach. The boat lurches toward the beach and soon the bow touches the beach. The five men in the boat jump out grabbing the cork and lead line still on the boat and quickly pull it to the beach. Three on the lead line and two on the cork, the men on the head rope does the same. Usually there are at least six on each end of the seine, more on the lead line because it is harder to pull. One person has to hold the lead line down with his foot while it is pulled, so the fish don't go under the net. They pull equally on each end of the seine working it gradually toward the beach. Every so often you hear "cut", which means move both ends of the net toward each other. This is moving the fish toward the pocket which is in the middle of the seine. Gradually the net is moved closer to shore, suddenly the fish realize they are trapped and brake on the net or panic, they try to escape by jumping, some do make it but most do not. Three or four of the hands wade out in hip deep water, grab the cork line and hold it high above their heads, the cork line is always a small ways ahead of the lead line, finally the fish are corralled in the pocket. The net reaches the beach to where it cannot be pulled any further at this point. The lead line and cork line are brought together and the hands back out of the water with the seine in their hands. The water the net pushes ahead of it helps them to pull it upon the shore. At this point they drop the lead line and roll the fish out, this time at a guess we only caught about six or seven hundred pounds. This was a small lick to show you how it was done but there were many licks with a hundred thousand caught at one time in those early days. When this many were caught the net was pulled as close to shore as possible, then each end was staked down until the tide left it. There would be dozens of small piles stacked up like a haystack, only this would be fish. As soon as possible the fish would be moved to the fish scaffold where they were split, the roe removed, the fish and roe were salted and packed into barrels to preserve them.

I could tell you many more things about fishing but hope this story gives you an insight to your past and your heritage, whether you have lived in Wakulla County one day or all of your life. Fishing is part of your heritage, "The oldest profession in the County", now, ALMOST FORGOTTEN.

Submitted and written by: Carlos Taff. 291 Bostic Pelt Road, Crawfordville, FL 32327 A special thanks to Ms. Carolyn W. Olah, for her many hours of hard work, typing and correcting this story.

Wakulla Springs Picnic

The Wakulla Springs picnics were started long before my time. I'd go out there with my daddy and momma when I was about six years old, every first Saturday in May. There'd be big crowds. There were more horse and buggies and wagons tied up than there were cars. The cars were old Model A Fords and 1932 Chevrolets. While they were all parked out there, somebody would come along and tie a big banner to all the front bumpers with string. It said, "See Wakulla Springs." This was before the hotel was built.

Every two years they'd have political rallies there. The people would come to hear the candidates speak. The thing that impressed me more than anything was a man on a big old motorcycle. It was loud! He'd announce that he would burst through a wall about 12 feet wide and 8 feet high made of pine boards up and down. He'd say, "I'm gonna run this motor cycle through that wall!" Every few minutes he'd rev his motor cycle up real loud to remind people that he was going to do that. I was six years old, and I was so excited I was about to pee in my britches! Anyway, after the last speech was made, he revved that thing up and took off like a bat out of hell, and through that wall. Boards flew, some of them thirty feet in the air, and then he turned around and came back to let everybody see that he wasn't hurt, to loud applause. I'll never forget that!

Tarzan, played by Jonny Weissmuller, made several movies over there. One time a group of us students from Crawfordville School went over there and he came out and would make a weird sound with his mouth in the water and then the principal, who stood in for Tarzan in several scenes, made a sound that was just like it. Bob Altman, a student at Sopchoppy High School, would dive out of 50-foot-high cypress trees there as Tarzan.

When I was in high school they hired me and several other students to work in the concession stand on Saturdays and Sundays. You talk about a mess! Five hundred soldiers from Camp Gordon Johnston and Dale Mabry Field, and every one of them wanting a bag of peanuts, a Coca Cola. We made it! They swam there.

Later on, Omar Bradley, Commander of the 28th Infantry Division at Camp Gordon Johnston, stayed at Wakulla Springs. He would work with his troops during the day and spend nights with his wife at Wakulla Springs. He was at Camp Gordon Johnston for six months of amphibious training, and while he was there the Pentagon called him to Washington, D.C. and moved him up, having recognized his abilities. He was second in command to Eisenhower and the brains of World War II. There is a good book about him at the library.

Submitted By: Clayton Taff. Permission to print granted by Patty Taff, 29 Benton Rd, Crawfordville, FL 32327

Magnolia Expedition

The date was October 25, 1958. At the age of 14 I was a member of Explorer Post 106 in Tallahassee. Our post Advisor was Ney C. Landrum, an officer in the US Marine Corps, and expert in map reading and orienteering. We decided to utilize his expertise and attempt to find the town site of Magnolia. At that time

Magnolia Expedition_1958_Explorer Scout Post 106

the Magnolia Cemetery was pretty much undisturbed with even the gate lock still in place.

Early Saturday morning our party including Mr. Landrum, Bill Cunningham, Gary Cook, one other scout and myself set out on our expedition. Base camp was off the first dirt road north of the cemetery near the river. We spent most of the morning walking a game trail down the west bank of the St Marks River. In the process we disturbed a very large Cottonmouth under some palmettos, which flashed its white mouth. With our group not yet having a thorough appreciation of the ecosystem, the poor snake was dispatched with quite some fanfare. A little further downstream we found ourselves across the river from a makeshift camp with a shelter constructed of logs, limbs and old metal signs and scrap tin. The owner was in camp. After introducing ourselves, he introduced himself as Cane Strickland.

Mr. Strickland was deadheading logs from the river. His equipment consisted of two wooden jon boats connected across the gunwale's by heavy timbers. Between the boats was a hand cranked winch with his "dogs" for lifting logs from the bottom. He inquired as to the day of the week. When told it was Saturday, he walked out on his boats declaring it was time for his bath. He hesitated, saying I see something on the bottom, and jumped into just over waist deep water. He went under and came up with a mastodon tooth. We said our good-byes and resumed our search for Magnolia. To this day I'm not sure if we were set up by Mr. Strickland or if all that unfolded was genuinely spontaneous. What I do know is we had met a truly friendly man who was part of Wakulla County's rich folk heritage. Not long afterwards an article featuring Mr. Strickland appeared in the Tallahassee Democrat. It authenticated our impression of this man as the real deal.

Magnolia Expedition; 1958; Ney Landrum; Magnolia Cemetery

Now back to the search for Magnolia. We did find the town site and collected many artifacts from a small stream that ran through or along the edge of town. There were signs of an old wharf or bridge on the river bank near the confluence of the stream and river. The area west of the stream had recently been cleared with heavy equipment. At the north end of the clearing was a scattering of old glass, earthenware and other debris, probably the town refuse site. We probably weren't the first explorers to locate the town of Magnolia, but it sure was a great adventure for a group of 14 year olds.

Submitted by: George E. Apthorp, 2888 Spring Creek Hwy, Crawfordville, FL 32327

The Little Family of Wakulla Springs

People make up my memories of Wakulla Springs and the Guy Little family was the best part of the Springs for me. The family was made up of; Mr. Guy, his wife Ms. Ferrell Little and their three daughters, Mary, Ginger and Carol. Mr. Little was the Springs Manager under Mr. Ed Ball. Mr. Guy was a big man in my eyes, because he seemed very tall and strong, with a big smile, a hearty laugh and a kind word. By comparison Miss Ferrell was petite and she had beautiful hair, she was always full of fun and I think that was why she was such a good friend of my mother's.

I was a bit younger than Ginger and Carol, but we had loads of fun and were allowed to roam all over the Springs, if Mr. Ball was not in residence. In other words, if the King was in, the subjects minded their manners. While Ginger, Carol and I roamed the Springs, Mary had little to do with us; we were just the younger kids. Thinking back, I realize that while she was never with us, she was always around close, now I wonder how much she had to do with keeping us out of trouble.

The Littles lived in The Lodge during their time at the Springs. That is the big two story house you see when you first arrive inside the Springs. It was called The Lodge since the managers family lived there on the first floor and sometimes unmarried employees had rooms upstairs. I don't remember a lot about the upstairs because we were not allowed to go up there. I remember the Little's residence and how wonderful it smelled because of all the wood used in it. The floors were hardwood and all the walls were paneled in wood, it was decorated in what now would be termed rustic. I was introduced to tuna salad with apples, celery and raisins in that house and that is still my favorite way to make tuna salad.

There was a big building between The Lodge and The Hotel full of huge pieces of machinery, we would look in the windows, but under threat of paddling, we were not allowed to go in there. I think that is where they built and maintained the boats. Also, there was a building housing the water pump and there were long pipes to The Lodge and The Hotel.

It was great fun to walk back and forth from The Lodge and The Hotel through the tall pines and smell the rich loam and see the little wildflowers growing along the path. The best time to make this trip was at night and we would scare ourselves silly with ghost stories.

If Mr. Ball was not in residence, we would go over to The Hotel at night and skate in our socks on the marble floors. Back then all the marble was kept smooth as glass and we could skate from the Dining Room, through the Hotel Lobby and into the fountain area. We would get a running start and fly from one end to the other. There wasn't as much furniture in the main hotel lobby and fountain as there is today or we would have hurt ourselves. (We used to do the same thing in the Courthouse on the weekends, because they didn't lock it up, we also slid down the banisters from the courtroom to the first floor.)

The fountain area had a long bar running the length of the room and served snacks, drinks, ice cream and a few "Wakulla Springs Souvenirs". You could go into the fountain in your bathing suit and get ice cream, the most wonderful ice cream, but you could not go into the hotel or the dining room unless you were properly dressed. They had real dipped ice cream and the strawberry was the best. I didn't eat in the dining room until many years later because we always ate in the kitchen, which was absolutely wonderful. We knew everyone and they treated us like family and fed us well. It was great fun to sit in the kitchen and watch the plates being served, then covered with a metal cover, placed on the cart and then it would go "clickety clackety" to the dining room. It didn't seem to matter which cart was used, they all went "clickety clackety", announcing their arrival.

The Wakulla Spring souvenirs were all typical Florida trinkets, lots of alligators, tomahawks, bows and arrows, plastic knives, shot glasses with "Florida" or "Wakulla Springs" emblazoned across the front, but they sold like hotcakes.

Guy Little

There was a concession stand at the entrance to Springs swimming area. It was also floored in marble, just as it is today. It had bathrooms on each side, one for the boys and one for the girls, there were dressing rooms and showers, where the floor was always wet and sandy. The concession stand was open all the way around and had huge glass windows that closed when the Springs was closed. I don't know where the Juke Box came from, but it could rival anything the kids have today for being loud and it was always on.

I think all the young people in Wakulla County at some time or other worked at the Springs, mostly at the concession stand. The concession stand was where you purchased your ticket to into the swimming area and for the boat rides. They also had all kinds of water toys like floats and goggles and beach towels and the best hotdogs and hamburgers. This was where you went to see and be seen, you didn't have to pay to get into Wakulla Springs at this time, just into the swimming area, and so lots of kids drove through to see who was there. Maybe that is where we learned to circle McDonalds!

To this day, when I go to the Springs, all the smells brings back the wonderful memories of the Little family and I often wonder where they are now. I seem to remember Mr. Guy passing away. My cousin, Tommy Raker had a terrific crush on Ginger, I don't know if that was her given name, or her nickname, she had glorious auburn hair. About 20 years ago I ran into Carol and she was a nurse in Tallahassee. I would love to hear from them.

I am sure that every kid growing up and going to Wakulla Springs remembers the Cypress tree roots that covered the ground and stumping their toes, no matter how careful, it always happened.

After Daddy (H. T. Adams) brought me a vehicle of my own, actually an old Willis Jeep (which I still have), outfitted to hold way more kids than was legal, I would gather all my friends and tell my mother (Gladys Adams) that we were going to run over to the Springs. Then I could go from Crawfordville to Wakulla Springs on dirt roads and only have to cross State Road 61 once. Well, to keep from being totally a sneak, we did run over to the Springs and then right on back to Cherokee Sink. My mother would have killed me if she had known we were swimming in Cherokee and I never told her. I knew I would not get caught because it was a long distance call from any and everywhere to the Springs. Their telephone provider was St. Joe Telephone Company, since Wakulla Springs belonged to St. Joe Paper Company, so you had to place a long distance call to St. Joe, Florida and it was then routed to Wakulla Springs. Long Distance calls were expensive and you didn't do that unless you had to, so I didn't think I would get caught, however, my mother was not above driving over there to see if I was where I was supposed to be, I just got lucky.

One of my fondest memories of the time I spent at the Springs isn't about the Springs, but about my brother-in-law, Jimmie Dykes. I was spending the night at the Springs and around 6:00pm, my mother arrived at the Springs all in a flutter. She was telling me to get in the car, we had to get home in a hurry, Jimmie was home from Korea. I don't actually remember all the particulars, I don't remember us expecting him, or maybe they just didn't tell me because I would have worried them to death until he got there. I just remember him coming home after being away so long and he had me a present, besides himself. He purchased me a tea set with all the plates, cups, saucers, bowls, serving dishes that matched the real size set of dishes that he brought my sister (Jean Dykes). I still have every single piece of the set in my china cabinet.

I hope that sharing these memories of Wakulla Springs will bring back some fond memories to others that have passed that way also.

Submitted By: Helen Adams Strickland, 138 H. T. Adams Ave., Crawfordville, FL 32327 April 12, 2011

Champion Trees of Wakulla Springs

In 2004 I began a search for the largest specimens of 42 species of trees in the upland hardwood forest of Wakulla Springs State Park. My inspiration came from the discovery of a huge Sassafras (the largest I had ever seen) on one of my wanderings through the woods. My wife Sandy Cook was Park Manager so I was very fortunate to live in the Park. Since I was retired, I had plenty of time to spend in the woods and it soon became evident that this park was full of very large

Champion Trees of Wakulla Springs_2005_White Oak Tree; Florida Champion, David Roddenberry

trees.

Having retired from the Florida Park Service in 2001, I was aware of a program to locate state and national champion trees in state parks. It didn't take long to realize I would need help to have any hope of "surveying" the hardwood portions of the original 2900 acre acquisition. I enlisted the expert assistance of David Roddenberry (also a FPS retiree), the foremost authority on big trees of Wakulla County. Due to other commitments and the park's heavy tick population, we confined our outings to the winter months. With 3 to 4 outings per year, we are now approximately 70% complete having GPSed and measured over 600 trees.

At the time of this writing we have found a total of 12 state champion trees, 2 of which are national champions and we have a couple more to nominate. Current champions include: Bluff Oak (national), Shumard Oak, Swamp Chestnut Oak, Swamp Laurel Oak, White Oak, Spruce Pine, Rusty Lyonia (national), Redbud, Sweetbay Magnolia, Sour Gum, American Basswood, and Sassafras. There are also 3 past champions which have either died or been replaced by other nominations. These include Southern Magnolia, Black Cherry and American Beech. Champion trees are often near the end of their vigorous life and susceptible to loosing large limbs or their tops.

Champion Trees of Wakulla Springs 2005; Rusty Lyonia Tree; National Champion; George Apthorp

This lowers their point totals making way for new champions. There are a few "champions-in-waiting" at Wakulla Springs.

The Champion Tree Program is administered by the Florida Division of Forestry. Check out their website for current champions and their measurements and the official Nomination Form. The points used to compare your tree with the current champion are determined as follows: Add the circumference in inches at 4.5 feet above the ground; the height in feet; and one fourth the average crown spread in feet. There are a few variations in determining total points. These mostly relate to the tree's structure near the ground (splits below 4.5 ft, etc.). Your county forester will be happy to assist in the nomination process.

Submitted by: George E. Apthorp, 2888 Spring Creek Hwy, Crawfordville, FL 32327

Sopchoppy School

She still stands, this mighty fortress, built so long ago, of limestone rock and mortar, so stately, and we know...

Ghostly shadows of the children still play upon her walls.

Voices from the past still echo from her halls. So many memories of this great old school.

This is where it started... where we learned the golden rule.

Now gone, the days of homework, English, literature and math...of misbehaving children, who stirred the teachers wrath.

Field days with bag races... they were so much fun, white, red or blue ribbons, to show off when we won.

Football games with Crawfordville, where the panthers felt the sting, of the mighty fighting yellow jackets, of victory we did sing.

May God bless this old school building and those who entered through her door. Her memories we will carry, in our hearts forevermore.

Submitted and Written By: Louise Thomas, 419 Buckhorn Creek Rd., Sopchoppy, FL 32358

Wakulla Beach Misery

Our weekend family outings (we called it "exploring") didn't often take us to Wakulla Beach, but one such outing remains vivid in my memory. The year was around 1950 and I was 6 or 7 years old. My dad, mother, brother and I arrived at the beach late on a hot summer afternoon. After poking around the old hotel (pictured below) it was time to head home. Much to our dismay, in the process of turning around, we got stuck. With about an hour of daylight left, Dad struck out walking for help at the small community a mile or so away. The sand gnats and mosquitoes were as bad as I have ever experienced. We didn't have our 6-12 bug repellant and it was too hot to take

1950s Wakulla Beach Hotel

refuge in the car which, as you know, was not air conditioned. Luckily, Dad did find help to pull us out of the mud and we were finally able to escape the Wakulla Beach misery.

Submitted by: George E. Apthorp, 2888 Spring Creek Hwy, Crawfordville, FL 32327

History of The St. Marks Yacht Club

Boat owners in the St. Marks area informally discussed the idea of a yacht club during 1959 and 1960. In the fall of 1960, Ed Miller and Cliff Chavez learned that land would be given to a group for the construction of a yacht club. Cliff and Ed took the initiative of contacting every person that had a boat in St. Marks with the idea of forming such a club in St. Marks. By the end of the year it was determined that a club would be feasible and desirable and the St. Marks Yacht Club was officially founded.

The first meeting was held at the Silver Slipper in Tallahassee with approximately twelve interested persons attending. Elections were held in January of 1961 with the following officers elected.

Harold Becklin - Commodore
Ed Miller - Vice Commodore
Cliff Chavez - Scribe
Max Lewis - Purser
Bill Hutchinson and Edwin Culbreath - Rear Commodores.

The Club was incorporated later that year with the adoption of its articles of constitution and by-laws.

Ed Miller had designed a club burgee in 1960 and it was adopted by the Club in 1961 and registered with Lloyds of London. The burgee colors are royal blue and gold. The burgee has a royal blue field with gold device.

The original land offer was found to be unsuitable for the construction of a yacht club so Ed Miller and Harold Becklin arranged to lease the boathouse on the St. Marks River that belonged to Mrs. Roberts and is now part of Shields Marina. The yacht club members took all of the slips in the Roberts boathouse so there was now an active club, a "clubhouse" and membership began to grow.

Harold Becklin moved quickly to establish an active social organization with parties, parades, fish-fries, formal dinners and dances and always boating get-togethers in the Appalachee Bay area. Making up the nucleus of the first members were Bill Snowden, Jack Leffler, Harold Becklin, Bill Hutchinson, Ed Miller, Hugh Williams, Peter Fenn, Max Lewis, Edwin Culbreath and Cliff Chavez.

Before the building of the first clubhouse, some of the affairs were held at the Kingfish Lodge, a ramshackle fish camp a little north of the Yacht Club property. One such event was a Predicted Log Contest with approximately twenty boats participating. There were other events such as Dead-Reckoning contests and treasure hunts with authentic looking pirate maps of the Wakulla and St. Marks Rivers with marks showing where treasure and hints of treasure could be found.

The dream of owning its own land and clubhouse never died and a constant search for suitable land led the Club to many possible locations. However, the membership always came back to the St. Marks area. When, in late 1961, land became available north of and including part of the old fort, seven members of the Club joined in partnership to purchase the land. They in turn conveyed the land to the Yacht Club in exchange for a waiver of their dues. With this turn of luck the "dream" was on the way to becoming a reality.

The first clubhouse was a ground level concrete block building constructed in 1964 on the same site as the current building. The first phase of the boathouse, which was a floating pier, was constructed in 1965 and the boathouse, lockers and parking lot were completed in 1966. The Gazebo was added to the boathouse in 1970 and the swimming pool was built in 1971.

During the years that followed several storms affected our area. The clubhouse and docks were damaged by several of these storms and tides flooded the clubhouse more than once. Then in November of 1985, Hurricane Kate hit land around Mexico Beach. The St. Marks area was on the wrong side of the "eye of the storm" and the tides and winds pretty well destroyed the old clubhouse as well as the boathouse. Although this was an enormous ordeal for the members at the time, it turned out to be a blessing in disguise. Between the insurance money and a low interest loan from the Small Business Administration, a new and much larger facility, designed by member and architect, Harold Odom, was built. Bob Worrall was the Commodore at the time and was largely responsible for obtaining the financing for the new clubhouse and overseeing its construction. The docks were also rebuilt. In December of 1986 the first social, the Annual Christmas Party, was held in the new clubhouse. In January 1987 the official "Open House" was held and the new clubhouse dedicated. Although fully submerged, the swimming pool survived the hurricane and is still being used today.

A freak winter storm (Blizzard of 93) snuck up on the big bend area in March of 1993 bringing unusually high tides and eighty mile an hour winds. The clubhouse suffered some slight damage to its roof and the boathouse lost some metal and timbers. The "tropical storm summer" of 1994, hurricanes Erin and Opal of 1995, hurricane Earl in 1999 also brought high tides and winds into St. Marks causing some damage to the docks. However, members working together have always managed to overcome these events of nature and have always brought the facilities back to "better than new" condition.

During 2002 members accomplished much remodeling. The entrance Tower to the Club was rebuilt, new paint and wallpaper gave the interior a facelift, and a new entertainment area was added to the docks. In addition, Mrs. Myrtle Shields donated a beautiful oil painting of the St. Marks Lighthouse to the Club.

Dennis, the hurricane that became a flood in 2005, wreaked havoc upon the Club. Water lapped at the undersides of the Clubhouse, the pool was under water and the docks were in disarray. Had it not been for the foresight of the Board that year placing concerted effort to stabilize the docks prior to hurricane season, we may have completely lost the Dock house. Soon thereafter the membership noticed a leak from the roof. The Clubhouse received a fresh coat of paint, new screening on the porch, and a beautiful galvanized tin roof. The Dock house went through a hefty re-stabilization project; and the members used these "work weekends" as a good time to socialize as well as clean up the debris. Through the hard work and efforts of the membership, again the Club is restored to a "better than new" condition.

After forty plus years of existence, the St. Marks Yacht Club has a beautiful clubhouse location on the Wakulla River, a stable membership base and a promising future. Much is owed to the men and women who have worked and played over these four decades to make our Club what it is today.

Wakulla County Museum and Archives

Jail Dream Becomes a Reality

Posted 12/8/2009 on Facebook

Once in a while a crazy idea or a chance thought becomes a dream. And once in a while a dream becomes a reality. I watched that happen tonight. 18 years ago in October and November of 1991 a group of people had the idea that they wanted a museum. They felt a little used old run down county building, the old jail, could be a potential place for it. It was a dream spun by my husband, Pete Gerrell, Betty Green, M. Gray, Doug Jones and a few others. After 18 years of hard work, scraping together pennies, playing politics and lots of elbow grease, it happened. The museum opened tonight officially for the public. It is still a work in progress but, it is a museum. My thanks to all who helped. I know my husband would have been pleased. I am thrilled to have been a part of it.

Submitted by: Terri Gerrell/SYP Publishing, 4351 Natural Bridge Rd., Tallahassee, FL

Sunbeams at the Jail

My mother's paternal heritage in Wakulla County began in 1845 when Isom and Permilia Hall Strickland settled in Smith Creek. Their fourth son, William M. "Buck" and Idella (Stanaland) Strickland whose youngest son, Roy Bedford Strickland (1897-1976) was my grandfather. He was born near River Sink as was my mother.

In 1964, my parents, Max Neal and Doris G. (Strickland) Davis, bought a business and property from Mr. C. D. Peak and Dr. Thomas Head in Crawfordville. The "dry cleaner" was across the street from the Baptist church and we lived in the back of it for a year before moving into the house where I grew up. Today there is a log building where the dry cleaner stood.

Walking to places around town was an adventure for any girl of nearly seven years. This was especially true for me. In teaching me responsibility, Mama sent me on little errands-to the drug store for a ten-cent coke or the Suwanee Store for bread. My feet marched daily to and from school along the side walk next to Judge A. L. Porter's office. Mrs. Klink, whose white hair was always done up in a twisted knot, worked in the Judge's yellow block building and her early 1950s light-blue Chevrolet Coupe was always parked near the sidewalk. Each school trip caused me to walk along the short little paved street between Judge Porter's office and the west side of the new courthouse to the street south of the courthouse. That street (now High Drive) was paved only as far as the Jail and then it was dirt all the way beyond the school. In a small gray house like building was Mr. Jewel Hudson's law office directly on the corner in front of the Jail. Trees surrounded the yard around the Jail, except for a small opening where cars parked. I hadn't really thought too much about the Jail until the day a prisoner escaped. During the night we heard bloodhounds barking as they chased the convict through the woods toward Bream Fountain. This exciting event caused a multitude of questions for Mama and Daddy from my little brother and me.

I knew Mr. R.E. Whaley because he brought clothes to the dry cleaner and I saw him and Mrs. "Dean" at church. One day Mama told me I was to go to Mrs. Whaley's house for Sunbeams, a mission group for primary Aged children at our church. Going to new places was fun and each time I went on one of these adventures Mama said she was proud of me when I got home. Walking to get there was not as surprising to me as were her directions. "Walk by the Suwanee Store" she said, and then "where the pavement ends at the Jail."

Whatever directions after those were muddled in my listening ear. It was probably the first time I experienced a momentary lapse in memory. The glee and excitement left my countenance and with widened eyes I asked her "Why can't I go to the church?" Much to my chagrin, Mama assured me that this Sunbeam group was definitely at Mrs. Whaley's house. She again directed me to walk past Mr. Hudson's office and the little opening between the trees toward the school. I was to go to the door between the flower beds. The fact that my destination involved walking so close to the Jail was of grave concern. Mama watched me cross the street and until I turned the corner walking toward the familiar store. My trembling quickened with each step taken beyond the safety of the Suwanee Store. Mama must have sensed the severity of my fear because she suddenly appeared to walk with me the rest of the way.

Indeed, a door and steps were between two flower beds among bushes and trees around the corner from the Jail. Before we could knock, the door opened and Mrs. Whaley greeted me with her sweet smile. Once inside I joined the boys and girls from church sitting on the rug around a small table in front of the sofa across the room from the door. Mrs. Whaley directed our attention to the globe on the small table, turned it slightly and pointed to a place depicted in green. She said, "We are going to learn about the missionaries who live and work there." She told a story and we sang a couple of Sunday school songs. I pushed the pennies Mama had given me into the slot atop the "missionary collection box." We prayed for the missionaries and then Mrs. Whaley announced it was time for refreshments and she led us to the kitchen.

As we stood in line for refreshments just outside the kitchen, the exterior door window caught my attention and I noticed the small opening between the trees where the pavement ended. The boys in the group looked in the other direction and I leaned that way to better see the stairs which went straight up. "That's where they keep the prisoners," one of the boys stated as a matter-of-fact. It started making sense to me that Mrs. Whaley's house was also the Jail. In the kitchen, Mrs. Whaley stood across the room at a table pouring Kool-Aid. I recognized her granddaughter who put cookies on napkins and slid them over to places on the table where we would stand to enjoy our refreshments. My curious widened eyes surveyed the kitchen from my place near the door. It slightly resembled the lunchroom kitchen at school. The white tiled walls sparkled, there was a very large sink under the window and I noticed the stove opposite the sink because steam was rising from something boiling in the biggest pot I'd ever seen. Everything in the room was very shiny stainless steel-the pots, the huge stove, the sink and even the table. When only crumbs were left, Mrs. Whaley's granddaughter showed us the trash can and we filed by depositing used napkins and cups. We were dismissed from Sunbeams and the boys ahead of me bounced through the door just outside the kitchen directly into the Jail yard. Even more interesting was the line of several men in disheveled but matching clothes standing outside. They all seemed to smile kindly at us while making pleasant comments as we passed. I thought I recognized one of them but not from church. The boys proceeded to play "cops and robbers" in the Jail yard, which seemed risky to me, so I began my walk home. I ventured toward the small opening between the trees and as soon as I could see the Suwanee Store all was well once again. That evening I had a million questions for Mama and Daddy after supper.

On Tuesday afternoon each week following, I confidently walked through the opening between the trees and made my way to the door in front of the stairs that went up to where "they kept the prisoners." Mrs. Whaley taught us about missionaries in her living room and served refreshments in the kitchen where she cooked meals for the prisoners. Mama had explained to me that Mr. and Mrs. Whaley lived there because he was "the jailer"' and their family visited them just as if it were a regular house. The prisoner I had recognized was a "trustee" who walked by the dry cleaner every afternoon on his way to feed those bloodhounds penned somewhere near Bream Fountain.

Submitted By: Sandra Davis Vidak, 396 J. K. Moore Rd., Crawfordville, FL 32327

Touching Harvey Donation & Memories of Mr. Whaley 2010

As a child, I never dreamed of participating in anything at the Old Jail again, nor could I have imagined taking part in the effort to preserve the heritage of Wakulla County. Last evening, October 12, 2010 was the annual Historical Society banquet at the Wakulla Springs Lodge. It was my second time attending the event. It's always nice to dine overlooking the famous spring. I casually noticed that all around were people of particular importance to me, though I had not expected some of them to be there. On my right was my sweet husband, Walter, who chatted and entertained the others at our table while attending to fetch extra ice and such. To my left was a well-acquainted local architect. Across the table were four "of Sandra's church ladies" as Walter introduced them to Randy Lewis. These ladies, "Mrs. Sheryl, Mrs. Helen, Mrs. Valda and Mrs. Alethea" are, indeed, some of my church ladies. As Sunday school teachers and role models, I admired the way they dressed, talked, and their infectious laughter. I learned benevolence from them. In joy and sorrow, these ladies are always around. They quickly acknowledge birthdays and give wedding showers just as they are the first to visit, send a card or bring food if there is sickness or grief in someone's home. In fact, I just received a birthday card from Mrs. Helen on behalf of the "Young at Heart" senior citizens group from church and she calls when she needs me to bake a cake. On this evening they seemed a bit enchanted with the conversation between Walter and Randy about a particular historical renovation project in Tallahassee. One of the ladies leaned over to Walter and whispered, "You need to get me a brick from there." As the evening progressed, folks finished dinner and began milling around and some walked across the marbled floor of the Lodge to the "rooms," returning to "take a seat waiting for the program to begin. We had a little business to be done before the keynote speakers presentation. Dignitaries and guests were welcomed by WCHS President Cathy Frank. Due to time constraints, the reports to be given were limited Terri Gerrell reported on the treasury. The nominating committee chair made her way to the podium, cautious that the microphone was correctly adjusted before she began the enormous task of introducing 19 board members with a biography of each.- She had requested that all of us submit to her in advance a little information about ourselves. There she stood in confidence and deliberate speech reading notes with her fingers! This speaker drew laughter when she paused and read, "...and her favorite quotation is the 1978 ' I do' of her husband, Walter." She finished the biographies with her own and announced "the office of secretary is still open." The President asked for nominations from the floor. The impulse was automatic for me to rise and state, "I wish to nominate Arlene Vause for the position of Secretary." For this lady, in her uniqueness, had just demonstrated that no excuse is excusable and in her way she inspired all of us to give and do our very best. She graciously accepted the position before sitting down. Hers is a hard act to follow, as they say, and my nervous report seemed trivial in comparison, but I guess it was a little respite between Arlene's and the Sheriff. Vice-president Richard Harden introduced Sheriff David F. Harvey in all of his accomplishment. His topic, "History of Wakulla Sheriffs and Jails" drew a lot of interest, since the meeting was so well attended. The sheriff absolutely captivated the audience with his power point pictures and stories. It turns out there were two jails prior to "The Old Jail" (1949-1972) which the Wakulla County Historical Society, Museum and Archives proudly calls "home". When the jail before "ours" was razed to make way for a new jail, the red brick from it was salvaged by Jimmie Dykes for his home near the cemetery on Shadeville Highway. As a child, I lived close to it and had heard many admire the remarkable attractive house he and his wife, Jean, built. There are probably a thousand of those bricks left the sheriff said, to suggest a possible fund-raising activity for the Society. Sheriff Harvey made a point to discuss the need for, and importance of, jailers. There are five jailers of the newest facility since it takes that many for 24/7 coverage of inmates. The youngest jailer, Jared Miller, was introduced. Sheriff Harvey had coached him on a "pee-wee ball team." He talked about all five jails, the number of beds and how the inmates were situated

R E. Whaley, 1960s

in each. Until 1949, no one was left in charge of the inmates at night, consequently there had been several suicides which might have been prevented. There was a time when inmates went outside fetching firewood to keep themselves warm through the night. We perched tall on our seats as the building plan was shown on the screen, especially me. I was anxious to see if my childhood memory was

Cathy Frank, President accepting the gift of Mr. Whaley's gun from Sheriff David Harvey.

correct of the room where I had attended Sunbeams and, indeed, it was. Mr. and Mrs. R. E. Whaley, the jailer and matron lived on the first floor with his mother and her mother for 18 years. There was a lovely picture of those four in coats and smiles standing at the High Drive entrance. Today's genealogy archives room was Mr. Whaley's office for dispatch and booking. There are a couple of closets in that room, one with remnants of a tiled shower, which may have served inmates.

The new "Betty Oaks Green" room had been a kitchen for the family. The second floor plan was interesting too. The Society is seeking a grant to restore it for future exhibits and an elevator is needed so that everyone can go up there. Not a person in the audience expected what Sheriff Harvey did next. He said, "Sometime before she died Mrs. Dean called me to her house and she insisted on giving me R. E.'s gun." Some of us wondered if Mr. Whaley ever needed a gun since he also carried that slap stick on his belt which had earlier been passed through the audience. The Sheriff continued, "the rightful place for this gun is the old jail" and he presented to the Wakulla County Historical Society that priceless artifact, a service revolver, which had presided there so many years ago.

It was truly a "shock and awe" moment for the WCHS Board when our adopted motto "A morsel of genuine history is a thing so rare as to be always valuable" because of Sheriff Harvey's generosity. Mr. R.E. Whaley's memory evokes some from my own childhood. He was familiar to me since he brought uniforms to the dry cleaner (my parents) and he seemed friendly enough. I remember catching a glimpse of him being serious in his office once when the Sunbeams ate cookies at the jail. Today I remembered an occasion of witnessing his serious demeanor. I practiced piano at the church across the street. My church key was on a chain from the Great Smokey Mountains and was kept with the money. I usually went over there every day for about an hour and I was supposed to let Mama know when I left. If she wasn't in front at the counter, I might have left her a note and thought she'd notice the missing key. On one particular day, I hadn't been at the piano for very long when something scared me. The door between the choir loft and the anteroom opened and quickly closed. I caught a glimpse of a relatively bald head but it didn't seem as tall or shiny enough to be the preacher's. I grabbed my piano books and ran for the door, knowing the Lord would forgive me for running through the sanctuary and praying He would just get me back across the street! Without breath, I was telling Mama that something had scared me when Mr. Whaley walked in the door. In his serious countenance, he leaned forward and placed each hand broadly on the counter. I had never noticed he could take up that much space. He looked straight at me and then said to Mama, " I understand there's a missing little girl." My eyes became wide like saucers and I wasn't sure what would happen next. "Can't you see that I'm right here(?)" is what I thought. I dared to speak since this situation didn't seem too good for me. I think Mama said something about my being at church without telling her. He looked at me again and reiterated the need for parents to know the whereabouts of their children. Before taking his leave, he told Mama to always call the jail if a child went missing. I don't know if it was Mr. Whaley's balding head I saw at church, but it might as well have been. Never again did I go to the church without making sure Mama knew where I'd be. I'm very sure that was the year I got for Christmas a piano on which to practice at home. It was definitely an inspiring evening at Wakulla Springs, not to be soon forgotten. I hope the Society has a chance to do something with all of those bricks!

Submitted By: Sandra Davis Vidak, 396 J. K. Moore Rd., Crawfordville, FL 32327

Wakulla County Historical Society
24 High Drive • Post Office Box 151
Crawfordville, Florida 32326
850-926-1110 • 24research@gmail.com

A morsel of genuine history is a thing so rare as to be always valuable.
Thomas Jefferson

Dear Friends of Wakulla County Historical Society,

Thank you for your support by purchasing this book. I gratefully acknowledge the contribution of all of you who donated your memories to be preserved in our book. I appreciate the intrinsic value of these stories to the history of Wakulla County. I also want to thank our book committee of Tanya Lynn, Terri Gerrell, Carolyn Harvey, Linda Thompson and Betty Green.

I am proud to be the president of the Wakulla County Historical Society. It is exciting to see what we have accomplished over the years. First, with the opening of our Wakulla County Museum and Archives, home of the Historical Society. The Betty Green Room, Pete Gerrell Room, and McLeod Room feature historic exhibits of Wakulla County and the surrounding area. Our genealogy suite is complete with resource library and genealogy research assistance from our well qualified volunteers. The museum has become a tourist destination like no other in Wakulla County.

Our latest land donation of 40 acres from the Ben and Anne Boynton Family, will enable us to work toward the vision of a Heritage Village Park where we can preserve historic homes and artifacts from our county.

In order for us to continue to preserve Wakulla County History through research, exhibits, and displays, it takes support through financial contributions and volunteerism. If you haven't joined us, contact the museum for a membership application.

In closing, I want to say that we should remember to appreciate what we have in Wakulla County. We are surrounded by good friends and people that care about each other and our county. Realize the beauty that surrounds us in Wakulla County, enjoy today, remember your history, and learn from it. If our history is lost it is tragic. Take time to write it down.

I am grateful for all my blessings and especially the gift of all of you, the friends of Wakulla County Historical Society.

Cathy Frank, President
Wakulla County Historical Society

Mission: Founded in 1991, Wakulla County Historical Society collects, preserves, exhibits, and interprets the heritage of Wakulla County and surrounding areas. Through exhibits, educational programs, research, & collection, we promote knowledge and appreciation for the events that have shaped our lives.

Executive Officers: President, Cathy Frank, Vice-President, Richard Harden, Secretary, Arlene Vause, and Treasurer, Terri Gerrell. Board Members: Past-President, Betty Green, Cal Jamison, Jim Calhoun, Murray McLaughlin, Carolyn Harvey, Scott Joyner, Tanya Lynn, Mark Perrin, Ryan Laird, and John Y. Roberts. Associate member: Clerk of Court, Brent Thurmond.

Index